SIMPSONS™
COMICS

COLOSSAL COMPENDIUM
VOLUME FOUR

MATT GROENING

HARPER

NEW YORK · LONDON · TORONTO · SYDNEY

**SIMPSONS COMICS COLOSSAL COMPENDIUM
VOLUME FOUR**

Materials previously published in
Bart Simpson's Pal Milhouse #1, Duffman Adventures #1, Li'l Homer #1, Maggie #1,
The Malevolent Mr. Burns #1, Ralph Wiggum Comics #1, Simpsons Comics #194, #198,
Simpsons Summer Shindig #5, #7, #8, Simpsons Winter Wingding #5, #8,
The Wonderful World of Lisa Simpson #1

FIRST EDITION
ISBN 978-0-06-242326-9
16 17 18 19 20 TC 10 9 8 7 6 5 4 3 2 1

Publisher: Matt Groening

Creative Director: Nathan Kane
Managing Editor: Terry Delegeane
Director of Operations: Robert Zaugh
Art Director: Jason Ho
Art Director Special Projects: Serban Cristescu
Assistant Art Director: Mike Rote
Production Manager: Christopher Ungar
Assistant Editor: Karen Bates
Production: Art Villanueva
Administration: Ruth Waytz
Legal Guardian: Susan A. Grode

Printed by TC Transcontinental, Beauceville, QC, Canada. 4/29/16

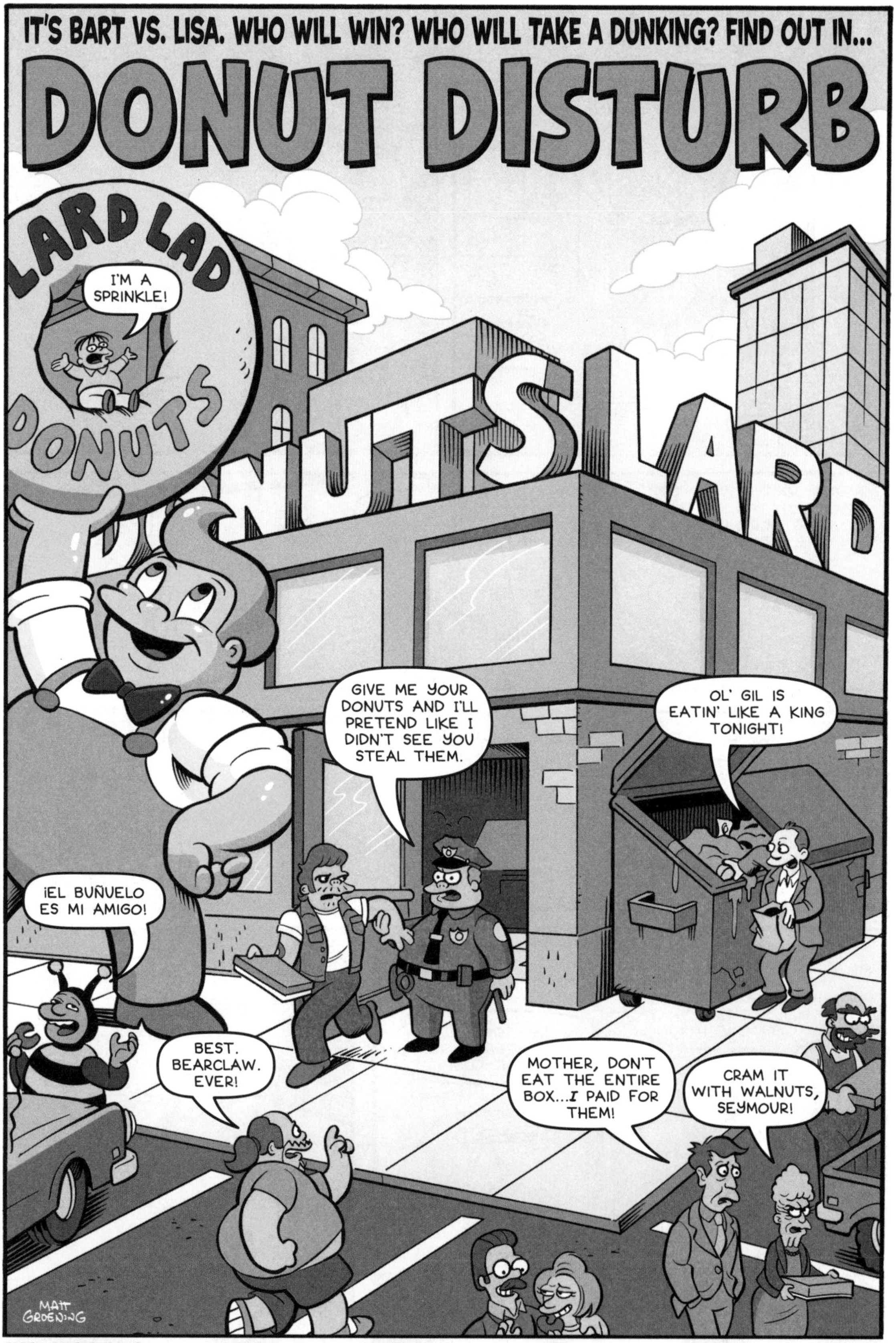
IT'S BART VS. LISA. WHO WILL WIN? WHO WILL TAKE A DUNKING? FIND OUT IN...
DONUT DISTURB
LARD LAD DONUTS
I'M A SPRINKLE!
DONUTS LARD
GIVE ME YOUR DONUTS AND I'LL PRETEND LIKE I DIDN'T SEE YOU STEAL THEM.
OL' GIL IS EATIN' LIKE A KING TONIGHT!
¡EL BUÑUELO ES MI AMIGO!
BEST. BEARCLAW. EVER!
MOTHER, DON'T EAT THE ENTIRE BOX...I PAID FOR THEM!
CRAM IT WITH WALNUTS, SEYMOUR!
MATT GROENING

TOM GAMMILL & HENRY GAMMILL *STORY* | **JOHN DELANEY** *PENCILS* | **ANDREW PEPOY** *INKS* | **ART VILLANUEVA** *COLORS* | **KAREN BATES** *LETTERS* | **NATHAN KANE** *EDITOR*

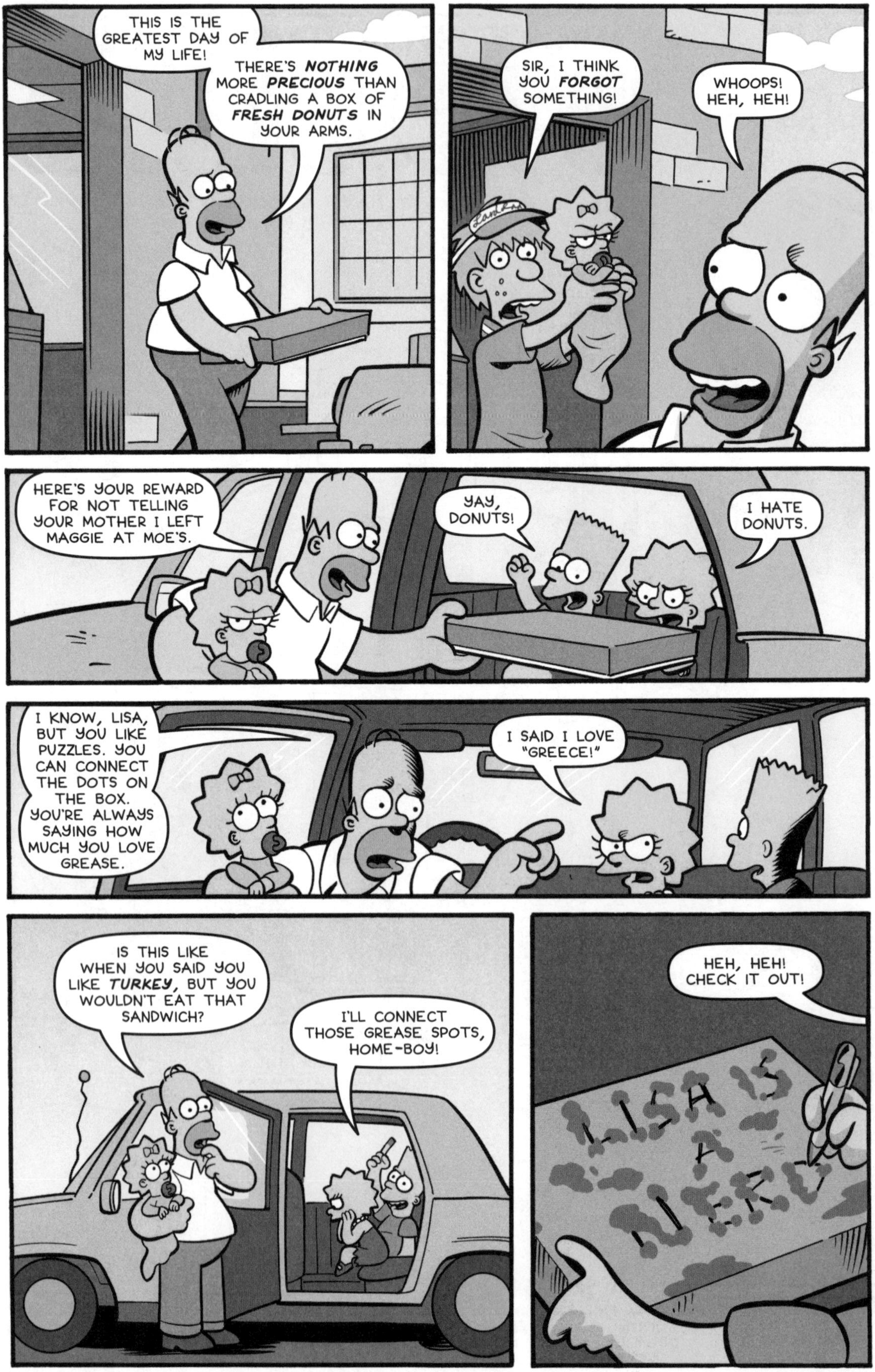
THIS IS THE GREATEST DAY OF MY LIFE!
THERE'S NOTHING MORE PRECIOUS THAN CRADLING A BOX OF FRESH DONUTS IN YOUR ARMS.
SIR, I THINK YOU FORGOT SOMETHING!
WHOOPS! HEH, HEH!
HERE'S YOUR REWARD FOR NOT TELLING YOUR MOTHER I LEFT MAGGIE AT MOE'S.
YAY, DONUTS!
I HATE DONUTS.
I KNOW, LISA, BUT YOU LIKE PUZZLES. YOU CAN CONNECT THE DOTS ON THE BOX. YOU'RE ALWAYS SAYING HOW MUCH YOU LOVE GREASE.
I SAID I LOVE "GREECE!"
IS THIS LIKE WHEN YOU SAID YOU LIKE TURKEY, BUT YOU WOULDN'T EAT THAT SANDWICH?
I'LL CONNECT THOSE GREASE SPOTS, HOME-BOY!
HEH, HEH! CHECK IT OUT!
LISA IS A NERD

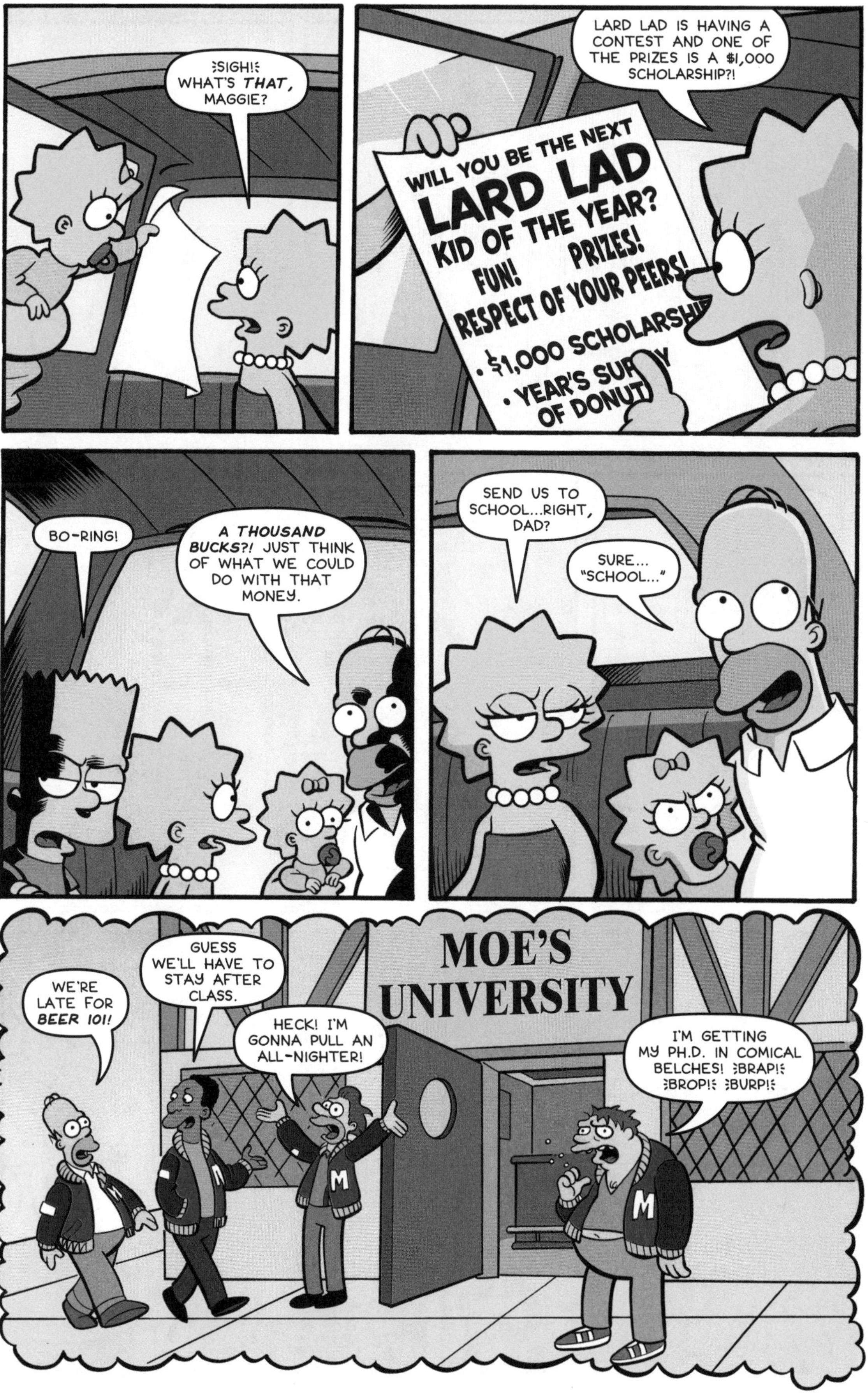

⁝SIGH!⁝ WHAT'S THAT, MAGGIE?
LARD LAD IS HAVING A CONTEST AND ONE OF THE PRIZES IS A $1,000 SCHOLARSHIP?!
WILL YOU BE THE NEXT LARD LAD KID OF THE YEAR?
FUN! PRIZES!
RESPECT OF YOUR PEERS!
• $1,000 SCHOLARSH
• YEAR'S SUP Y OF DONUT
BO-RING!
A THOUSAND BUCKS?! JUST THINK OF WHAT WE COULD DO WITH THAT MONEY.
SEND US TO SCHOOL...RIGHT, DAD?
SURE... "SCHOOL..."
MOE'S UNIVERSITY
WE'RE LATE FOR BEER 101!
GUESS WE'LL HAVE TO STAY AFTER CLASS.
HECK! I'M GONNA PULL AN ALL-NIGHTER!
I'M GETTING MY PH.D. IN COMICAL BELCHES! ⁝BRAP!⁝ ⁝BROP!⁝ ⁝BURP!⁝
M

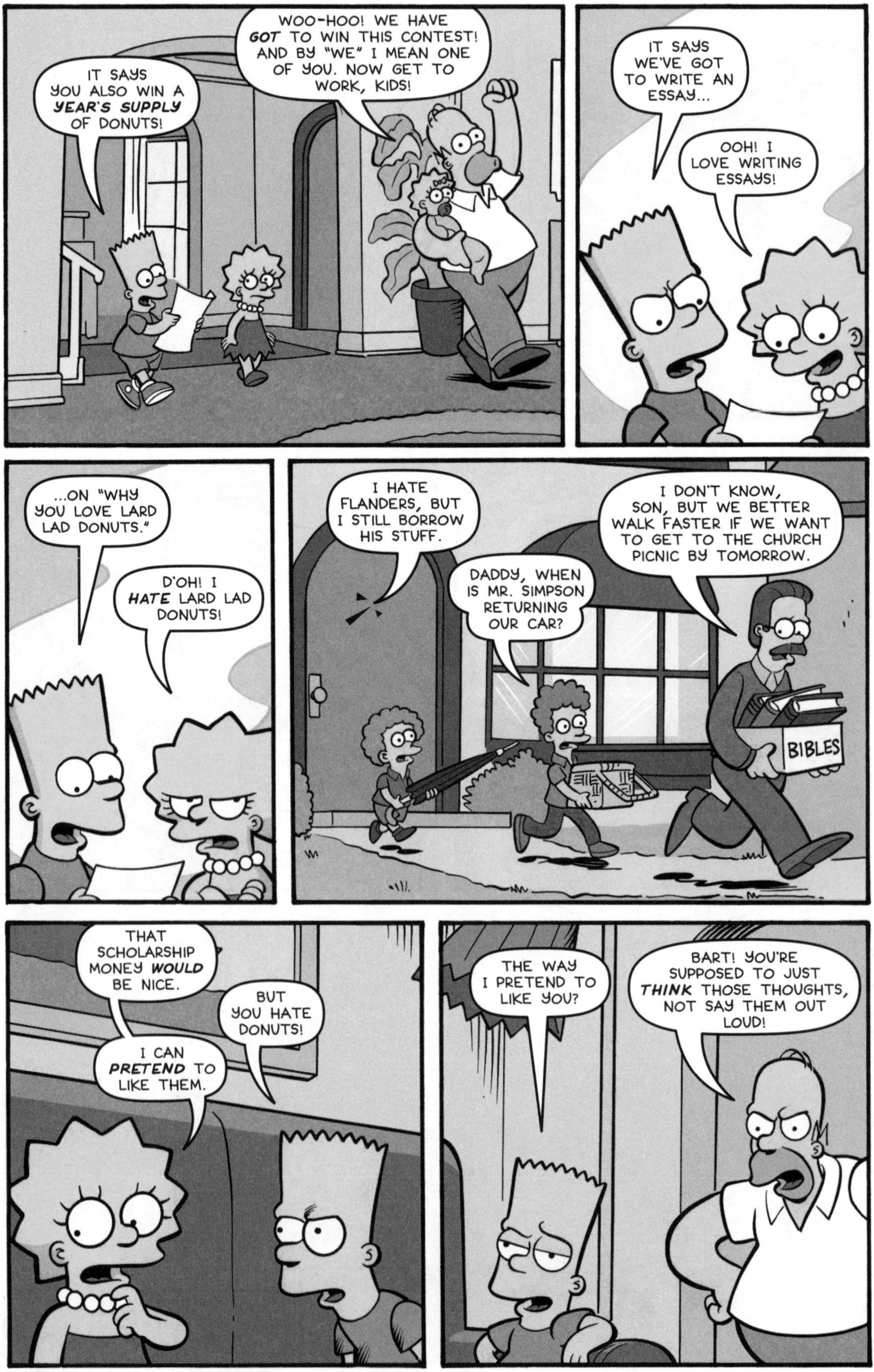
IT SAYS YOU ALSO WIN A YEAR'S SUPPLY OF DONUTS!
WOO-HOO! WE HAVE GOT TO WIN THIS CONTEST! AND BY "WE" I MEAN ONE OF YOU. NOW GET TO WORK, KIDS!
IT SAYS WE'VE GOT TO WRITE AN ESSAY...
OOH! I LOVE WRITING ESSAYS!
...ON "WHY YOU LOVE LARD LAD DONUTS."
D'OH! I HATE LARD LAD DONUTS!
I HATE FLANDERS, BUT I STILL BORROW HIS STUFF.
DADDY, WHEN IS MR. SIMPSON RETURNING OUR CAR?
I DON'T KNOW, SON, BUT WE BETTER WALK FASTER IF WE WANT TO GET TO THE CHURCH PICNIC BY TOMORROW.
BIBLES
THAT SCHOLARSHIP MONEY WOULD BE NICE.
BUT YOU HATE DONUTS!
I CAN PRETEND TO LIKE THEM.
THE WAY I PRETEND TO LIKE YOU?
BART! YOU'RE SUPPOSED TO JUST THINK THOSE THOUGHTS, NOT SAY THEM OUT LOUD!

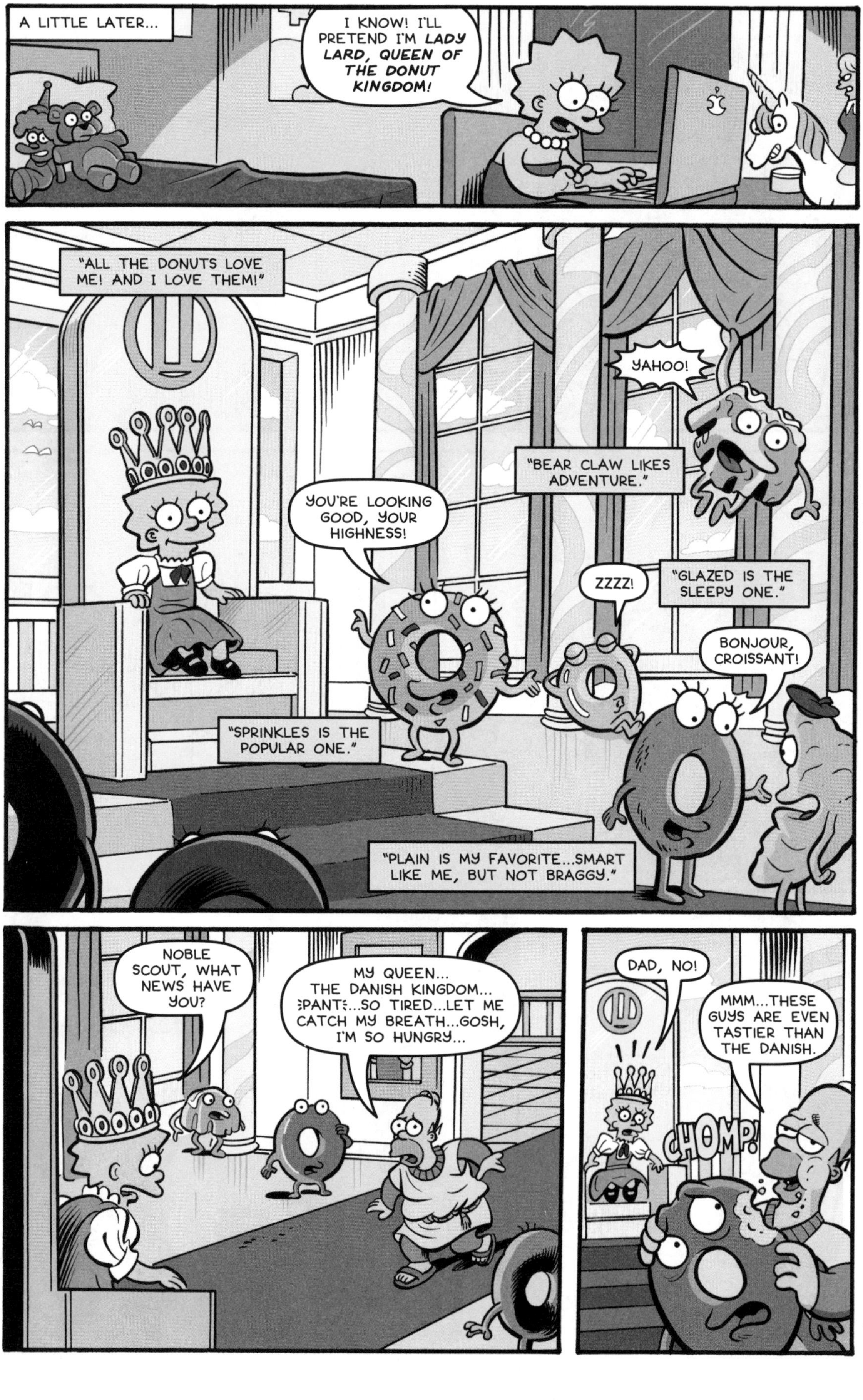
A LITTLE LATER...
I KNOW! I'LL PRETEND I'M *LADY LARD, QUEEN OF THE DONUT KINGDOM!*
"ALL THE DONUTS LOVE ME! AND I LOVE THEM!"
YAHOO!
"BEAR CLAW LIKES ADVENTURE."
YOU'RE LOOKING GOOD, YOUR HIGHNESS!
ZZZZ!
"GLAZED IS THE SLEEPY ONE."
BONJOUR, CROISSANT!
"SPRINKLES IS THE POPULAR ONE."
"PLAIN IS MY FAVORITE...SMART LIKE ME, BUT NOT BRAGGY."
NOBLE SCOUT, WHAT NEWS HAVE YOU?
MY QUEEN... THE DANISH KINGDOM... ⁝PANT⁝...SO TIRED...LET ME CATCH MY BREATH...GOSH, I'M SO HUNGRY...
DAD, NO!
MMM...THESE GUYS ARE EVEN TASTIER THAN THE DANISH.
CHOMP!

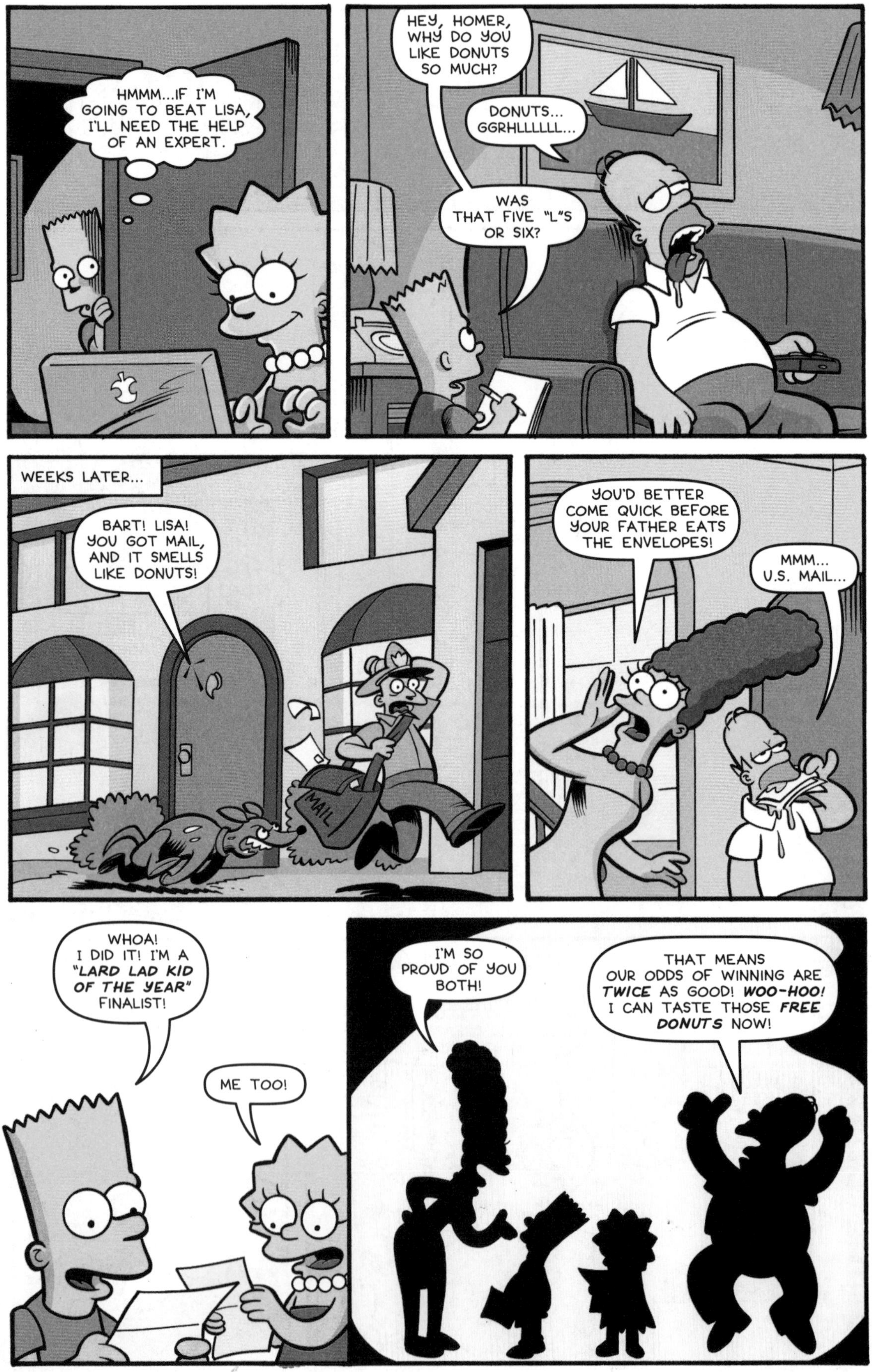
HMMM...IF I'M GOING TO BEAT LISA, I'LL NEED THE HELP OF AN EXPERT.
HEY, HOMER, WHY DO YOU LIKE DONUTS SO MUCH?
DONUTS... GGRHLLLLLL...
WAS THAT FIVE "L"S OR SIX?
WEEKS LATER...
BART! LISA! YOU GOT MAIL, AND IT SMELLS LIKE DONUTS!
MAIL
YOU'D BETTER COME QUICK BEFORE YOUR FATHER EATS THE ENVELOPES!
MMM... U.S. MAIL...
WHOA! I DID IT! I'M A "*LARD LAD KID OF THE YEAR*" FINALIST!
ME TOO!
I'M SO PROUD OF YOU BOTH!
THAT MEANS OUR ODDS OF WINNING ARE *TWICE* AS GOOD! *WOO-HOO!* I CAN TASTE THOSE *FREE DONUTS* NOW!

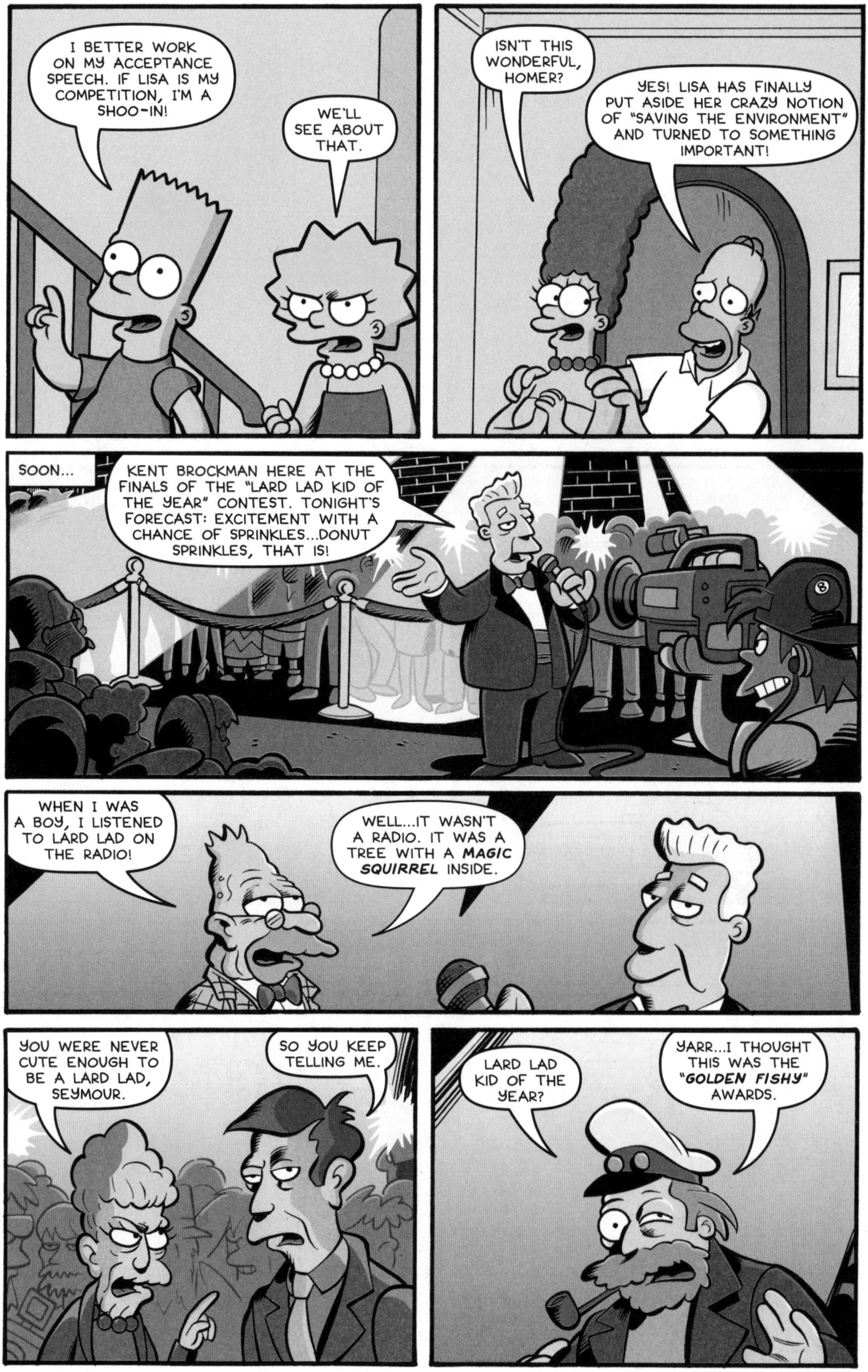
I BETTER WORK ON MY ACCEPTANCE SPEECH. IF LISA IS MY COMPETITION, I'M A SHOO-IN!
WE'LL SEE ABOUT THAT.
ISN'T THIS WONDERFUL, HOMER?
YES! LISA HAS FINALLY PUT ASIDE HER CRAZY NOTION OF "SAVING THE ENVIRONMENT" AND TURNED TO SOMETHING IMPORTANT!
SOON...
KENT BROCKMAN HERE AT THE FINALS OF THE "LARD LAD KID OF THE YEAR" CONTEST. TONIGHT'S FORECAST: EXCITEMENT WITH A CHANCE OF SPRINKLES...DONUT SPRINKLES, THAT IS!
WHEN I WAS A BOY, I LISTENED TO LARD LAD ON THE RADIO!
WELL...IT WASN'T A RADIO. IT WAS A TREE WITH A MAGIC SQUIRREL INSIDE.
YOU WERE NEVER CUTE ENOUGH TO BE A LARD LAD, SEYMOUR.
SO YOU KEEP TELLING ME.
LARD LAD KID OF THE YEAR?
YARR...I THOUGHT THIS WAS THE "GOLDEN FISHY" AWARDS.

THIS IS SO FANCY. I FEEL LIKE I'M AT THE OSCARS!

ME, TOO! GOOD THING I BROUGHT ROTTEN FRUIT TO THROW IN CASE *BILLY CRYSTAL* SHOWS UP!

EVERYONE IN TOWN IS HERE!

THIS IS THE BIGGEST THING TO HAPPEN TO SPRINGFIELD SINCE THE LAST BIG THING THAT HAPPENED TO SPRINGFIELD!

SMITHERS, DO I UNDERSTAND CORRECTLY THAT THE WINNING CHILD WILL BE KILLED, STIRRED INTO BATTER, AND THEN MADE INTO DONUTS?

I DON'T BELIEVE DONUTS ARE MADE FROM CHILDREN, SIR.

THEN WHAT HAVE I BEEN *EATING* ALL THESE YEARS?

ISN'T IT KIND OF ODD WE'RE AT A CHILDREN'S PAGEANT AND WE DON'T HAVE ANY KIDS OF OUR OWN?

I'LL SAY. ESPECIALLY CONSIDERING THE *SUPER BOWL* IS GOING ON RIGHT NOW.

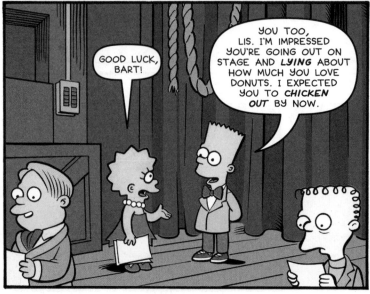

GOOD LUCK, BART!

YOU TOO, LIS. I'M IMPRESSED YOU'RE GOING OUT ON STAGE AND *LYING* ABOUT HOW MUCH YOU LOVE DONUTS. I EXPECTED YOU TO *CHICKEN OUT* BY NOW.

...LYING ABOUT DONUTS...LYING ABOUT DONUTS.. LYING ABOUT...

HMMM...

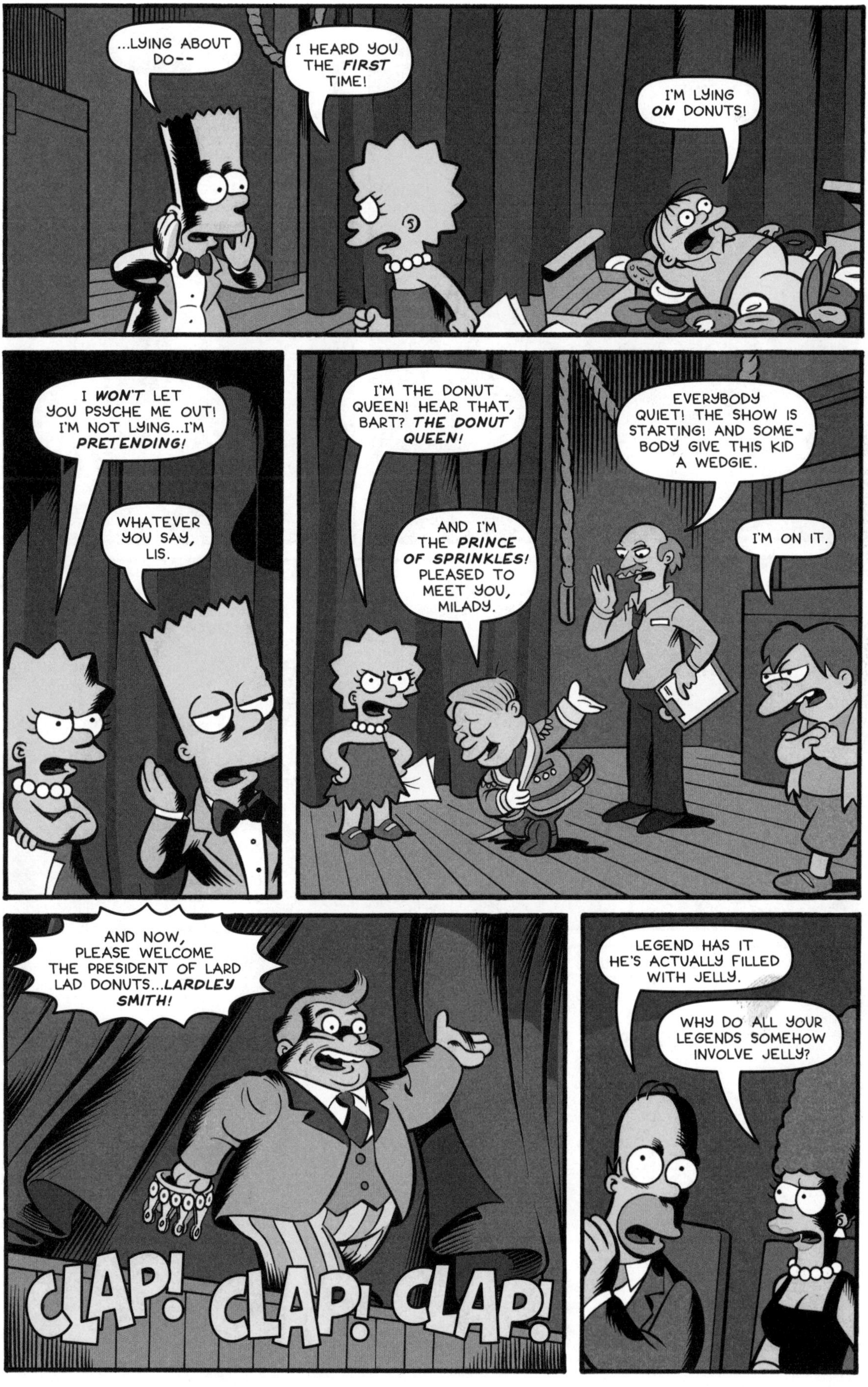
...LYING ABOUT DO--
I HEARD YOU THE FIRST TIME!
I'M LYING ON DONUTS!
I WON'T LET YOU PSYCHE ME OUT! I'M NOT LYING...I'M PRETENDING!
WHATEVER YOU SAY, LIS.
I'M THE DONUT QUEEN! HEAR THAT, BART? THE DONUT QUEEN!
AND I'M THE PRINCE OF SPRINKLES! PLEASED TO MEET YOU, MILADY.
EVERYBODY QUIET! THE SHOW IS STARTING! AND SOMEBODY GIVE THIS KID A WEDGIE.
I'M ON IT.
AND NOW, PLEASE WELCOME THE PRESIDENT OF LARD LAD DONUTS...LARDLEY SMITH!
CLAP! CLAP! CLAP!
LEGEND HAS IT HE'S ACTUALLY FILLED WITH JELLY.
WHY DO ALL YOUR LEGENDS SOMEHOW INVOLVE JELLY?

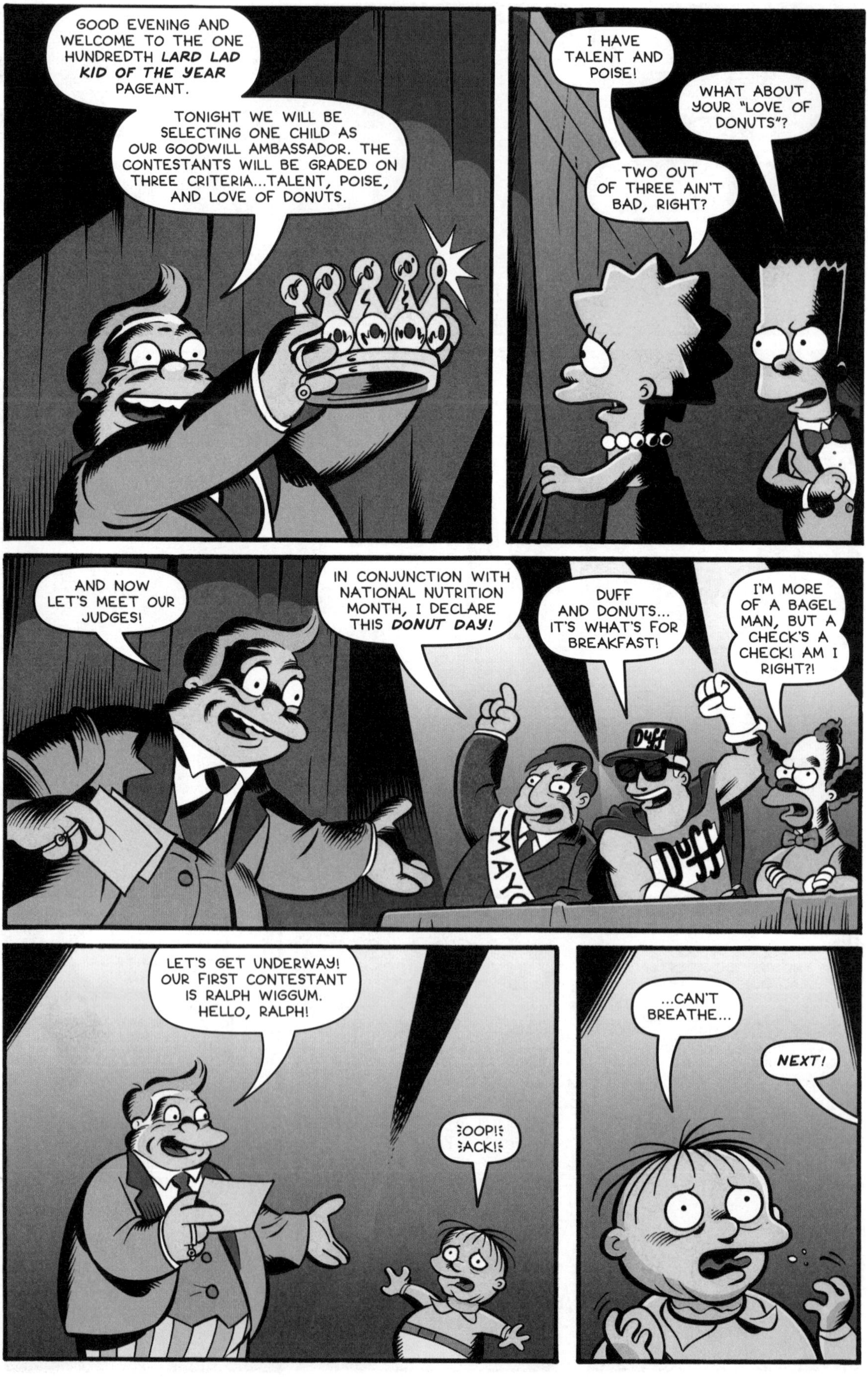
GOOD EVENING AND WELCOME TO THE ONE HUNDREDTH **LARD LAD KID OF THE YEAR** PAGEANT.
TONIGHT WE WILL BE SELECTING ONE CHILD AS OUR GOODWILL AMBASSADOR. THE CONTESTANTS WILL BE GRADED ON THREE CRITERIA...TALENT, POISE, AND LOVE OF DONUTS.
I HAVE TALENT AND POISE!
WHAT ABOUT YOUR "LOVE OF DONUTS"?
TWO OUT OF THREE AIN'T BAD, RIGHT?
AND NOW LET'S MEET OUR JUDGES!
IN CONJUNCTION WITH NATIONAL NUTRITION MONTH, I DECLARE THIS **DONUT DAY!**
DUFF AND DONUTS... IT'S WHAT'S FOR BREAKFAST!
I'M MORE OF A BAGEL MAN, BUT A CHECK'S A CHECK! AM I RIGHT?!
LET'S GET UNDERWAY! OUR FIRST CONTESTANT IS RALPH WIGGUM. HELLO, RALPH!
OOP!
ACK!
...CAN'T BREATHE...
NEXT!

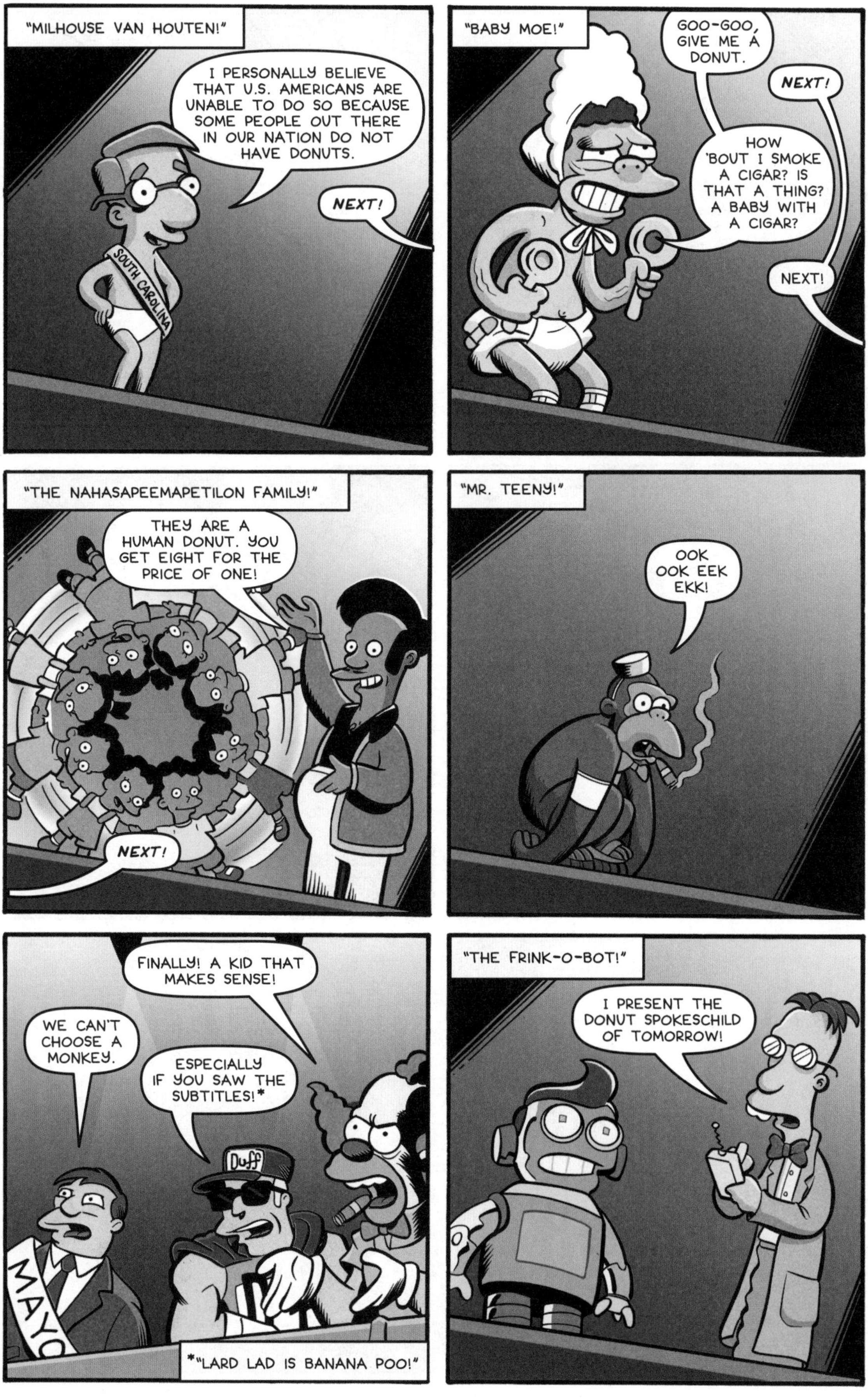
"MILHOUSE VAN HOUTEN!"
I PERSONALLY BELIEVE THAT U.S. AMERICANS ARE UNABLE TO DO SO BECAUSE SOME PEOPLE OUT THERE IN OUR NATION DO NOT HAVE DONUTS.
SOUTH CAROLINA
NEXT!
"BABY MOE!"
GOO-GOO, GIVE ME A DONUT.
HOW 'BOUT I SMOKE A CIGAR? IS THAT A THING? A BABY WITH A CIGAR?
NEXT!
NEXT!
"THE NAHASAPEEMAPETILON FAMILY!"
THEY ARE A HUMAN DONUT. YOU GET EIGHT FOR THE PRICE OF ONE!
NEXT!
"MR. TEENY!"
OOK OOK EEK EKK!
FINALLY! A KID THAT MAKES SENSE!
WE CAN'T CHOOSE A MONKEY.
ESPECIALLY IF YOU SAW THE SUBTITLES!*
Duff
MAYO
*"LARD LAD IS BANANA POO!"
"THE FRINK-O-BOT!"
I PRESENT THE DONUT SPOKESCHILD OF TOMORROW!

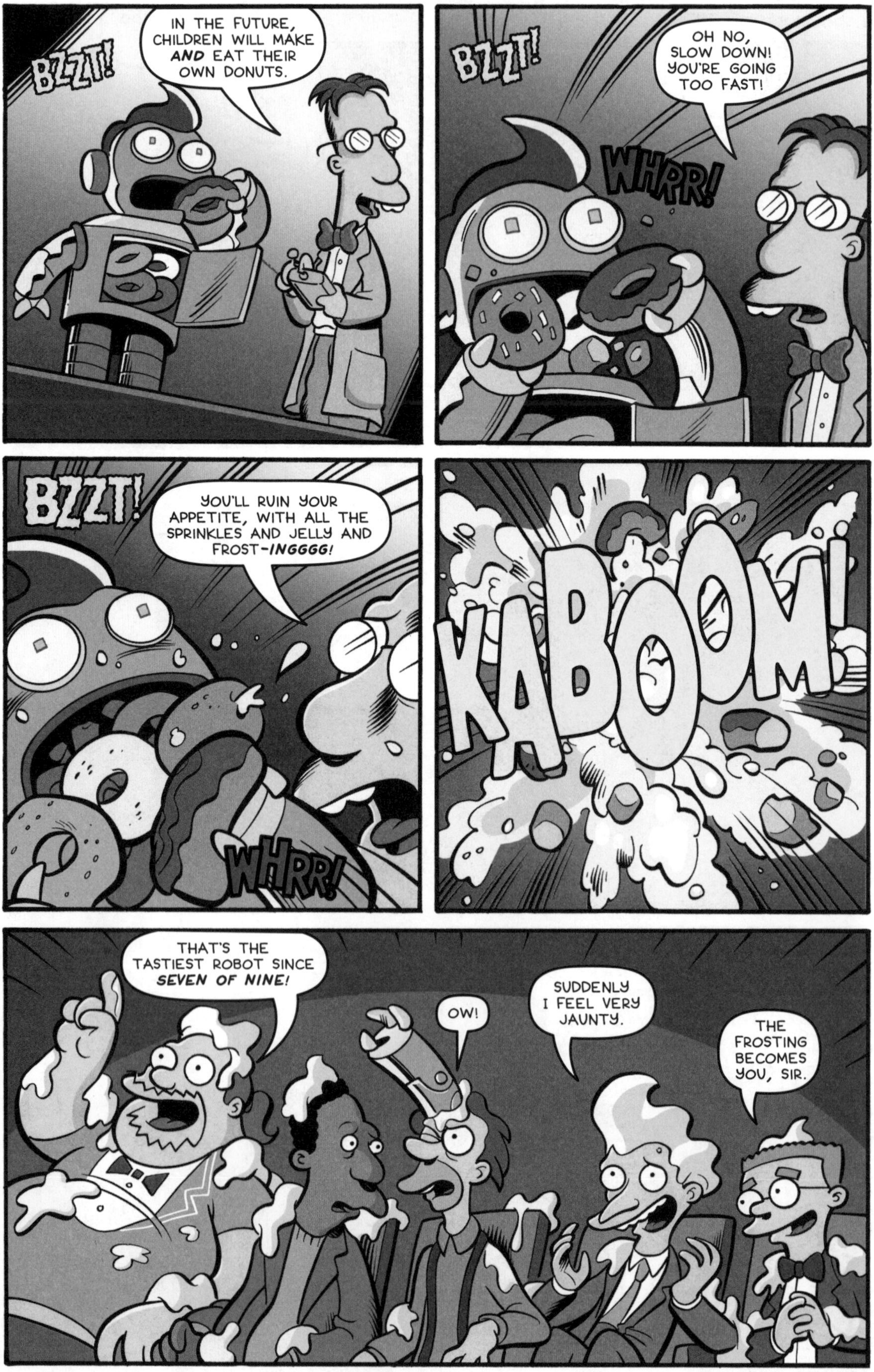
BZZT!
IN THE FUTURE, CHILDREN WILL MAKE *AND* EAT THEIR OWN DONUTS.
BZZT!
OH NO, SLOW DOWN! YOU'RE GOING TOO FAST!
WHRR!
BZZT!
YOU'LL RUIN YOUR APPETITE, WITH ALL THE SPRINKLES AND JELLY AND FROST-*INGGGG!*
WHRR!
KABOOM!
THAT'S THE TASTIEST ROBOT SINCE *SEVEN OF NINE!*
OW!
SUDDENLY I FEEL VERY JAUNTY.
THE FROSTING BECOMES YOU, SIR.

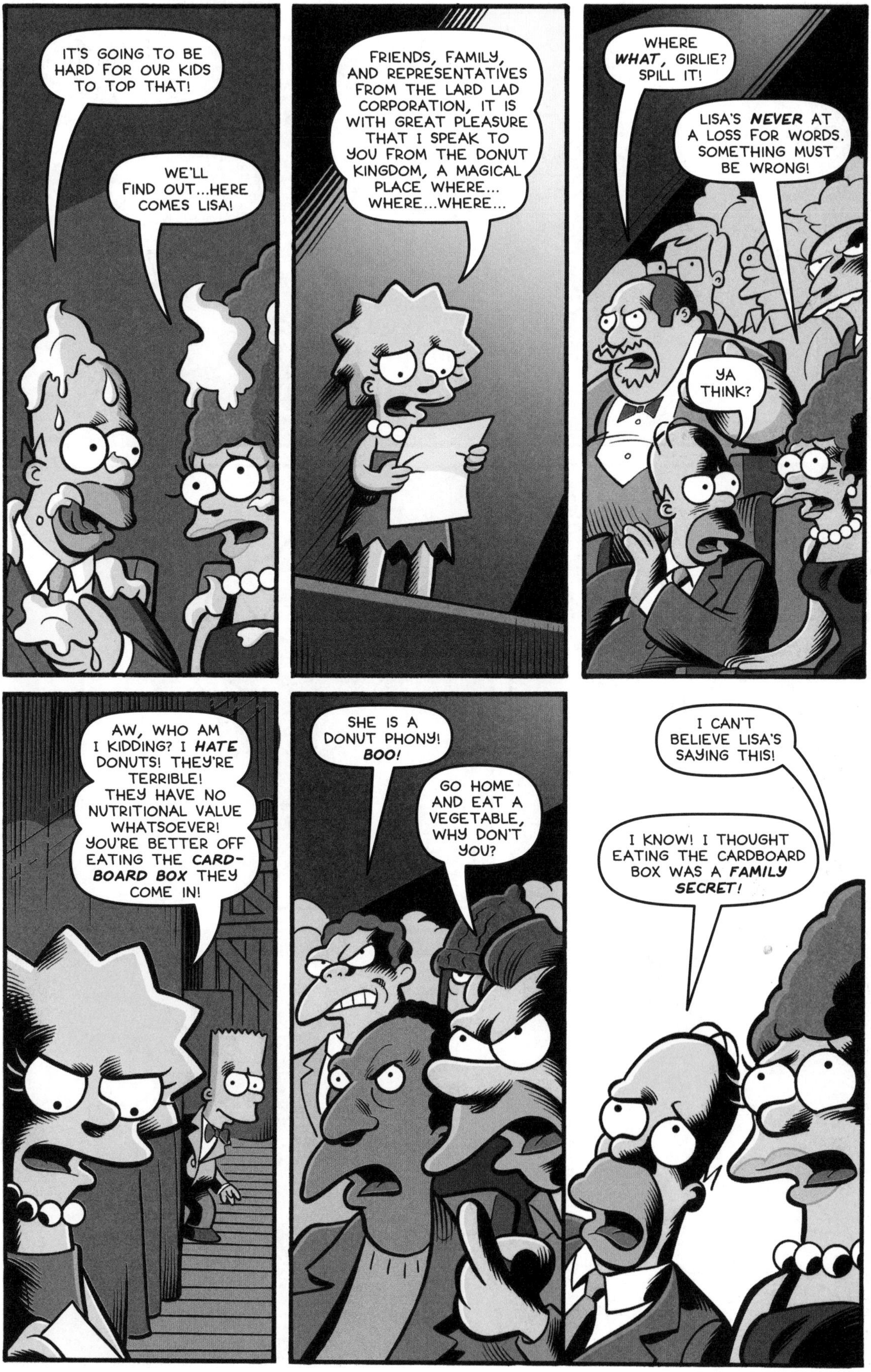
IT'S GOING TO BE HARD FOR OUR KIDS TO TOP THAT!
WE'LL FIND OUT...HERE COMES LISA!
FRIENDS, FAMILY, AND REPRESENTATIVES FROM THE LARD LAD CORPORATION, IT IS WITH GREAT PLEASURE THAT I SPEAK TO YOU FROM THE DONUT KINGDOM, A MAGICAL PLACE WHERE... WHERE...WHERE...
WHERE *WHAT*, GIRLIE? SPILL IT!
LISA'S *NEVER* AT A LOSS FOR WORDS. SOMETHING MUST BE WRONG!
YA THINK?
AW, WHO AM I KIDDING? I *HATE* DONUTS! THEY'RE TERRIBLE! THEY HAVE NO NUTRITIONAL VALUE WHATSOEVER! YOU'RE BETTER OFF EATING THE *CARD-BOARD BOX* THEY COME IN!
SHE IS A DONUT PHONY! *BOO!*
GO HOME AND EAT A VEGETABLE, WHY DON'T YOU?
I CAN'T BELIEVE LISA'S SAYING THIS!
I KNOW! I THOUGHT EATING THE CARDBOARD BOX WAS A *FAMILY SECRET*!

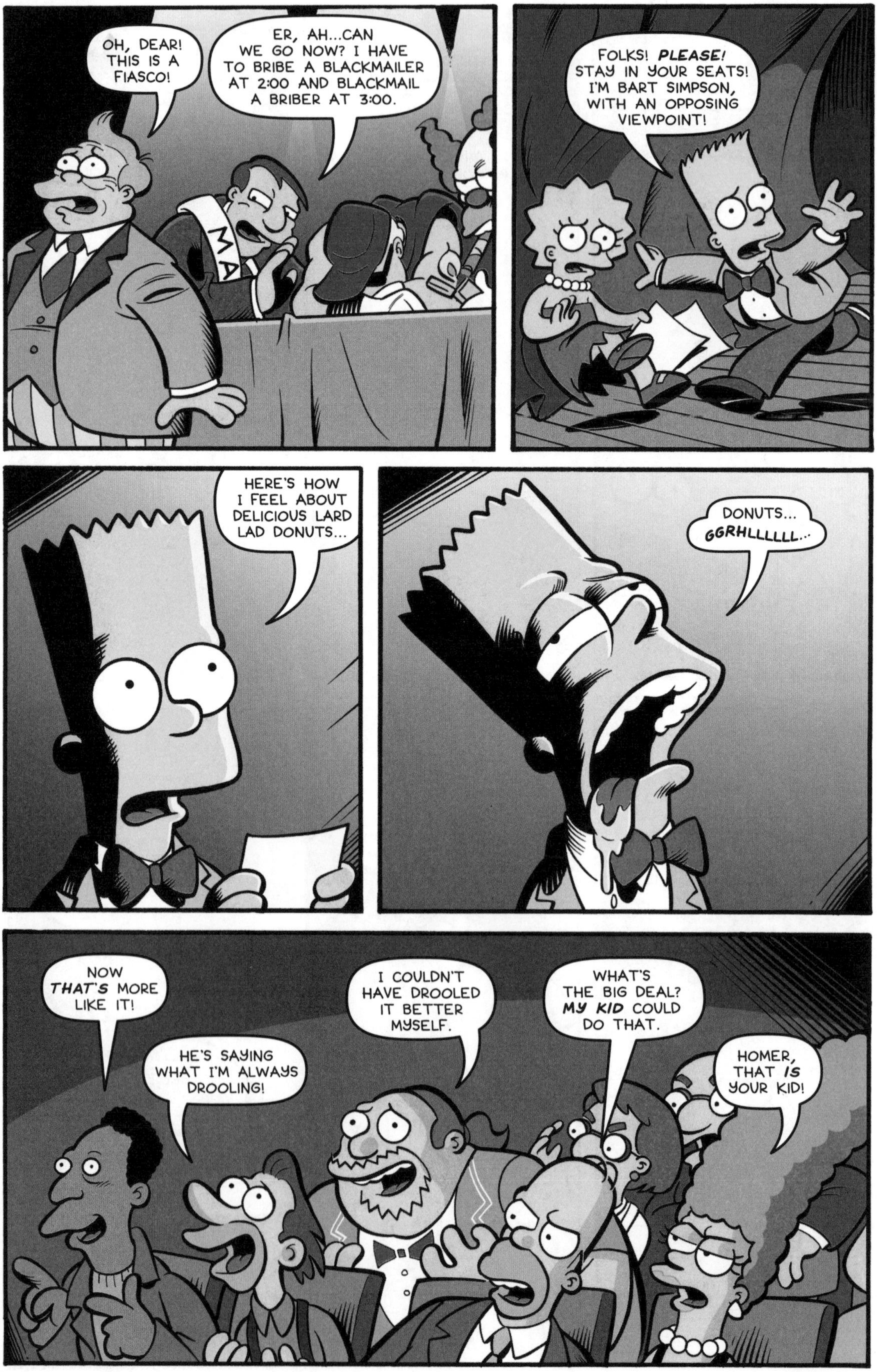
OH, DEAR! THIS IS A FIASCO!
ER, AH...CAN WE GO NOW? I HAVE TO BRIBE A BLACKMAILER AT 2:00 AND BLACKMAIL A BRIBER AT 3:00.
MA
FOLKS! PLEASE! STAY IN YOUR SEATS! I'M BART SIMPSON, WITH AN OPPOSING VIEWPOINT!
HERE'S HOW I FEEL ABOUT DELICIOUS LARD LAD DONUTS...
DONUTS... GGRHLLLLLLL...
NOW THAT'S MORE LIKE IT!
HE'S SAYING WHAT I'M ALWAYS DROOLING!
I COULDN'T HAVE DROOLED IT BETTER MYSELF.
WHAT'S THE BIG DEAL? MY KID COULD DO THAT.
HOMER, THAT IS YOUR KID!

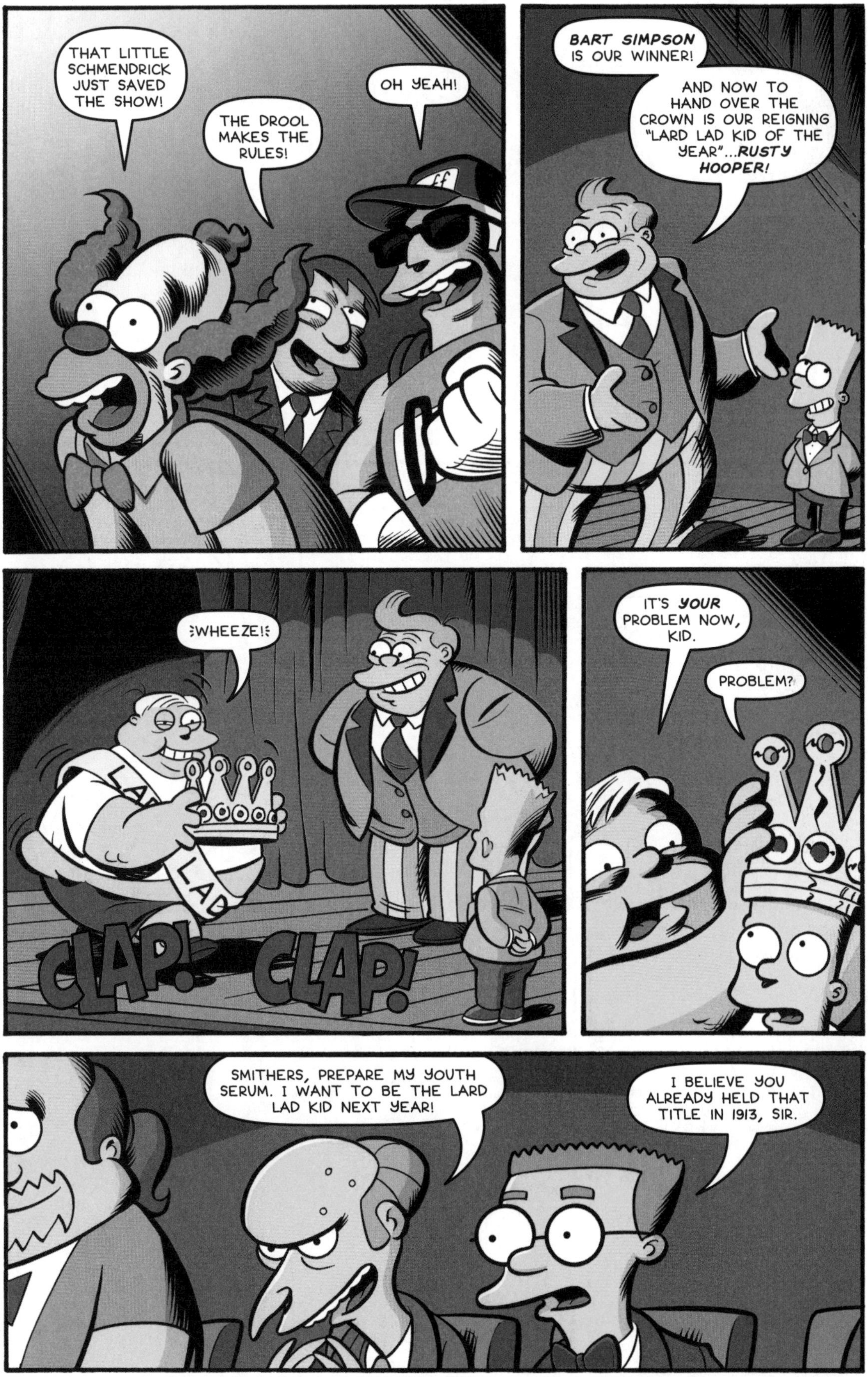
THAT LITTLE SCHMENDRICK JUST SAVED THE SHOW!
THE DROOL MAKES THE RULES!
OH YEAH!
BART SIMPSON IS OUR WINNER!
AND NOW TO HAND OVER THE CROWN IS OUR REIGNING "LARD LAD KID OF THE YEAR"...**RUSTY HOOPER!**
WHEEZE!
CLAP! CLAP!
IT'S **YOUR** PROBLEM NOW, KID.
PROBLEM?
SMITHERS, PREPARE MY YOUTH SERUM. I WANT TO BE THE LARD LAD KID NEXT YEAR!
I BELIEVE YOU ALREADY HELD THAT TITLE IN 1913, SIR.

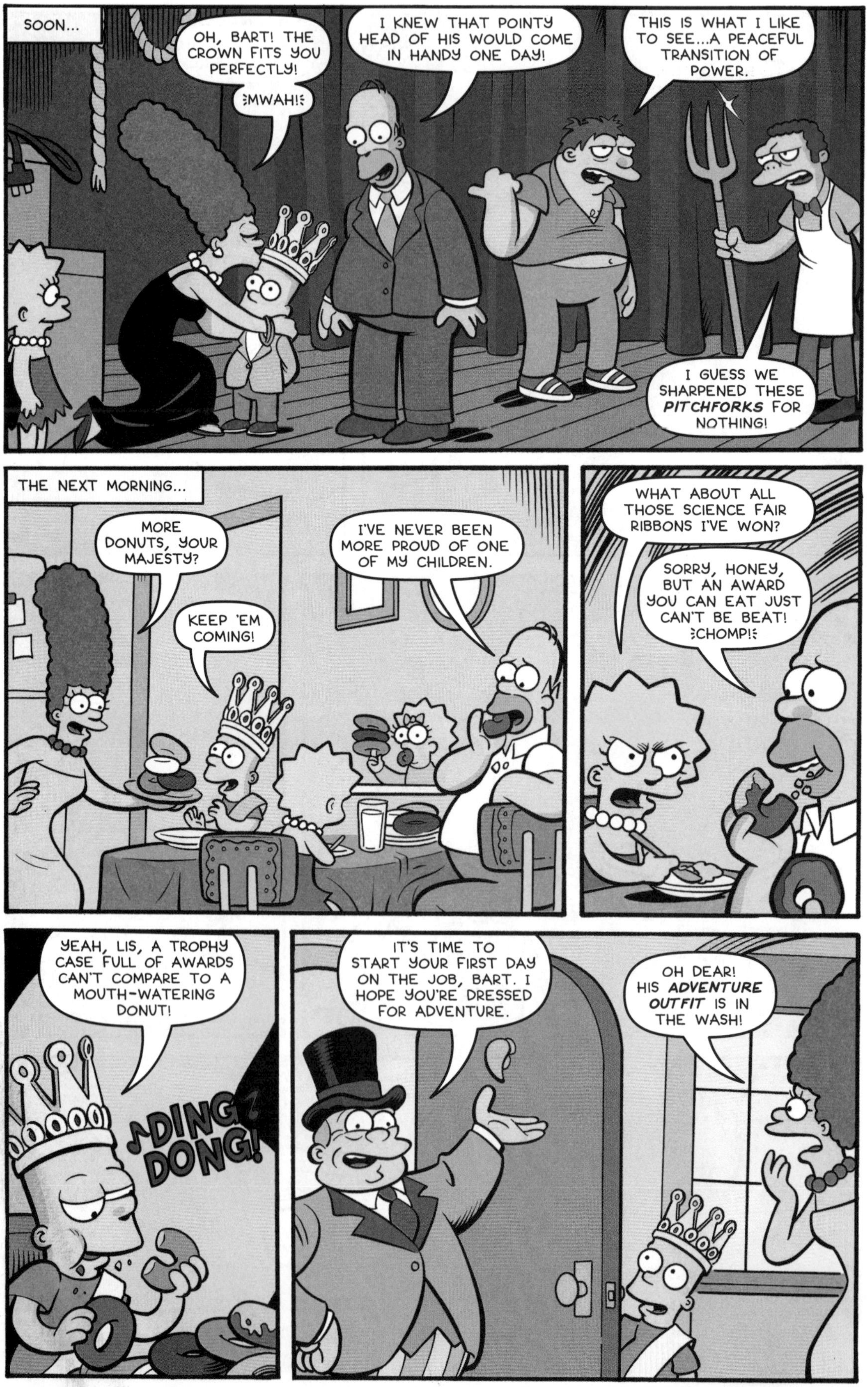
SOON...
OH, BART! THE CROWN FITS YOU PERFECTLY!
MWAH!
I KNEW THAT POINTY HEAD OF HIS WOULD COME IN HANDY ONE DAY!
THIS IS WHAT I LIKE TO SEE...A PEACEFUL TRANSITION OF POWER.
I GUESS WE SHARPENED THESE **PITCHFORKS** FOR NOTHING!
THE NEXT MORNING...
MORE DONUTS, YOUR MAJESTY?
KEEP 'EM COMING!
I'VE NEVER BEEN MORE PROUD OF ONE OF MY CHILDREN.
WHAT ABOUT ALL THOSE SCIENCE FAIR RIBBONS I'VE WON?
SORRY, HONEY, BUT AN AWARD YOU CAN EAT JUST CAN'T BE BEAT!
CHOMP!
YEAH, LIS, A TROPHY CASE FULL OF AWARDS CAN'T COMPARE TO A MOUTH-WATERING DONUT!
DING DONG!
IT'S TIME TO START YOUR FIRST DAY ON THE JOB, BART. I HOPE YOU'RE DRESSED FOR ADVENTURE.
OH DEAR! HIS **ADVENTURE OUTFIT** IS IN THE WASH!

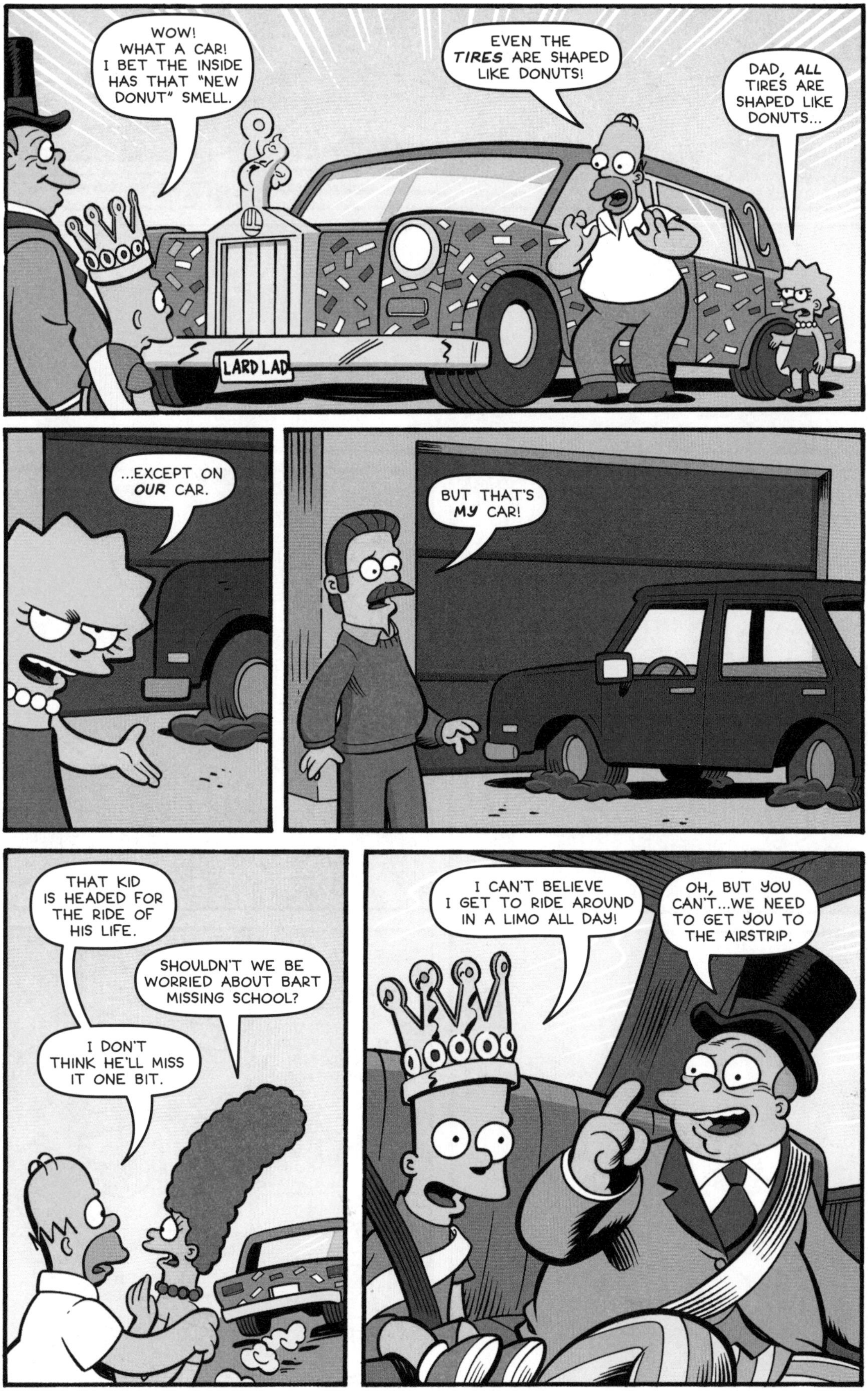

WOW! WHAT A CAR! I BET THE INSIDE HAS THAT "NEW DONUT" SMELL.
LARD LAD
EVEN THE *TIRES* ARE SHAPED LIKE DONUTS!
DAD, **ALL** TIRES ARE SHAPED LIKE DONUTS...
...EXCEPT ON ***OUR*** CAR.
BUT THAT'S ***MY*** CAR!
THAT KID IS HEADED FOR THE RIDE OF HIS LIFE.
SHOULDN'T WE BE WORRIED ABOUT BART MISSING SCHOOL?
I DON'T THINK HE'LL MISS IT ONE BIT.
I CAN'T BELIEVE I GET TO RIDE AROUND IN A LIMO ALL DAY!
OH, BUT YOU CAN'T...WE NEED TO GET YOU TO THE AIRSTRIP.

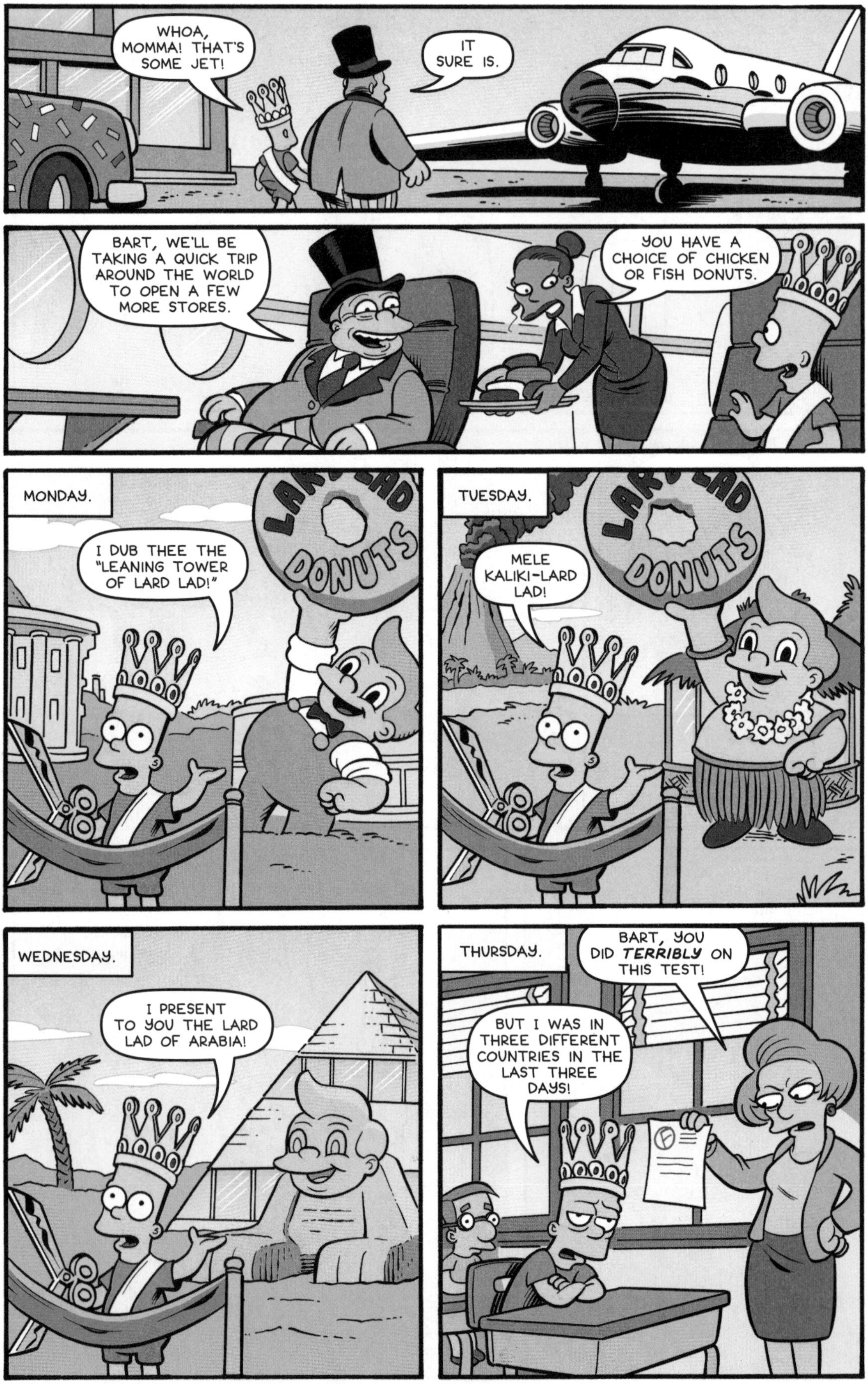

WHOA, MOMMA! THAT'S SOME JET!
IT SURE IS.
BART, WE'LL BE TAKING A QUICK TRIP AROUND THE WORLD TO OPEN A FEW MORE STORES.
YOU HAVE A CHOICE OF CHICKEN OR FISH DONUTS.
MONDAY.
LARD LAD DONUTS
I DUB THEE THE "LEANING TOWER OF LARD LAD!"
TUESDAY.
LARD LAD DONUTS
MELE KALIKI-LARD LAD!
WEDNESDAY.
I PRESENT TO YOU THE LARD LAD OF ARABIA!
THURSDAY.
BART, YOU DID *TERRIBLY* ON THIS TEST!
BUT I WAS IN THREE DIFFERENT COUNTRIES IN THE LAST THREE DAYS!
F

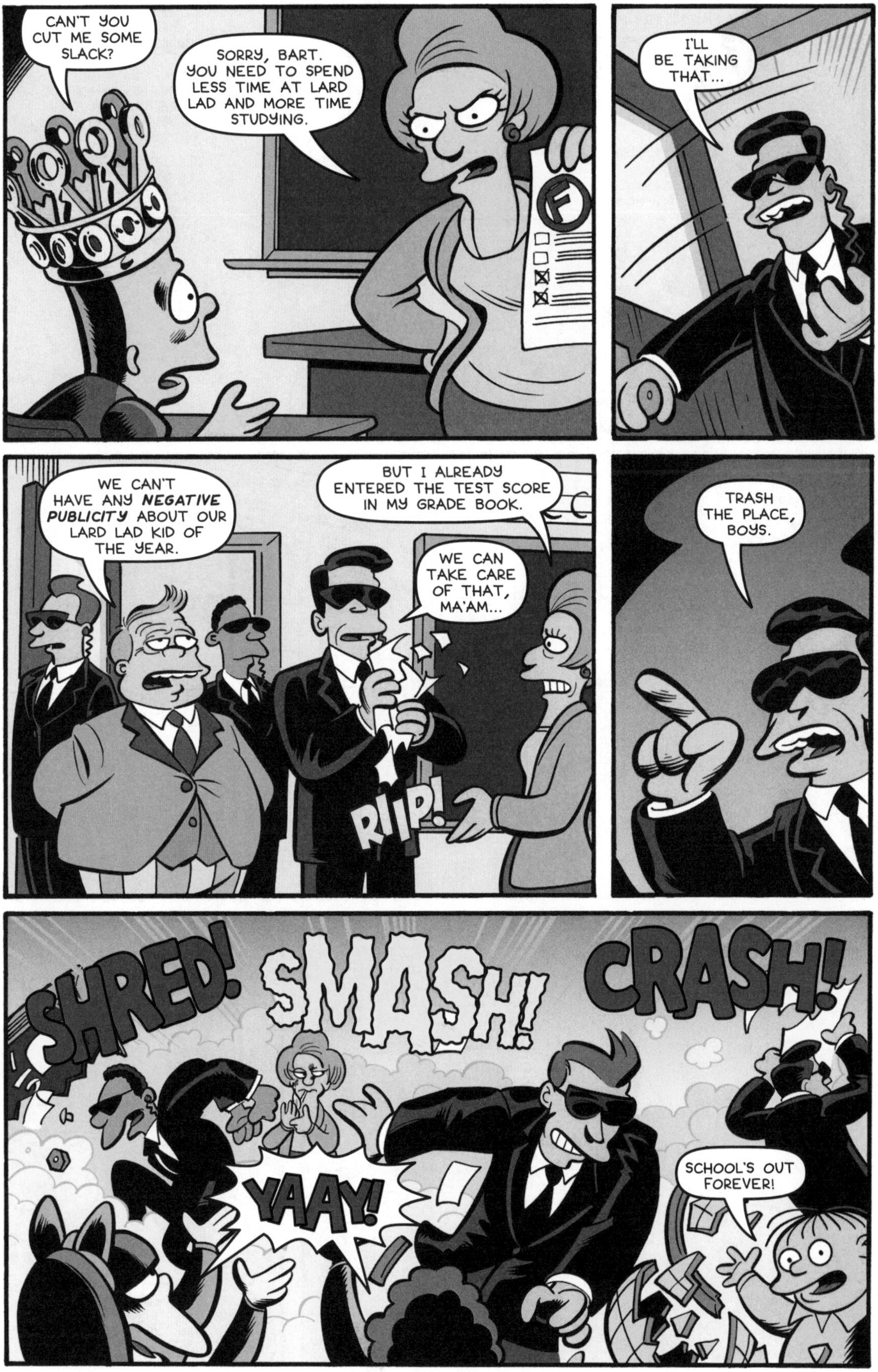
CAN'T YOU CUT ME SOME SLACK?
SORRY, BART. YOU NEED TO SPEND LESS TIME AT LARD LAD AND MORE TIME STUDYING.
F
I'LL BE TAKING THAT...
WE CAN'T HAVE ANY **NEGATIVE PUBLICITY** ABOUT OUR LARD LAD KID OF THE YEAR.
BUT I ALREADY ENTERED THE TEST SCORE IN MY GRADE BOOK.
WE CAN TAKE CARE OF THAT, MA'AM...
RIIP!
TRASH THE PLACE, BOYS.
SHRED!
SMASH!
CRASH!
YAAY!
SCHOOL'S OUT FOREVER!

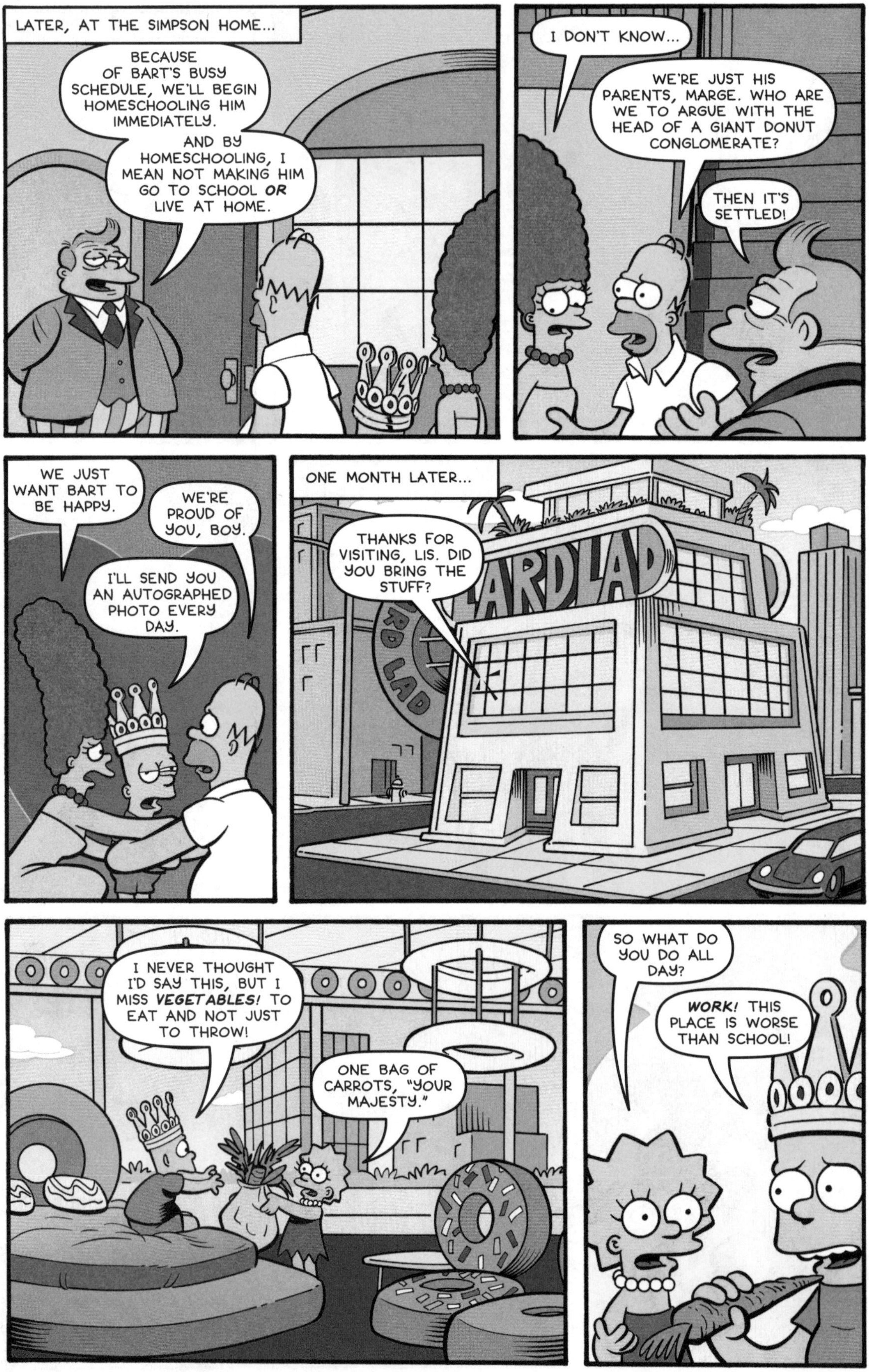
LATER, AT THE SIMPSON HOME...
BECAUSE OF BART'S BUSY SCHEDULE, WE'LL BEGIN HOMESCHOOLING HIM IMMEDIATELY.
AND BY HOMESCHOOLING, I MEAN NOT MAKING HIM GO TO SCHOOL *OR* LIVE AT HOME.
I DON'T KNOW...
WE'RE JUST HIS PARENTS, MARGE. WHO ARE WE TO ARGUE WITH THE HEAD OF A GIANT DONUT CONGLOMERATE?
THEN IT'S SETTLED!
WE JUST WANT BART TO BE HAPPY.
WE'RE PROUD OF YOU, BOY.
I'LL SEND YOU AN AUTOGRAPHED PHOTO EVERY DAY.
ONE MONTH LATER...
THANKS FOR VISITING, LIS. DID YOU BRING THE STUFF?
LARD LAD
I NEVER THOUGHT I'D SAY THIS, BUT I MISS ***VEGETABLES!*** TO EAT AND NOT JUST TO THROW!
ONE BAG OF CARROTS, "YOUR MAJESTY."
SO WHAT DO YOU DO ALL DAY?
WORK! THIS PLACE IS WORSE THAN SCHOOL!

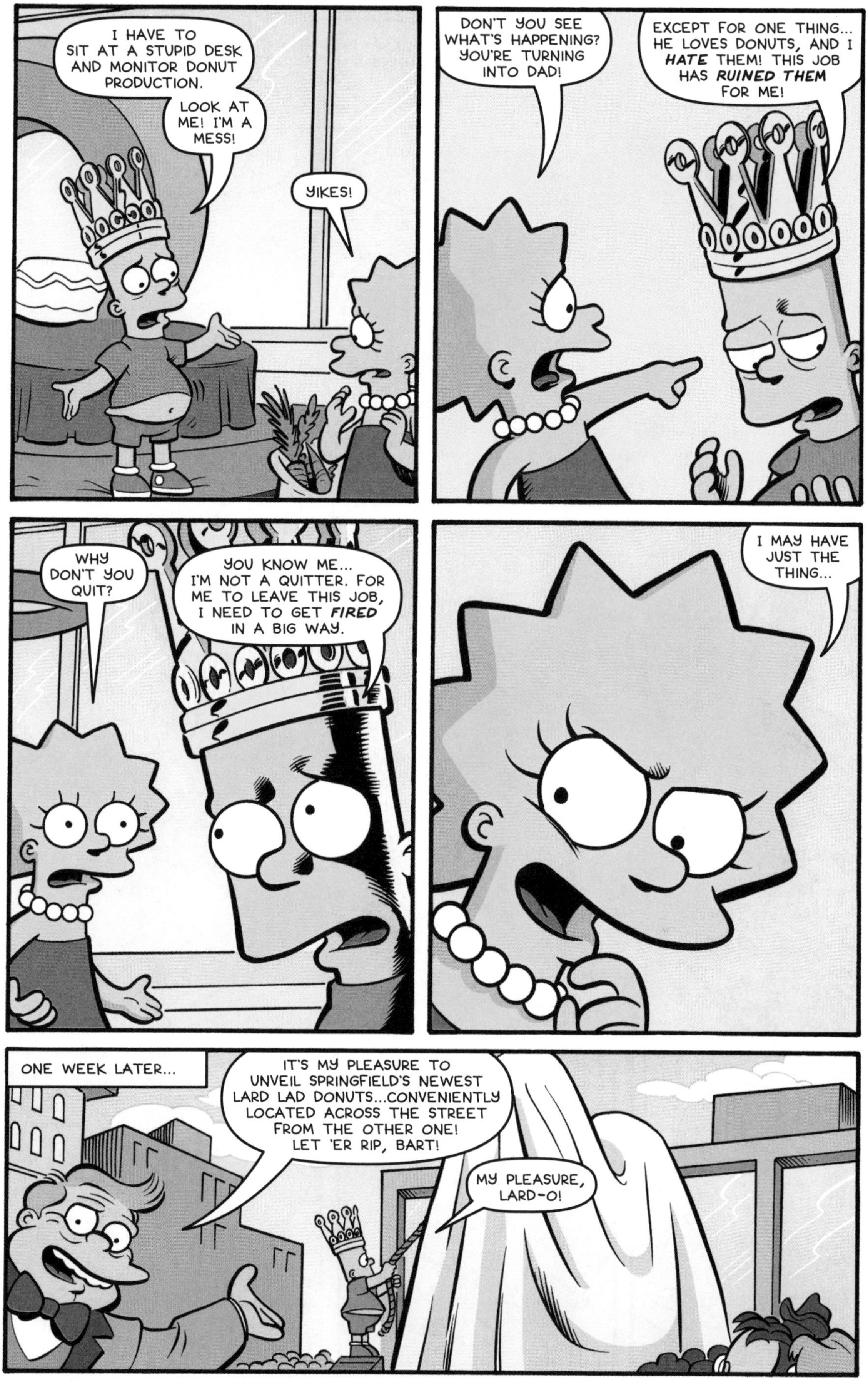

I HAVE TO SIT AT A STUPID DESK AND MONITOR DONUT PRODUCTION.
LOOK AT ME! I'M A MESS!
YIKES!
DON'T YOU SEE WHAT'S HAPPENING? YOU'RE TURNING INTO DAD!
EXCEPT FOR ONE THING... HE LOVES DONUTS, AND I *HATE* THEM! THIS JOB HAS *RUINED THEM* FOR ME!
WHY DON'T YOU QUIT?
YOU KNOW ME... I'M NOT A QUITTER. FOR ME TO LEAVE THIS JOB, I NEED TO GET *FIRED* IN A BIG WAY.
I MAY HAVE JUST THE THING...
ONE WEEK LATER...
IT'S MY PLEASURE TO UNVEIL SPRINGFIELD'S NEWEST LARD LAD DONUTS...CONVENIENTLY LOCATED ACROSS THE STREET FROM THE OTHER ONE! LET 'ER RIP, BART!
MY PLEASURE, LARD-O!

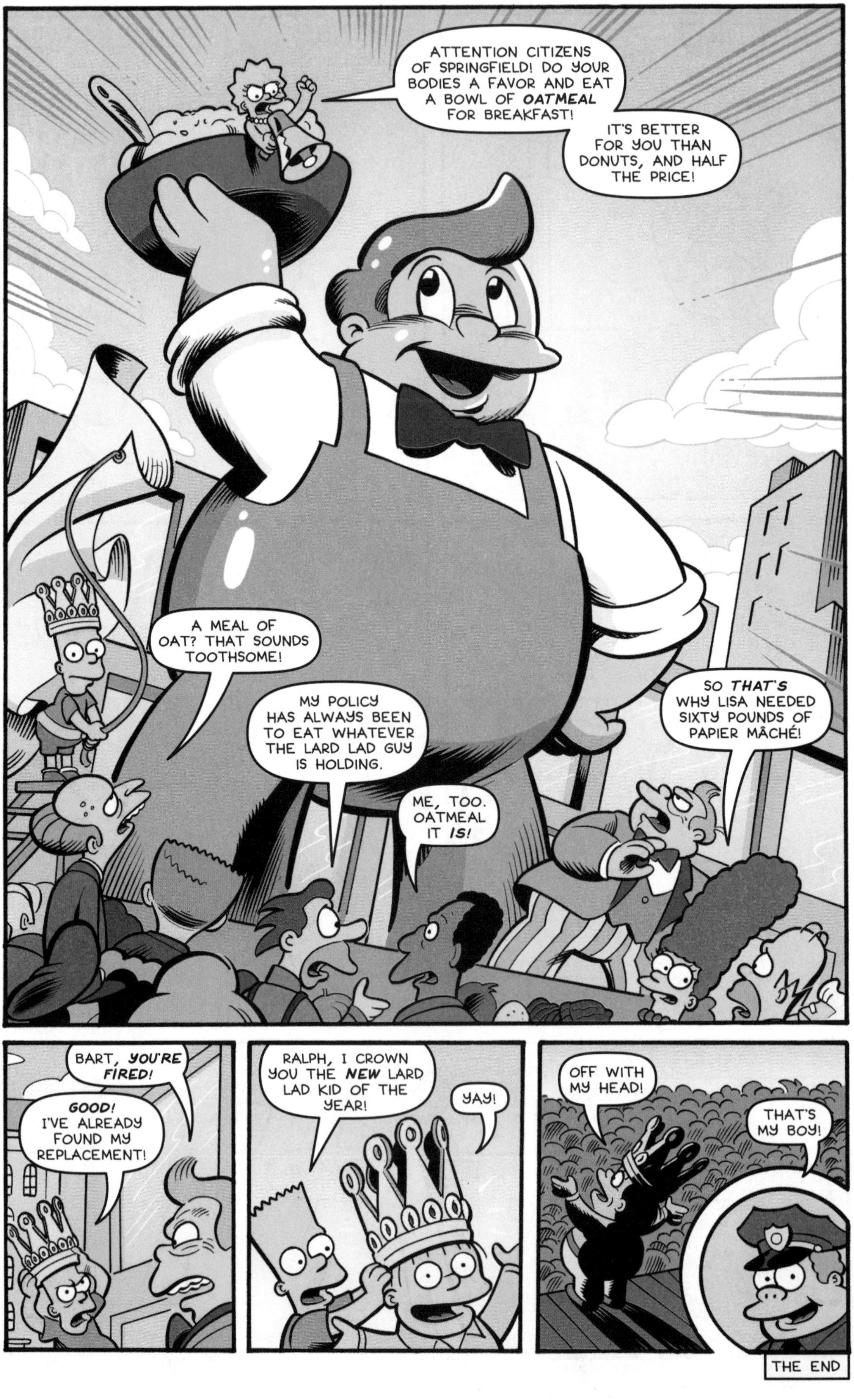
ATTENTION CITIZENS OF SPRINGFIELD! DO YOUR BODIES A FAVOR AND EAT A BOWL OF **OATMEAL** FOR BREAKFAST!
IT'S BETTER FOR YOU THAN DONUTS, AND HALF THE PRICE!
A MEAL OF OAT? THAT SOUNDS TOOTHSOME!
MY POLICY HAS ALWAYS BEEN TO EAT WHATEVER THE LARD LAD GUY IS HOLDING.
ME, TOO. OATMEAL IT ***IS!***
SO ***THAT'S*** WHY LISA NEEDED SIXTY POUNDS OF PAPIER MÂCHÉ!
BART, ***YOU'RE FIRED!***
GOOD! I'VE ALREADY FOUND MY REPLACEMENT!
RALPH, I CROWN YOU THE ***NEW*** LARD LAD KID OF THE YEAR!
YAY!
OFF WITH MY HEAD!
THAT'S MY BOY!
THE END

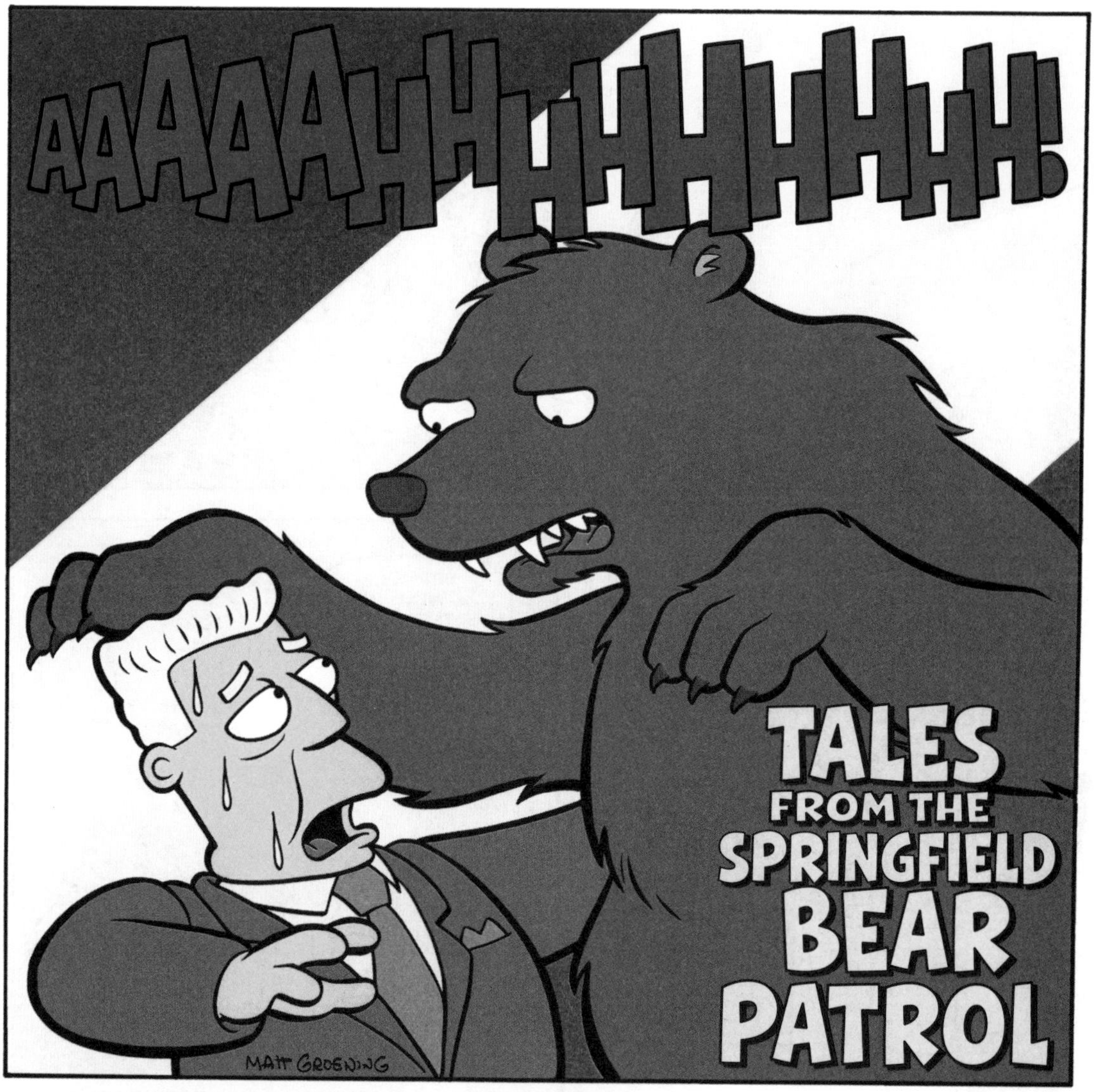
AAAAAHHHHHHHHHH!
TALES FROM THE SPRINGFIELD BEAR PATROL
MATT GROENING

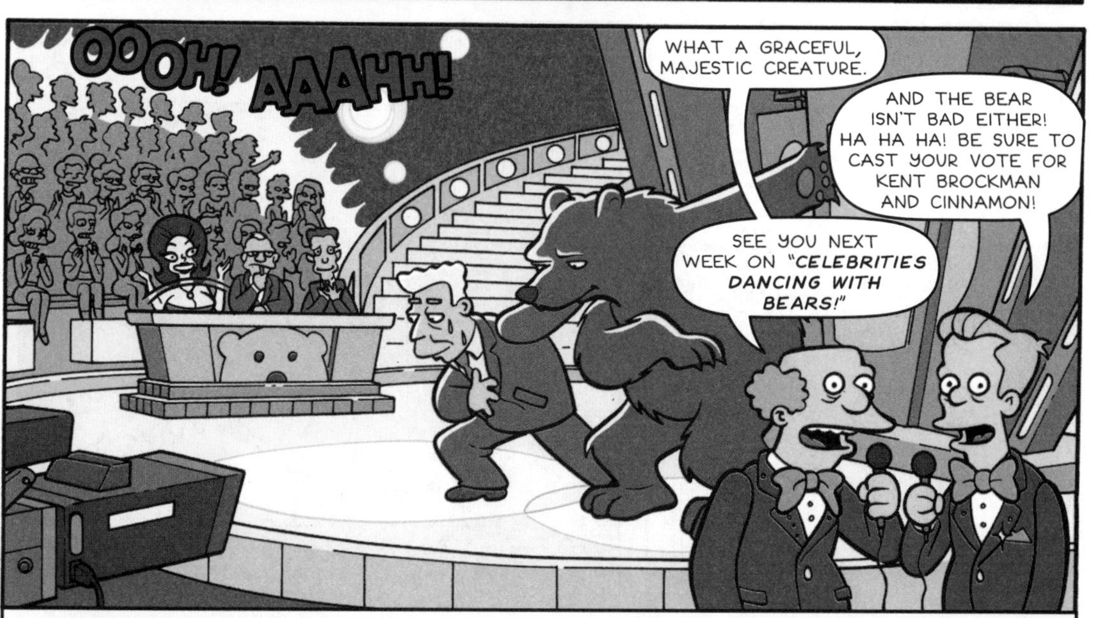
OOOH! AAAHH!
WHAT A GRACEFUL, MAJESTIC CREATURE.
AND THE BEAR ISN'T BAD EITHER! HA HA HA! BE SURE TO CAST YOUR VOTE FOR KENT BROCKMAN AND CINNAMON!
SEE YOU NEXT WEEK ON "*CELEBRITIES DANCING WITH BEARS!*"

BRIAN HOULIHAN SCRIPT ***JAMES LLOYD*** PENCILS ***ANDREW PEPOY*** INKS ***NATHAN HAMILL*** COLORS ***KAREN BATES*** LETTERS ***BILL MORRISON*** EDITOR

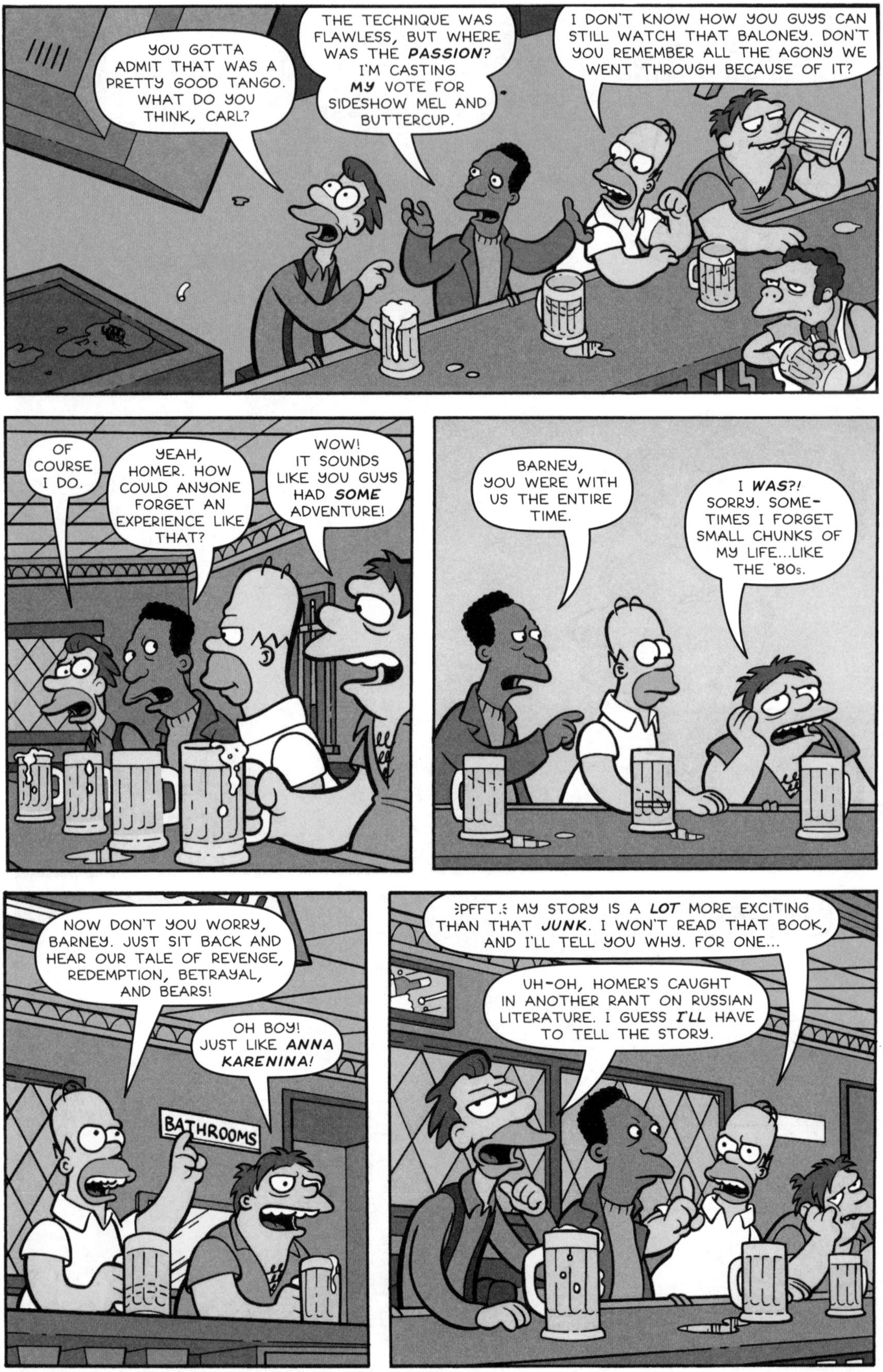
YOU GOTTA ADMIT THAT WAS A PRETTY GOOD TANGO. WHAT DO YOU THINK, CARL?
THE TECHNIQUE WAS FLAWLESS, BUT WHERE WAS THE ***PASSION***? I'M CASTING ***MY*** VOTE FOR SIDESHOW MEL AND BUTTERCUP.
I DON'T KNOW HOW YOU GUYS CAN STILL WATCH THAT BALONEY. DON'T YOU REMEMBER ALL THE AGONY WE WENT THROUGH BECAUSE OF IT?
OF COURSE I DO.
YEAH, HOMER. HOW COULD ANYONE FORGET AN EXPERIENCE LIKE THAT?
WOW! IT SOUNDS LIKE YOU GUYS HAD ***SOME*** ADVENTURE!
BARNEY, YOU WERE WITH US THE ENTIRE TIME.
I ***WAS?!*** SORRY. SOME-TIMES I FORGET SMALL CHUNKS OF MY LIFE...LIKE THE '80s.
NOW DON'T YOU WORRY, BARNEY. JUST SIT BACK AND HEAR OUR TALE OF REVENGE, REDEMPTION, BETRAYAL, AND BEARS!
OH BOY! JUST LIKE ***ANNA KARENINA!***
BATHROOMS
PFFT. MY STORY IS A ***LOT*** MORE EXCITING THAN THAT ***JUNK***. I WON'T READ THAT BOOK, AND I'LL TELL YOU WHY. FOR ONE...
UH-OH, HOMER'S CAUGHT IN ANOTHER RANT ON RUSSIAN LITERATURE. I GUESS ***I'LL*** HAVE TO TELL THE STORY.

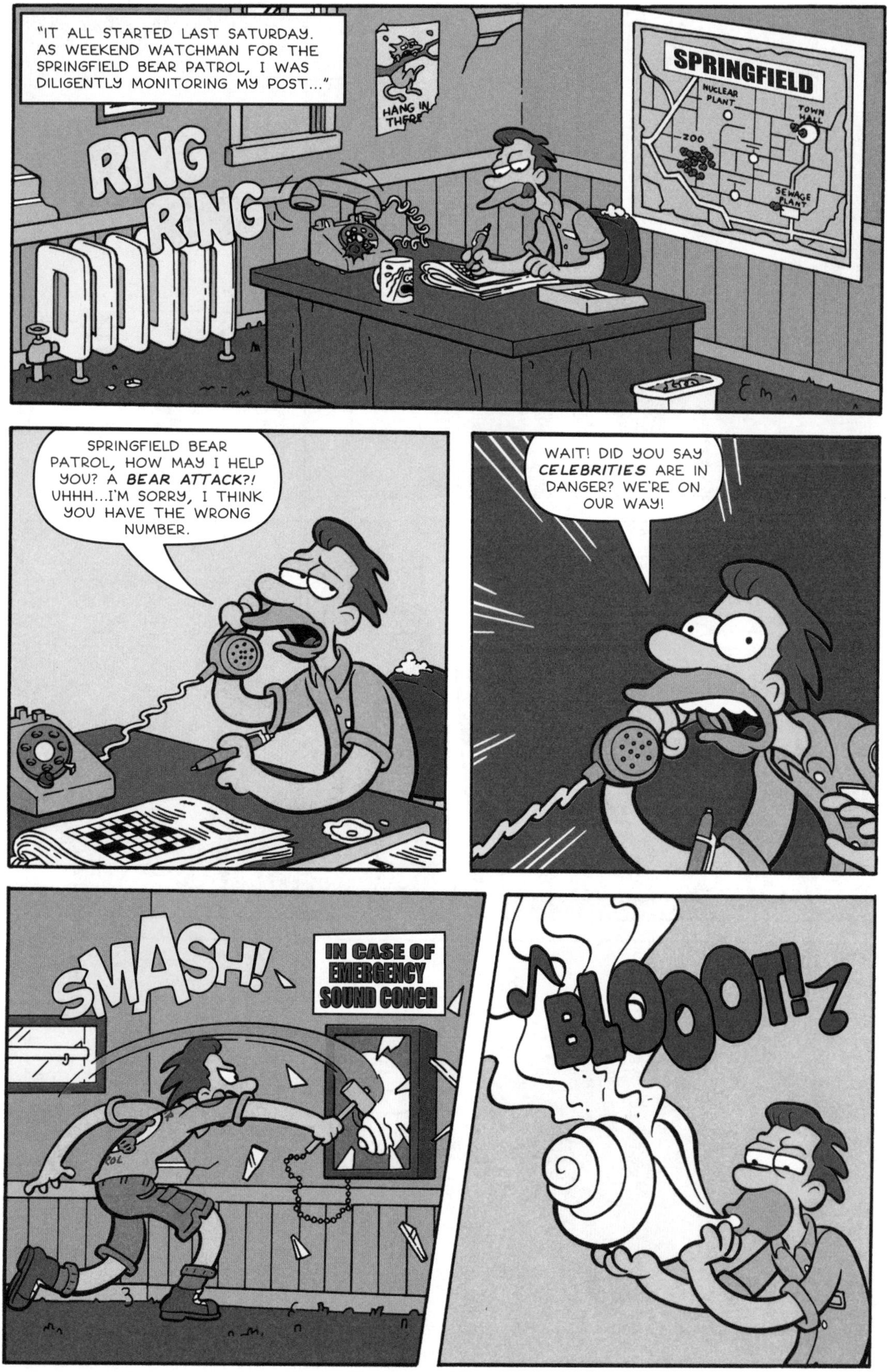
"IT ALL STARTED LAST SATURDAY. AS WEEKEND WATCHMAN FOR THE SPRINGFIELD BEAR PATROL, I WAS DILIGENTLY MONITORING MY POST..."
HANG IN THERE
SPRINGFIELD
NUCLEAR PLANT
TOWN HALL
ZOO
SEWAGE PLANT
RING
RING
SPRINGFIELD BEAR PATROL, HOW MAY I HELP YOU? A BEAR ATTACK?! UHHH...I'M SORRY, I THINK YOU HAVE THE WRONG NUMBER.
WAIT! DID YOU SAY CELEBRITIES ARE IN DANGER? WE'RE ON OUR WAY!
SMASH!
IN CASE OF EMERGENCY SOUND CONCH
BLOOOT!

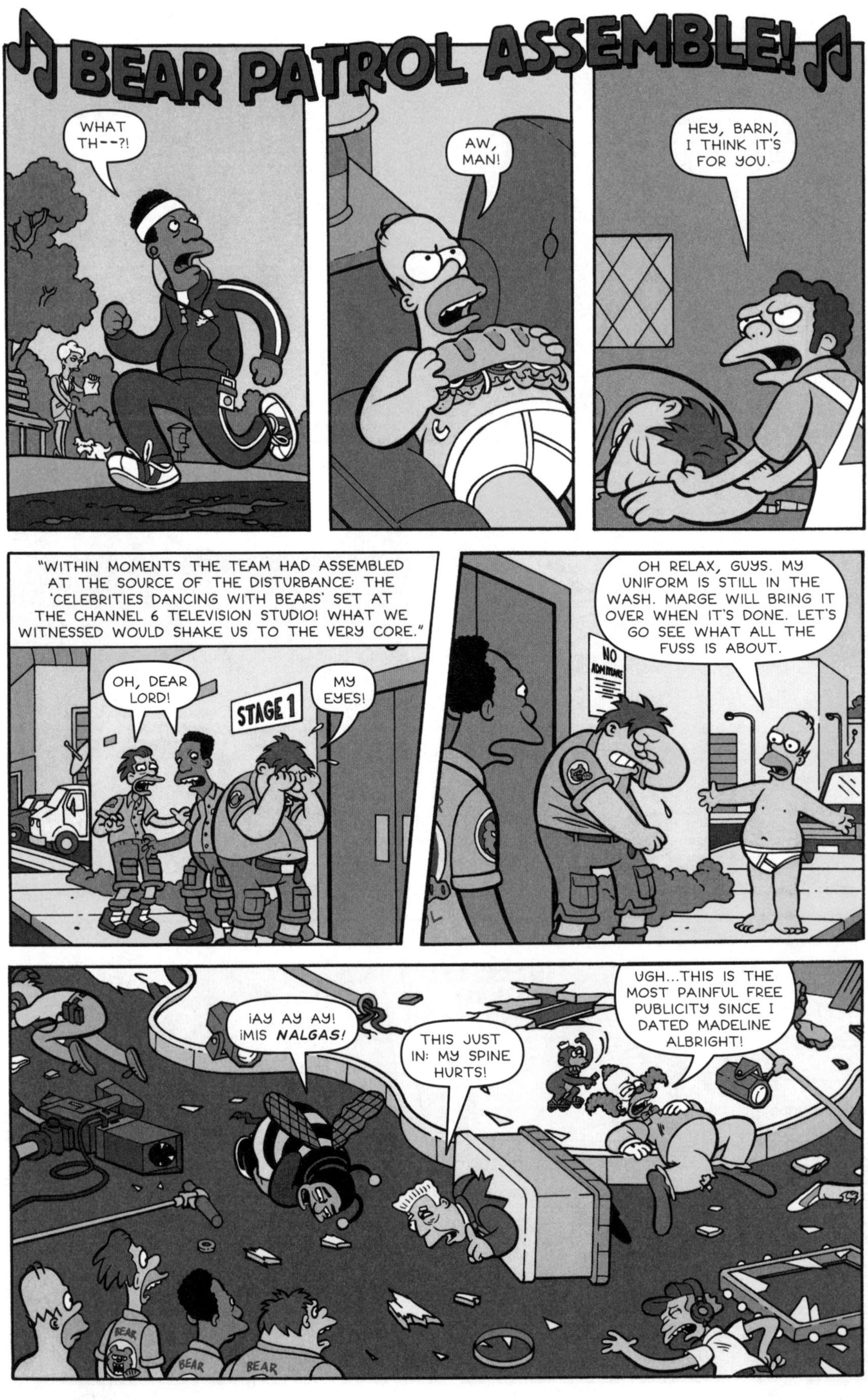
BEAR PATROL ASSEMBLE!
WHAT TH--?!
AW, MAN!
HEY, BARN, I THINK IT'S FOR YOU.
"WITHIN MOMENTS THE TEAM HAD ASSEMBLED AT THE SOURCE OF THE DISTURBANCE: THE 'CELEBRITIES DANCING WITH BEARS' SET AT THE CHANNEL 6 TELEVISION STUDIO! WHAT WE WITNESSED WOULD SHAKE US TO THE VERY CORE."
OH, DEAR LORD!
STAGE 1
MY EYES!
OH RELAX, GUYS. MY UNIFORM IS STILL IN THE WASH. MARGE WILL BRING IT OVER WHEN IT'S DONE. LET'S GO SEE WHAT ALL THE FUSS IS ABOUT.
NO
¡AY AY AY! ¡MIS NALGAS!
THIS JUST IN: MY SPINE HURTS!
UGH...THIS IS THE MOST PAINFUL FREE PUBLICITY SINCE I DATED MADELINE ALBRIGHT!
BEAR
BEAR
BEAR

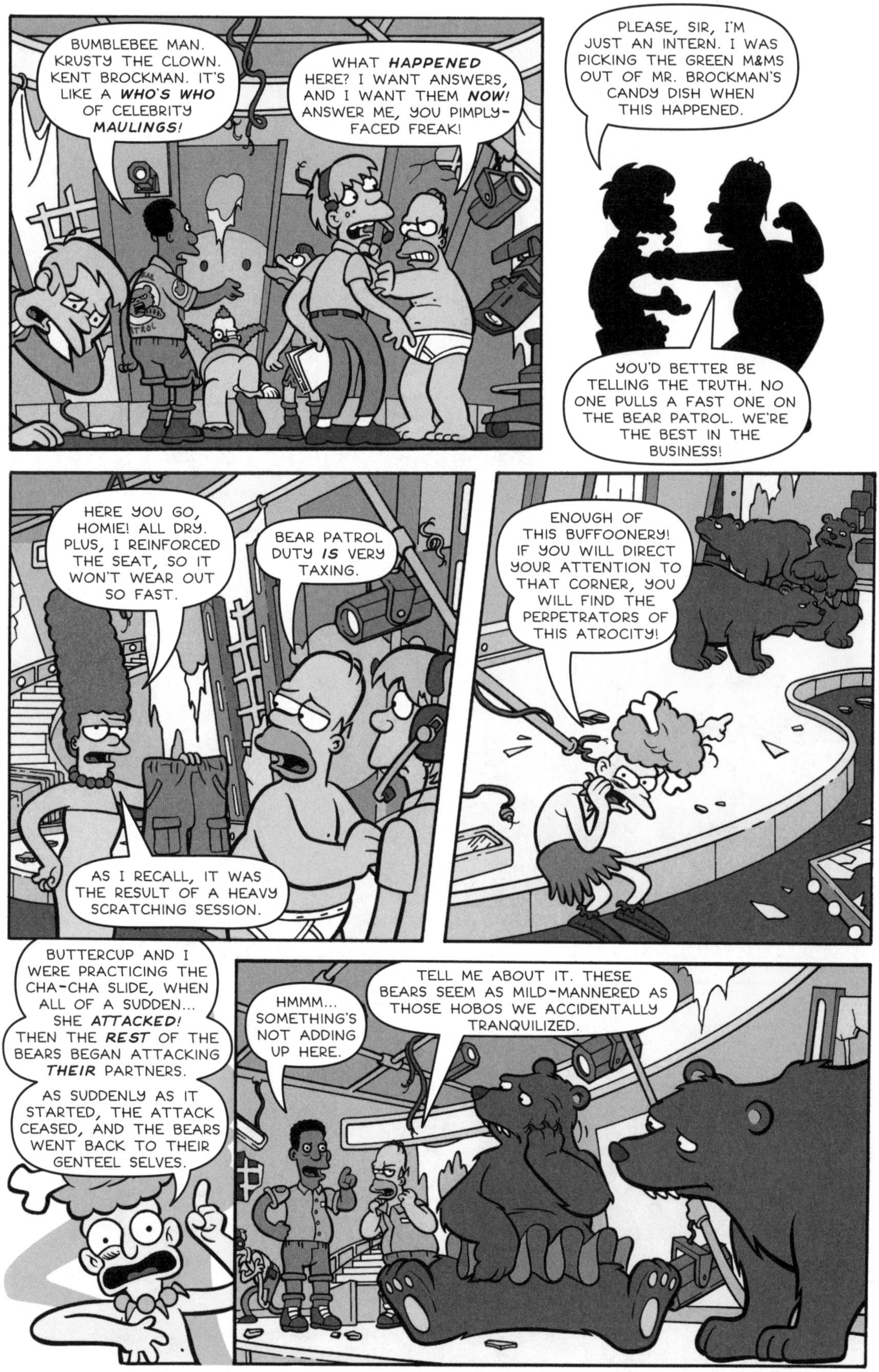
BUMBLEBEE MAN. KRUSTY THE CLOWN. KENT BROCKMAN. IT'S LIKE A **WHO'S WHO** OF CELEBRITY **MAULINGS!**
WHAT **HAPPENED** HERE? I WANT ANSWERS, AND I WANT THEM **NOW!** ANSWER ME, YOU PIMPLY-FACED FREAK!
PLEASE, SIR, I'M JUST AN INTERN. I WAS PICKING THE GREEN M&MS OUT OF MR. BROCKMAN'S CANDY DISH WHEN THIS HAPPENED.
YOU'D BETTER BE TELLING THE TRUTH. NO ONE PULLS A FAST ONE ON THE BEAR PATROL. WE'RE THE BEST IN THE BUSINESS!
HERE YOU GO, HOMIE! ALL DRY. PLUS, I REINFORCED THE SEAT, SO IT WON'T WEAR OUT SO FAST.
BEAR PATROL DUTY **IS** VERY TAXING.
AS I RECALL, IT WAS THE RESULT OF A HEAVY SCRATCHING SESSION.
ENOUGH OF THIS BUFFOONERY! IF YOU WILL DIRECT YOUR ATTENTION TO THAT CORNER, YOU WILL FIND THE PERPETRATORS OF THIS ATROCITY!
BUTTERCUP AND I WERE PRACTICING THE CHA-CHA SLIDE, WHEN ALL OF A SUDDEN... SHE **ATTACKED!** THEN THE **REST** OF THE BEARS BEGAN ATTACKING **THEIR** PARTNERS.
AS SUDDENLY AS IT STARTED, THE ATTACK CEASED, AND THE BEARS WENT BACK TO THEIR GENTEEL SELVES.
HMMM... SOMETHING'S NOT ADDING UP HERE.
TELL ME ABOUT IT. THESE BEARS SEEM AS MILD-MANNERED AS THOSE HOBOS WE ACCIDENTALLY TRANQUILIZED.

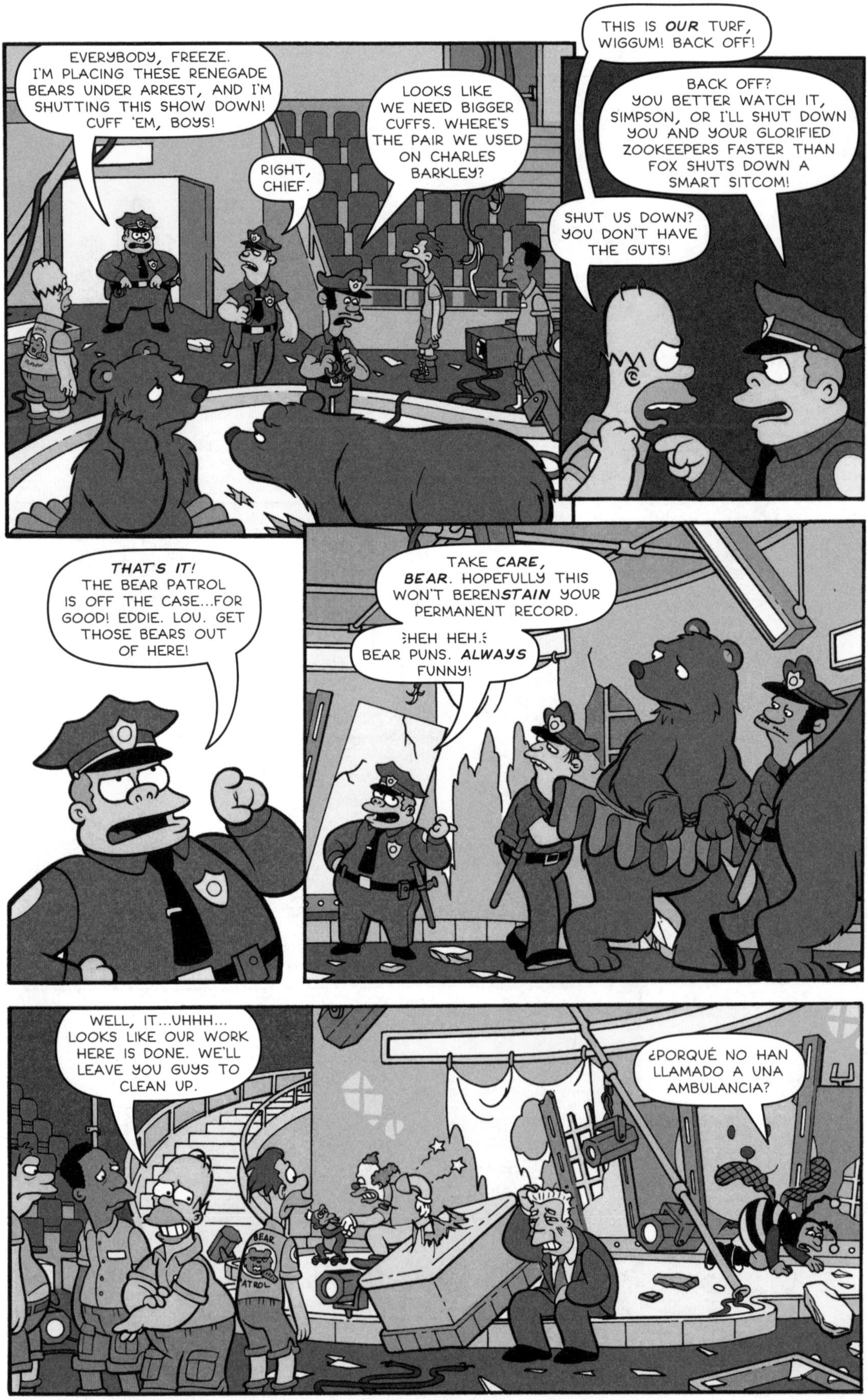
EVERYBODY, FREEZE. I'M PLACING THESE RENEGADE BEARS UNDER ARREST, AND I'M SHUTTING THIS SHOW DOWN! CUFF 'EM, BOYS!
RIGHT, CHIEF.
LOOKS LIKE WE NEED BIGGER CUFFS. WHERE'S THE PAIR WE USED ON CHARLES BARKLEY?
THIS IS **OUR** TURF, WIGGUM! BACK OFF!
BACK OFF? YOU BETTER WATCH IT, SIMPSON, OR I'LL SHUT DOWN YOU AND YOUR GLORIFIED ZOOKEEPERS FASTER THAN FOX SHUTS DOWN A SMART SITCOM!
SHUT US DOWN? YOU DON'T HAVE THE GUTS!
THAT'S IT! THE BEAR PATROL IS OFF THE CASE...FOR GOOD! EDDIE. LOU. GET THOSE BEARS OUT OF HERE!
TAKE ***CARE, BEAR***. HOPEFULLY THIS WON'T BEREN***STAIN*** YOUR PERMANENT RECORD.
HEH HEH. BEAR PUNS. ***ALWAYS*** FUNNY!
WELL, IT...UHHH... LOOKS LIKE OUR WORK HERE IS DONE. WE'LL LEAVE YOU GUYS TO CLEAN UP.
BEAR PATROL
¿PORQUÉ NO HAN LLAMADO A UNA AMBULANCIA?

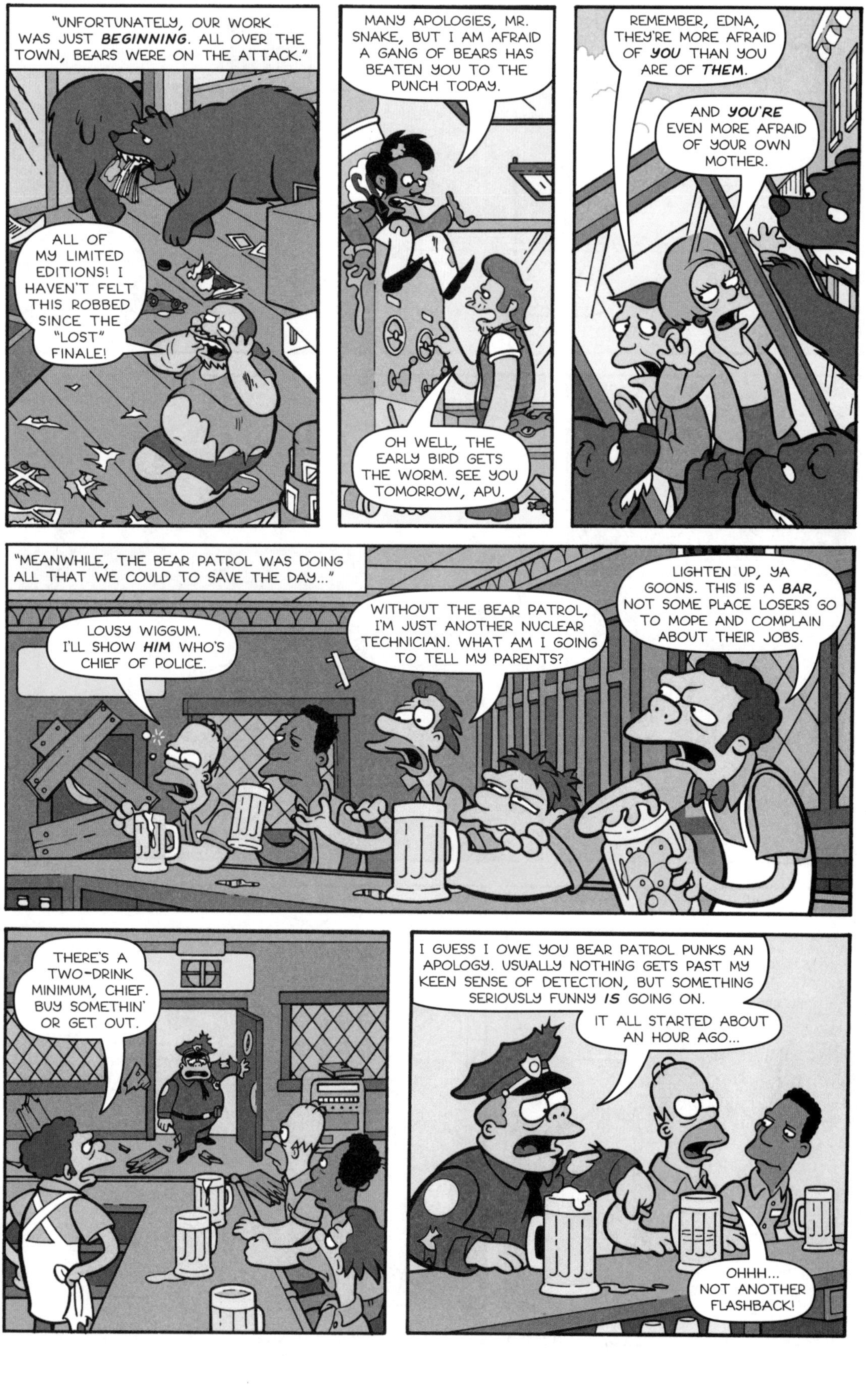
"UNFORTUNATELY, OUR WORK WAS JUST BEGINNING. ALL OVER THE TOWN, BEARS WERE ON THE ATTACK."
ALL OF MY LIMITED EDITIONS! I HAVEN'T FELT THIS ROBBED SINCE THE "LOST" FINALE!
MANY APOLOGIES, MR. SNAKE, BUT I AM AFRAID A GANG OF BEARS HAS BEATEN YOU TO THE PUNCH TODAY.
OH WELL, THE EARLY BIRD GETS THE WORM. SEE YOU TOMORROW, APU.
REMEMBER, EDNA, THEY'RE MORE AFRAID OF YOU THAN YOU ARE OF THEM.
AND YOU'RE EVEN MORE AFRAID OF YOUR OWN MOTHER.
"MEANWHILE, THE BEAR PATROL WAS DOING ALL THAT WE COULD TO SAVE THE DAY..."
LOUSY WIGGUM. I'LL SHOW HIM WHO'S CHIEF OF POLICE.
WITHOUT THE BEAR PATROL, I'M JUST ANOTHER NUCLEAR TECHNICIAN. WHAT AM I GOING TO TELL MY PARENTS?
LIGHTEN UP, YA GOONS. THIS IS A BAR, NOT SOME PLACE LOSERS GO TO MOPE AND COMPLAIN ABOUT THEIR JOBS.
THERE'S A TWO-DRINK MINIMUM, CHIEF. BUY SOMETHIN' OR GET OUT.
I GUESS I OWE YOU BEAR PATROL PUNKS AN APOLOGY. USUALLY NOTHING GETS PAST MY KEEN SENSE OF DETECTION, BUT SOMETHING SERIOUSLY FUNNY IS GOING ON.
IT ALL STARTED ABOUT AN HOUR AGO...
OHHH... NOT ANOTHER FLASHBACK!

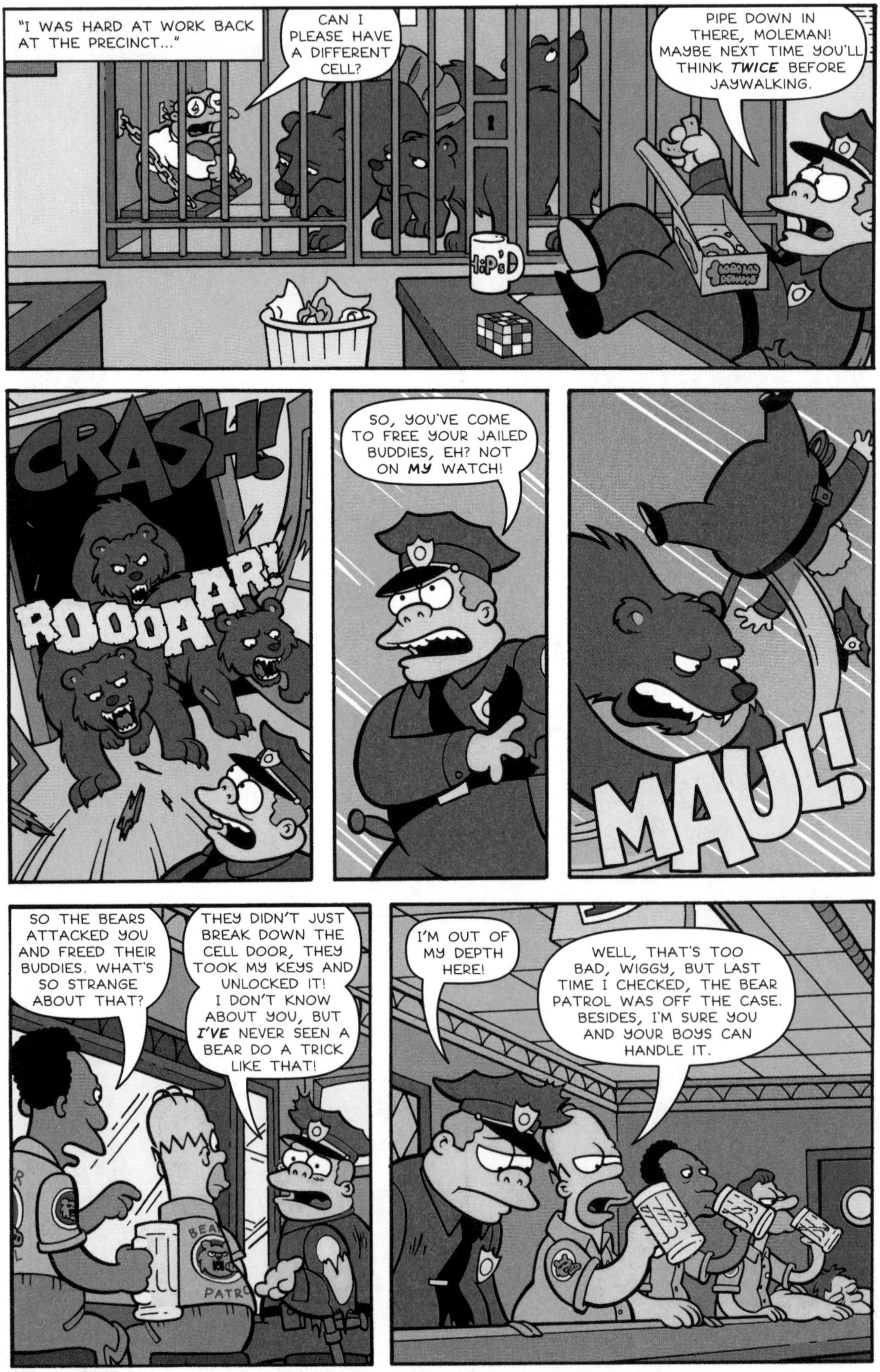

"I WAS HARD AT WORK BACK AT THE PRECINCT..."
CAN I PLEASE HAVE A DIFFERENT CELL?
PIPE DOWN IN THERE, MOLEMAN! MAYBE NEXT TIME YOU'LL THINK *TWICE* BEFORE JAYWALKING.
CRASH!
ROOOAAR!
SO, YOU'VE COME TO FREE YOUR JAILED BUDDIES, EH? NOT ON *MY* WATCH!
MAUL!
SO THE BEARS ATTACKED YOU AND FREED THEIR BUDDIES. WHAT'S SO STRANGE ABOUT THAT?
THEY DIDN'T JUST BREAK DOWN THE CELL DOOR, THEY TOOK MY KEYS AND UNLOCKED IT! I DON'T KNOW ABOUT YOU, BUT *I'VE* NEVER SEEN A BEAR DO A TRICK LIKE THAT!
I'M OUT OF MY DEPTH HERE!
WELL, THAT'S TOO BAD, WIGGY, BUT LAST TIME I CHECKED, THE BEAR PATROL WAS OFF THE CASE. BESIDES, I'M SURE YOU AND YOUR BOYS CAN HANDLE IT.

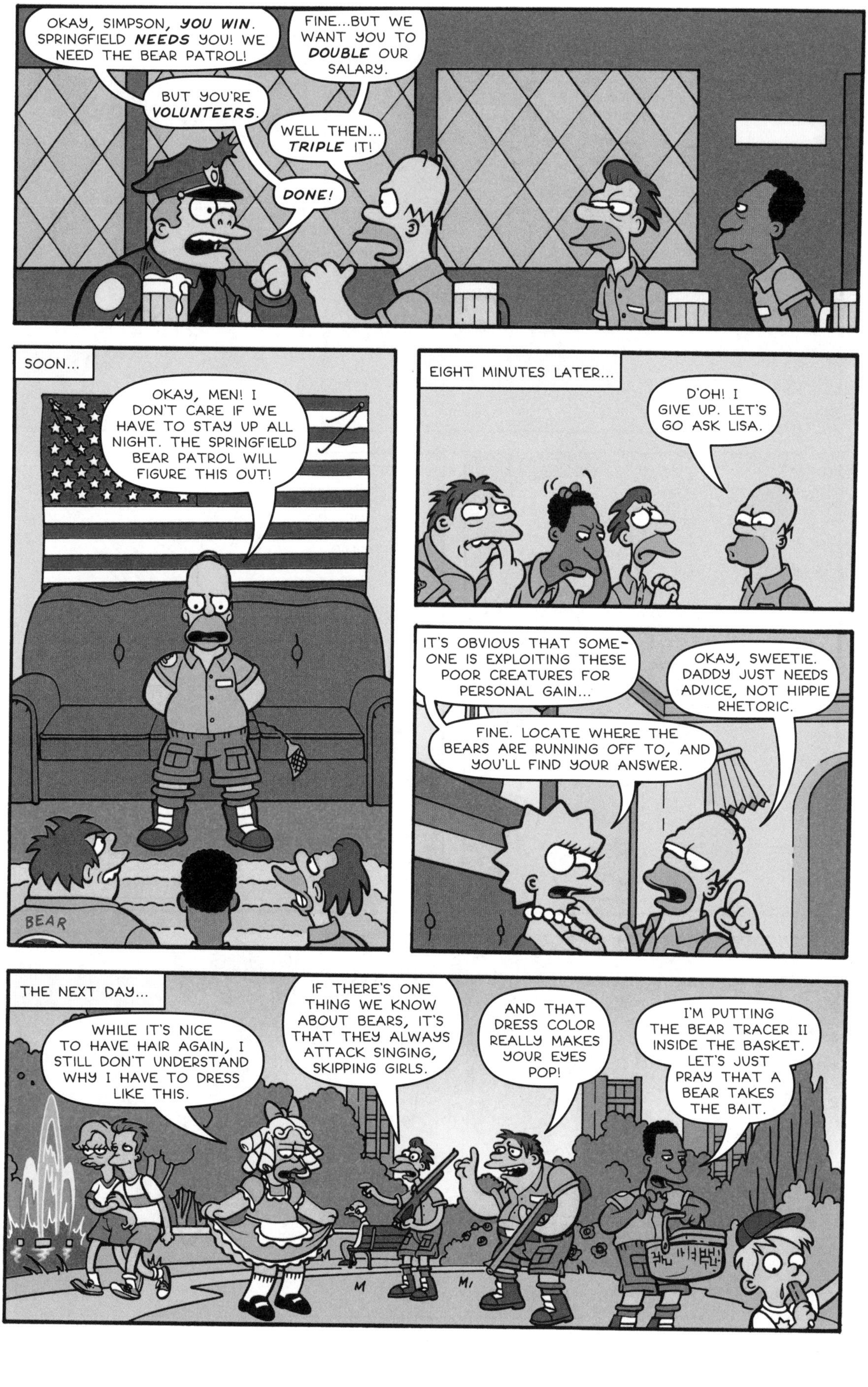

OKAY, SIMPSON, ***YOU WIN***. SPRINGFIELD ***NEEDS*** YOU! WE NEED THE BEAR PATROL!
FINE...BUT WE WANT YOU TO ***DOUBLE*** OUR SALARY.
BUT YOU'RE ***VOLUNTEERS***.
WELL THEN... ***TRIPLE*** IT!
DONE!
SOON...
OKAY, MEN! I DON'T CARE IF WE HAVE TO STAY UP ALL NIGHT. THE SPRINGFIELD BEAR PATROL WILL FIGURE THIS OUT!
BEAR
EIGHT MINUTES LATER...
D'OH! I GIVE UP. LET'S GO ASK LISA.
IT'S OBVIOUS THAT SOME-ONE IS EXPLOITING THESE POOR CREATURES FOR PERSONAL GAIN...
OKAY, SWEETIE. DADDY JUST NEEDS ADVICE, NOT HIPPIE RHETORIC.
FINE. LOCATE WHERE THE BEARS ARE RUNNING OFF TO, AND YOU'LL FIND YOUR ANSWER.
THE NEXT DAY...
WHILE IT'S NICE TO HAVE HAIR AGAIN, I STILL DON'T UNDERSTAND WHY I HAVE TO DRESS LIKE THIS.
IF THERE'S ONE THING WE KNOW ABOUT BEARS, IT'S THAT THEY ALWAYS ATTACK SINGING, SKIPPING GIRLS.
AND THAT DRESS COLOR REALLY MAKES YOUR EYES POP!
I'M PUTTING THE BEAR TRACER II INSIDE THE BASKET. LET'S JUST PRAY THAT A BEAR TAKES THE BAIT.

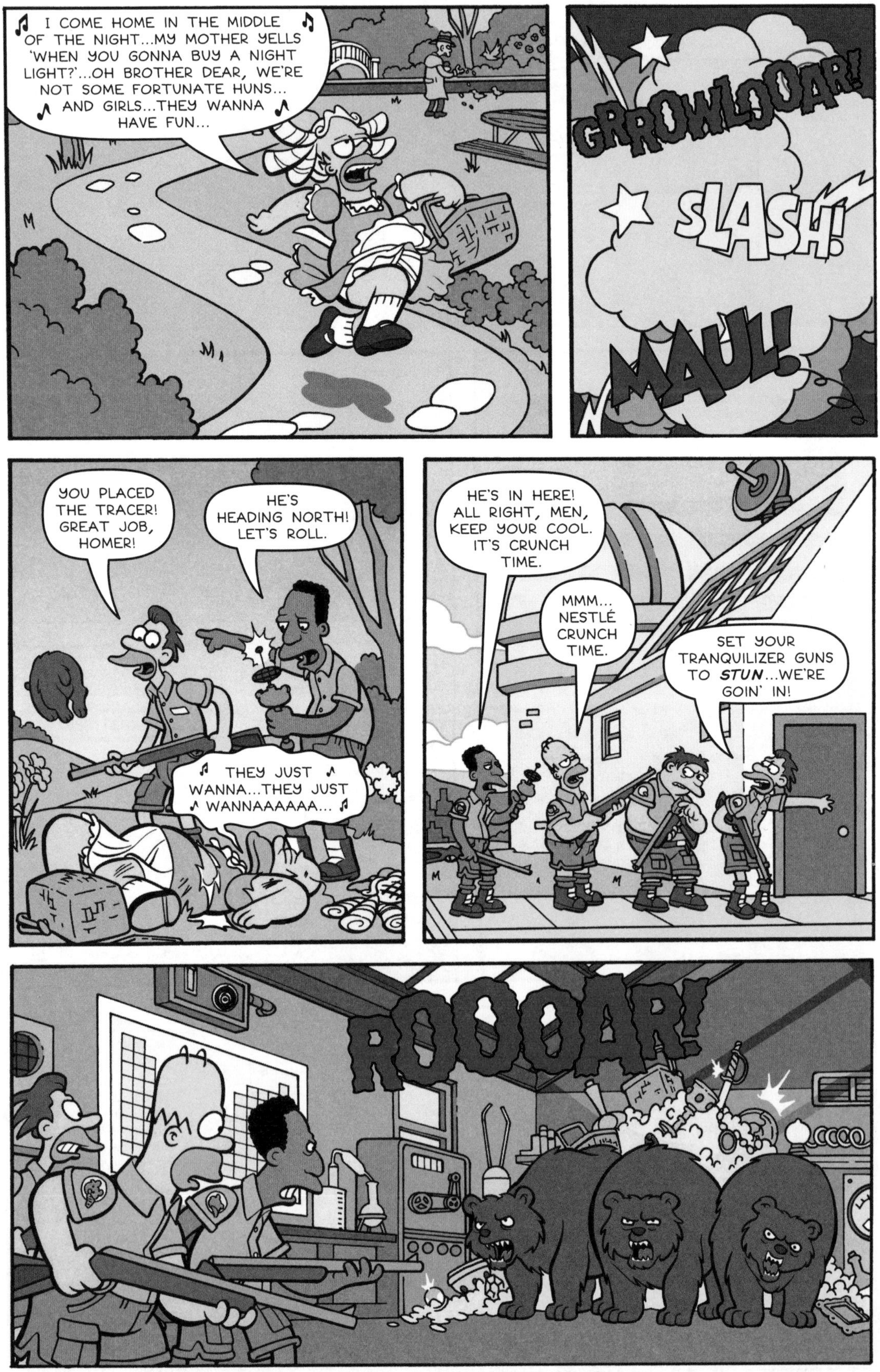
♫ I COME HOME IN THE MIDDLE OF THE NIGHT...MY MOTHER YELLS 'WHEN YOU GONNA BUY A NIGHT LIGHT?'...OH BROTHER DEAR, WE'RE NOT SOME FORTUNATE HUNS... AND GIRLS...THEY WANNA HAVE FUN... ♫
GRROWLOOAR!
SLASH!
MAUL!
YOU PLACED THE TRACER! GREAT JOB, HOMER!
HE'S HEADING NORTH! LET'S ROLL.
♪ THEY JUST WANNA...THEY JUST WANNAAAAAA... ♫
HE'S IN HERE! ALL RIGHT, MEN, KEEP YOUR COOL. IT'S CRUNCH TIME.
MMM... NESTLÉ CRUNCH TIME.
SET YOUR TRANQUILIZER GUNS TO ***STUN***...WE'RE GOIN' IN!
ROOOAR!

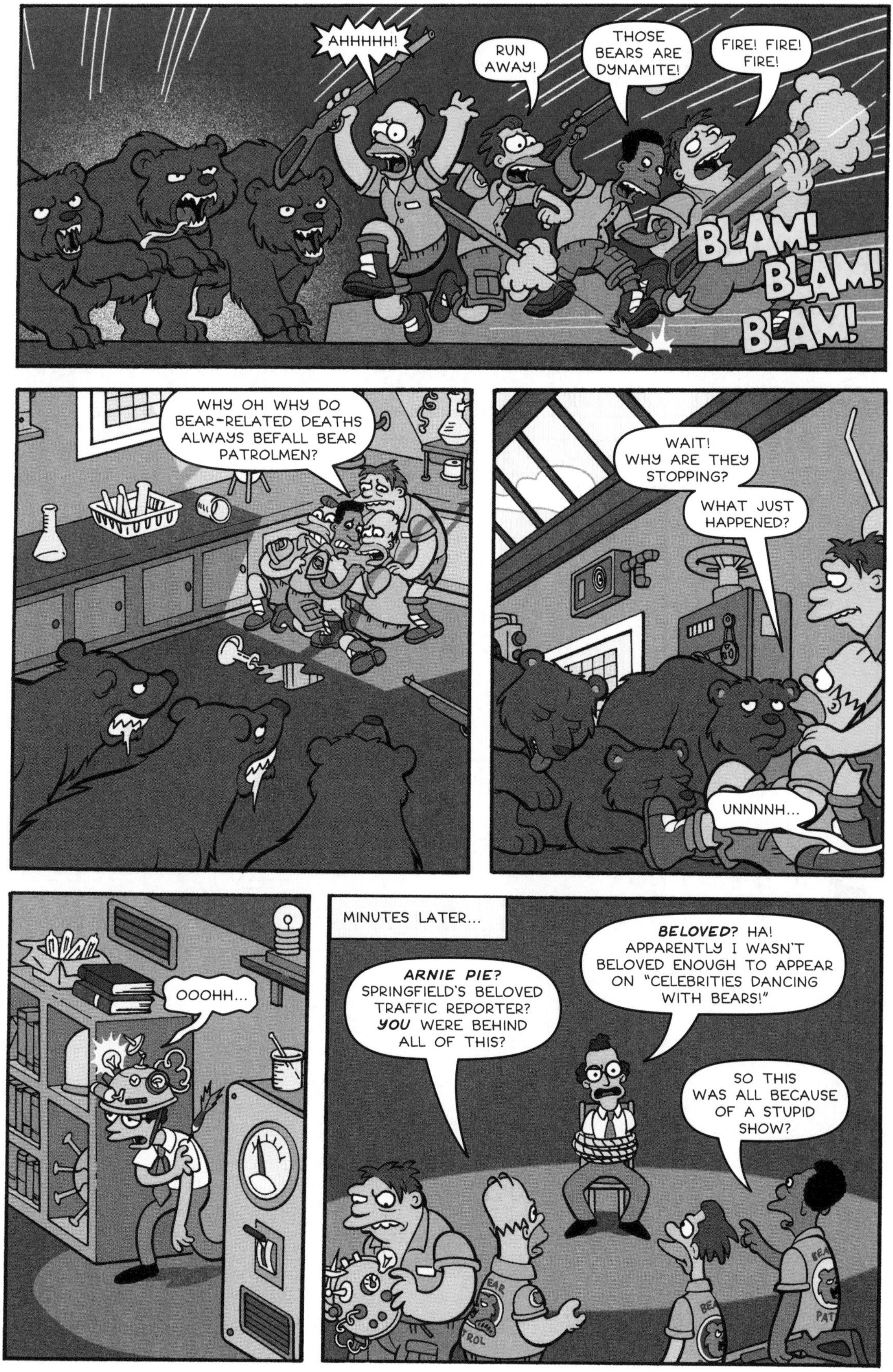
AHHHHH!
RUN AWAY!
THOSE BEARS ARE DYNAMITE!
FIRE! FIRE! FIRE!
BLAM! BLAM! BLAM!
WHY OH WHY DO BEAR-RELATED DEATHS ALWAYS BEFALL BEAR PATROLMEN?
WAIT! WHY ARE THEY STOPPING?
WHAT JUST HAPPENED?
UNNNNH...
OOOHH...
MINUTES LATER...
ARNIE PIE? SPRINGFIELD'S BELOVED TRAFFIC REPORTER? *YOU* WERE BEHIND ALL OF THIS?
BELOVED? HA! APPARENTLY I WASN'T BELOVED ENOUGH TO APPEAR ON "CELEBRITIES DANCING WITH BEARS!"
SO THIS WAS ALL BECAUSE OF A STUPID SHOW?

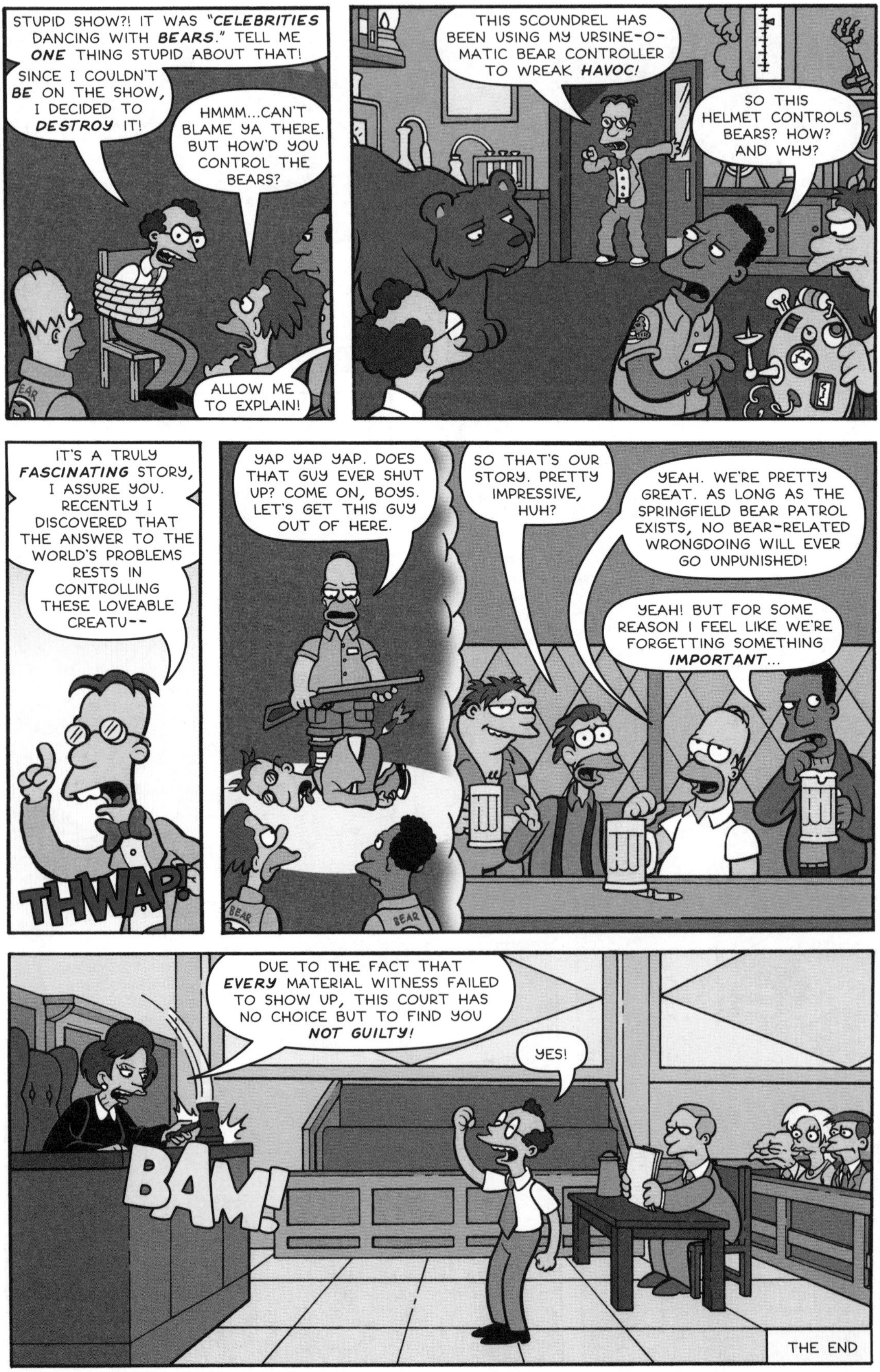

STUPID SHOW?! IT WAS "CELEBRITIES DANCING WITH BEARS." TELL ME ONE THING STUPID ABOUT THAT!
SINCE I COULDN'T BE ON THE SHOW, I DECIDED TO DESTROY IT!
HMMM...CAN'T BLAME YA THERE. BUT HOW'D YOU CONTROL THE BEARS?
ALLOW ME TO EXPLAIN!
THIS SCOUNDREL HAS BEEN USING MY URSINE-O-MATIC BEAR CONTROLLER TO WREAK HAVOC!
SO THIS HELMET CONTROLS BEARS? HOW? AND WHY?
IT'S A TRULY FASCINATING STORY, I ASSURE YOU. RECENTLY I DISCOVERED THAT THE ANSWER TO THE WORLD'S PROBLEMS RESTS IN CONTROLLING THESE LOVEABLE CREATU--
THWAP!
YAP YAP YAP. DOES THAT GUY EVER SHUT UP? COME ON, BOYS. LET'S GET THIS GUY OUT OF HERE.
SO THAT'S OUR STORY. PRETTY IMPRESSIVE, HUH?
YEAH. WE'RE PRETTY GREAT. AS LONG AS THE SPRINGFIELD BEAR PATROL EXISTS, NO BEAR-RELATED WRONGDOING WILL EVER GO UNPUNISHED!
YEAH! BUT FOR SOME REASON I FEEL LIKE WE'RE FORGETTING SOMETHING IMPORTANT...
DUE TO THE FACT THAT EVERY MATERIAL WITNESS FAILED TO SHOW UP, THIS COURT HAS NO CHOICE BUT TO FIND YOU NOT GUILTY!
YES!
BAM!
THE END

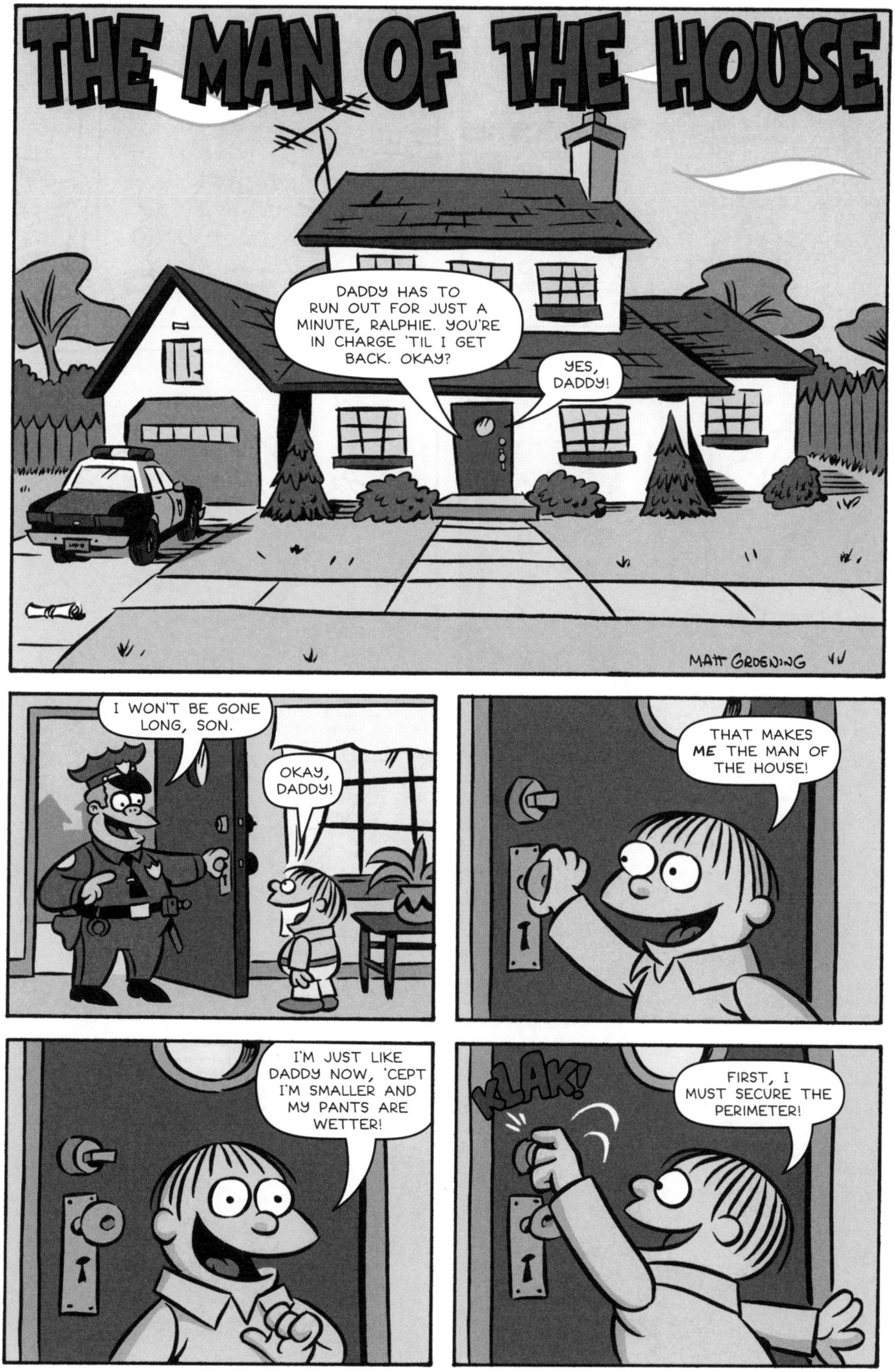
THE MAN OF THE HOUSE
DADDY HAS TO RUN OUT FOR JUST A MINUTE, RALPHIE. YOU'RE IN CHARGE 'TIL I GET BACK. OKAY?
YES, DADDY!
MATT GROENING
I WON'T BE GONE LONG, SON.
OKAY, DADDY!
THAT MAKES *ME* THE MAN OF THE HOUSE!
I'M JUST LIKE DADDY NOW, 'CEPT I'M SMALLER AND MY PANTS ARE WETTER!
KLAK!
FIRST, I MUST SECURE THE PERIMETER!

MARY TRAINOR SCRIPT | *MIKE KAZALEH* PENCILS & INKS | *NATHAN HAMILL* COLORS | *KAREN BATES* LETTERS | *BILL MORRISON* EDITOR

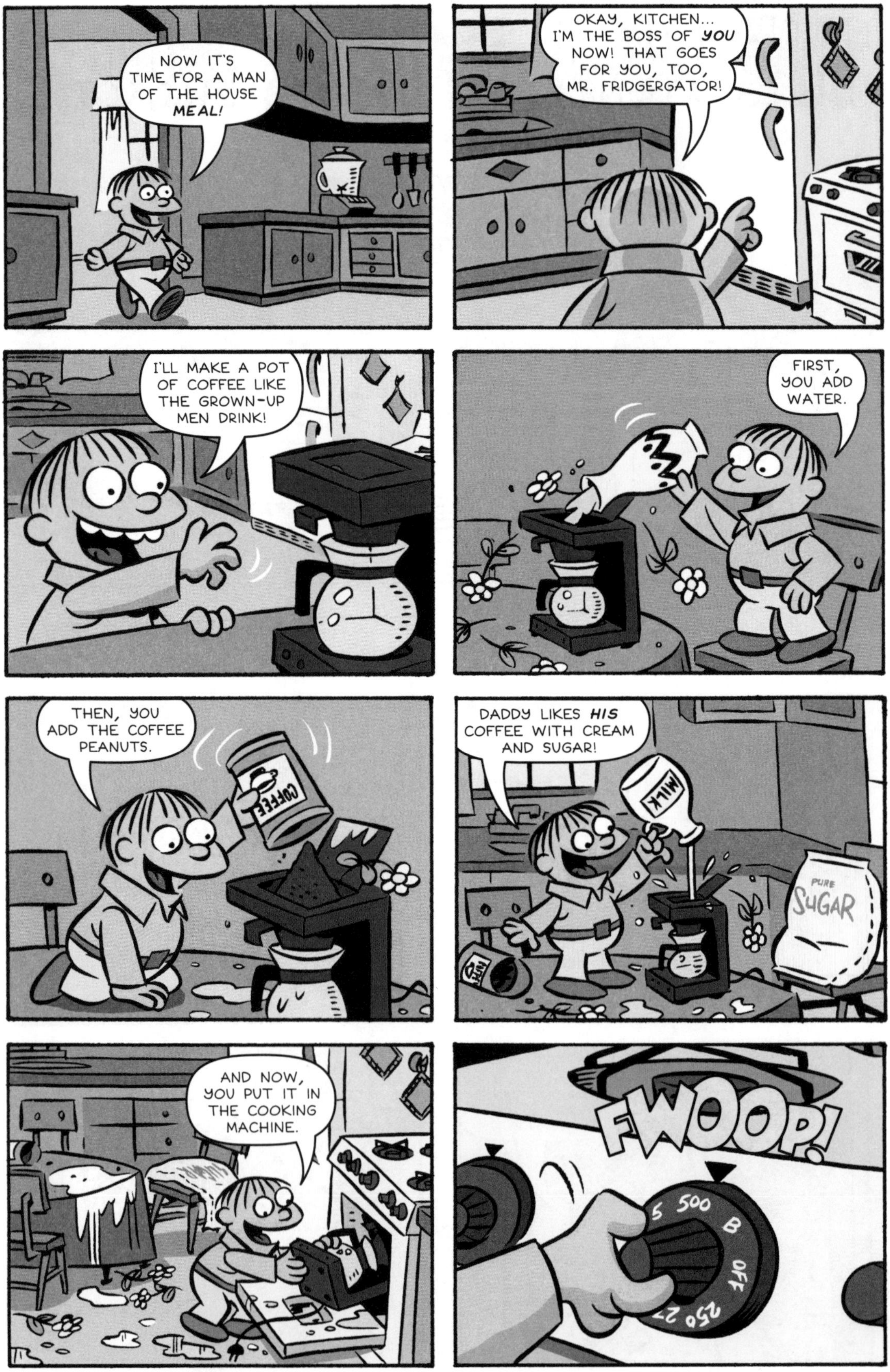

NOW IT'S TIME FOR A MAN OF THE HOUSE MEAL!
OKAY, KITCHEN... I'M THE BOSS OF YOU NOW! THAT GOES FOR YOU, TOO, MR. FRIDGERGATOR!
I'LL MAKE A POT OF COFFEE LIKE THE GROWN-UP MEN DRINK!
FIRST, YOU ADD WATER.
THEN, YOU ADD THE COFFEE PEANUTS.
COFFEE
DADDY LIKES HIS COFFEE WITH CREAM AND SUGAR!
MILK
PURE SUGAR
AND NOW, YOU PUT IT IN THE COOKING MACHINE.
FWOOP!
5 500 B OFF 250 27

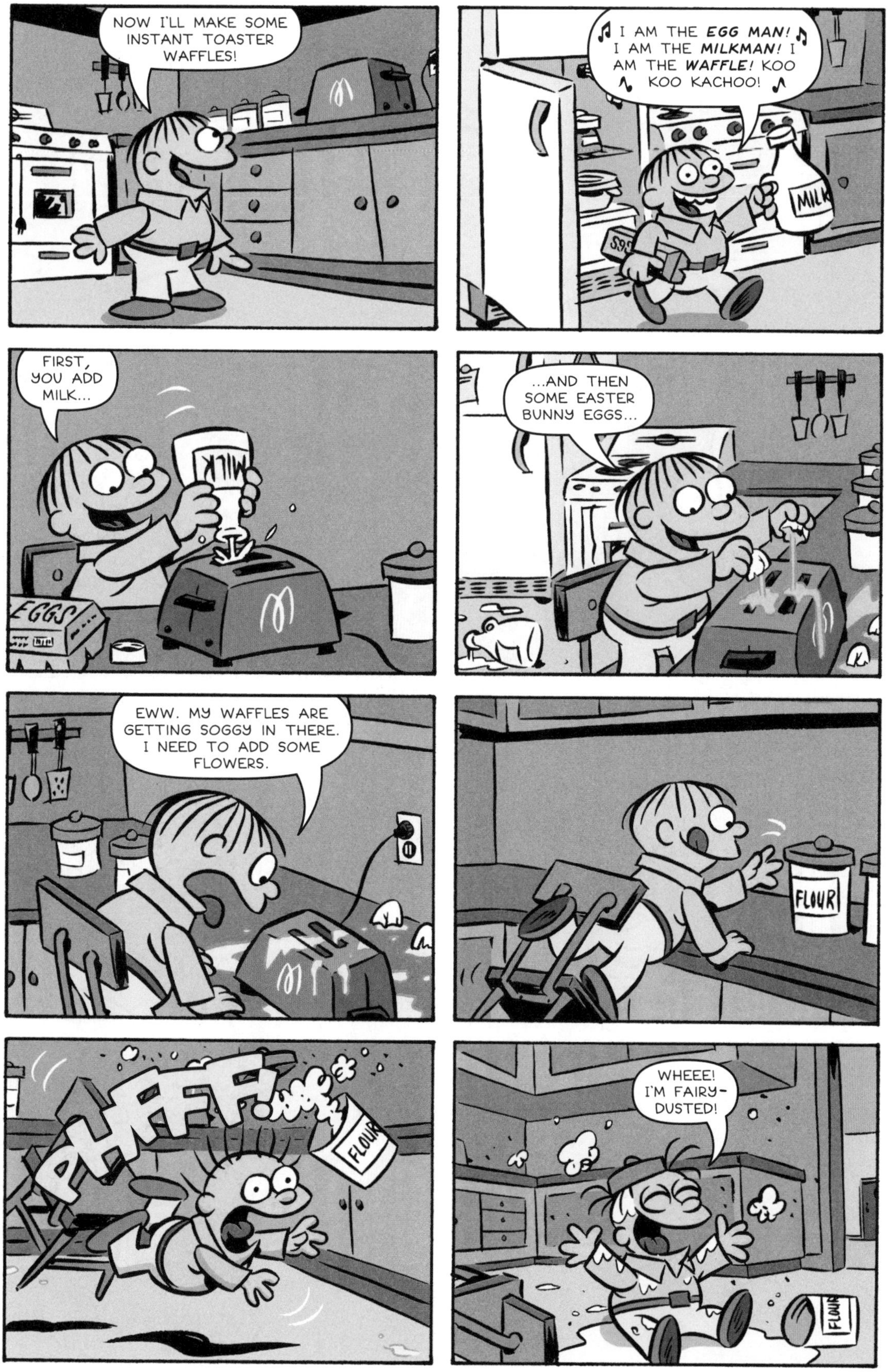
NOW I'LL MAKE SOME INSTANT TOASTER WAFFLES!
♪ I AM THE **EGG MAN!** ♪ I AM THE **MILKMAN!** I AM THE **WAFFLE!** KOO KOO KACHOO! ♪
MILK
SSS
FIRST, YOU ADD MILK...
MILK
EGGS
...AND THEN SOME EASTER BUNNY EGGS...
EWW. MY WAFFLES ARE GETTING SOGGY IN THERE. I NEED TO ADD SOME FLOWERS.
FLOUR
PHFFF!
FLOUR
WHEEE! I'M FAIRY-DUSTED!
FLOUR

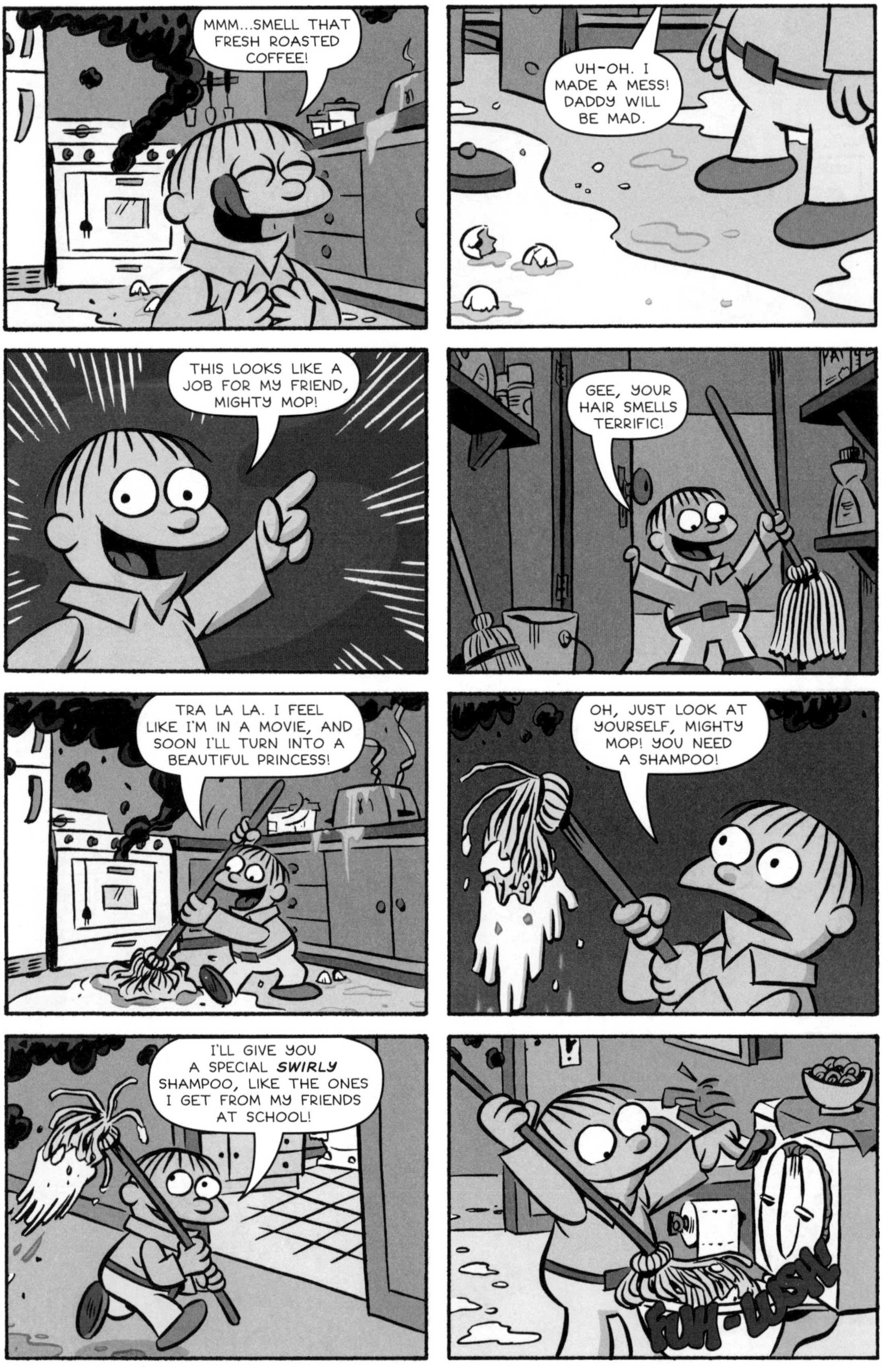
MMM...SMELL THAT FRESH ROASTED COFFEE!
UH-OH. I MADE A MESS! DADDY WILL BE MAD.
THIS LOOKS LIKE A JOB FOR MY FRIEND, MIGHTY MOP!
GEE, YOUR HAIR SMELLS TERRIFIC!
TRA LA LA. I FEEL LIKE I'M IN A MOVIE, AND SOON I'LL TURN INTO A BEAUTIFUL PRINCESS!
OH, JUST LOOK AT YOURSELF, MIGHTY MOP! YOU NEED A SHAMPOO!
I'LL GIVE YOU A SPECIAL *SWIRLY* SHAMPOO, LIKE THE ONES I GET FROM MY FRIENDS AT SCHOOL!
FLUH-LUSH!

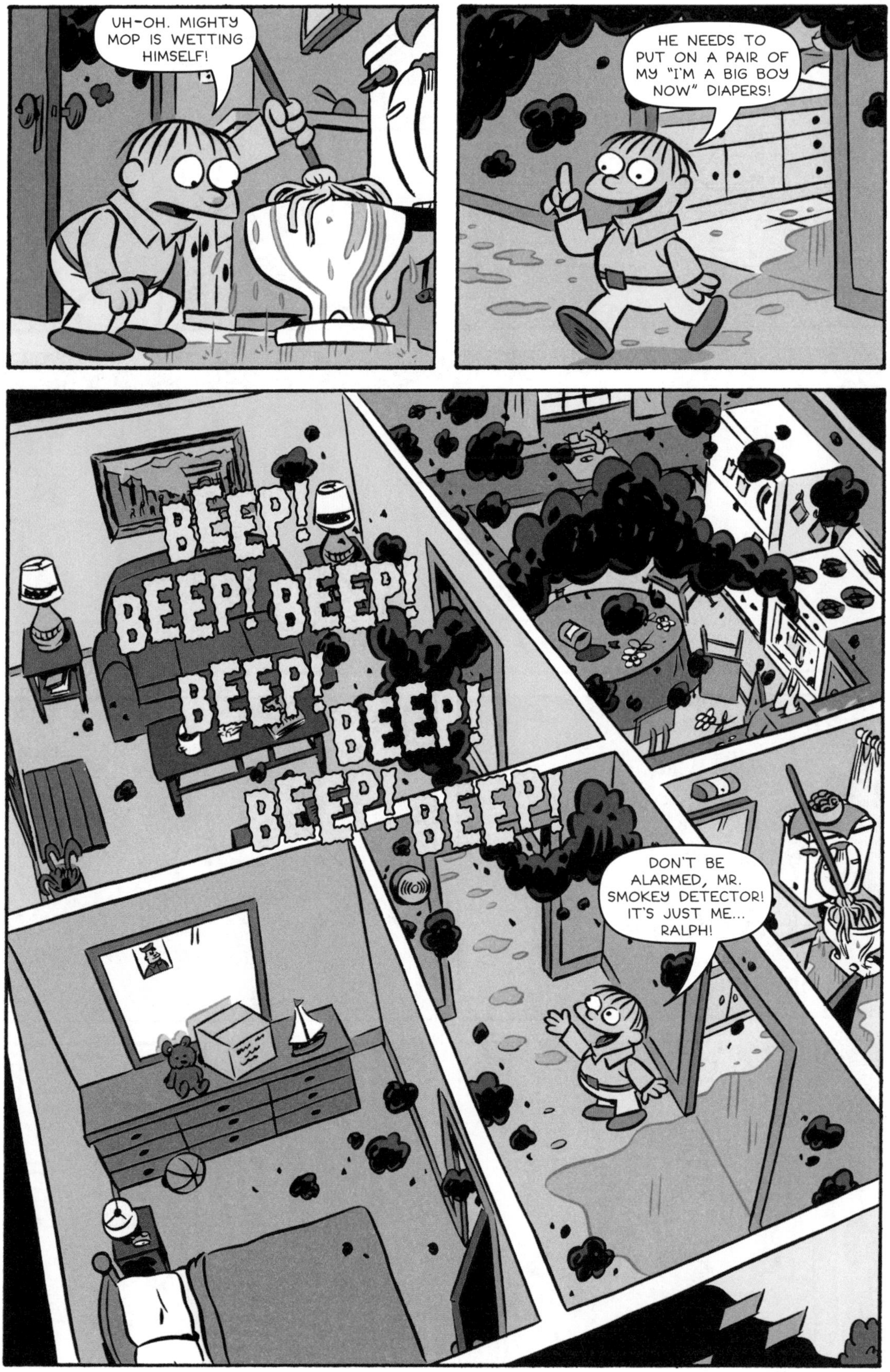
UH-OH. MIGHTY MOP IS WETTING HIMSELF!
HE NEEDS TO PUT ON A PAIR OF MY "I'M A BIG BOY NOW" DIAPERS!
BEEP! BEEP! BEEP! BEEP! BEEP! BEEP! BEEP!
DON'T BE ALARMED, MR. SMOKEY DETECTOR! IT'S JUST ME... RALPH!

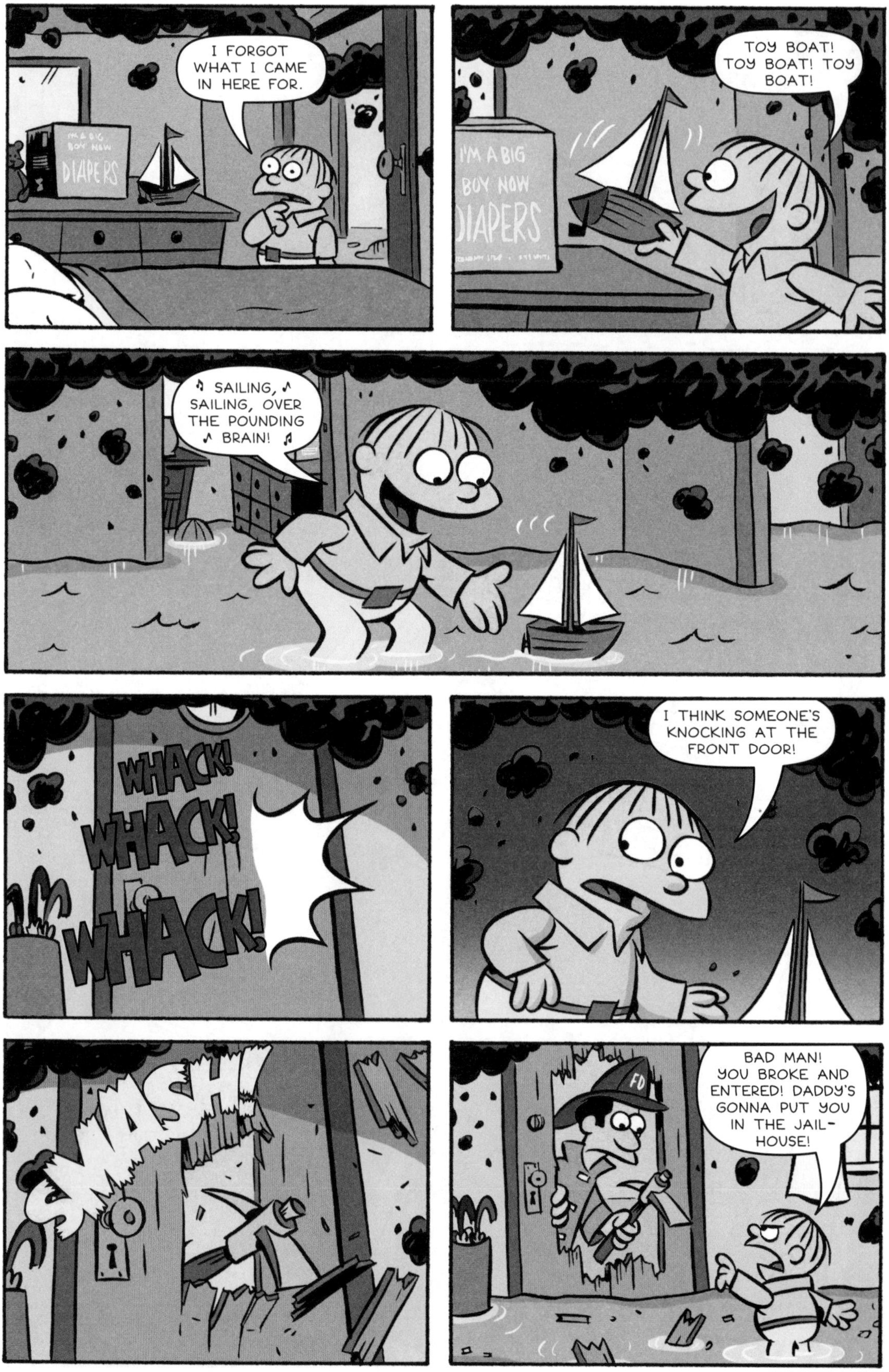

I FORGOT WHAT I CAME IN HERE FOR.
I'M A BIG BOY NOW DIAPERS
TOY BOAT! TOY BOAT! TOY BOAT!
I'M A BIG BOY NOW DIAPERS
♪ SAILING, ♪ SAILING, OVER THE POUNDING ♪ BRAIN! ♫
WHACK! WHACK! WHACK!
I THINK SOMEONE'S KNOCKING AT THE FRONT DOOR!
SMASH!
FD
BAD MAN! YOU BROKE AND ENTERED! DADDY'S GONNA PUT YOU IN THE JAIL-HOUSE!

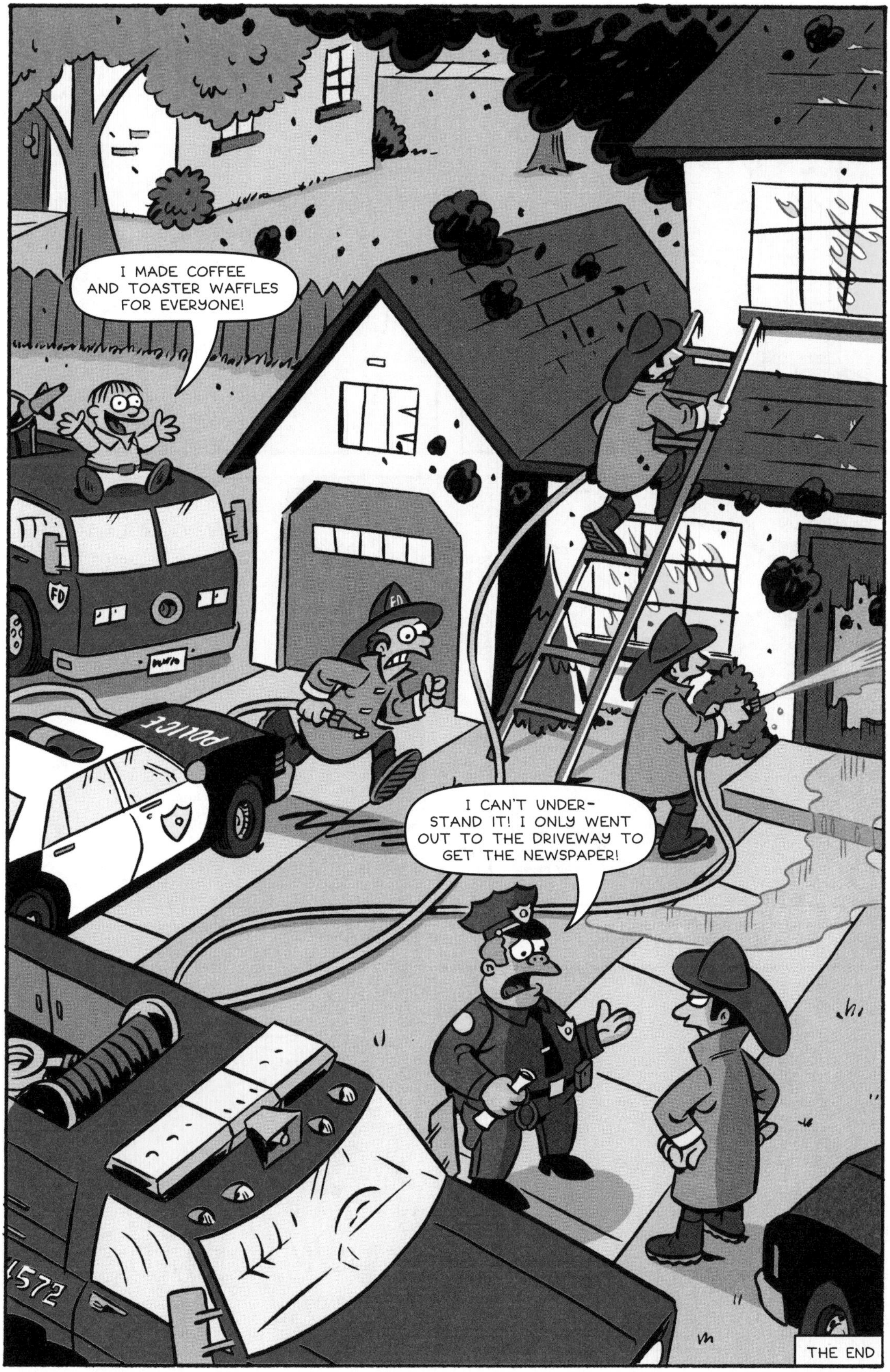
I MADE COFFEE AND TOASTER WAFFLES FOR EVERYONE!
POLICE
I CAN'T UNDER-STAND IT! I ONLY WENT OUT TO THE DRIVEWAY TO GET THE NEWSPAPER!
THE END

McBAIN in "A HERO'S HERO"

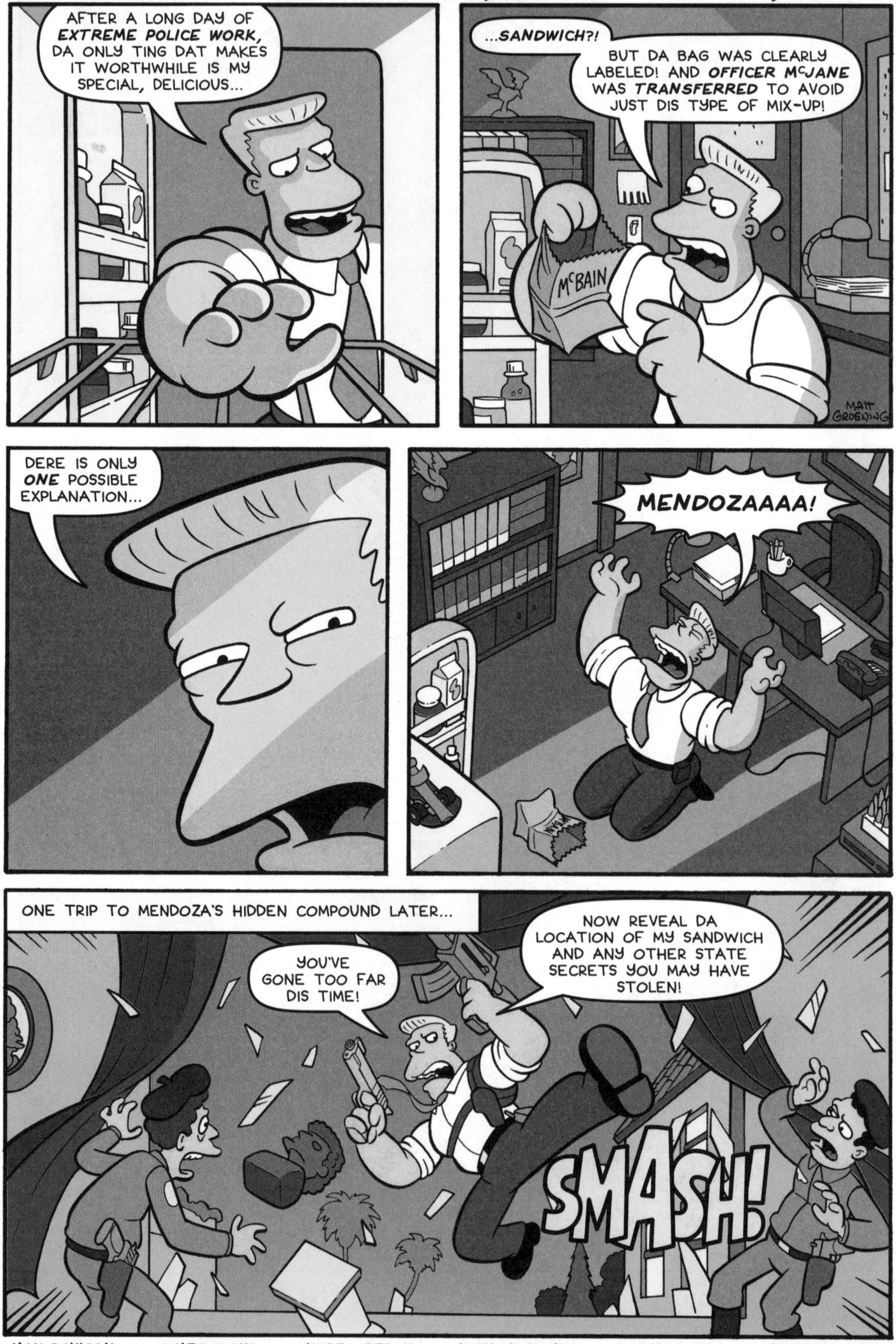

AFTER A LONG DAY OF **EXTREME POLICE WORK,** DA ONLY TING DAT MAKES IT WORTHWHILE IS MY SPECIAL, DELICIOUS...
...**SANDWICH**?!
BUT DA BAG WAS CLEARLY LABELED! AND **OFFICER McJANE** WAS **TRANSFERRED** TO AVOID JUST DIS TYPE OF MIX-UP!
McBAIN
MATT GROENING
DERE IS ONLY **ONE** POSSIBLE EXPLANATION...
MENDOZAAAAA!
ONE TRIP TO MENDOZA'S HIDDEN COMPOUND LATER...
YOU'VE GONE TOO FAR DIS TIME!
NOW REVEAL DA LOCATION OF MY SANDWICH AND ANY OTHER STATE SECRETS YOU MAY HAVE STOLEN!
SMASH!

MAX DAVISON SCRIPT | **JAMES LLOYD** PENCILS | **ANDREW PEPOY** INKS | **NATHAN HAMILL** COLORS | **KAREN BATES** LETTERS | **NATHAN KANE** EDITOR

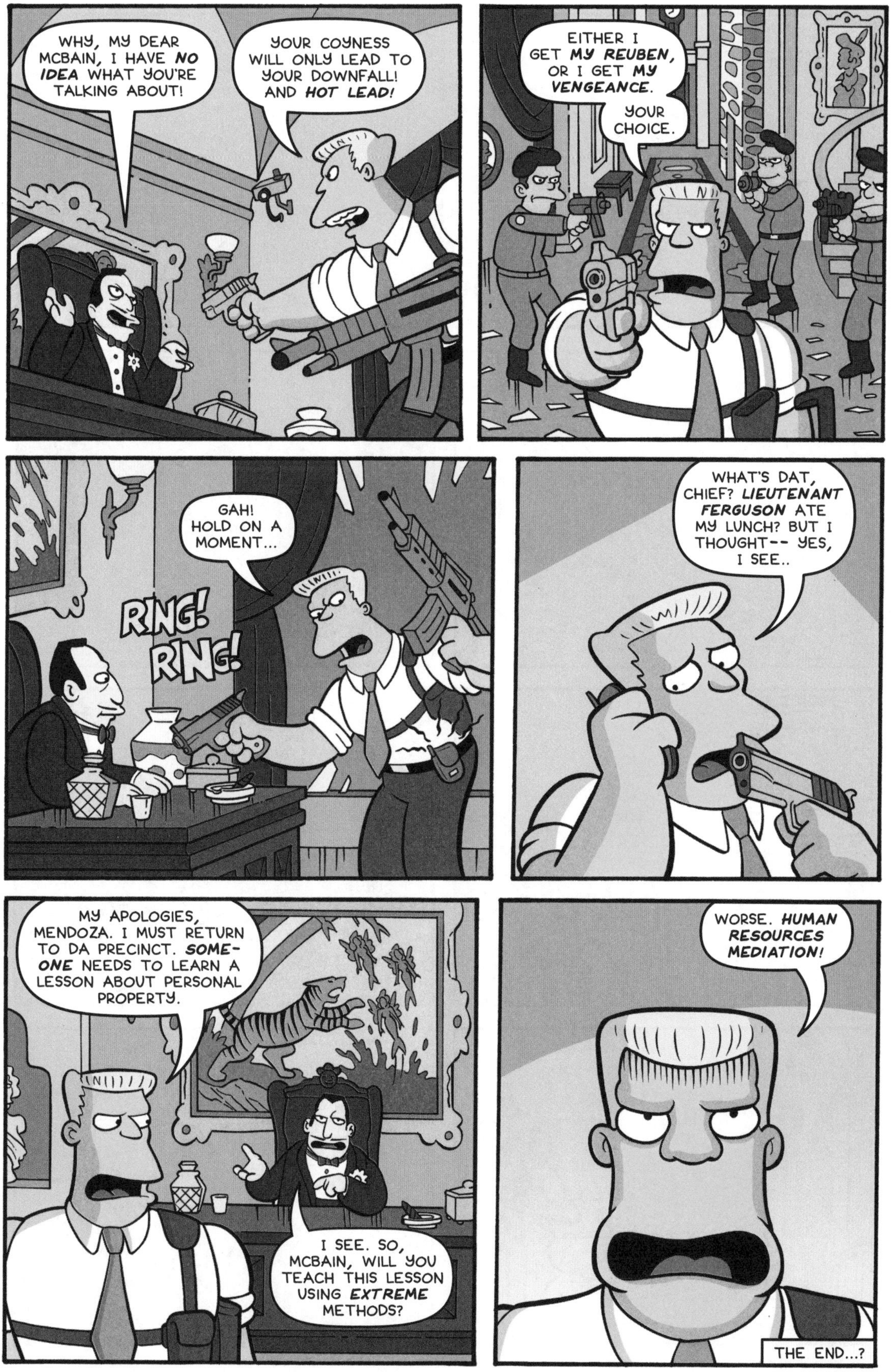
WHY, MY DEAR MCBAIN, I HAVE NO IDEA WHAT YOU'RE TALKING ABOUT!
YOUR COYNESS WILL ONLY LEAD TO YOUR DOWNFALL! AND HOT LEAD!
EITHER I GET MY REUBEN, OR I GET MY VENGEANCE.
YOUR CHOICE.
GAH! HOLD ON A MOMENT...
RING! RING!
WHAT'S DAT, CHIEF? LIEUTENANT FERGUSON ATE MY LUNCH? BUT I THOUGHT-- YES, I SEE..
MY APOLOGIES, MENDOZA. I MUST RETURN TO DA PRECINCT. SOME-ONE NEEDS TO LEARN A LESSON ABOUT PERSONAL PROPERTY.
I SEE. SO, MCBAIN, WILL YOU TEACH THIS LESSON USING EXTREME METHODS?
WORSE. HUMAN RESOURCES MEDIATION!
THE END...?

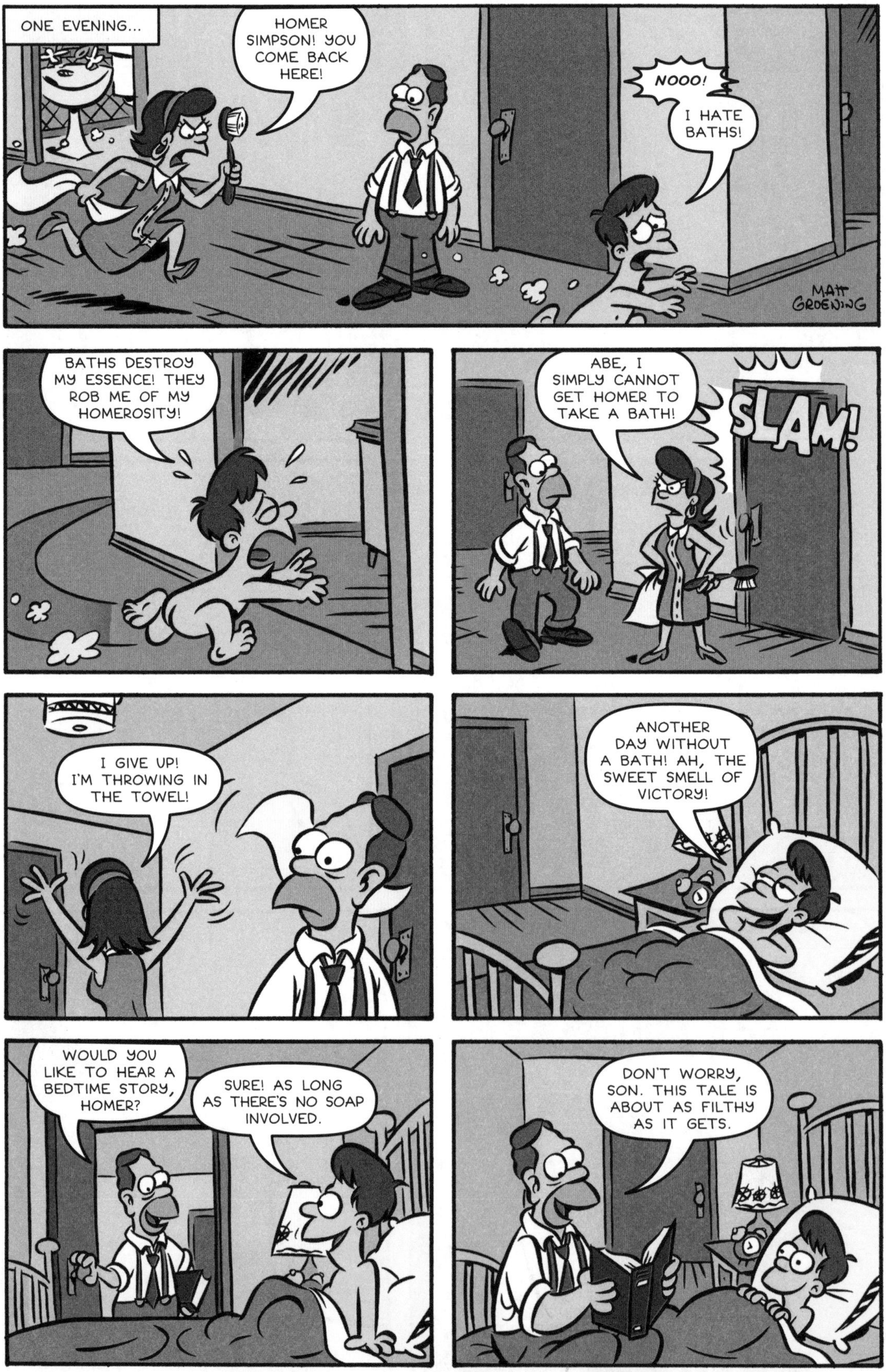
ONE EVENING...
HOMER SIMPSON! YOU COME BACK HERE!
NOOO!
I HATE BATHS!
MATT GROENING
BATHS DESTROY MY ESSENCE! THEY ROB ME OF MY HOMEROSITY!
ABE, I SIMPLY CANNOT GET HOMER TO TAKE A BATH!
SLAM!
I GIVE UP! I'M THROWING IN THE TOWEL!
ANOTHER DAY WITHOUT A BATH! AH, THE SWEET SMELL OF VICTORY!
WOULD YOU LIKE TO HEAR A BEDTIME STORY, HOMER?
SURE! AS LONG AS THERE'S NO SOAP INVOLVED.
DON'T WORRY, SON. THIS TALE IS ABOUT AS FILTHY AS IT GETS.

MARY TRAINOR STORY | **MIKE KAZALEH** ART | **NATHAN HAMILL** COLORS | **KAREN BATES** LETTERS | **NATHAN KANE** EDITOR

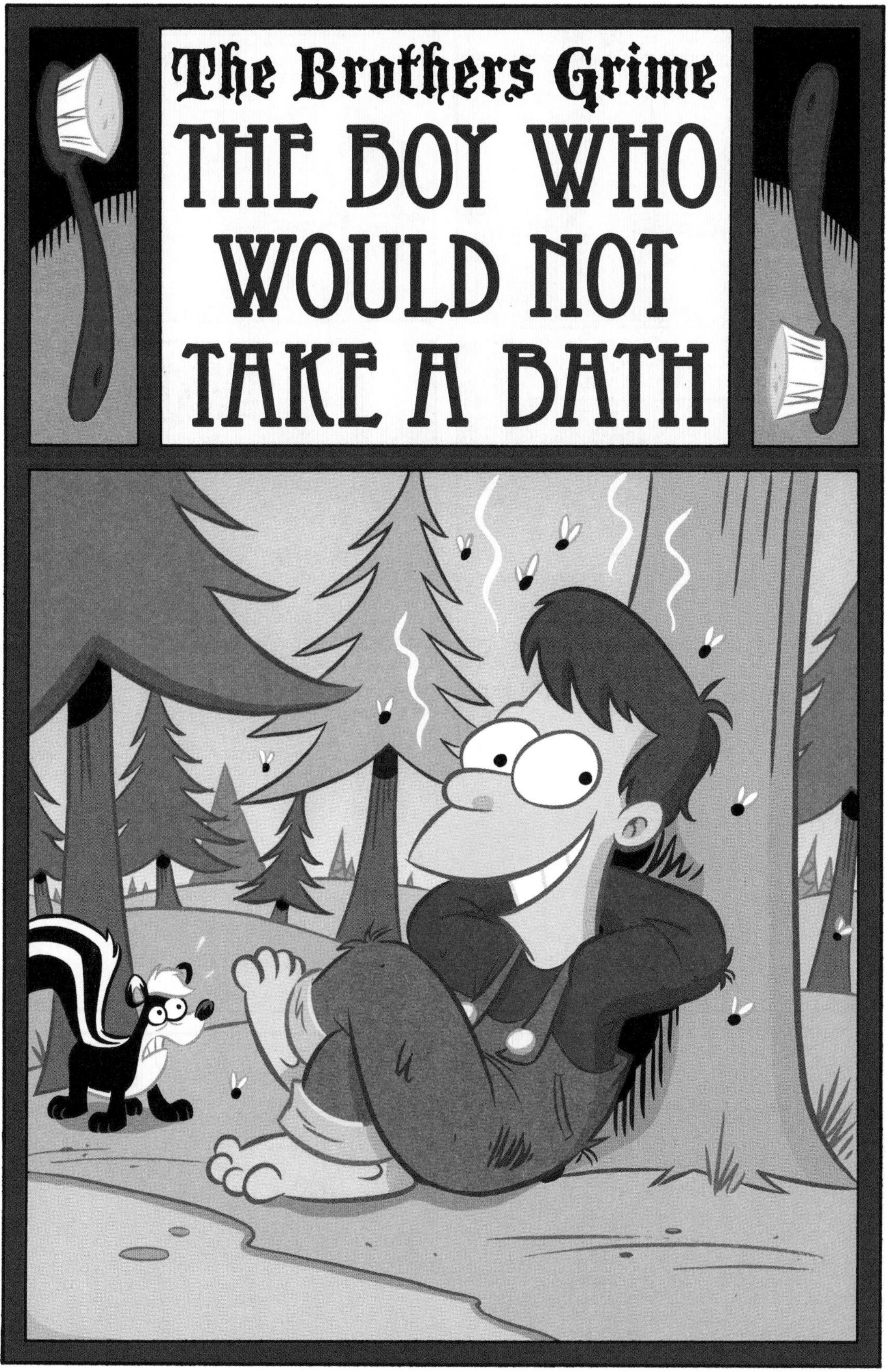
The Brothers Grime
THE BOY WHO
WOULD NOT
TAKE A BATH

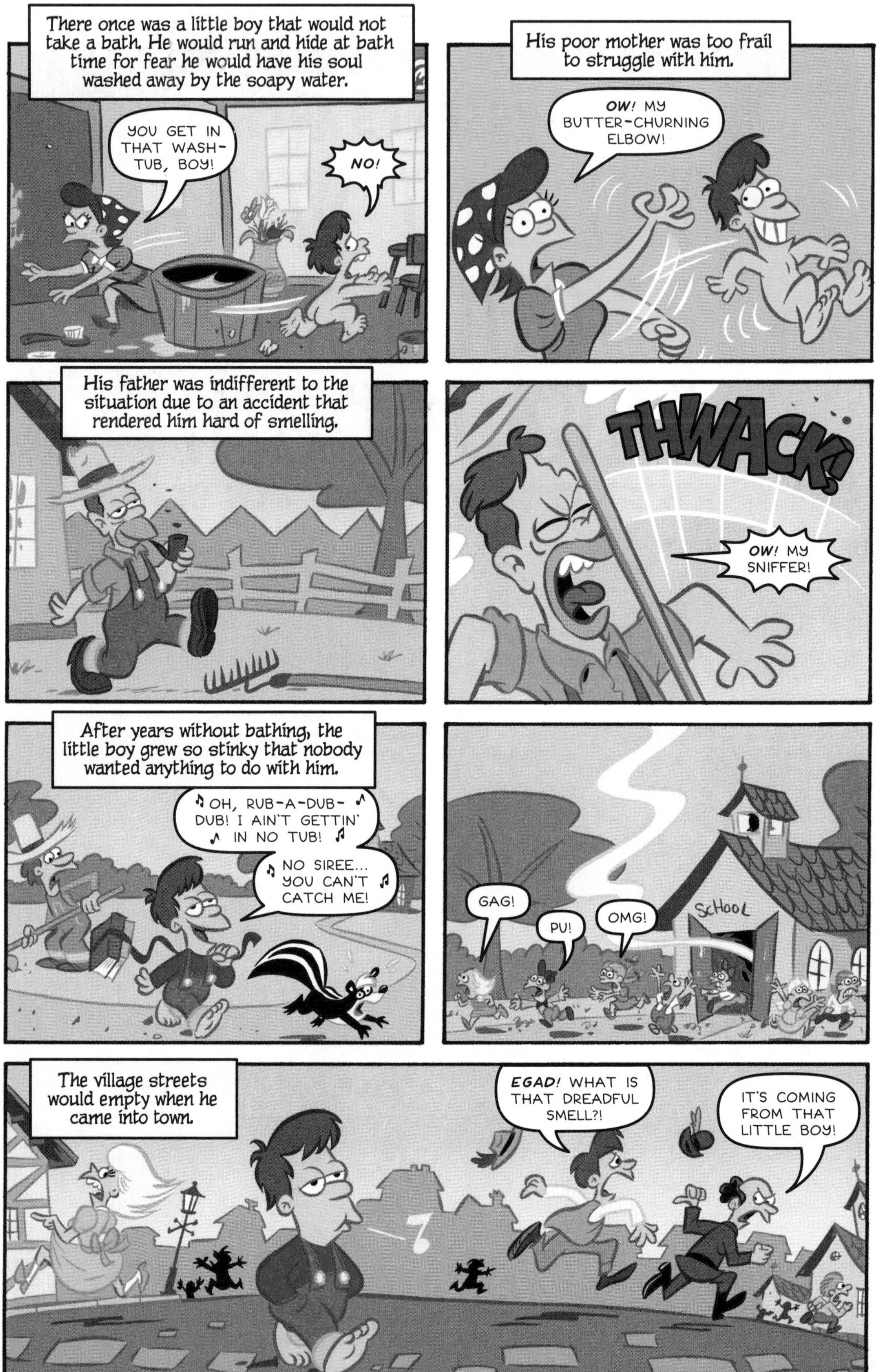

There once was a little boy that would not take a bath. He would run and hide at bath time for fear he would have his soul washed away by the soapy water.
YOU GET IN THAT WASH-TUB, BOY!
NO!
His poor mother was too frail to struggle with him.
OW! MY BUTTER-CHURNING ELBOW!
His father was indifferent to the situation due to an accident that rendered him hard of smelling.
THWACK!
OW! MY SNIFFER!
After years without bathing, the little boy grew so stinky that nobody wanted anything to do with him.
OH, RUB-A-DUB-DUB! I AIN'T GETTIN' IN NO TUB!
NO SIREE... YOU CAN'T CATCH ME!
SCHOOL
GAG!
PU!
OMG!
The village streets would empty when he came into town.
EGAD! WHAT IS THAT DREADFUL SMELL?!
IT'S COMING FROM THAT LITTLE BOY!

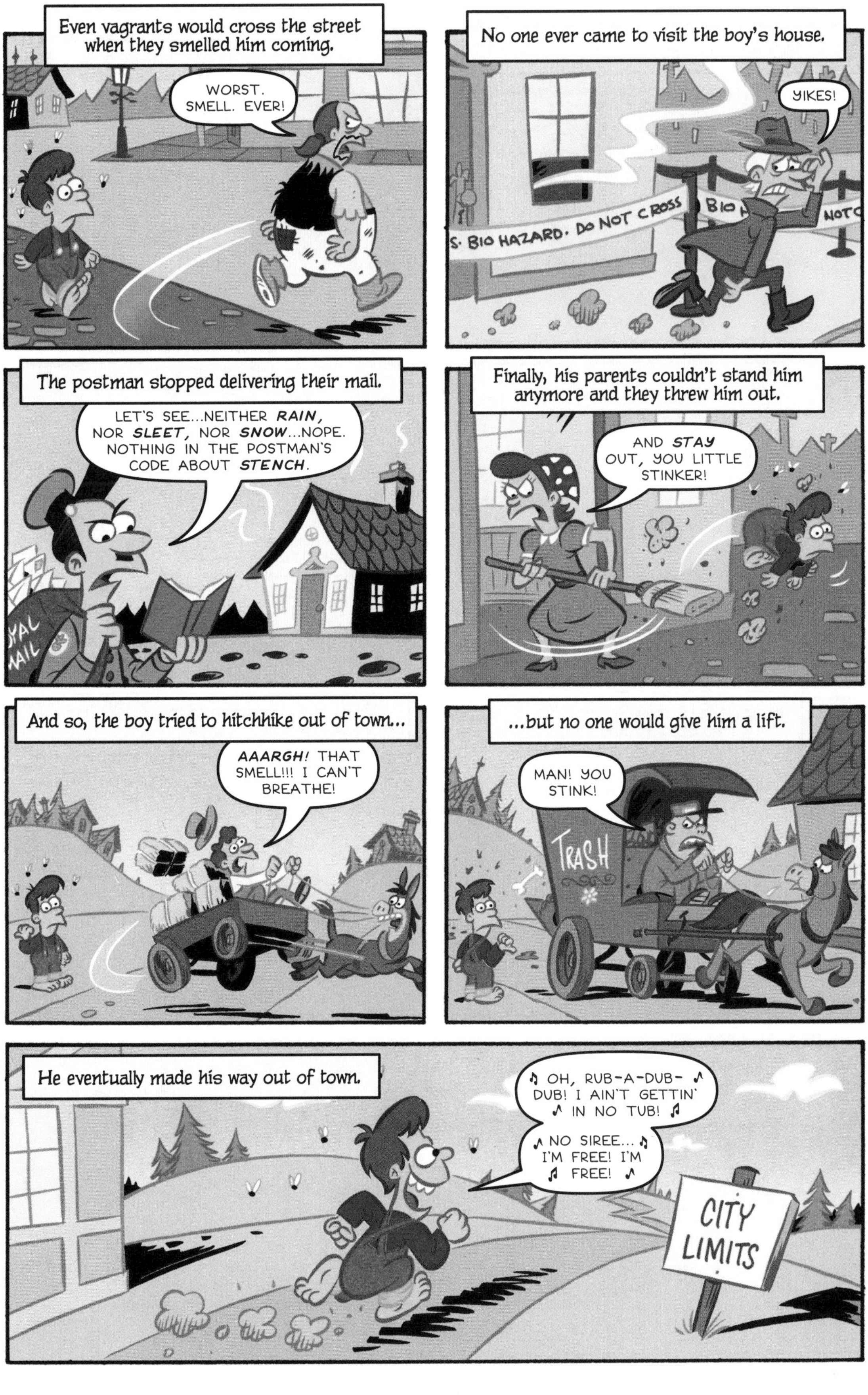

Even vagrants would cross the street when they smelled him coming.
WORST. SMELL. EVER!
No one ever came to visit the boy's house.
S. BIO HAZARD. DO NOT CROSS
YIKES!
The postman stopped delivering their mail.
LET'S SEE...NEITHER *RAIN,* NOR *SLEET,* NOR *SNOW*...NOPE. NOTHING IN THE POSTMAN'S CODE ABOUT *STENCH*.
Finally, his parents couldn't stand him anymore and they threw him out.
AND *STAY* OUT, YOU LITTLE STINKER!
And so, the boy tried to hitchhike out of town...
AAARGH! THAT SMELL!!! I CAN'T BREATHE!
...but no one would give him a lift.
MAN! YOU STINK!
TRASH
He eventually made his way out of town.
♪ OH, RUB-A-DUB-DUB! I AIN'T GETTIN' IN NO TUB! ♪
♪ NO SIREE... I'M FREE! I'M FREE! ♪
CITY LIMITS

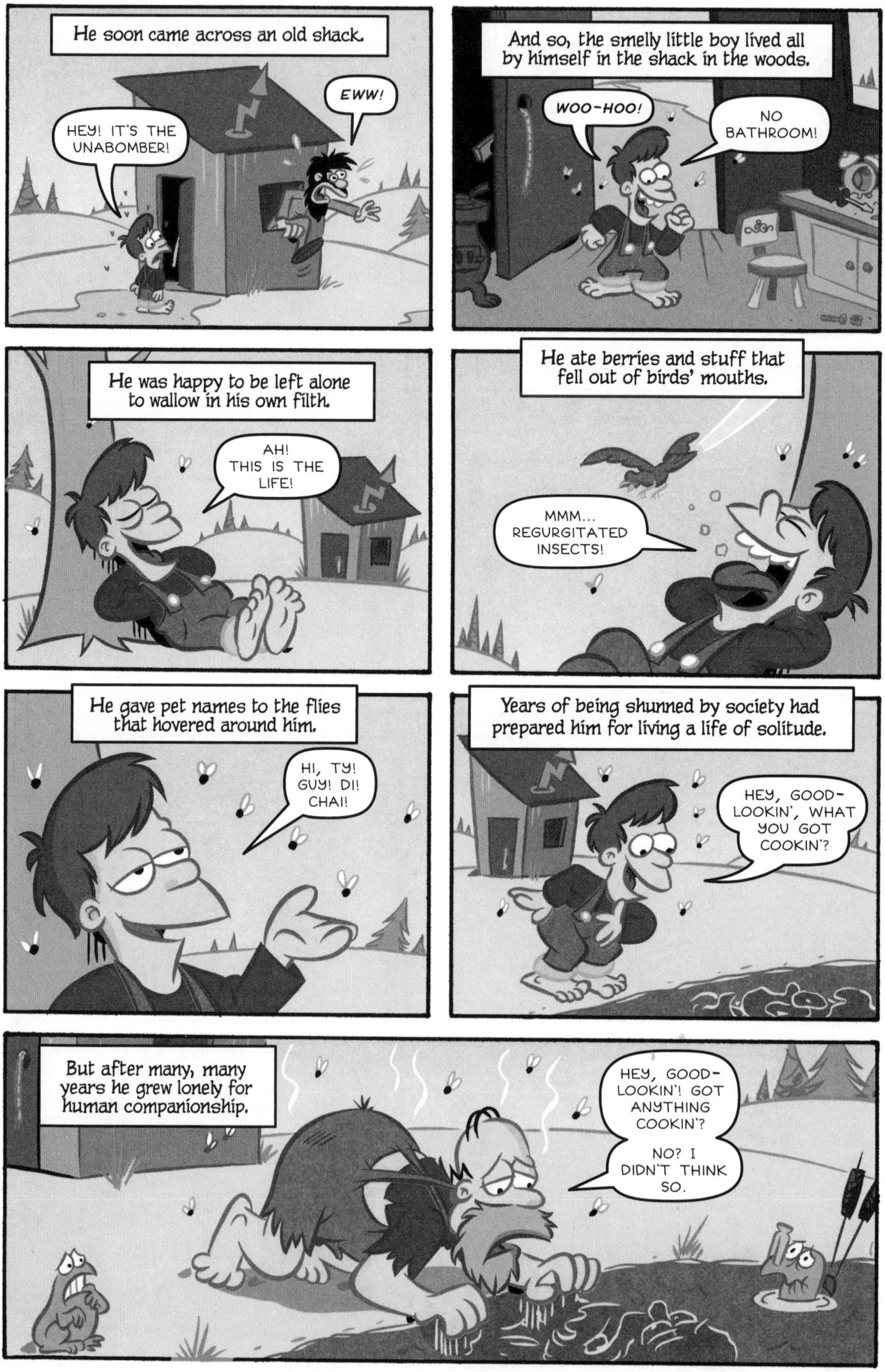
He soon came across an old shack.
HEY! IT'S THE UNABOMBER!
EWW!
And so, the smelly little boy lived all by himself in the shack in the woods.
WOO-HOO!
NO BATHROOM!
He was happy to be left alone to wallow in his own filth.
AH! THIS IS THE LIFE!
He ate berries and stuff that fell out of birds' mouths.
MMM... REGURGITATED INSECTS!
He gave pet names to the flies that hovered around him.
HI, TY! GUY! DI! CHAI!
Years of being shunned by society had prepared him for living a life of solitude.
HEY, GOOD-LOOKIN', WHAT YOU GOT COOKIN'?
But after many, many years he grew lonely for human companionship.
HEY, GOOD-LOOKIN'! GOT ANYTHING COOKIN'?
NO? I DIDN'T THINK SO.

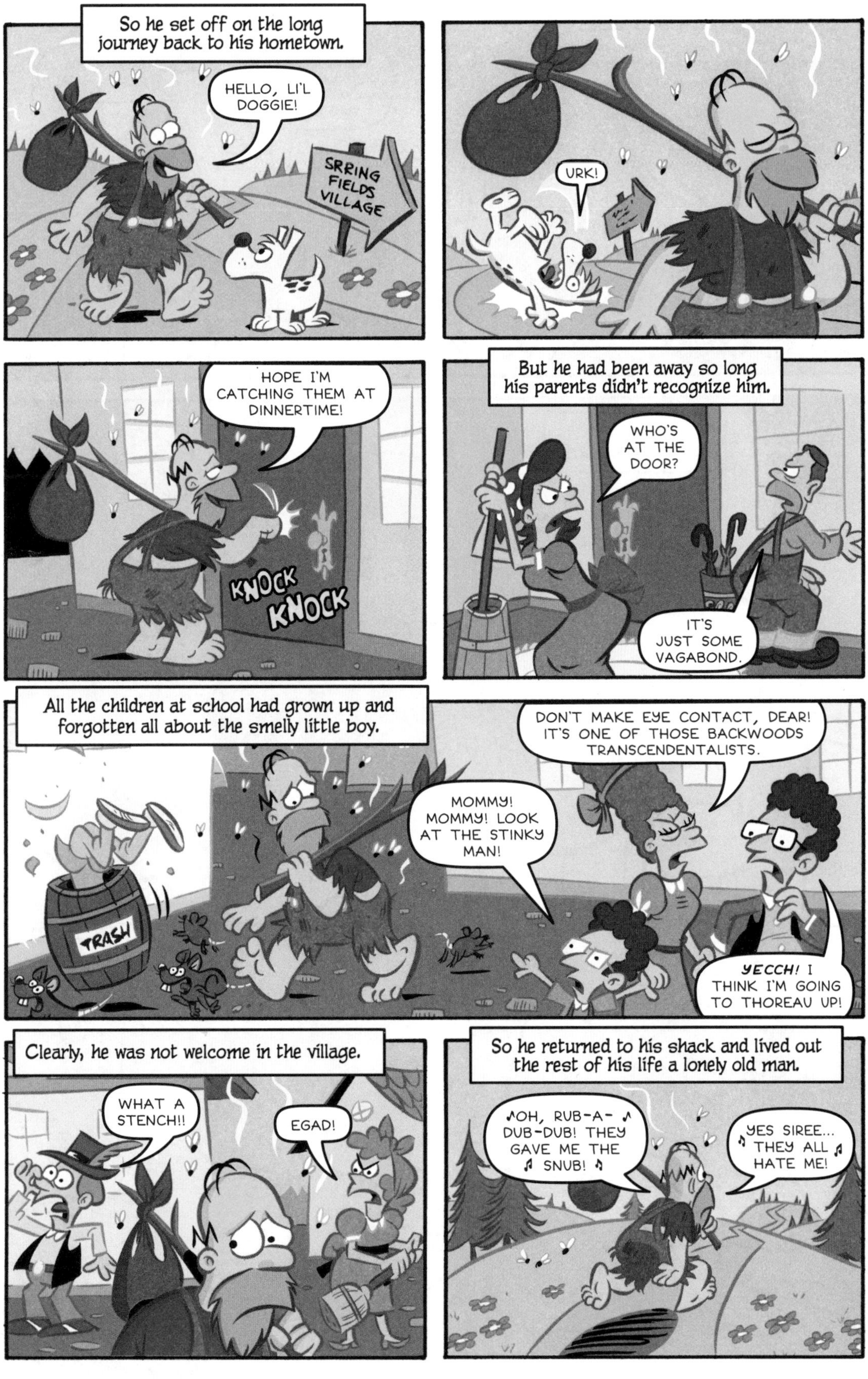
So he set off on the long journey back to his hometown.
HELLO, LI'L DOGGIE!
SRRING FIELDS VILLAGE
URK!
HOPE I'M CATCHING THEM AT DINNERTIME!
KNOCK KNOCK
But he had been away so long his parents didn't recognize him.
WHO'S AT THE DOOR?
IT'S JUST SOME VAGABOND.
All the children at school had grown up and forgotten all about the smelly little boy.
DON'T MAKE EYE CONTACT, DEAR! IT'S ONE OF THOSE BACKWOODS TRANSCENDENTALISTS.
MOMMY! MOMMY! LOOK AT THE STINKY MAN!
TRASH
YECCH! I THINK I'M GOING TO THOREAU UP!
Clearly, he was not welcome in the village.
WHAT A STENCH!!
EGAD!
So he returned to his shack and lived out the rest of his life a lonely old man.
♪OH, RUB-A-DUB-DUB! THEY GAVE ME THE SNUB! ♪
YES SIREE... ♪ THEY ALL HATE ME! ♪

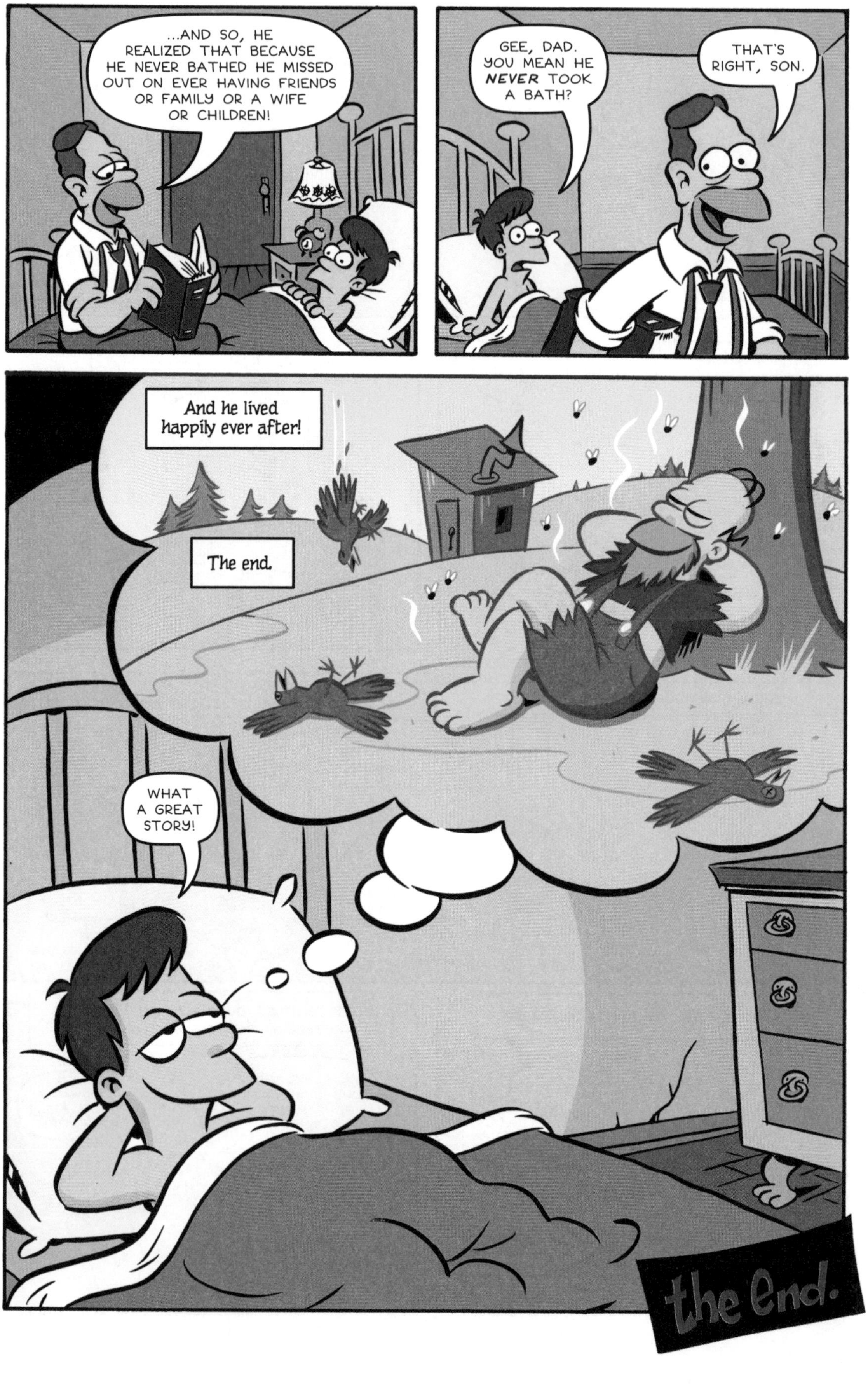
...AND SO, HE REALIZED THAT BECAUSE HE NEVER BATHED HE MISSED OUT ON EVER HAVING FRIENDS OR FAMILY OR A WIFE OR CHILDREN!
GEE, DAD. YOU MEAN HE NEVER TOOK A BATH?
THAT'S RIGHT, SON.
And he lived happily ever after!
The end.
WHAT A GREAT STORY!
the end.

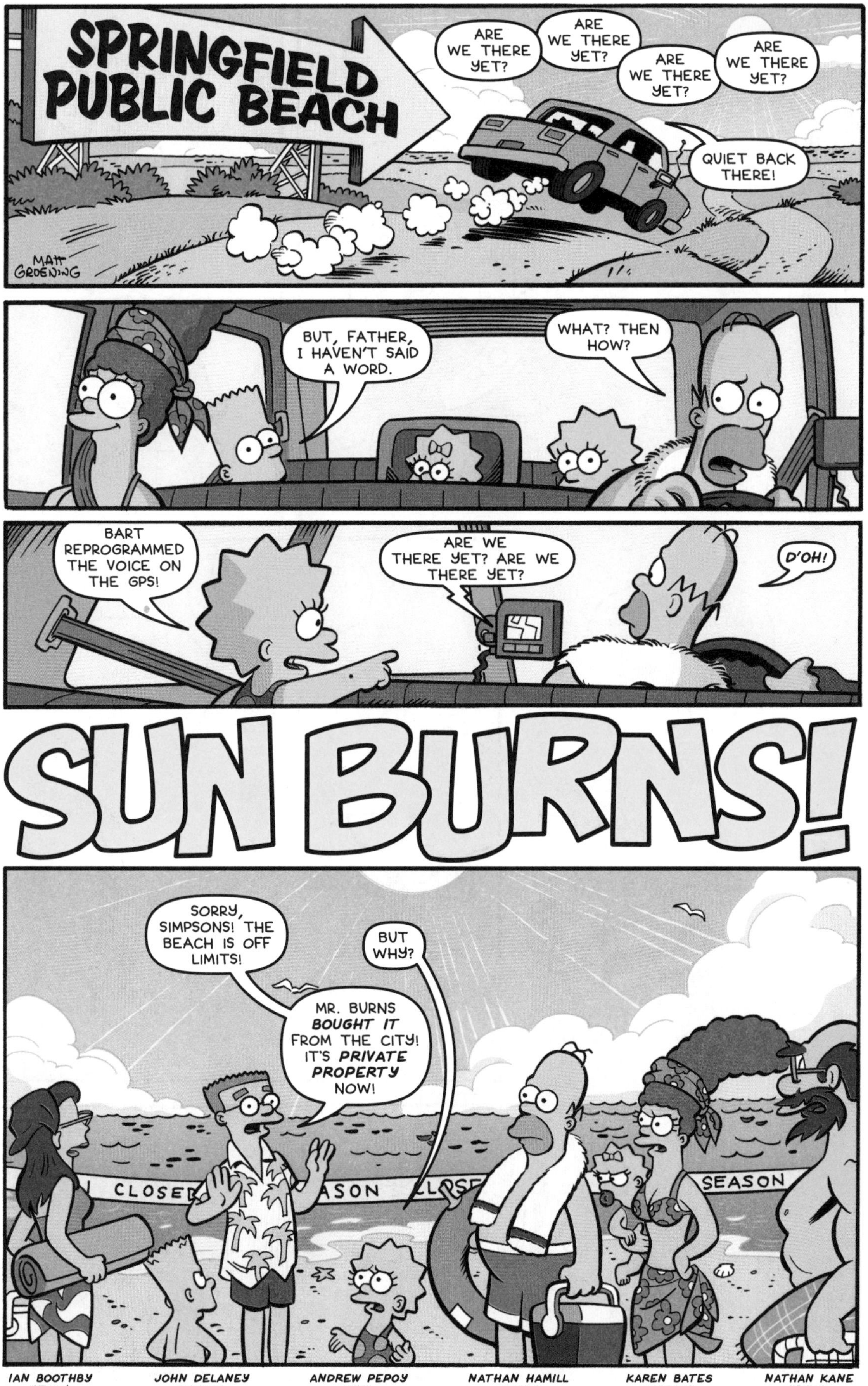

SPRINGFIELD PUBLIC BEACH
ARE WE THERE YET?
ARE WE THERE YET?
ARE WE THERE YET?
ARE WE THERE YET?
QUIET BACK THERE!
MATT GROENING
BUT, FATHER, I HAVEN'T SAID A WORD.
WHAT? THEN HOW?
BART REPROGRAMMED THE VOICE ON THE GPS!
ARE WE THERE YET? ARE WE THERE YET?
D'OH!
SUN BURNS!
SORRY, SIMPSONS! THE BEACH IS OFF LIMITS!
BUT WHY?
MR. BURNS **BOUGHT IT** FROM THE CITY! IT'S **PRIVATE PROPERTY** NOW!
CLOSED SEASON CLOSED SEASON

IAN BOOTHBY STORY · **JOHN DELANEY** PENCILS · **ANDREW PEPOY** INKS · **NATHAN HAMILL** COLORS · **KAREN BATES** LETTERS · **NATHAN KANE** EDITOR

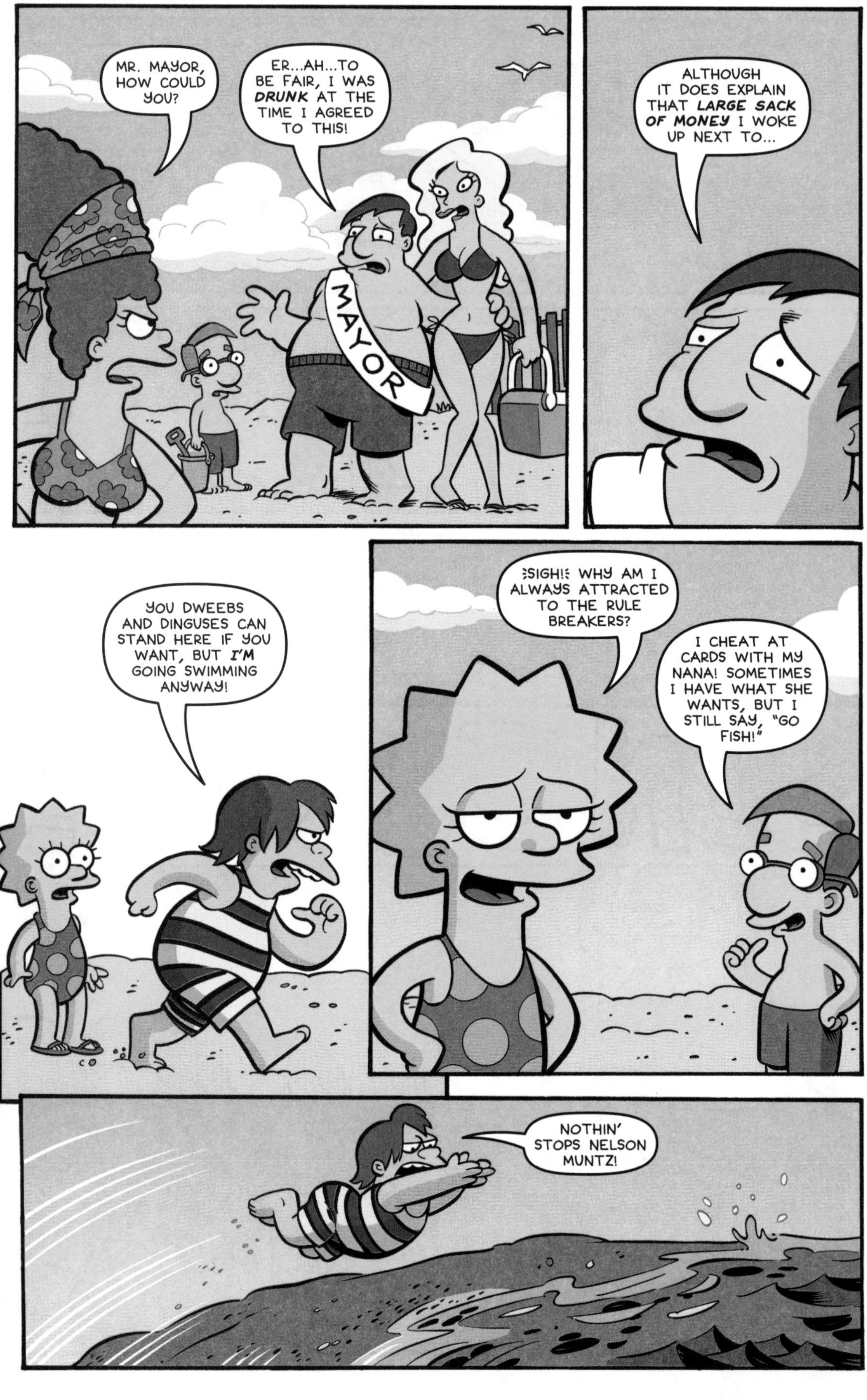
MR. MAYOR, HOW COULD YOU?
ER...AH...TO BE FAIR, I WAS DRUNK AT THE TIME I AGREED TO THIS!
MAYOR
ALTHOUGH IT DOES EXPLAIN THAT LARGE SACK OF MONEY I WOKE UP NEXT TO...
YOU DWEEBS AND DINGUSES CAN STAND HERE IF YOU WANT, BUT I'M GOING SWIMMING ANYWAY!
SIGH! WHY AM I ALWAYS ATTRACTED TO THE RULE BREAKERS?
I CHEAT AT CARDS WITH MY NANA! SOMETIMES I HAVE WHAT SHE WANTS, BUT I STILL SAY, "GO FISH!"
NOTHIN' STOPS NELSON MUNTZ!

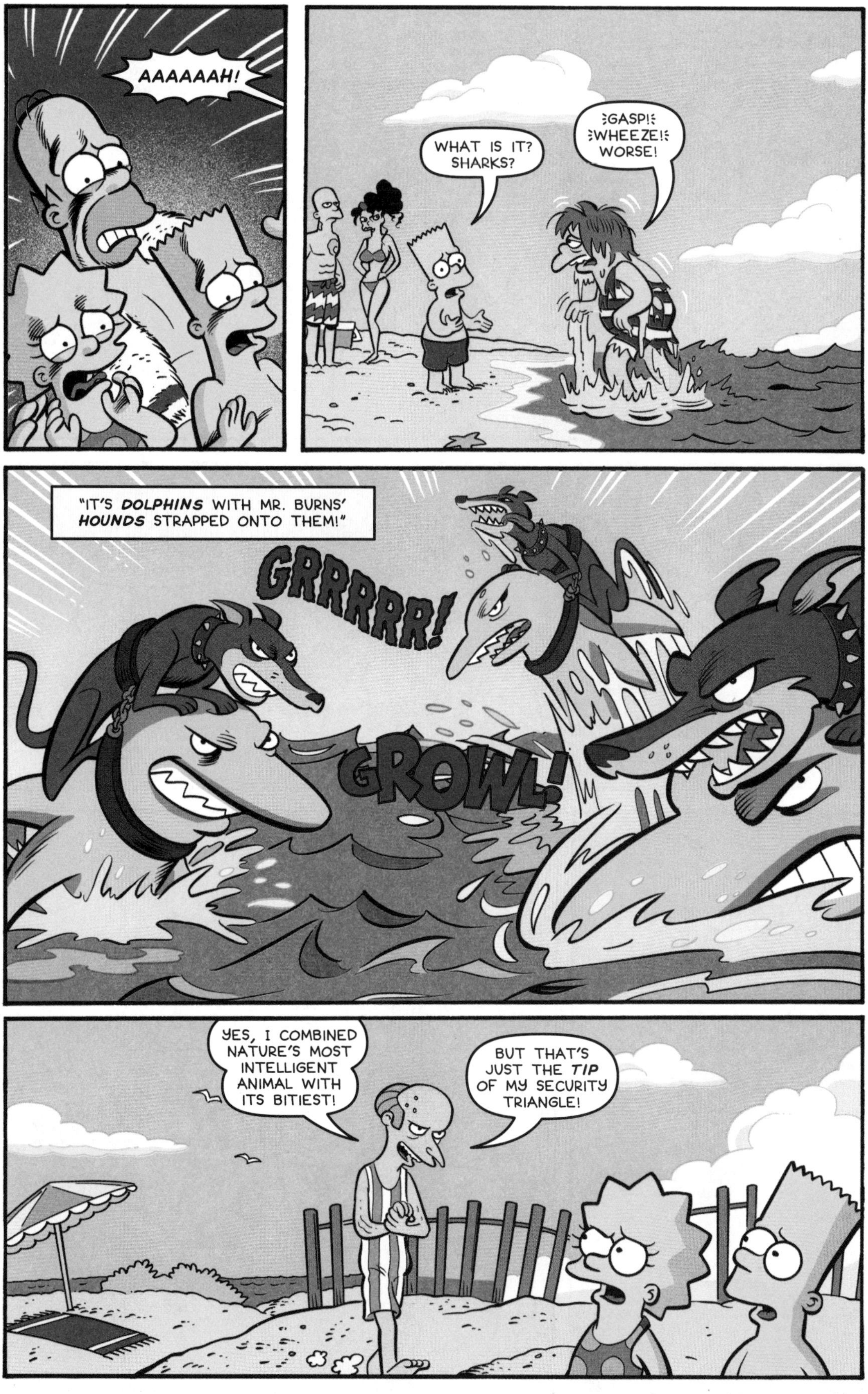
AAAAAAH!
WHAT IS IT? SHARKS?
GASP! WHEEZE! WORSE!
"IT'S DOLPHINS WITH MR. BURNS' HOUNDS STRAPPED ONTO THEM!"
GRRRRRR!
GROWL!
YES, I COMBINED NATURE'S MOST INTELLIGENT ANIMAL WITH ITS BITIEST!
BUT THAT'S JUST THE TIP OF MY SECURITY TRIANGLE!

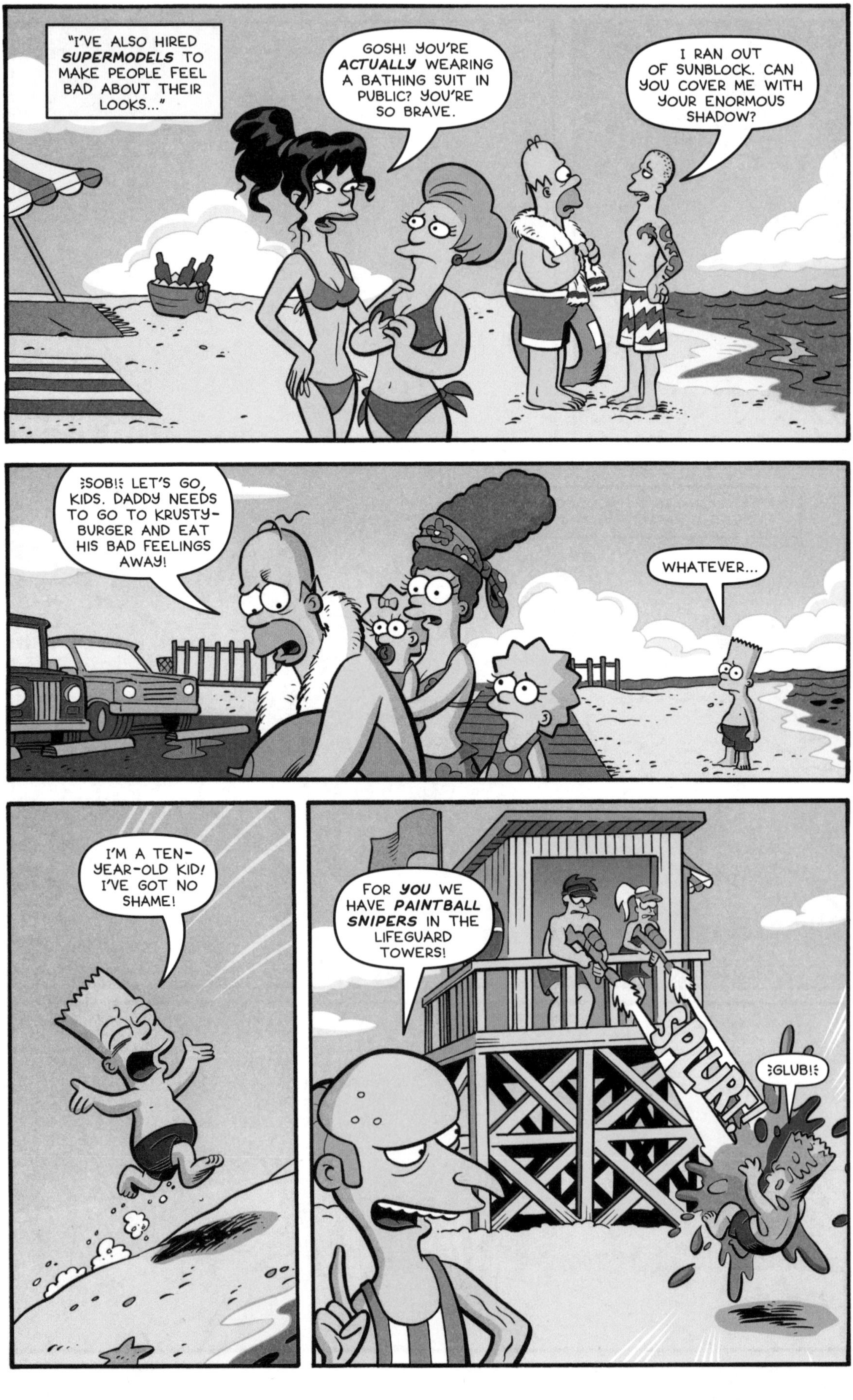
"I'VE ALSO HIRED SUPERMODELS TO MAKE PEOPLE FEEL BAD ABOUT THEIR LOOKS..."
GOSH! YOU'RE ACTUALLY WEARING A BATHING SUIT IN PUBLIC? YOU'RE SO BRAVE.
I RAN OUT OF SUNBLOCK. CAN YOU COVER ME WITH YOUR ENORMOUS SHADOW?
SOB! LET'S GO, KIDS. DADDY NEEDS TO GO TO KRUSTY-BURGER AND EAT HIS BAD FEELINGS AWAY!
WHATEVER...
I'M A TEN-YEAR-OLD KID! I'VE GOT NO SHAME!
FOR YOU WE HAVE PAINTBALL SNIPERS IN THE LIFEGUARD TOWERS!
SPLURT!
GLUB!

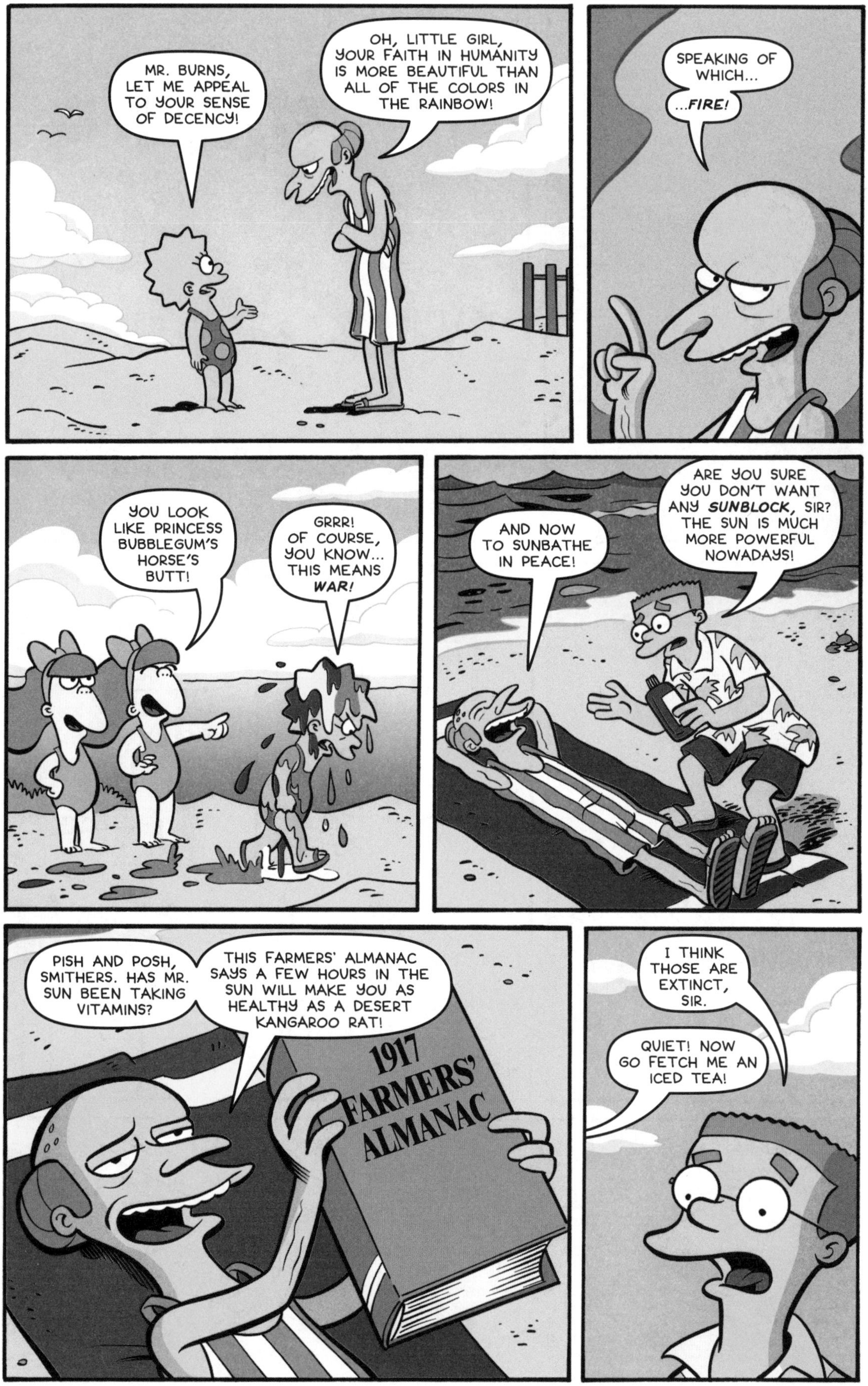

MR. BURNS, LET ME APPEAL TO YOUR SENSE OF DECENCY!
OH, LITTLE GIRL, YOUR FAITH IN HUMANITY IS MORE BEAUTIFUL THAN ALL OF THE COLORS IN THE RAINBOW!
SPEAKING OF WHICH...
...FIRE!
YOU LOOK LIKE PRINCESS BUBBLEGUM'S HORSE'S BUTT!
GRRR! OF COURSE, YOU KNOW... THIS MEANS WAR!
AND NOW TO SUNBATHE IN PEACE!
ARE YOU SURE YOU DON'T WANT ANY SUNBLOCK, SIR? THE SUN IS MUCH MORE POWERFUL NOWADAYS!
PISH AND POSH, SMITHERS. HAS MR. SUN BEEN TAKING VITAMINS?
THIS FARMERS' ALMANAC SAYS A FEW HOURS IN THE SUN WILL MAKE YOU AS HEALTHY AS A DESERT KANGAROO RAT!
1917 FARMERS' ALMANAC
I THINK THOSE ARE EXTINCT, SIR.
QUIET! NOW GO FETCH ME AN ICED TEA!

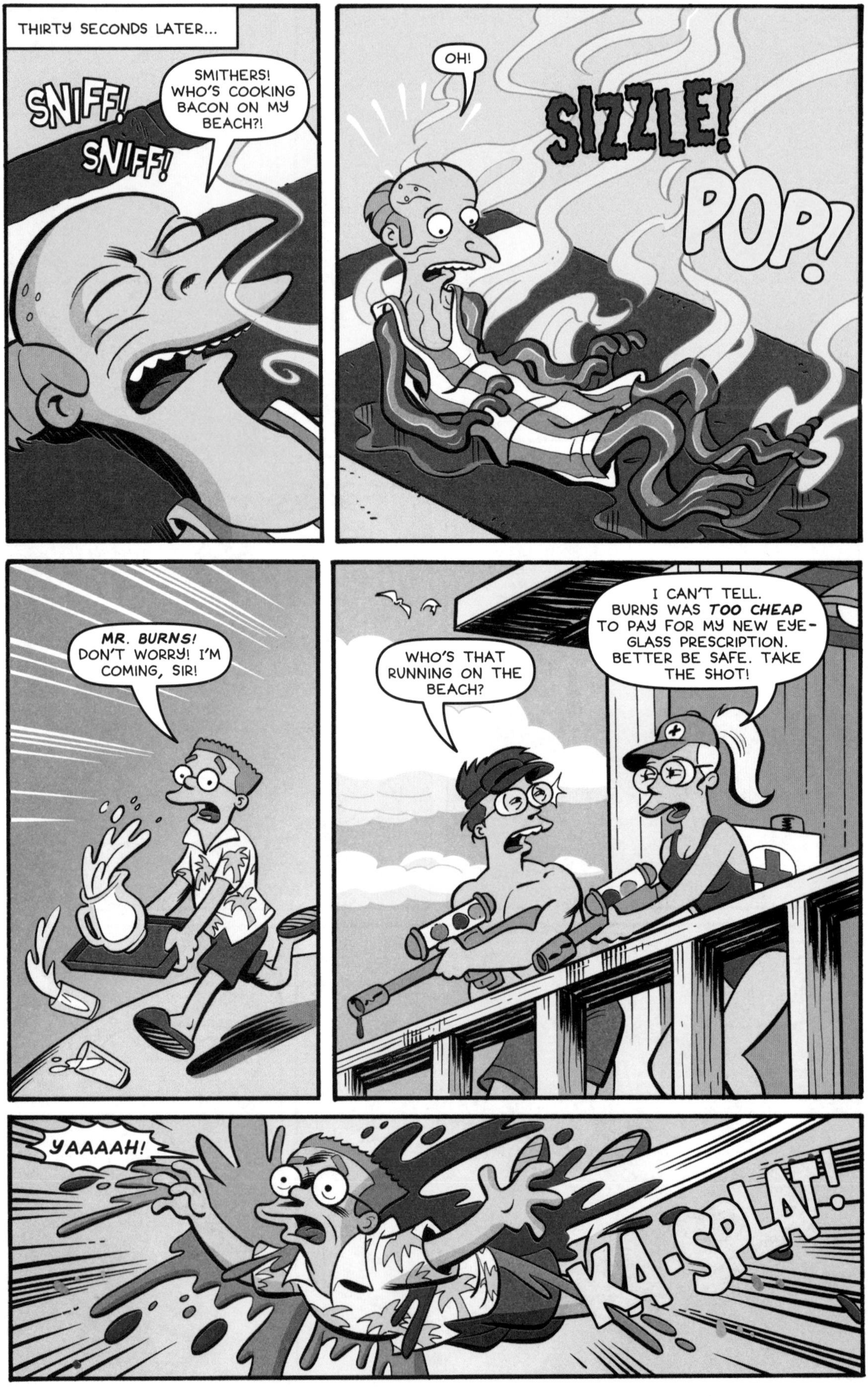
THIRTY SECONDS LATER...
SNIFF!
SNIFF!
SMITHERS! WHO'S COOKING BACON ON MY BEACH?!
OH!
SIZZLE!
POP!
MR. BURNS! DON'T WORRY! I'M COMING, SIR!
WHO'S THAT RUNNING ON THE BEACH?
I CAN'T TELL. BURNS WAS TOO CHEAP TO PAY FOR MY NEW EYE-GLASS PRESCRIPTION. BETTER BE SAFE. TAKE THE SHOT!
YAAAAH!
KA-SPLAT!

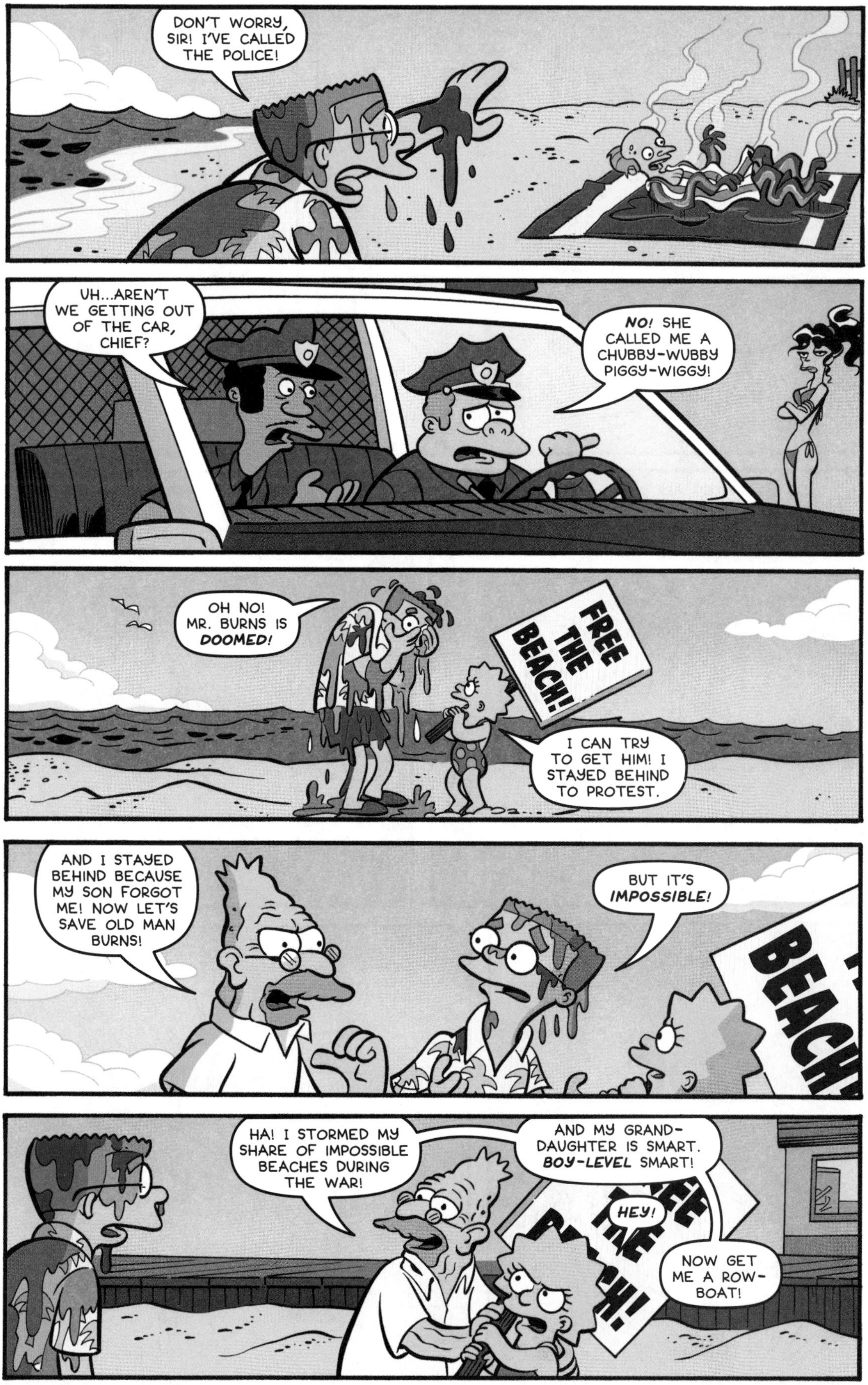
DON'T WORRY, SIR! I'VE CALLED THE POLICE!
UH...AREN'T WE GETTING OUT OF THE CAR, CHIEF?
NO! SHE CALLED ME A CHUBBY-WUBBY PIGGY-WIGGY!
OH NO! MR. BURNS IS DOOMED!
FREE THE BEACH!
I CAN TRY TO GET HIM! I STAYED BEHIND TO PROTEST.
AND I STAYED BEHIND BECAUSE MY SON FORGOT ME! NOW LET'S SAVE OLD MAN BURNS!
BUT IT'S IMPOSSIBLE!
BEACH
HA! I STORMED MY SHARE OF IMPOSSIBLE BEACHES DURING THE WAR!
AND MY GRAND-DAUGHTER IS SMART. BOY-LEVEL SMART!
HEY!
NOW GET ME A ROW-BOAT!

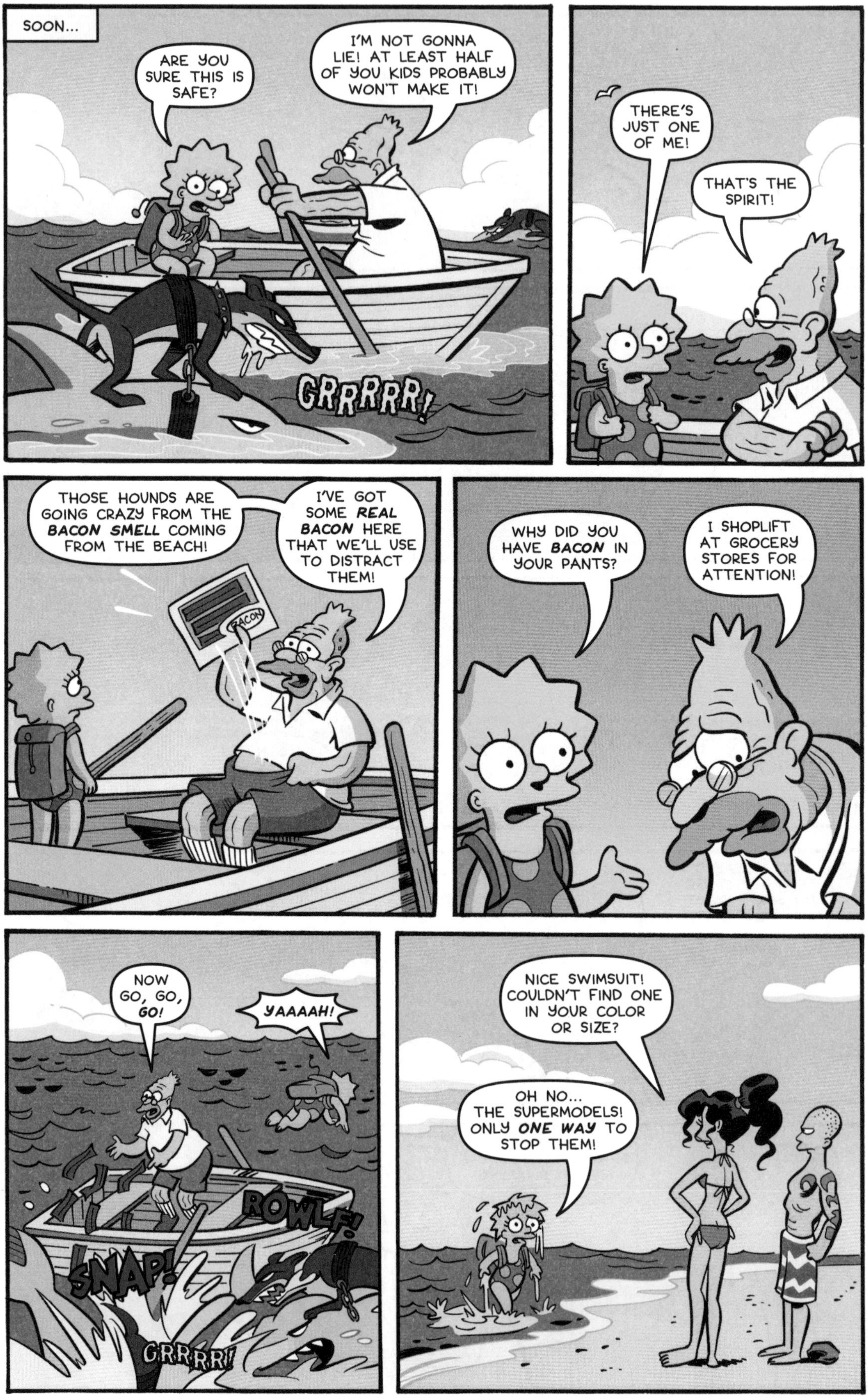
SOON...
ARE YOU SURE THIS IS SAFE?
I'M NOT GONNA LIE! AT LEAST HALF OF YOU KIDS PROBABLY WON'T MAKE IT!
GRRRRR!
THERE'S JUST ONE OF ME!
THAT'S THE SPIRIT!
THOSE HOUNDS ARE GOING CRAZY FROM THE BACON SMELL COMING FROM THE BEACH!
I'VE GOT SOME REAL BACON HERE THAT WE'LL USE TO DISTRACT THEM!
BACON
WHY DID YOU HAVE BACON IN YOUR PANTS?
I SHOPLIFT AT GROCERY STORES FOR ATTENTION!
NOW GO, GO, GO!
YAAAAH!
ROWLF!
SNAP!
GRRRR!
NICE SWIMSUIT! COULDN'T FIND ONE IN YOUR COLOR OR SIZE?
OH NO... THE SUPERMODELS! ONLY ONE WAY TO STOP THEM!

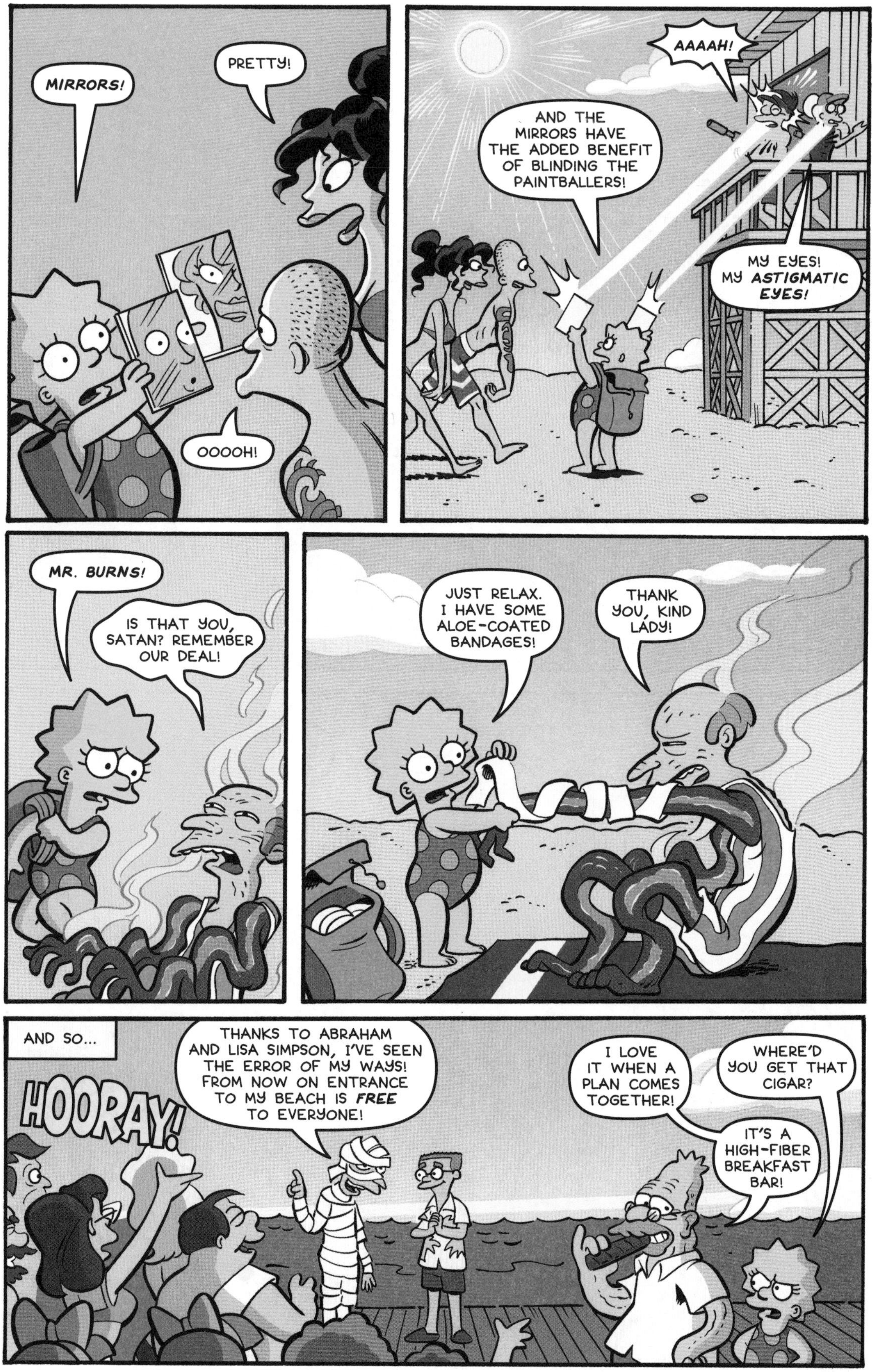
MIRRORS!
PRETTY!
OOOOH!
AAAAH!
AND THE MIRRORS HAVE THE ADDED BENEFIT OF BLINDING THE PAINTBALLERS!
MY EYES! MY ASTIGMATIC EYES!
MR. BURNS!
IS THAT YOU, SATAN? REMEMBER OUR DEAL!
JUST RELAX. I HAVE SOME ALOE-COATED BANDAGES!
THANK YOU, KIND LADY!
AND SO...
HOORAY!
THANKS TO ABRAHAM AND LISA SIMPSON, I'VE SEEN THE ERROR OF MY WAYS! FROM NOW ON ENTRANCE TO MY BEACH IS FREE TO EVERYONE!
I LOVE IT WHEN A PLAN COMES TOGETHER!
WHERE'D YOU GET THAT CIGAR?
IT'S A HIGH-FIBER BREAKFAST BAR!

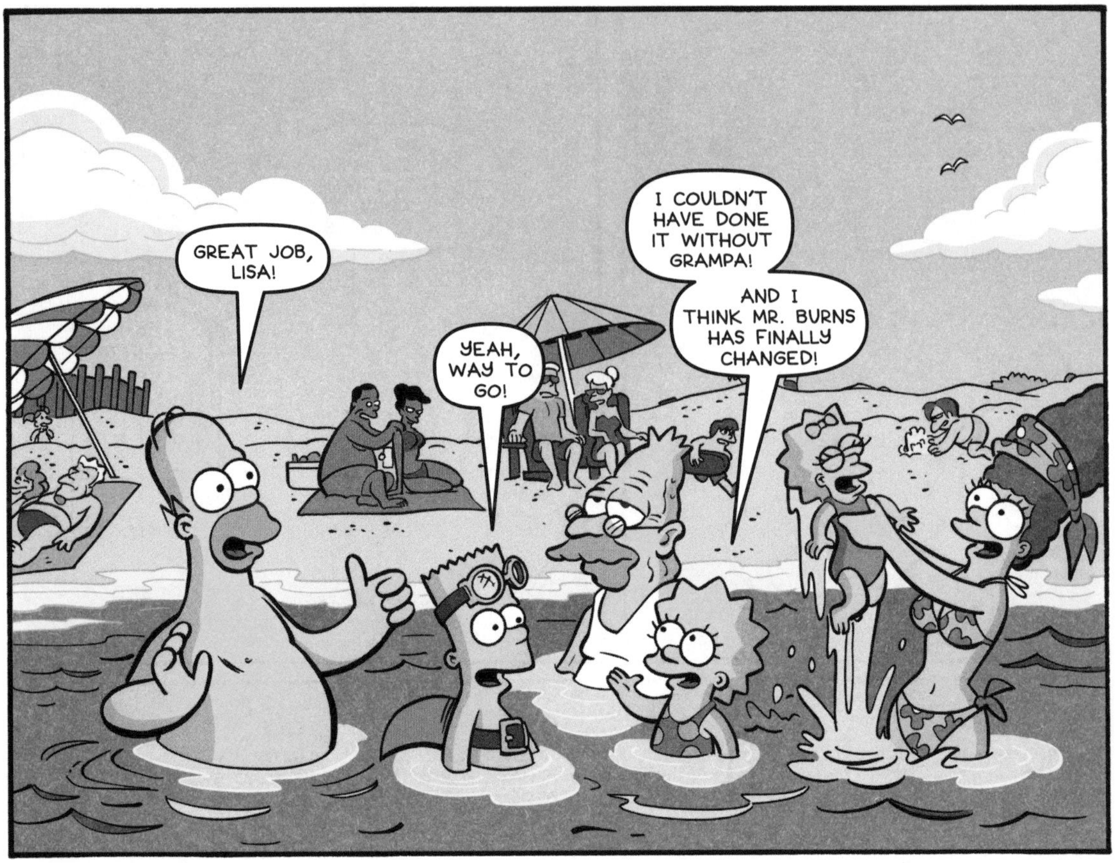
GREAT JOB, LISA!
YEAH, WAY TO GO!
I COULDN'T HAVE DONE IT WITHOUT GRAMPA!
AND I THINK MR. BURNS HAS FINALLY CHANGED!

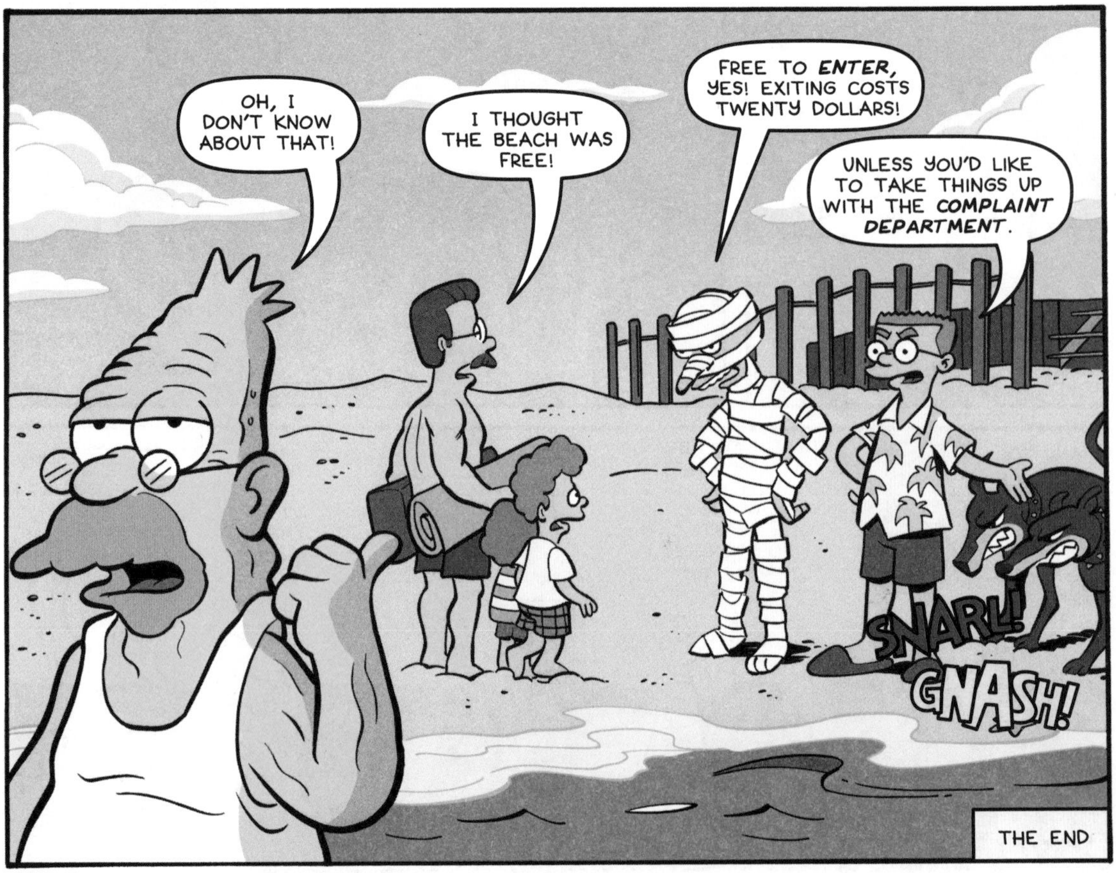
OH, I DON'T KNOW ABOUT THAT!
I THOUGHT THE BEACH WAS FREE!
FREE TO ENTER, YES! EXITING COSTS TWENTY DOLLARS!
UNLESS YOU'D LIKE TO TAKE THINGS UP WITH THE COMPLAINT DEPARTMENT.
SNARL!
GNASH!
THE END

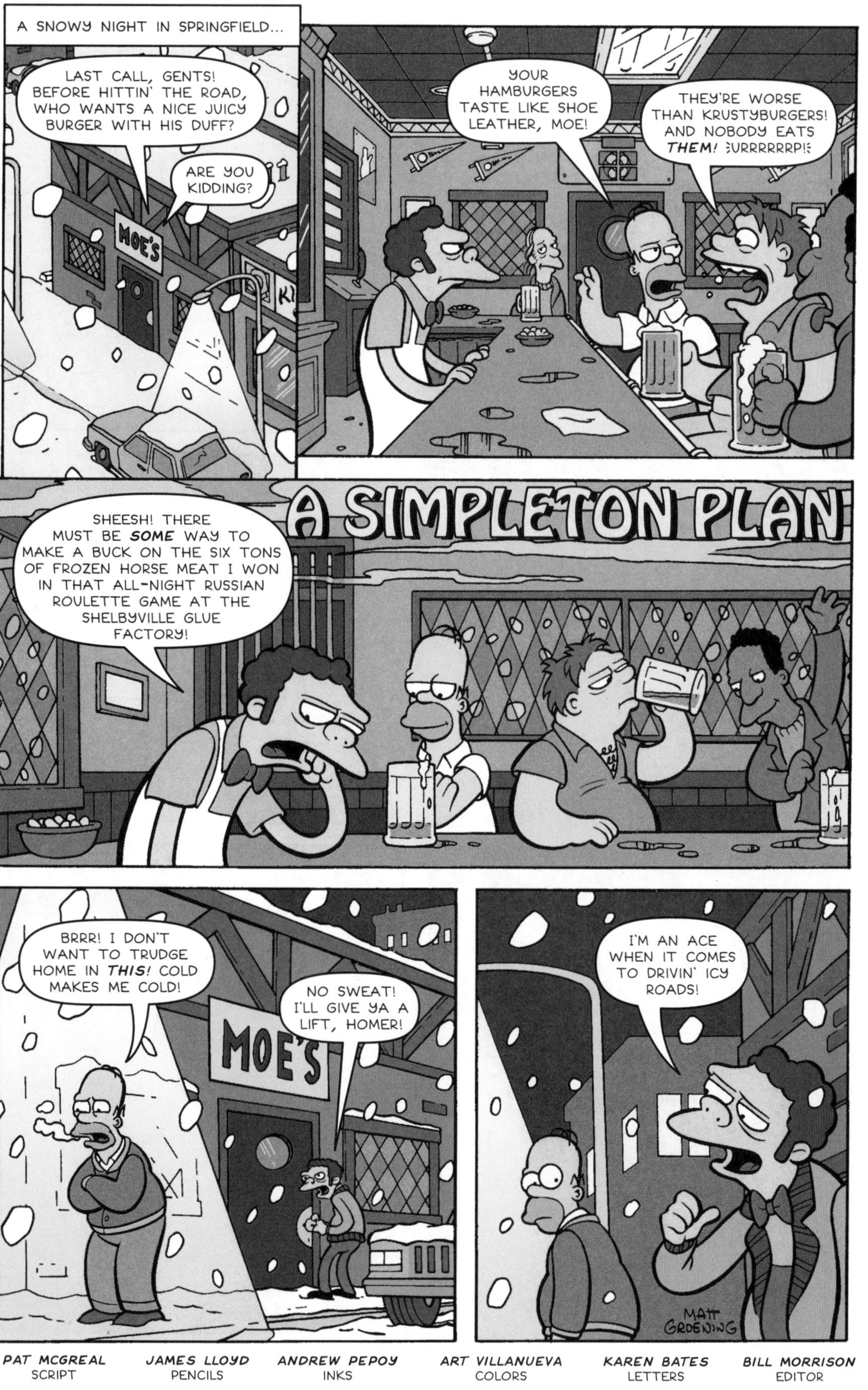
A SNOWY NIGHT IN SPRINGFIELD...
LAST CALL, GENTS! BEFORE HITTIN' THE ROAD, WHO WANTS A NICE JUICY BURGER WITH HIS DUFF?
ARE YOU KIDDING?
MOE'S
YOUR HAMBURGERS TASTE LIKE SHOE LEATHER, MOE!
THEY'RE WORSE THAN KRUSTYBURGERS! AND NOBODY EATS *THEM!* URRRRRRP!
A SIMPLETON PLAN
SHEESH! THERE MUST BE **SOME** WAY TO MAKE A BUCK ON THE SIX TONS OF FROZEN HORSE MEAT I WON IN THAT ALL-NIGHT RUSSIAN ROULETTE GAME AT THE SHELBYVILLE GLUE FACTORY!
BRRR! I DON'T WANT TO TRUDGE HOME IN *THIS!* COLD MAKES ME COLD!
MOE'S
NO SWEAT! I'LL GIVE YA A LIFT, HOMER!
I'M AN ACE WHEN IT COMES TO DRIVIN' ICY ROADS!
MATT GROENING

PAT MCGREAL SCRIPT

JAMES LLOYD PENCILS

ANDREW PEPOY INKS

ART VILLANUEVA COLORS

KAREN BATES LETTERS

BILL MORRISON EDITOR

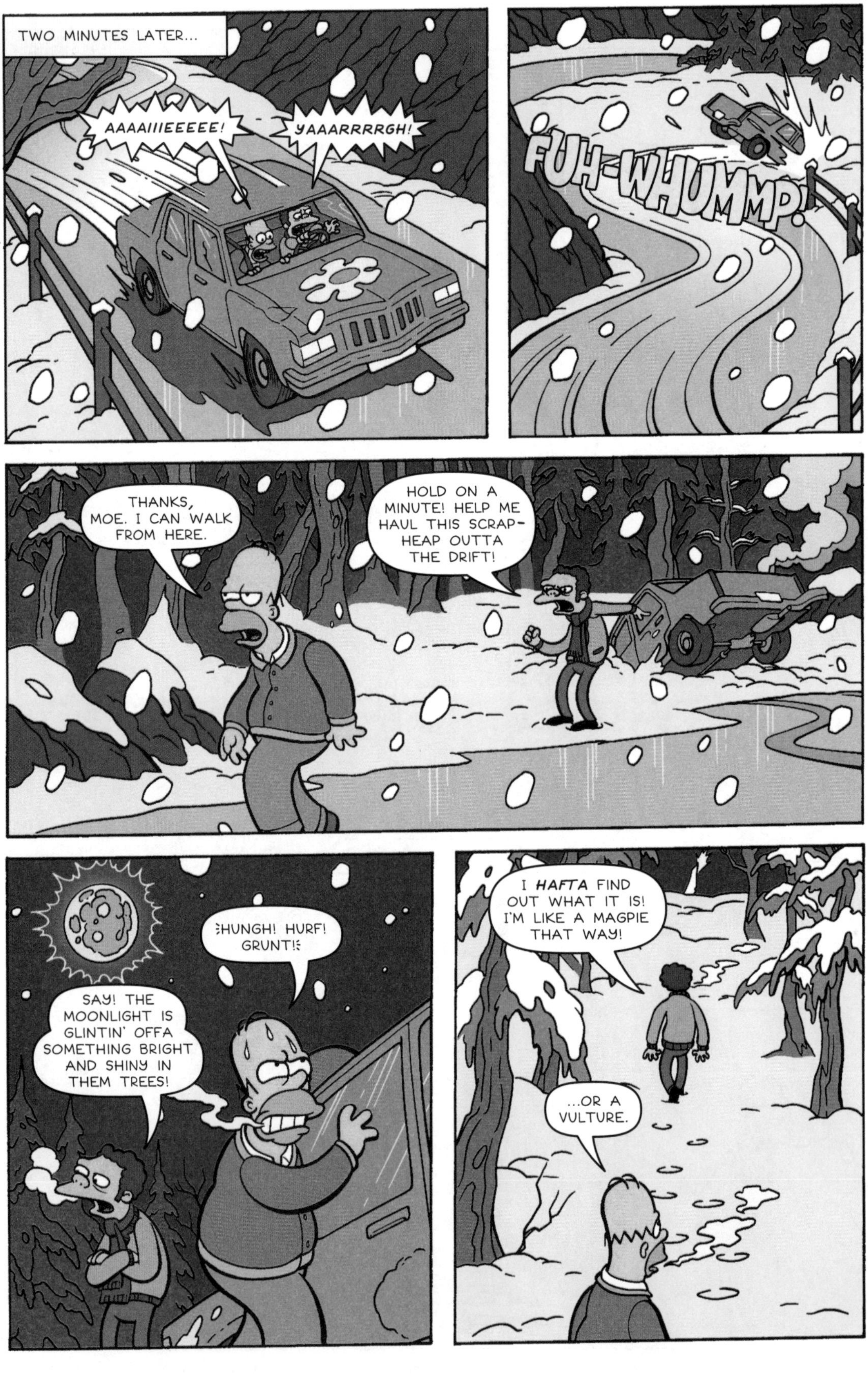
TWO MINUTES LATER...
AAAAIIIEEEEE!
YAAARRRRGH!
FUH-WHUMMP!
THANKS, MOE. I CAN WALK FROM HERE.
HOLD ON A MINUTE! HELP ME HAUL THIS SCRAP-HEAP OUTTA THE DRIFT!
HUNGH! HURF! GRUNT!
SAY! THE MOONLIGHT IS GLINTIN' OFFA SOMETHING BRIGHT AND SHINY IN THEM TREES!
I HAFTA FIND OUT WHAT IT IS! I'M LIKE A MAGPIE THAT WAY!
...OR A VULTURE.

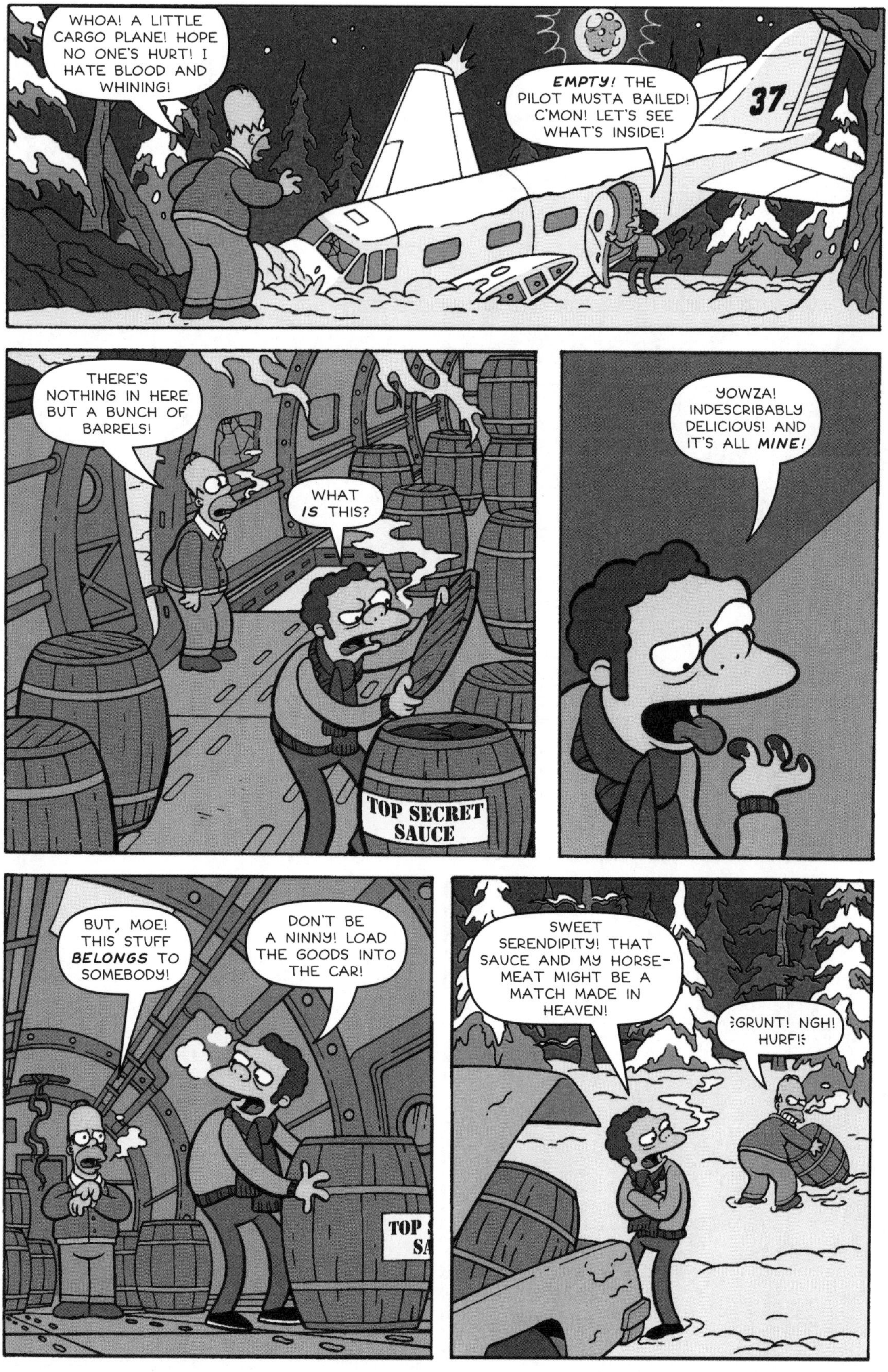

WHOA! A LITTLE CARGO PLANE! HOPE NO ONE'S HURT! I HATE BLOOD AND WHINING!
EMPTY! THE PILOT MUSTA BAILED! C'MON! LET'S SEE WHAT'S INSIDE!
37
THERE'S NOTHING IN HERE BUT A BUNCH OF BARRELS!
WHAT IS THIS?
TOP SECRET SAUCE
YOWZA! INDESCRIBABLY DELICIOUS! AND IT'S ALL MINE!
BUT, MOE! THIS STUFF BELONGS TO SOMEBODY!
DON'T BE A NINNY! LOAD THE GOODS INTO THE CAR!
SWEET SERENDIPITY! THAT SAUCE AND MY HORSE-MEAT MIGHT BE A MATCH MADE IN HEAVEN!
GRUNT! NGH! HURF!

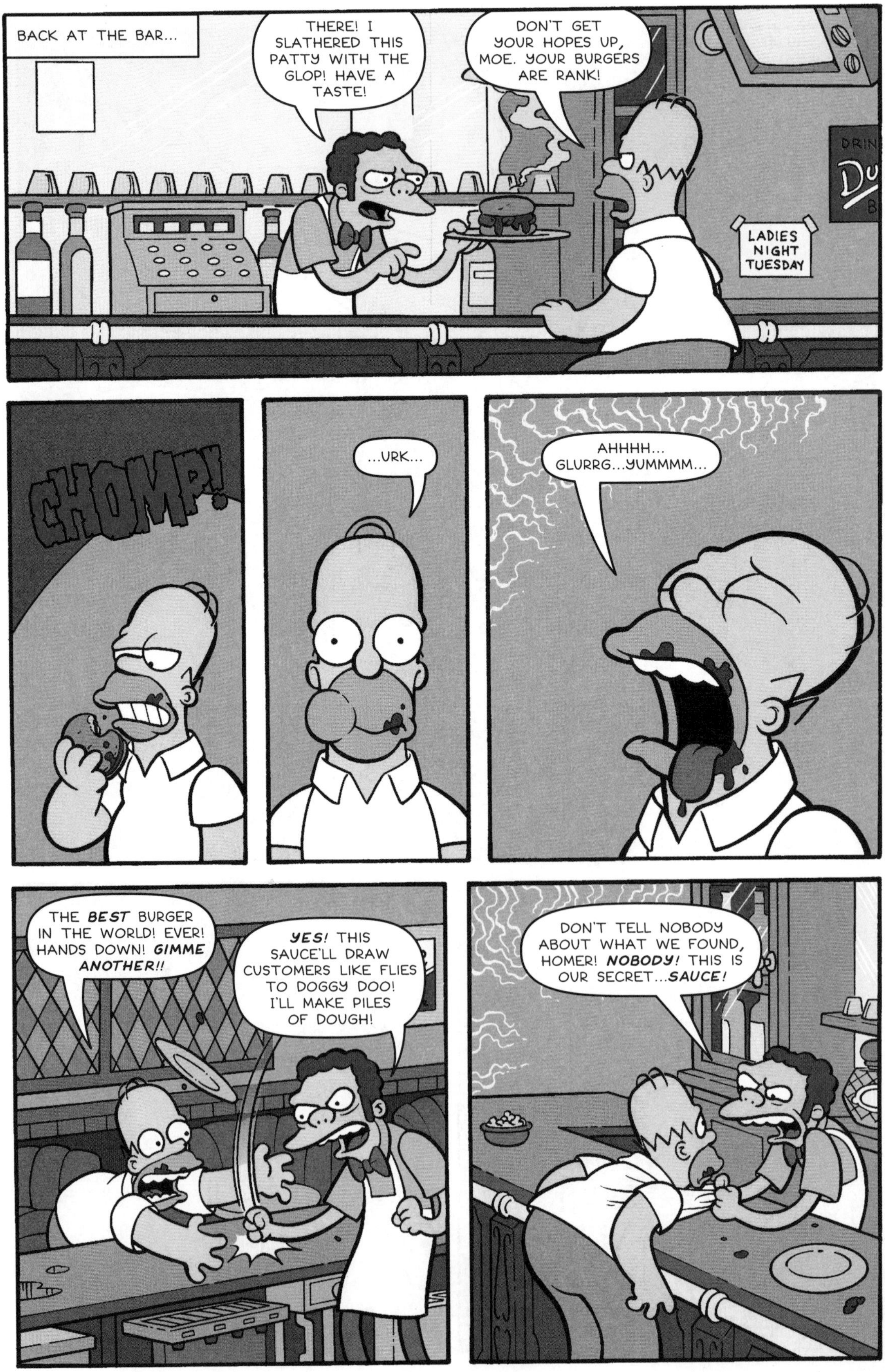

BACK AT THE BAR...
THERE! I SLATHERED THIS PATTY WITH THE GLOP! HAVE A TASTE!
DON'T GET YOUR HOPES UP, MOE. YOUR BURGERS ARE RANK!
LADIES NIGHT TUESDAY
CHOMP!
...URK...
AHHHH... GLURRG...YUMMMM...
THE **BEST** BURGER IN THE WORLD! EVER! HANDS DOWN! ***GIMME ANOTHER!!***
YES! THIS SAUCE'LL DRAW CUSTOMERS LIKE FLIES TO DOGGY DOO! I'LL MAKE PILES OF DOUGH!
DON'T TELL NOBODY ABOUT WHAT WE FOUND, HOMER! ***NOBODY!*** THIS IS OUR SECRET...***SAUCE!***

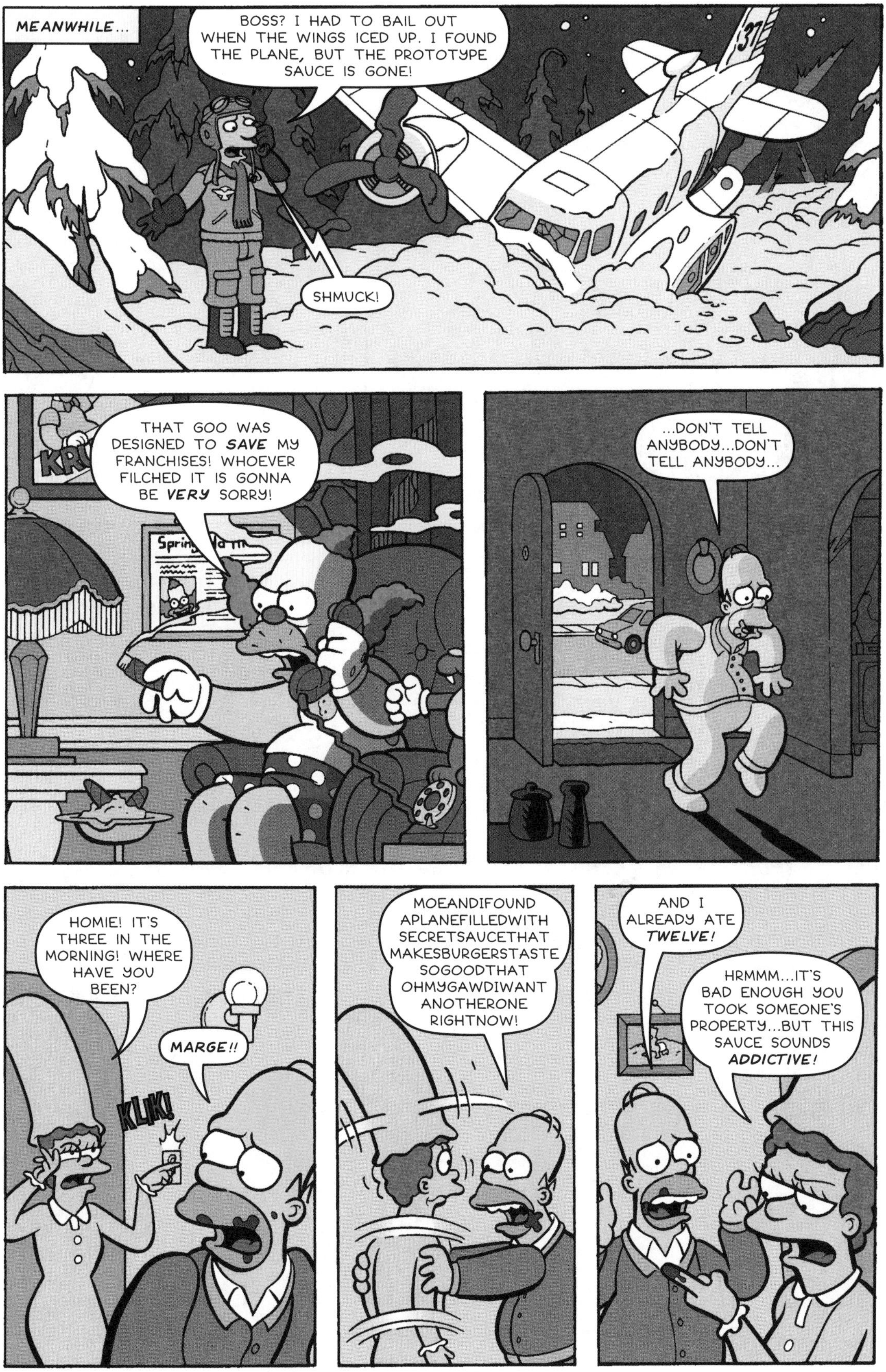
MEANWHILE...
BOSS? I HAD TO BAIL OUT WHEN THE WINGS ICED UP. I FOUND THE PLANE, BUT THE PROTOTYPE SAUCE IS GONE!
SHMUCK!
THAT GOO WAS DESIGNED TO SAVE MY FRANCHISES! WHOEVER FILCHED IT IS GONNA BE VERY SORRY!
...DON'T TELL ANYBODY...DON'T TELL ANYBODY...
HOMIE! IT'S THREE IN THE MORNING! WHERE HAVE YOU BEEN?
KLIK!
MARGE!!
MOEANDIFOUND APLANEFILLEDWITH SECRETSAUCETHAT MAKESBURGERSTASTE SOGOODTHAT OHMYGAWDIWANT ANOTHERONE RIGHTNOW!
AND I ALREADY ATE TWELVE!
HRMMM...IT'S BAD ENOUGH YOU TOOK SOMEONE'S PROPERTY...BUT THIS SAUCE SOUNDS ADDICTIVE!

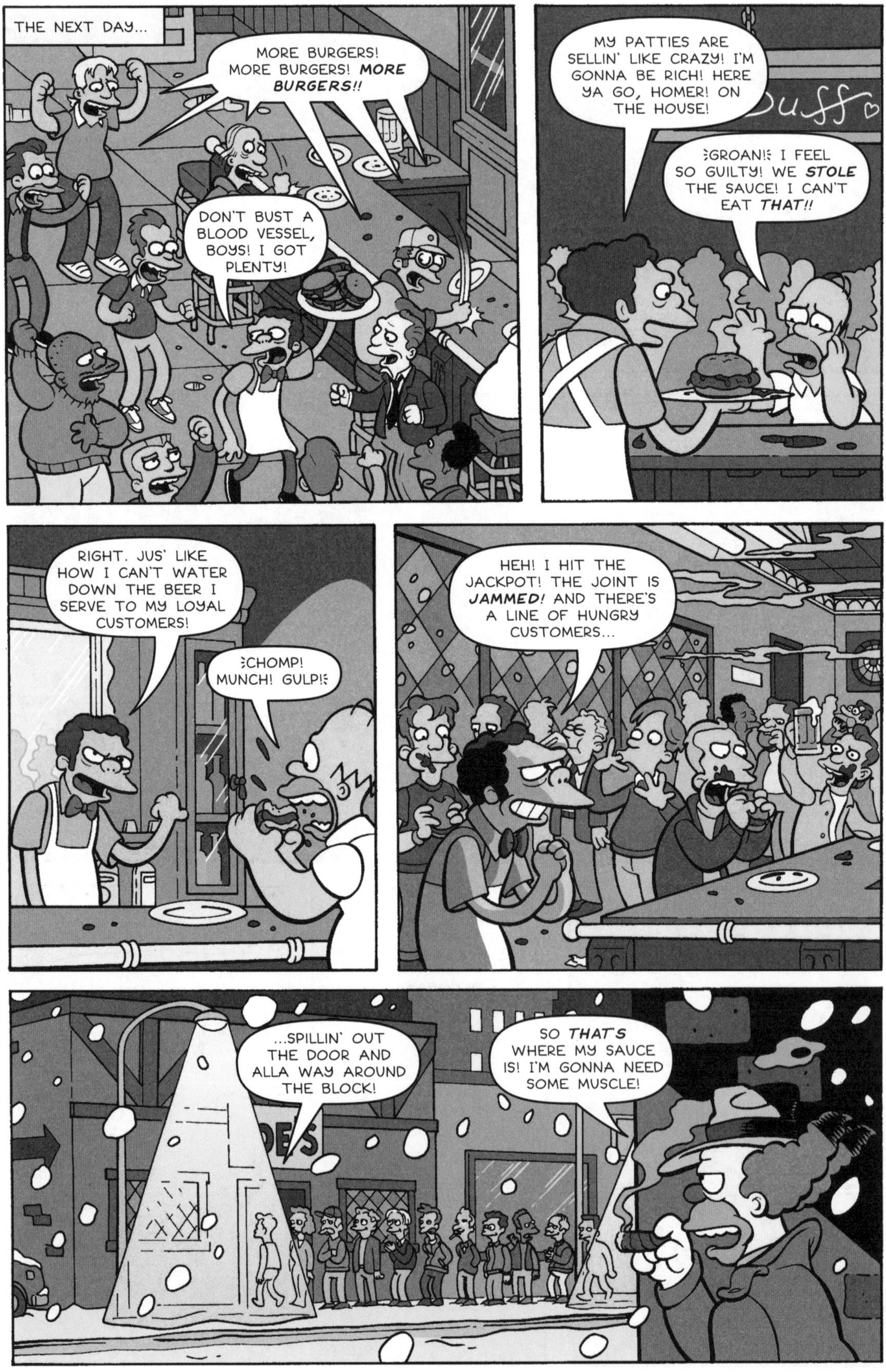
THE NEXT DAY...
MORE BURGERS! MORE BURGERS! MORE BURGERS!!
DON'T BUST A BLOOD VESSEL, BOYS! I GOT PLENTY!
MY PATTIES ARE SELLIN' LIKE CRAZY! I'M GONNA BE RICH! HERE YA GO, HOMER! ON THE HOUSE!
GROAN! I FEEL SO GUILTY! WE STOLE THE SAUCE! I CAN'T EAT THAT!!
RIGHT. JUS' LIKE HOW I CAN'T WATER DOWN THE BEER I SERVE TO MY LOYAL CUSTOMERS!
CHOMP! MUNCH! GULP!
HEH! I HIT THE JACKPOT! THE JOINT IS JAMMED! AND THERE'S A LINE OF HUNGRY CUSTOMERS...
...SPILLIN' OUT THE DOOR AND ALLA WAY AROUND THE BLOCK!
SO THAT'S WHERE MY SAUCE IS! I'M GONNA NEED SOME MUSCLE!

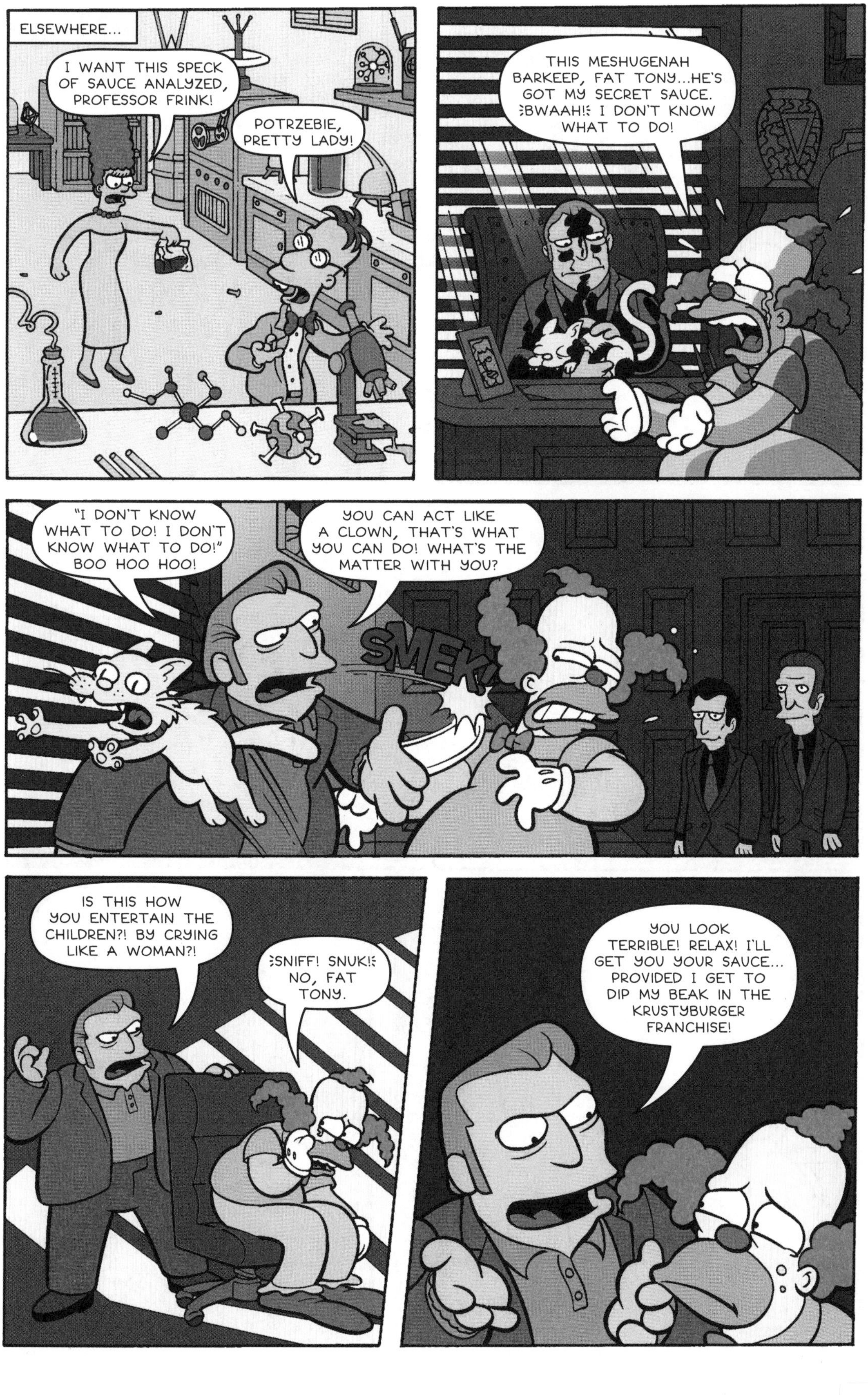

ELSEWHERE...
I WANT THIS SPECK OF SAUCE ANALYZED, PROFESSOR FRINK!
POTRZEBIE, PRETTY LADY!
THIS MESHUGENAH BARKEEP, FAT TONY...HE'S GOT MY SECRET SAUCE. BWAAH! I DON'T KNOW WHAT TO DO!
"I DON'T KNOW WHAT TO DO! I DON'T KNOW WHAT TO DO!" BOO HOO HOO!
YOU CAN ACT LIKE A CLOWN, THAT'S WHAT YOU CAN DO! WHAT'S THE MATTER WITH YOU?
SMEK!
IS THIS HOW YOU ENTERTAIN THE CHILDREN?! BY CRYING LIKE A WOMAN?!
SNIFF! SNUK! NO, FAT TONY.
YOU LOOK TERRIBLE! RELAX! I'LL GET YOU YOUR SAUCE... PROVIDED I GET TO DIP MY BEAK IN THE KRUSTYBURGER FRANCHISE!

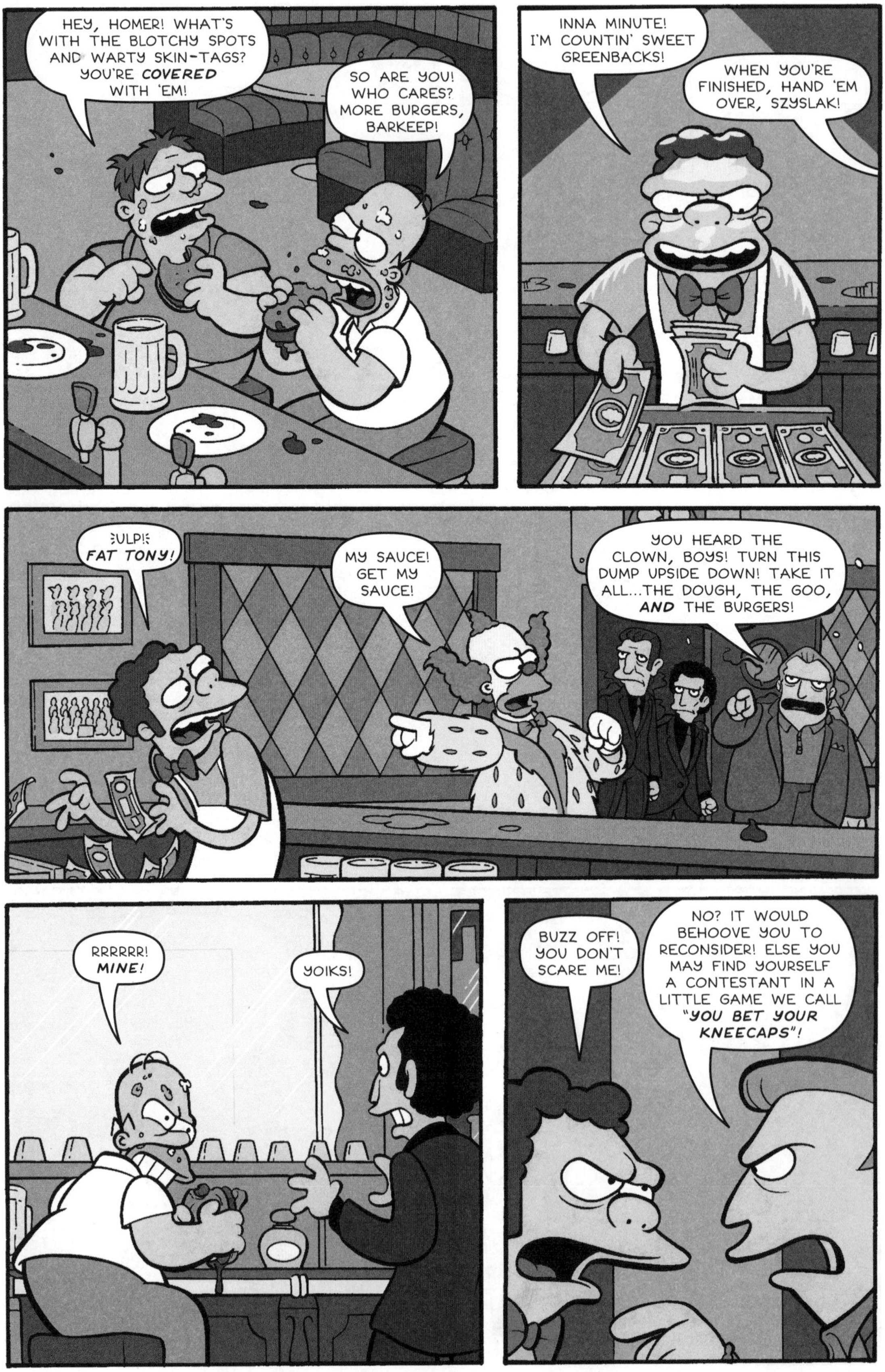
HEY, HOMER! WHAT'S WITH THE BLOTCHY SPOTS AND WARTY SKIN-TAGS? YOU'RE **COVERED** WITH 'EM!
SO ARE YOU! WHO CARES? MORE BURGERS, BARKEEP!
INNA MINUTE! I'M COUNTIN' SWEET GREENBACKS!
WHEN YOU'RE FINISHED, HAND 'EM OVER, SZYSLAK!
ULP! ***FAT TONY!***
MY SAUCE! GET MY SAUCE!
YOU HEARD THE CLOWN, BOYS! TURN THIS DUMP UPSIDE DOWN! TAKE IT ALL...THE DOUGH, THE GOO, **AND** THE BURGERS!
RRRRRR! ***MINE!***
YOIKS!
BUZZ OFF! YOU DON'T SCARE ME!
NO? IT WOULD BEHOOVE YOU TO RECONSIDER! ELSE YOU MAY FIND YOURSELF A CONTESTANT IN A LITTLE GAME WE CALL "***YOU BET YOUR KNEECAPS***"!

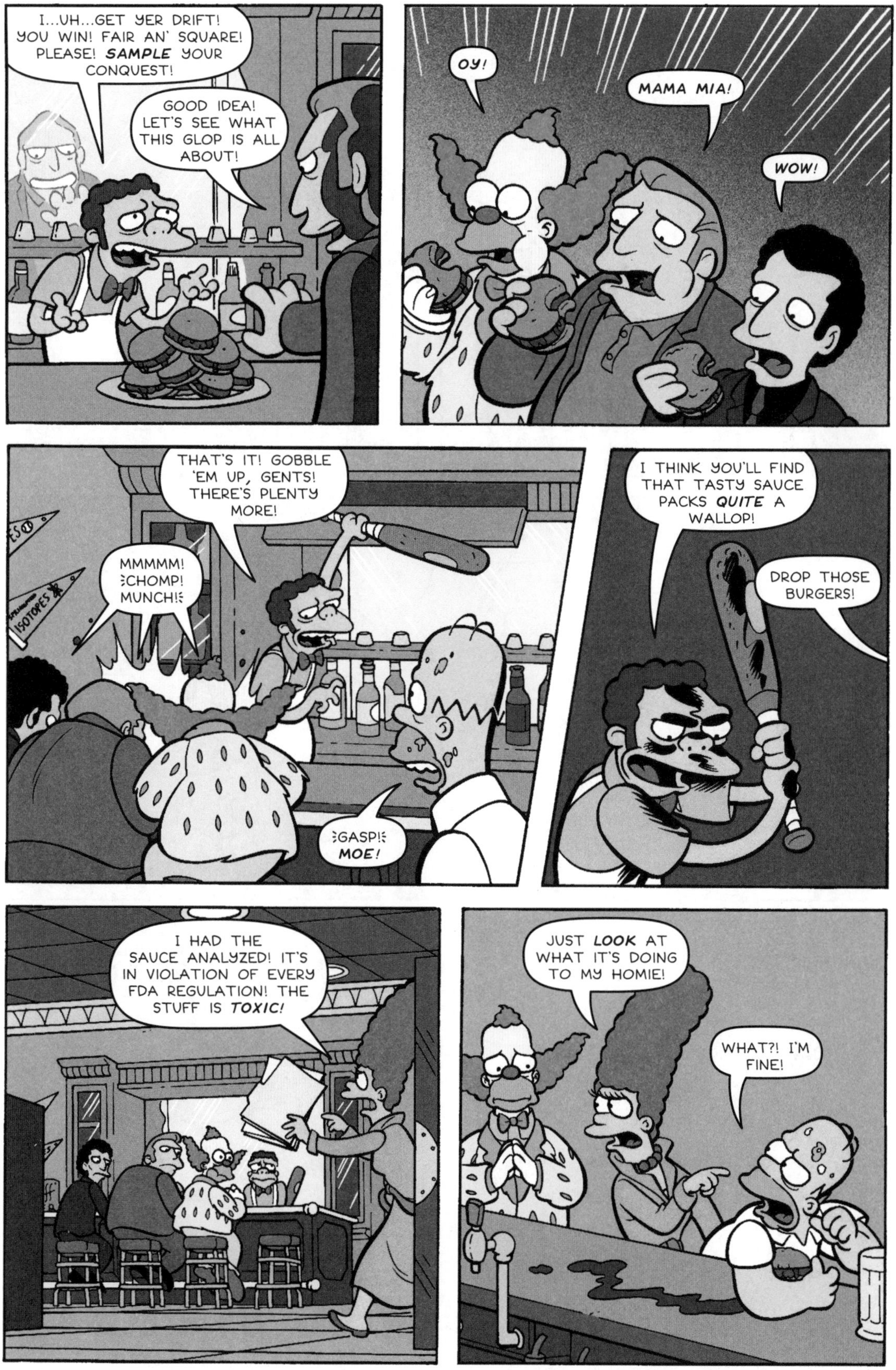
I...UH...GET YER DRIFT! YOU WIN! FAIR AN' SQUARE! PLEASE! **SAMPLE** YOUR CONQUEST!
GOOD IDEA! LET'S SEE WHAT THIS GLOP IS ALL ABOUT!
OY!
MAMA MIA!
WOW!
THAT'S IT! GOBBLE 'EM UP, GENTS! THERE'S PLENTY MORE!
MMMMM! CHOMP! MUNCH!
ISOTOPES
GASP! **MOE!**
I THINK YOU'LL FIND THAT TASTY SAUCE PACKS **QUITE** A WALLOP!
DROP THOSE BURGERS!
I HAD THE SAUCE ANALYZED! IT'S IN VIOLATION OF EVERY FDA REGULATION! THE STUFF IS **TOXIC!**
JUST **LOOK** AT WHAT IT'S DOING TO MY HOMIE!
WHAT?! I'M FINE!

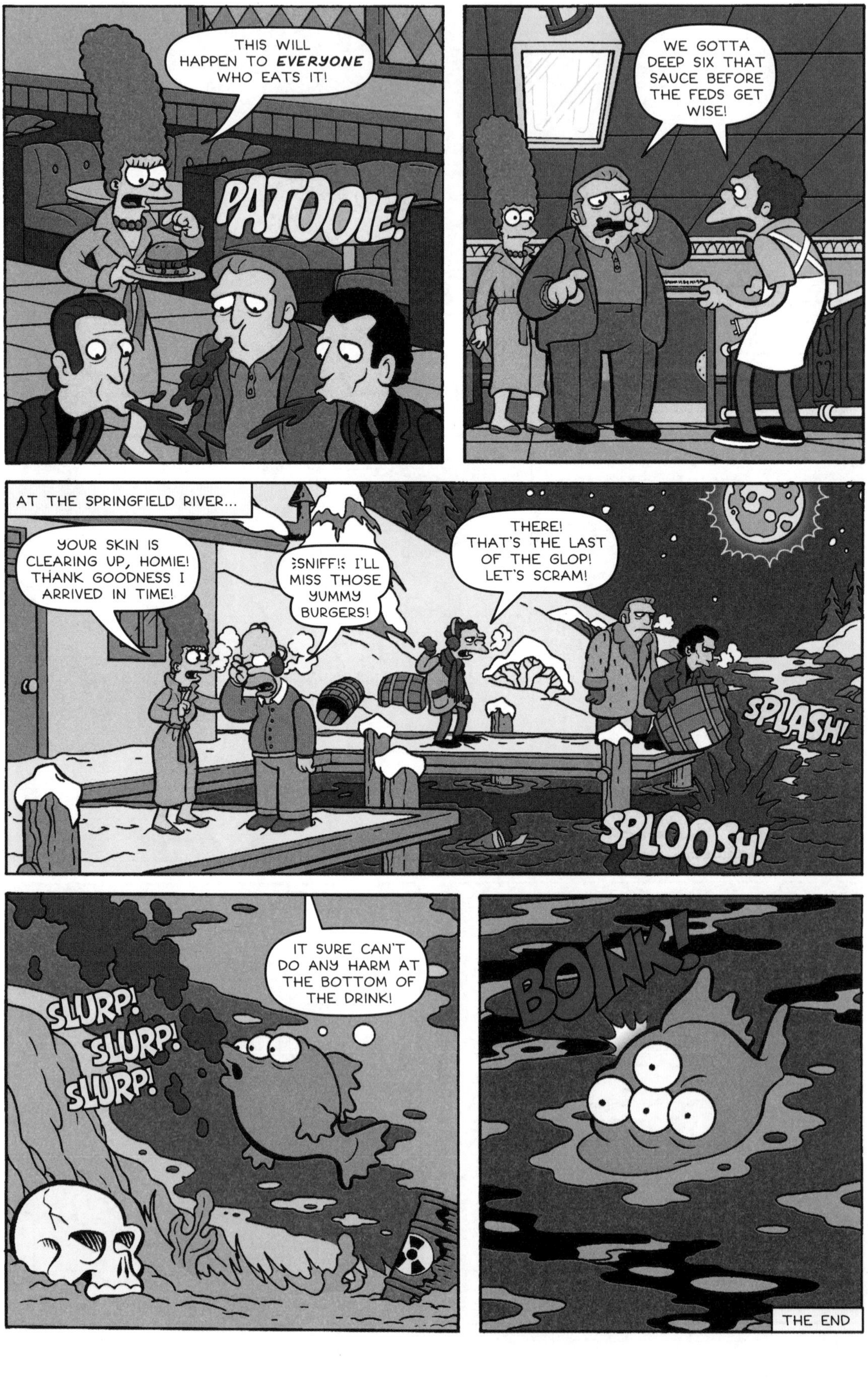
THIS WILL HAPPEN TO EVERYONE WHO EATS IT!
PATOOIE!
WE GOTTA DEEP SIX THAT SAUCE BEFORE THE FEDS GET WISE!
AT THE SPRINGFIELD RIVER...
YOUR SKIN IS CLEARING UP, HOMIE! THANK GOODNESS I ARRIVED IN TIME!
SNIFF! I'LL MISS THOSE YUMMY BURGERS!
THERE! THAT'S THE LAST OF THE GLOP! LET'S SCRAM!
SPLASH!
SPLOOSH!
IT SURE CAN'T DO ANY HARM AT THE BOTTOM OF THE DRINK!
SLURP! SLURP! SLURP!
BOINK!
THE END

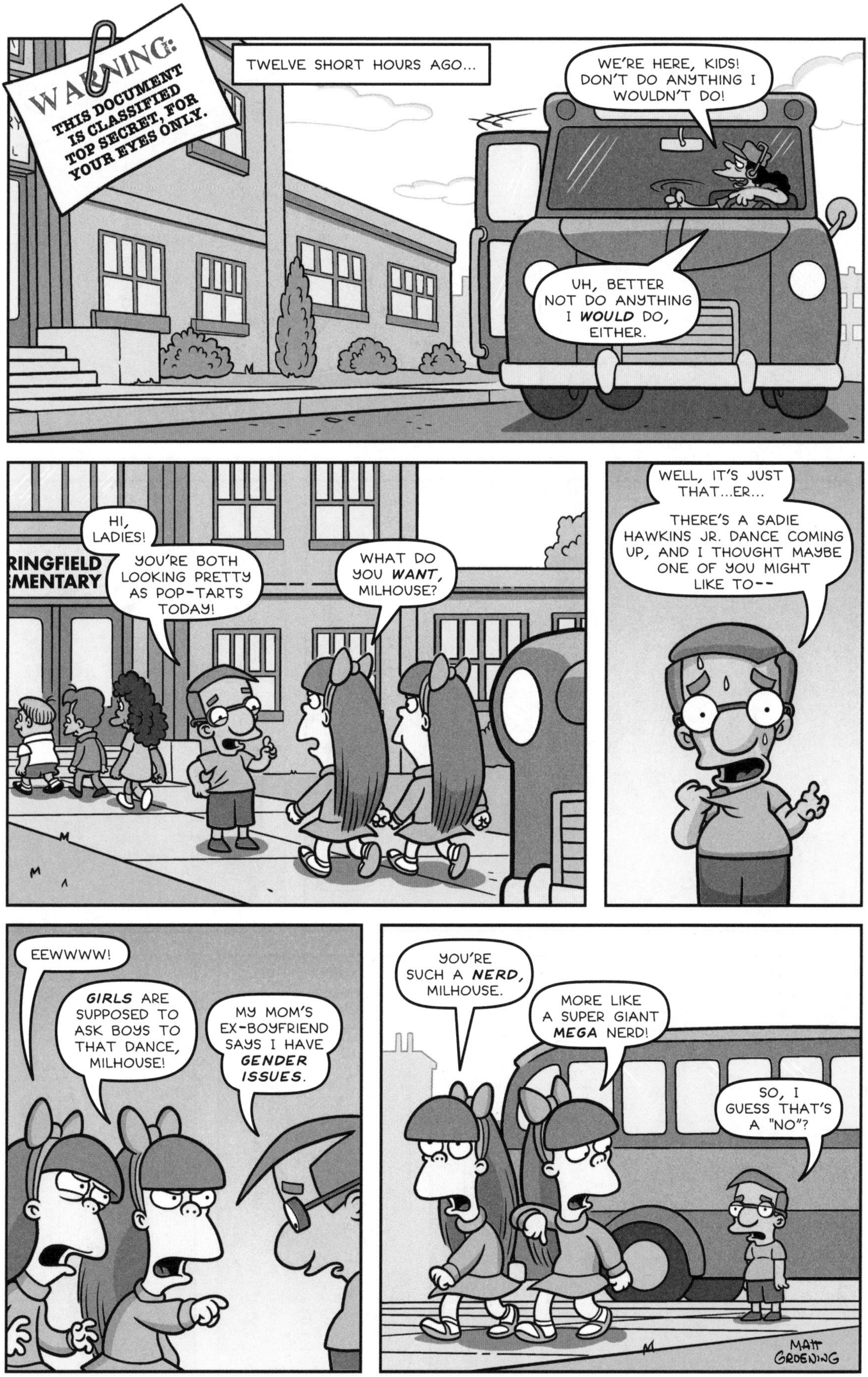
WARNING: THIS DOCUMENT IS CLASSIFIED TOP SECRET, FOR YOUR EYES ONLY.
TWELVE SHORT HOURS AGO...
WE'RE HERE, KIDS! DON'T DO ANYTHING I WOULDN'T DO!
UH, BETTER NOT DO ANYTHING I **WOULD** DO, EITHER.
RINGFIELD EMENTARY
HI, LADIES!
YOU'RE BOTH LOOKING PRETTY AS POP-TARTS TODAY!
WHAT DO YOU **WANT,** MILHOUSE?
WELL, IT'S JUST THAT...ER...
THERE'S A SADIE HAWKINS JR. DANCE COMING UP, AND I THOUGHT MAYBE ONE OF YOU MIGHT LIKE TO--
EEWWWW!
GIRLS ARE SUPPOSED TO ASK BOYS TO THAT DANCE, MILHOUSE!
MY MOM'S EX-BOYFRIEND SAYS I HAVE **GENDER ISSUES**.
YOU'RE SUCH A **NERD,** MILHOUSE.
MORE LIKE A SUPER GIANT **MEGA** NERD!
SO, I GUESS THAT'S A "NO"?
MATT GROENING

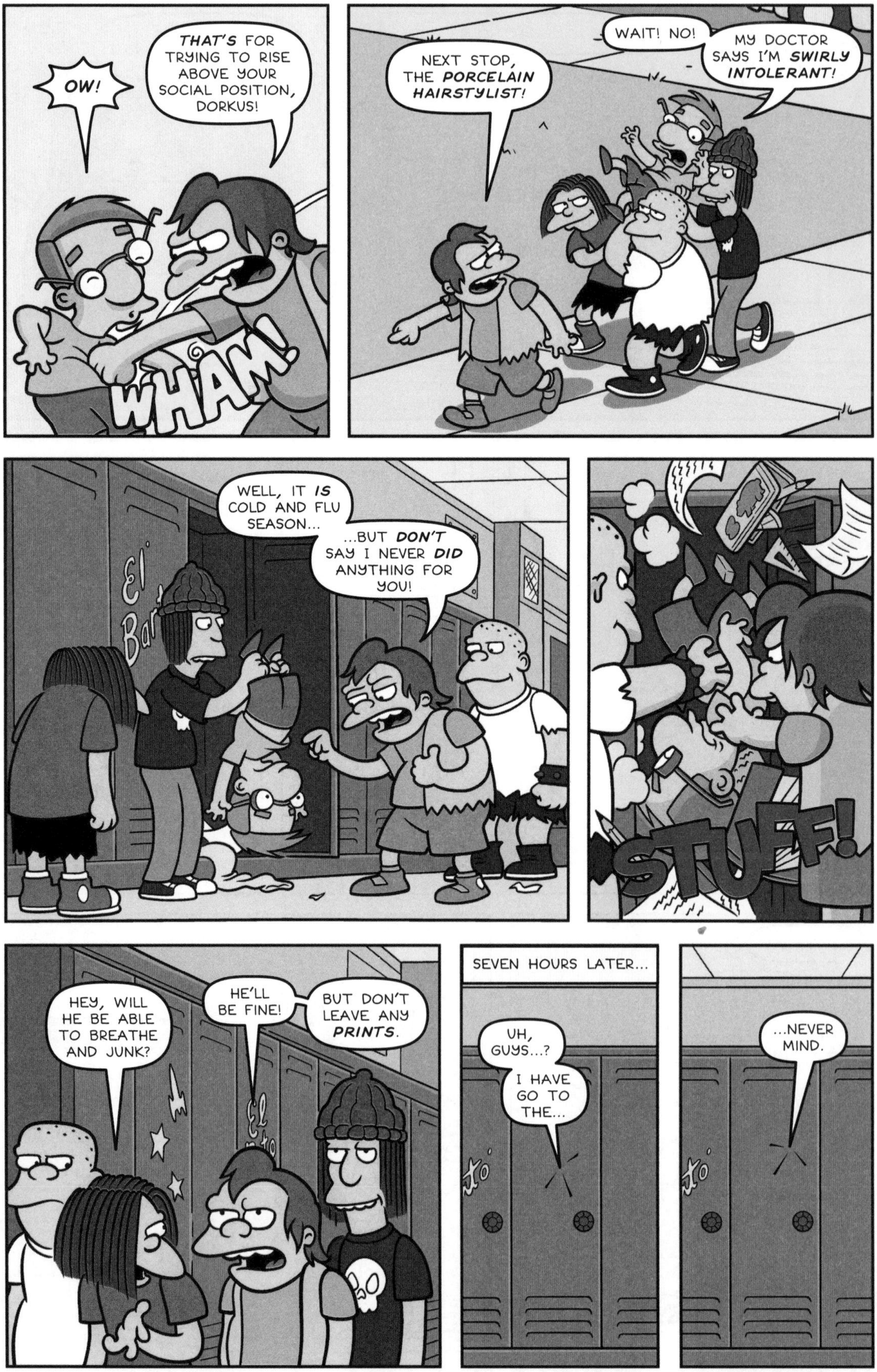
OW!
THAT'S FOR TRYING TO RISE ABOVE YOUR SOCIAL POSITION, DORKUS!
WHAM!
NEXT STOP, THE PORCELAIN HAIRSTYLIST!
WAIT! NO!
MY DOCTOR SAYS I'M SWIRLY INTOLERANT!
WELL, IT IS COLD AND FLU SEASON...
...BUT DON'T SAY I NEVER DID ANYTHING FOR YOU!
STUFF!
HEY, WILL HE BE ABLE TO BREATHE AND JUNK?
HE'LL BE FINE!
BUT DON'T LEAVE ANY PRINTS.
SEVEN HOURS LATER...
UH, GUYS...?
I HAVE GO TO THE...
...NEVER MIND.

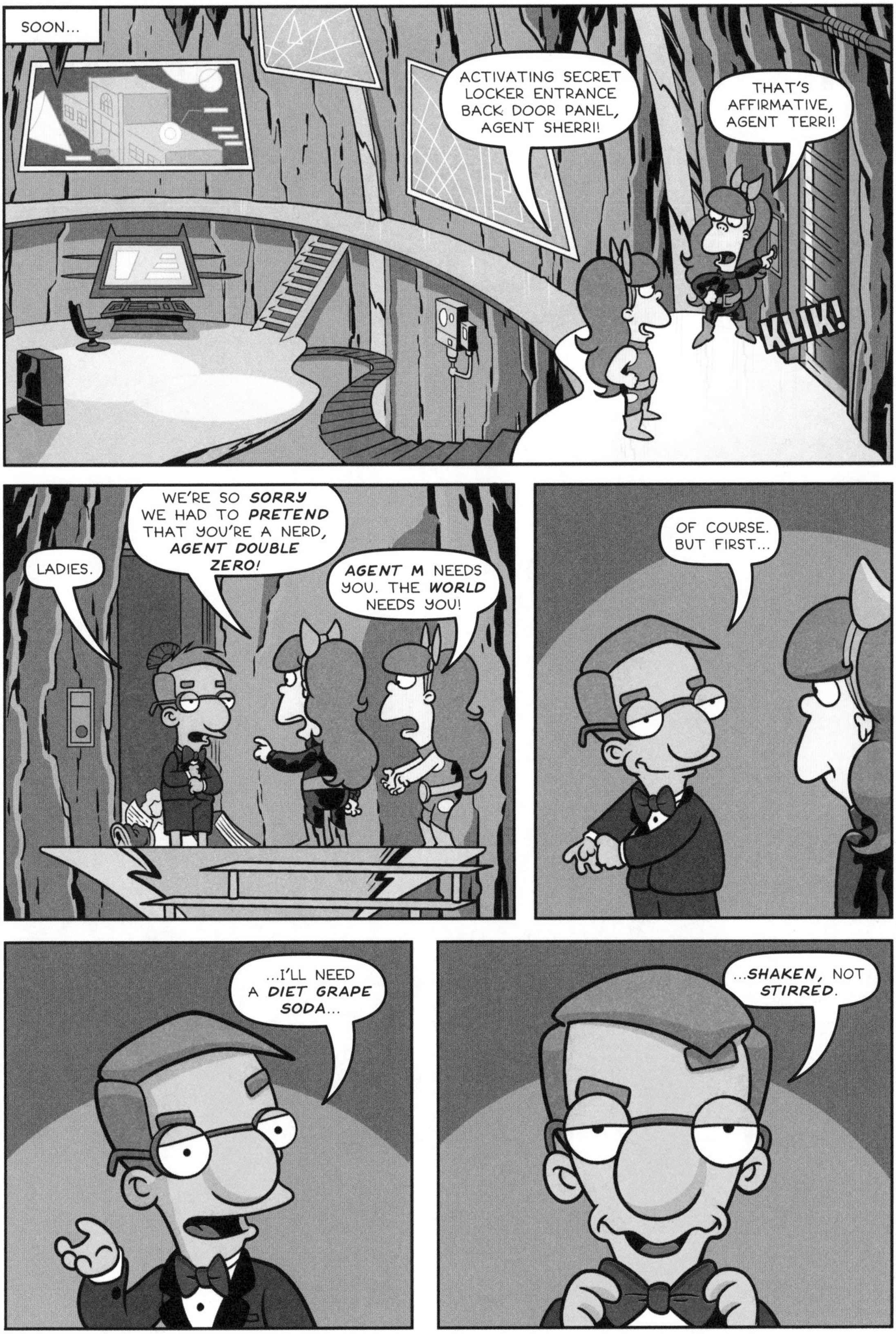
SOON...
ACTIVATING SECRET LOCKER ENTRANCE BACK DOOR PANEL, AGENT SHERRI!
THAT'S AFFIRMATIVE, AGENT TERRI!
KLIK!
LADIES.
WE'RE SO SORRY WE HAD TO PRETEND THAT YOU'RE A NERD, AGENT DOUBLE ZERO!
AGENT M NEEDS YOU. THE WORLD NEEDS YOU!
OF COURSE. BUT FIRST...
...I'LL NEED A DIET GRAPE SODA...
...SHAKEN, NOT STIRRED.

MILHOUSE VAN HOUTEN IS OCTO-WEENIE

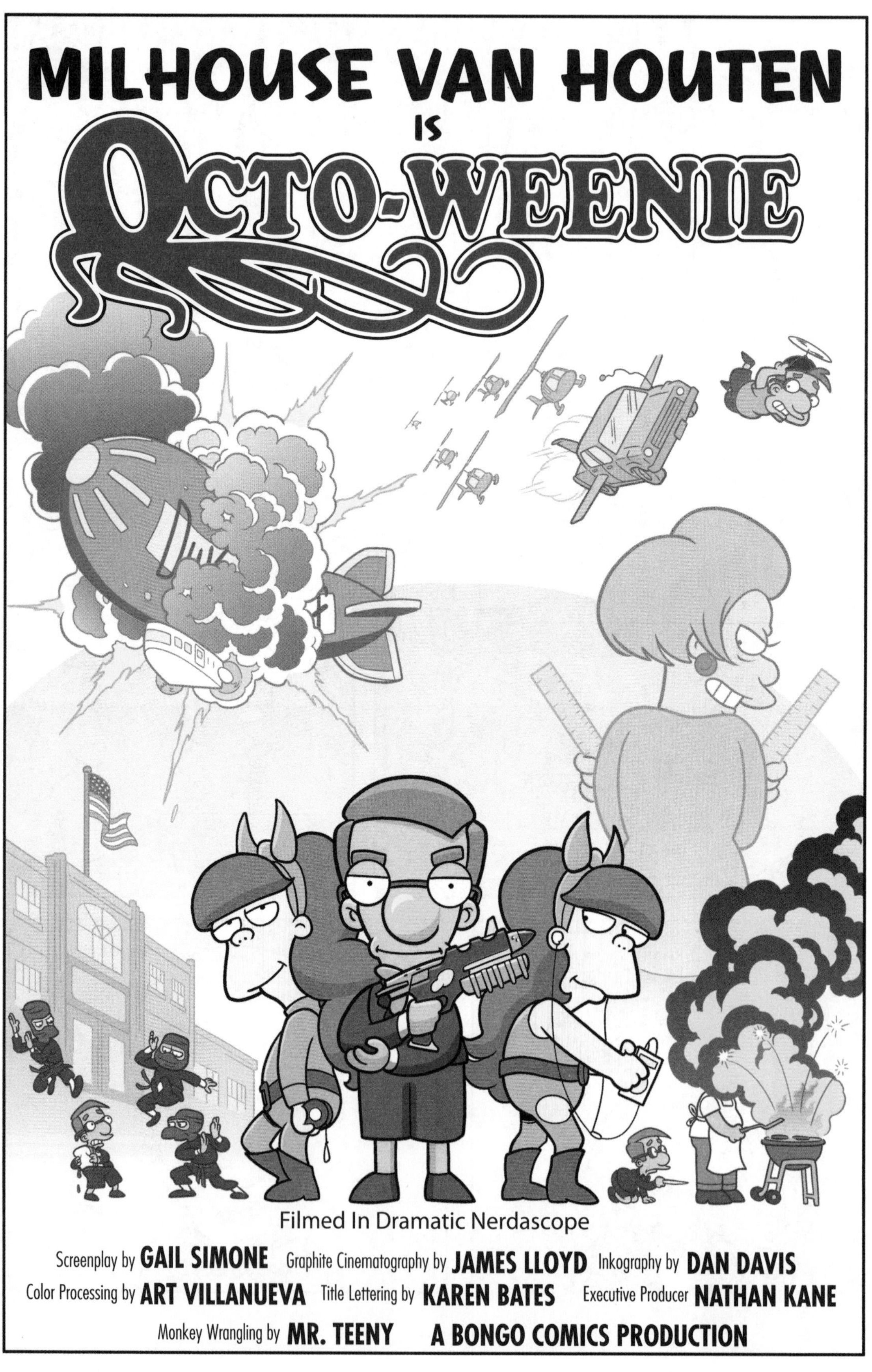

Filmed In Dramatic Nerdascope

Screenplay by **GAIL SIMONE** Graphite Cinematography by **JAMES LLOYD** Inkography by **DAN DAVIS**
Color Processing by **ART VILLANUEVA** Title Lettering by **KAREN BATES** Executive Producer **NATHAN KANE**
Monkey Wrangling by **MR. TEENY** **A BONGO COMICS PRODUCTION**

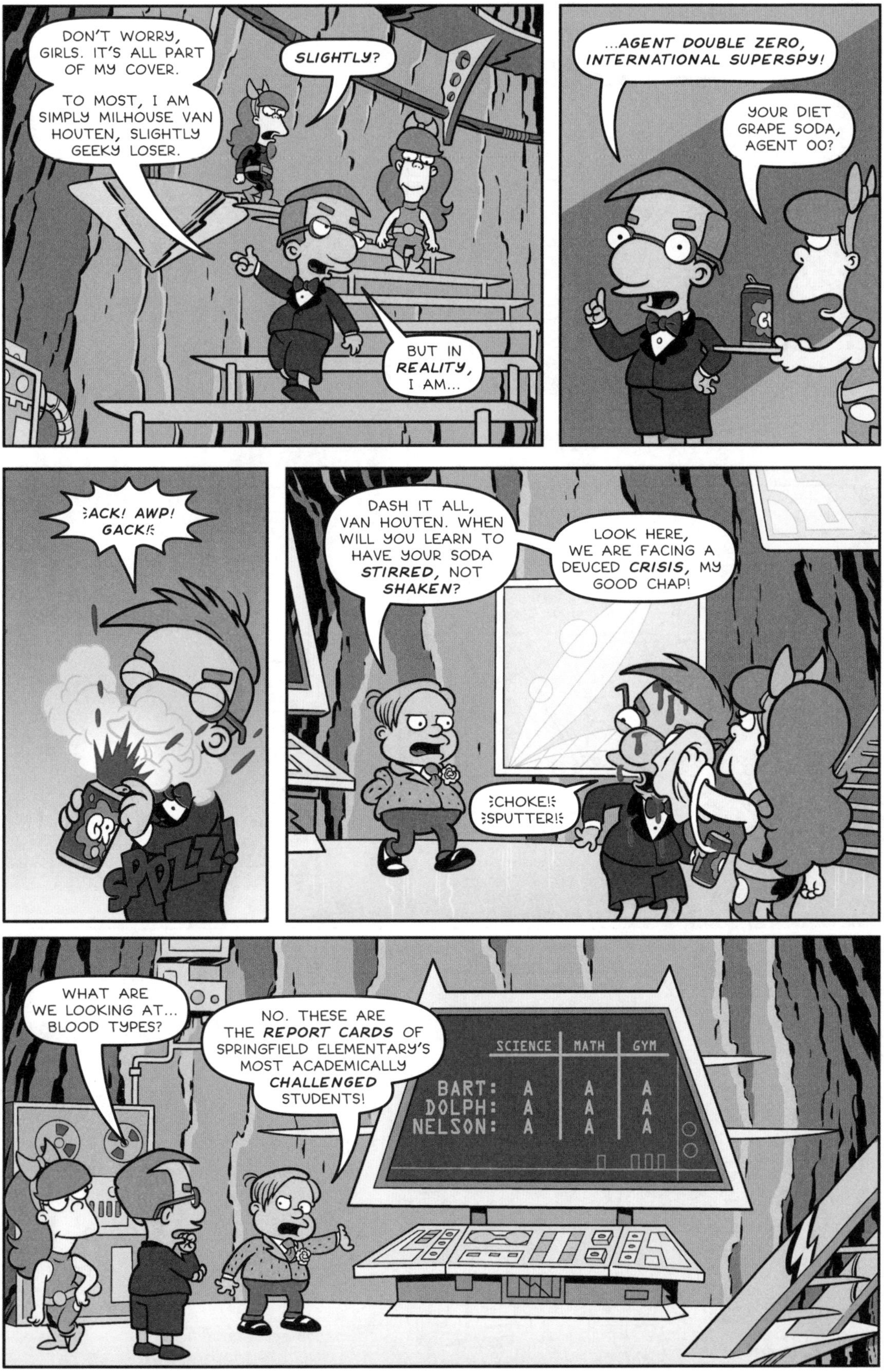

DON'T WORRY, GIRLS. IT'S ALL PART OF MY COVER.
TO MOST, I AM SIMPLY MILHOUSE VAN HOUTEN, SLIGHTLY GEEKY LOSER.
SLIGHTLY?
BUT IN REALITY, I AM...
...AGENT DOUBLE ZERO, INTERNATIONAL SUPERSPY!
YOUR DIET GRAPE SODA, AGENT 00?
ACK! AWP! GACK!
SPZZ!
DASH IT ALL, VAN HOUTEN. WHEN WILL YOU LEARN TO HAVE YOUR SODA STIRRED, NOT SHAKEN?
CHOKE! SPUTTER!
LOOK HERE, WE ARE FACING A DEUCED CRISIS, MY GOOD CHAP!
WHAT ARE WE LOOKING AT... BLOOD TYPES?
NO. THESE ARE THE REPORT CARDS OF SPRINGFIELD ELEMENTARY'S MOST ACADEMICALLY CHALLENGED STUDENTS!
SCIENCE MATH GYM
BART: A A A
DOLPH: A A A
NELSON: A A A

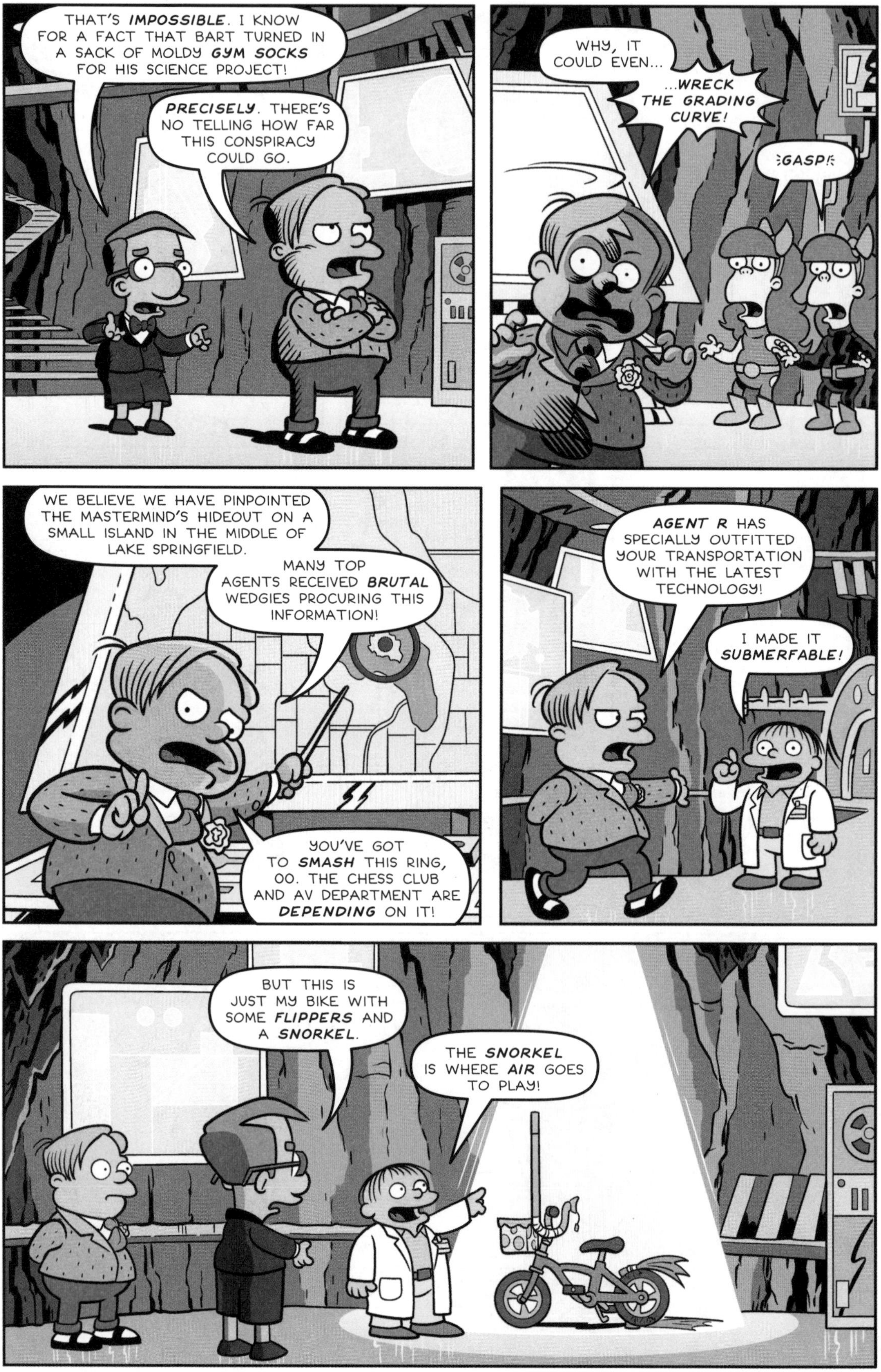
THAT'S IMPOSSIBLE. I KNOW FOR A FACT THAT BART TURNED IN A SACK OF MOLDY GYM SOCKS FOR HIS SCIENCE PROJECT!
PRECISELY. THERE'S NO TELLING HOW FAR THIS CONSPIRACY COULD GO.
WHY, IT COULD EVEN...
...WRECK THE GRADING CURVE!
GASP!
WE BELIEVE WE HAVE PINPOINTED THE MASTERMIND'S HIDEOUT ON A SMALL ISLAND IN THE MIDDLE OF LAKE SPRINGFIELD.
MANY TOP AGENTS RECEIVED BRUTAL WEDGIES PROCURING THIS INFORMATION!
YOU'VE GOT TO SMASH THIS RING, 00. THE CHESS CLUB AND AV DEPARTMENT ARE DEPENDING ON IT!
AGENT R HAS SPECIALLY OUTFITTED YOUR TRANSPORTATION WITH THE LATEST TECHNOLOGY!
I MADE IT SUBMERFABLE!
BUT THIS IS JUST MY BIKE WITH SOME FLIPPERS AND A SNORKEL.
THE SNORKEL IS WHERE AIR GOES TO PLAY!

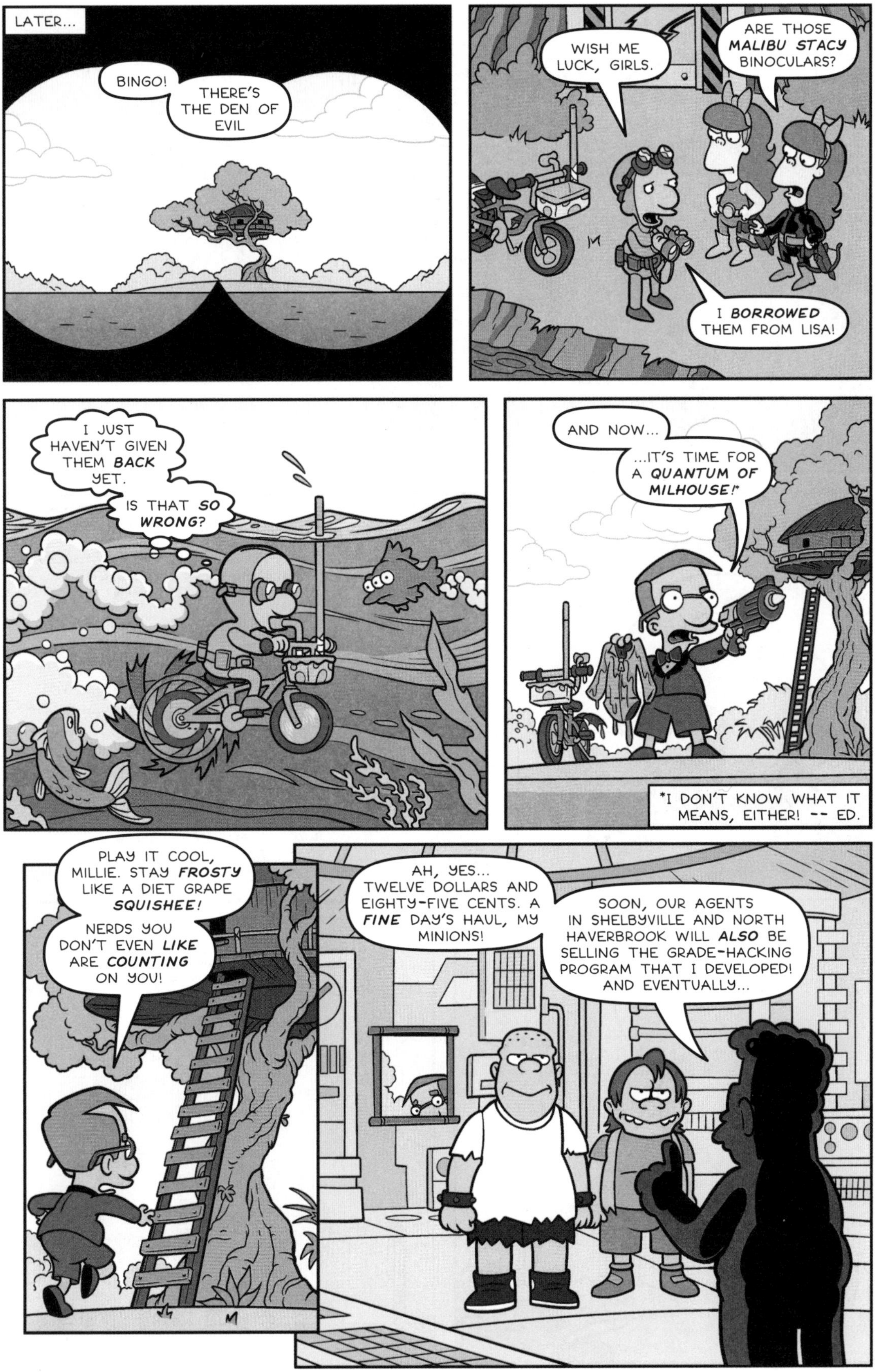
LATER...
BINGO!
THERE'S THE DEN OF EVIL
WISH ME LUCK, GIRLS.
ARE THOSE MALIBU STACY BINOCULARS?
I BORROWED THEM FROM LISA!
I JUST HAVEN'T GIVEN THEM BACK YET.
IS THAT SO WRONG?
AND NOW...
...IT'S TIME FOR A QUANTUM OF MILHOUSE!*
*I DON'T KNOW WHAT IT MEANS, EITHER! -- ED.
PLAY IT COOL, MILLIE. STAY FROSTY LIKE A DIET GRAPE SQUISHEE!
NERDS YOU DON'T EVEN LIKE ARE COUNTING ON YOU!
AH, YES... TWELVE DOLLARS AND EIGHTY-FIVE CENTS. A FINE DAY'S HAUL, MY MINIONS!
SOON, OUR AGENTS IN SHELBYVILLE AND NORTH HAVERBROOK WILL ALSO BE SELLING THE GRADE-HACKING PROGRAM THAT I DEVELOPED! AND EVENTUALLY...

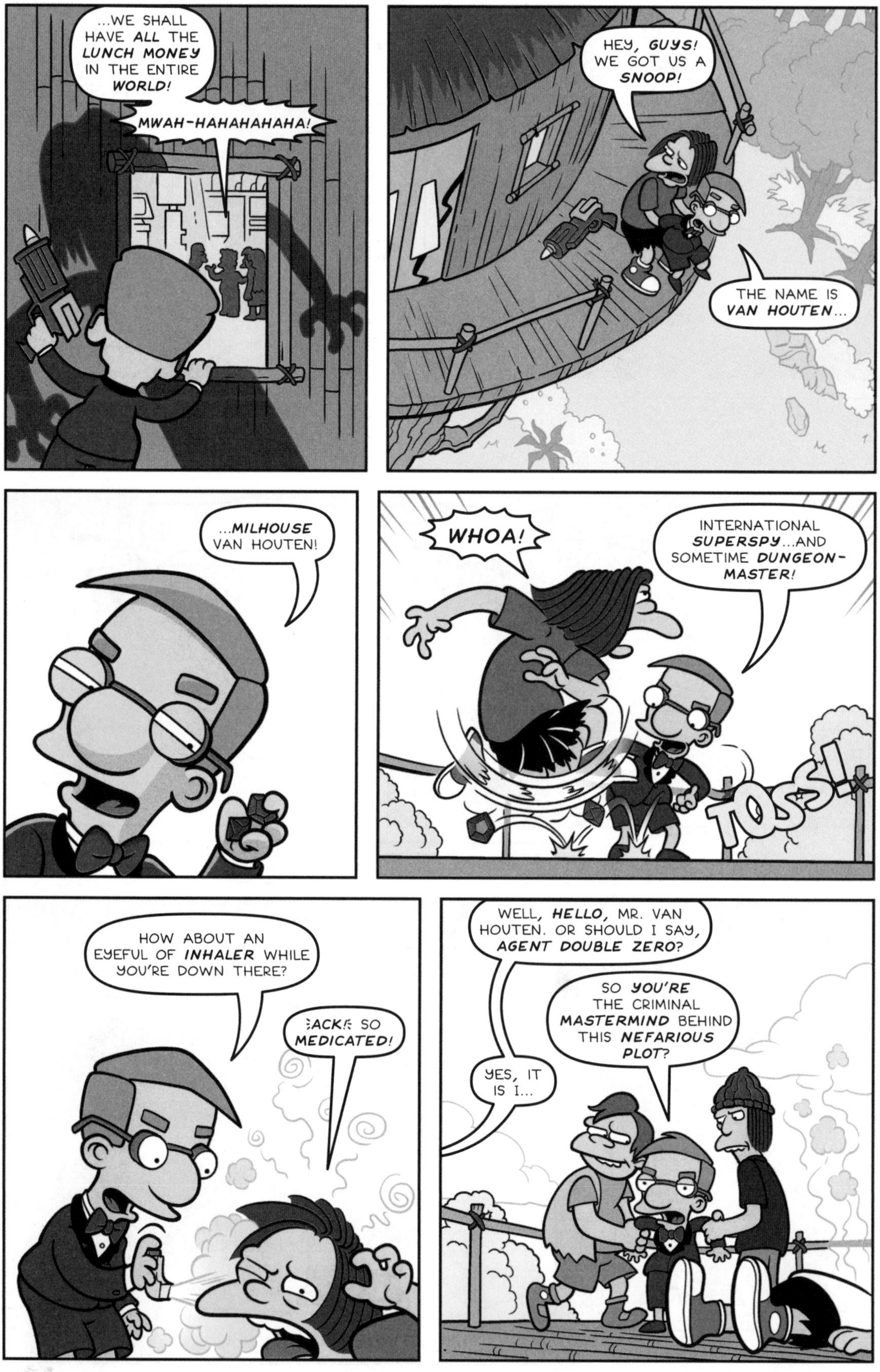

...WE SHALL HAVE ALL THE LUNCH MONEY IN THE ENTIRE WORLD!
MWAH-HAHAHAHAHA!
HEY, GUYS! WE GOT US A SNOOP!
THE NAME IS VAN HOUTEN...
...MILHOUSE VAN HOUTEN!
WHOA!
INTERNATIONAL SUPERSPY...AND SOMETIME DUNGEON-MASTER!
TOSS!
HOW ABOUT AN EYEFUL OF INHALER WHILE YOU'RE DOWN THERE?
ACK! SO MEDICATED!
WELL, HELLO, MR. VAN HOUTEN. OR SHOULD I SAY, AGENT DOUBLE ZERO?
SO YOU'RE THE CRIMINAL MASTERMIND BEHIND THIS NEFARIOUS PLOT?
YES, IT IS I...

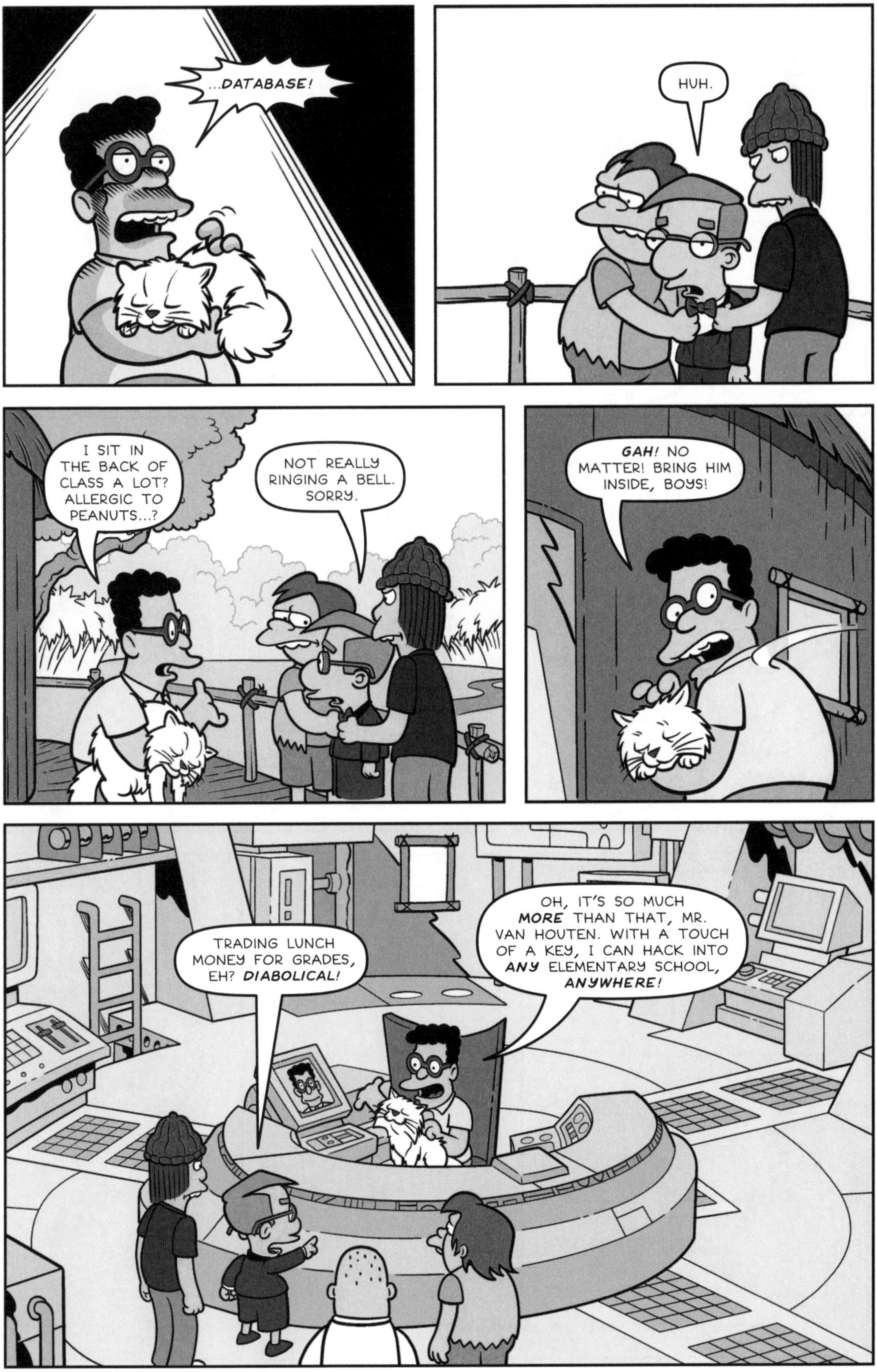

...DATABASE!
HUH.
I SIT IN THE BACK OF CLASS A LOT? ALLERGIC TO PEANUTS...?
NOT REALLY RINGING A BELL. SORRY.
GAH! NO MATTER! BRING HIM INSIDE, BOYS!
TRADING LUNCH MONEY FOR GRADES, EH? DIABOLICAL!
OH, IT'S SO MUCH MORE THAN THAT, MR. VAN HOUTEN. WITH A TOUCH OF A KEY, I CAN HACK INTO ANY ELEMENTARY SCHOOL, ANYWHERE!

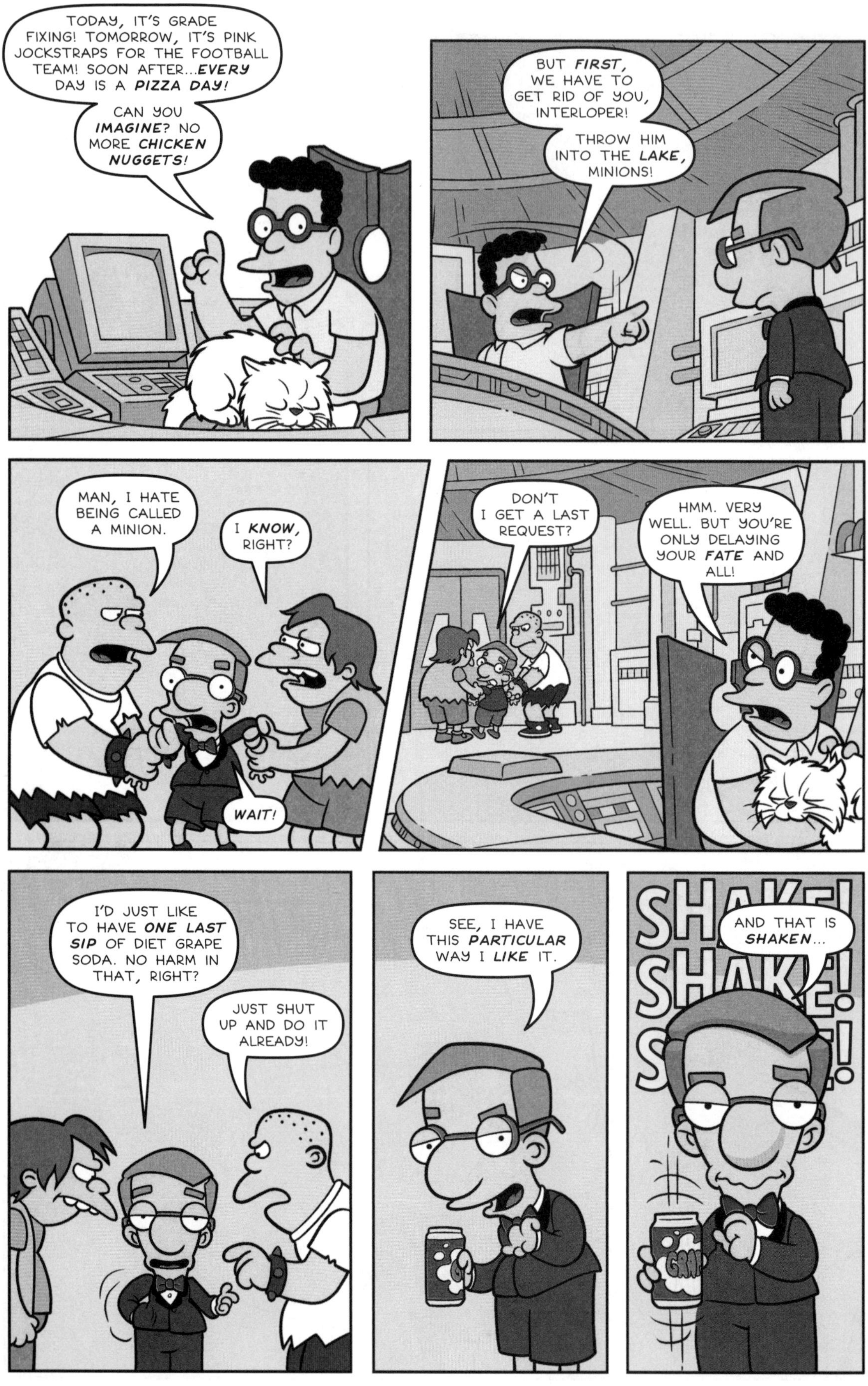
TODAY, IT'S GRADE FIXING! TOMORROW, IT'S PINK JOCKSTRAPS FOR THE FOOTBALL TEAM! SOON AFTER... **EVERY** DAY IS A **PIZZA DAY**!
CAN YOU **IMAGINE**? NO MORE **CHICKEN NUGGETS**!
BUT **FIRST**, WE HAVE TO GET RID OF YOU, INTERLOPER!
THROW HIM INTO THE **LAKE**, MINIONS!
MAN, I HATE BEING CALLED A MINION.
I **KNOW**, RIGHT?
WAIT!
DON'T I GET A LAST REQUEST?
HMM. VERY WELL. BUT YOU'RE ONLY DELAYING YOUR **FATE** AND ALL!
I'D JUST LIKE TO HAVE **ONE LAST SIP** OF DIET GRAPE SODA. NO HARM IN THAT, RIGHT?
JUST SHUT UP AND DO IT ALREADY!
SEE, I HAVE THIS **PARTICULAR** WAY I **LIKE** IT.
AND THAT IS **SHAKEN**...

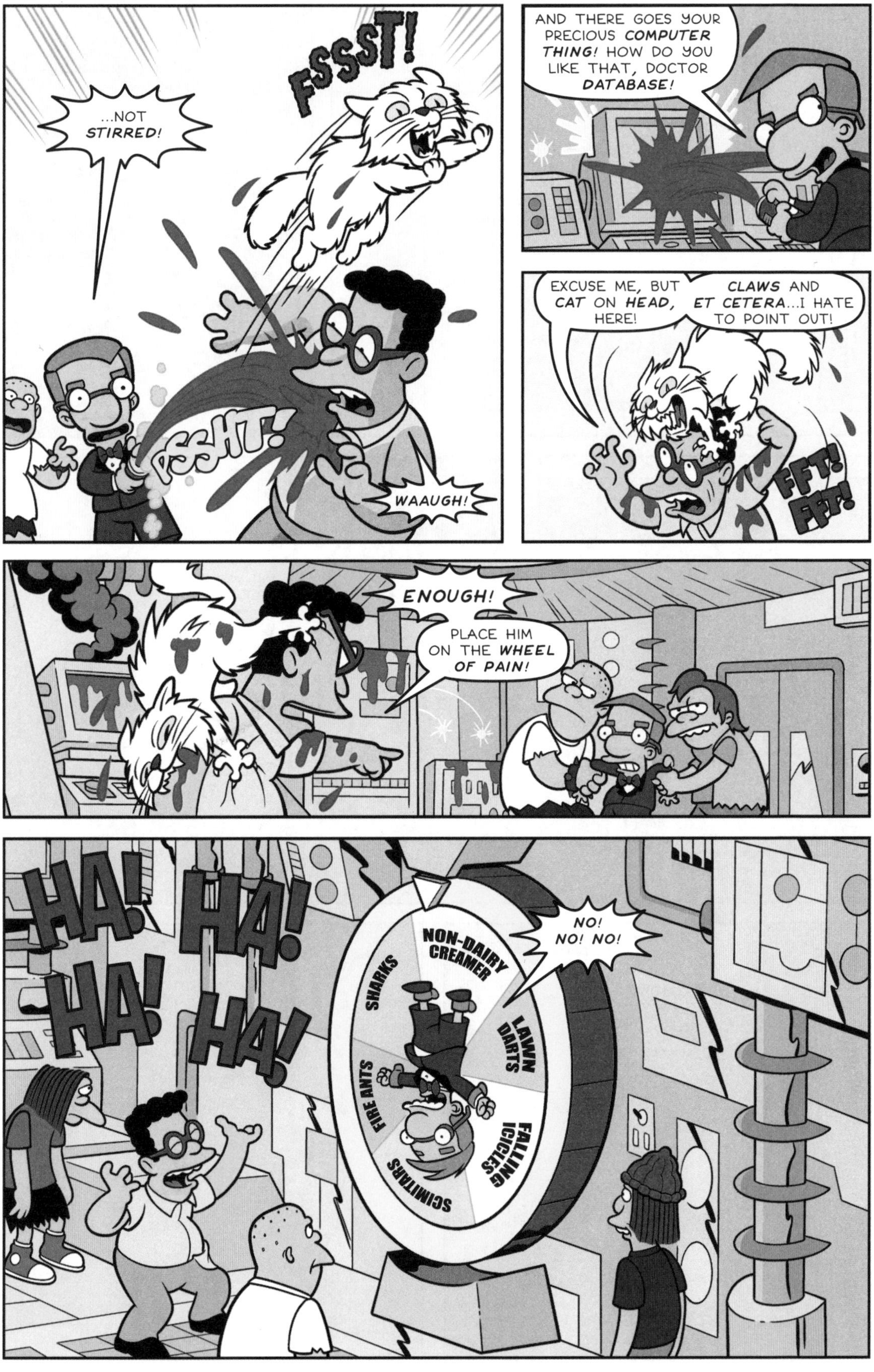
FSSST!
...NOT STIRRED!
PSSHT!
WAAUGH!
AND THERE GOES YOUR PRECIOUS COMPUTER THING! HOW DO YOU LIKE THAT, DOCTOR DATABASE!
EXCUSE ME, BUT CAT ON HEAD, HERE!
CLAWS AND ET CETERA...I HATE TO POINT OUT!
FFT! FFT!
ENOUGH!
PLACE HIM ON THE WHEEL OF PAIN!
HA! HA! HA! HA!
NON-DAIRY CREAMER
LAWN DARTS
FALLING ICICLES
SCIMITARS
FIRE ANTS
SHARKS
NO! NO! NO!

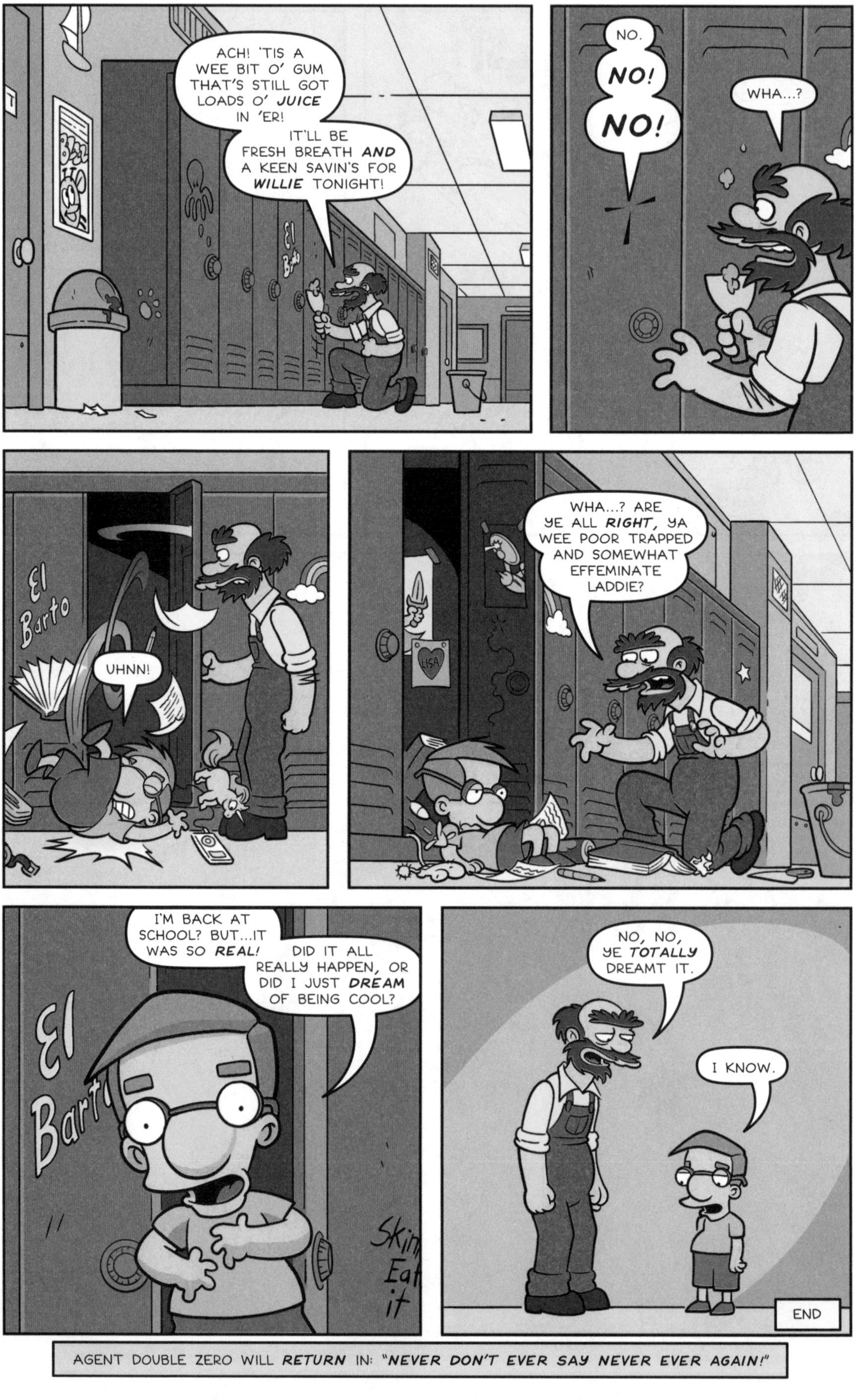

ACH! 'TIS A WEE BIT O' GUM THAT'S STILL GOT LOADS O' **JUICE** IN 'ER!
IT'LL BE FRESH BREATH **AND** A KEEN SAVIN'S FOR **WILLIE** TONIGHT!
NO.
NO!
NO!
WHA...?
UHNN!
WHA...? ARE YE ALL **RIGHT,** YA WEE POOR TRAPPED AND SOMEWHAT EFFEMINATE LADDIE?
I'M BACK AT SCHOOL? BUT...IT WAS SO **REAL!**
DID IT ALL REALLY HAPPEN, OR DID I JUST **DREAM** OF BEING COOL?
NO, NO, YE **TOTALLY** DREAMT IT.
I KNOW.
END
AGENT DOUBLE ZERO WILL **RETURN** IN: "***NEVER DON'T EVER SAY NEVER EVER AGAIN!***"

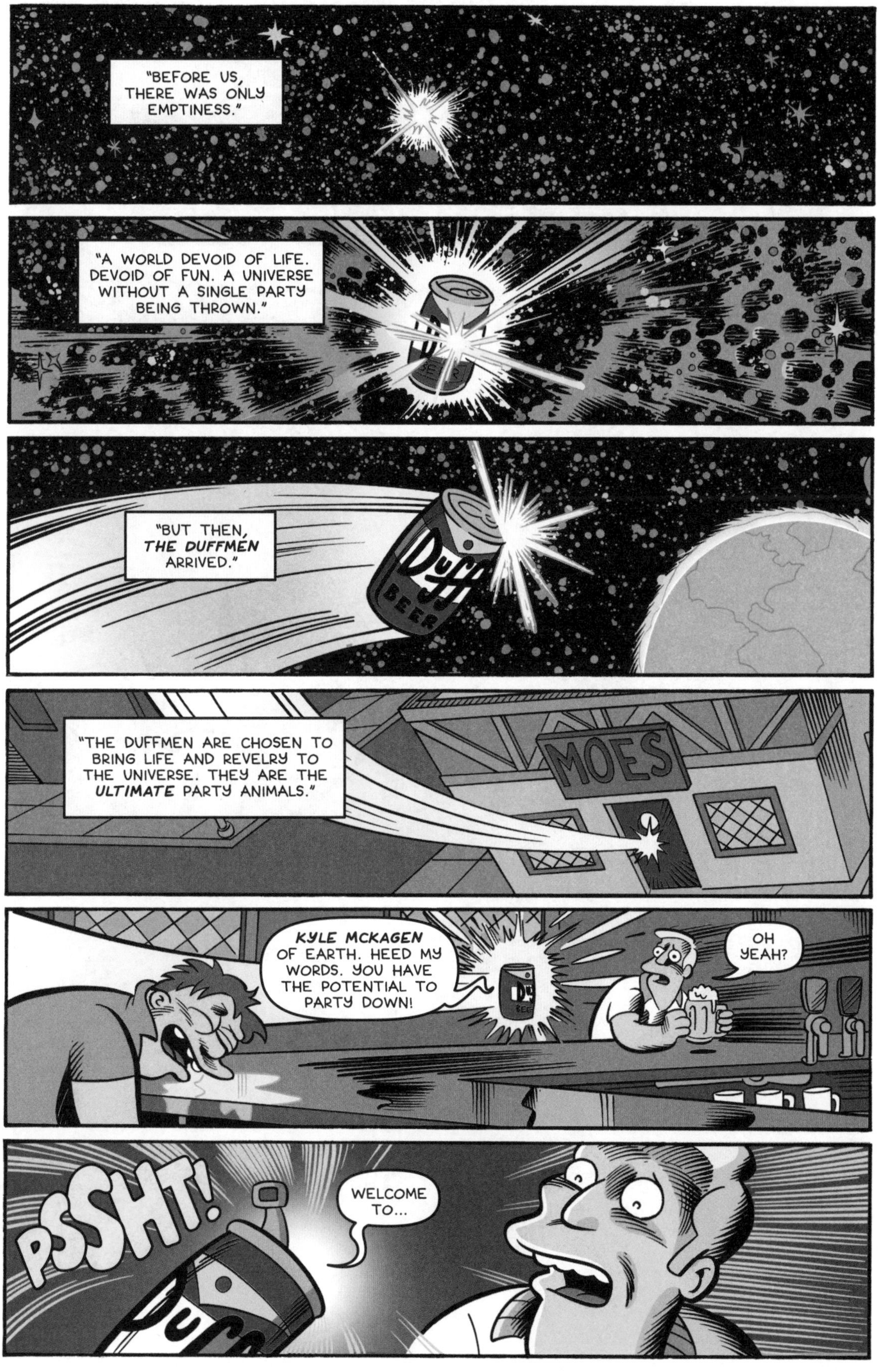
"BEFORE US, THERE WAS ONLY EMPTINESS."
"A WORLD DEVOID OF LIFE. DEVOID OF FUN. A UNIVERSE WITHOUT A SINGLE PARTY BEING THROWN."
DUFF BEER
"BUT THEN, THE DUFFMEN ARRIVED."
DUFF BEER
"THE DUFFMEN ARE CHOSEN TO BRING LIFE AND REVELRY TO THE UNIVERSE. THEY ARE THE ULTIMATE PARTY ANIMALS."
MOES
KYLE MCKAGEN OF EARTH. HEED MY WORDS. YOU HAVE THE POTENTIAL TO PARTY DOWN!
OH YEAH?
PSSHT!
WELCOME TO...

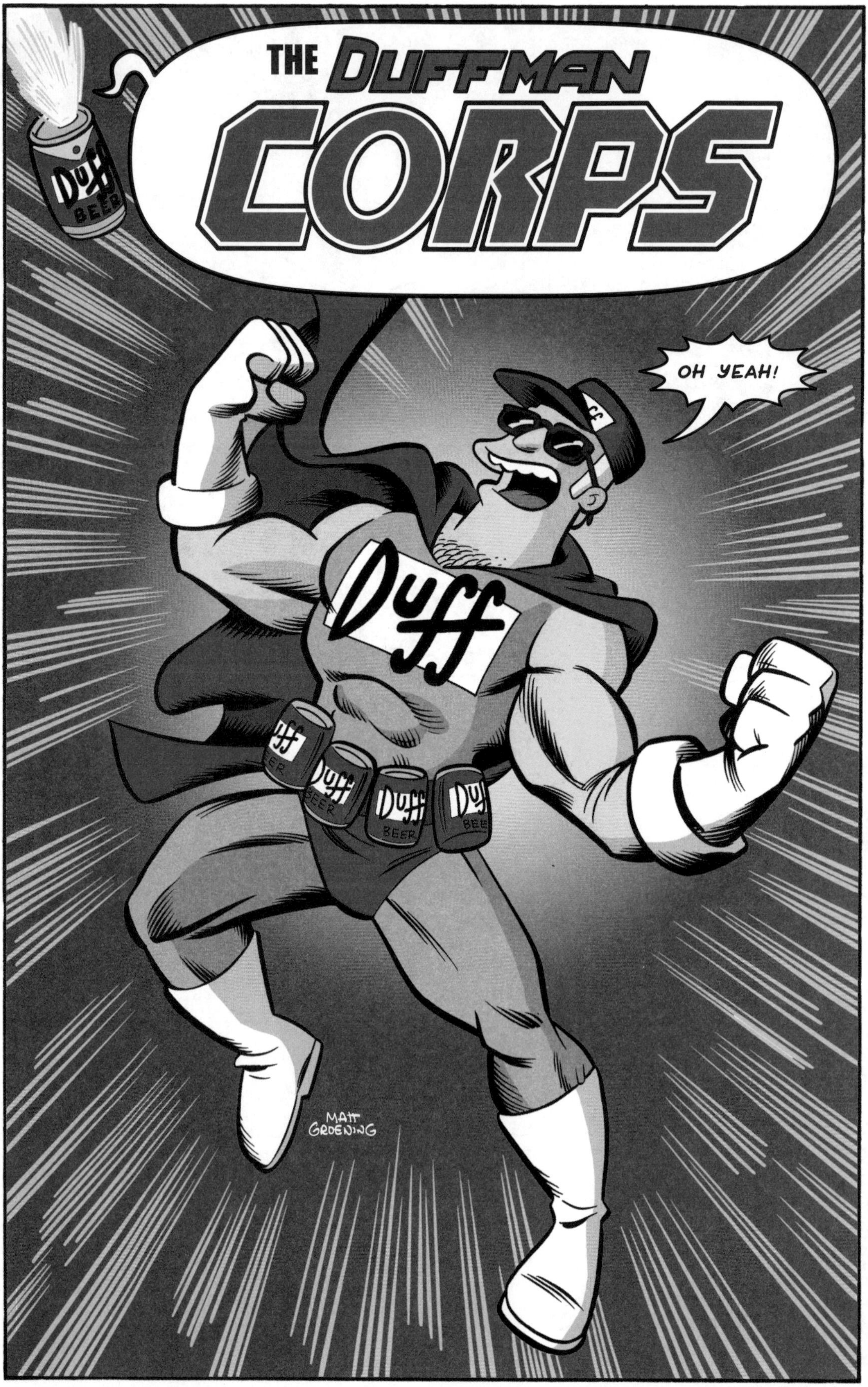
THE DUFFMAN CORPS
DUFF BEER
OH YEAH!
DUFF
DUFF BEER
MATT GROENING

MAX DAVISON
SCRIPT

JOHN DELANEY
PENCILS

ANDREW PEPOY
INKS

NATHAN HAMILL
COLORS

KAREN BATES
LETTERS

NATHAN KANE
EDITOR

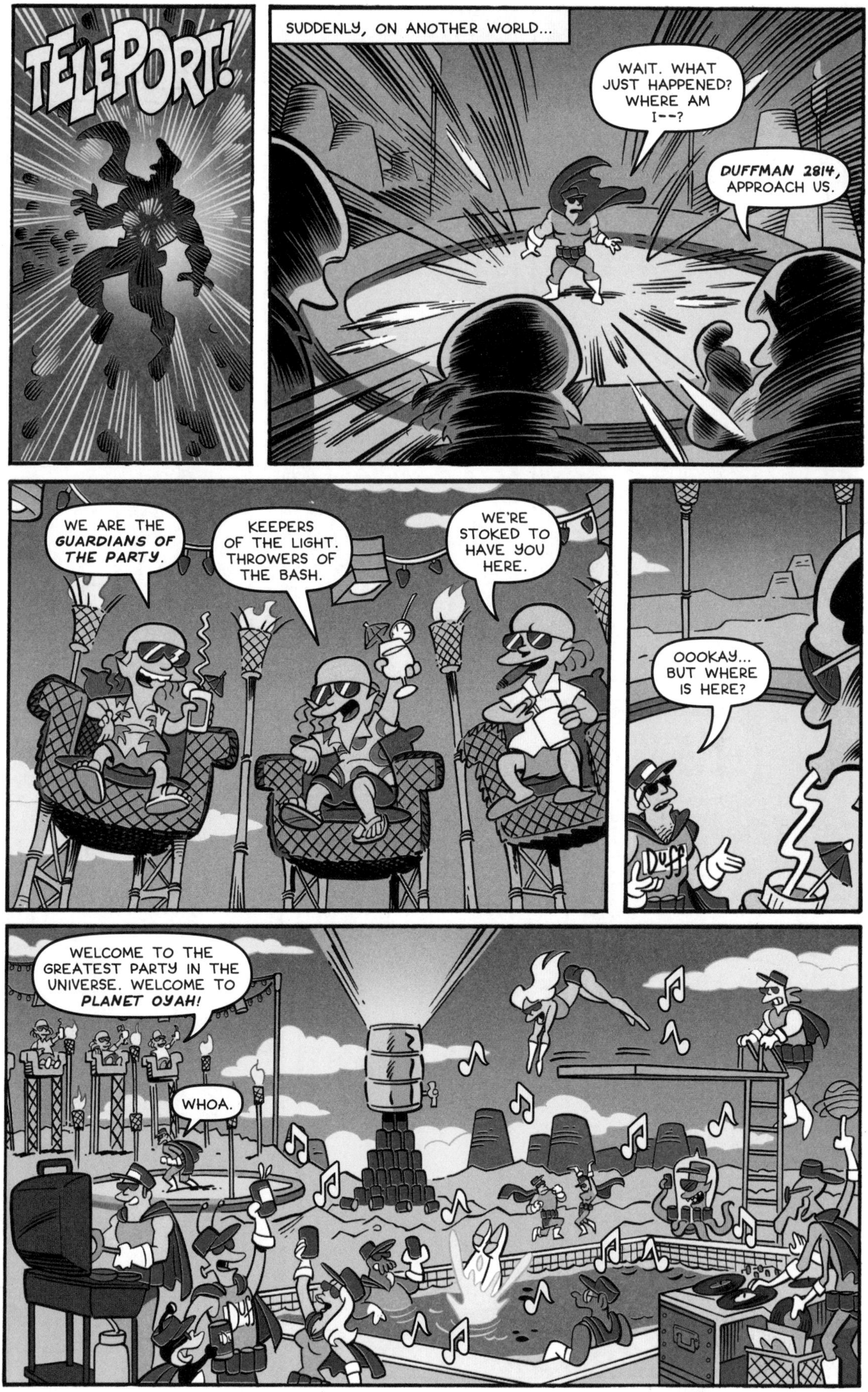
TELEPORT!
SUDDENLY, ON ANOTHER WORLD...
WAIT. WHAT JUST HAPPENED? WHERE AM I--?
DUFFMAN 2814, APPROACH US.
WE ARE THE GUARDIANS OF THE PARTY.
KEEPERS OF THE LIGHT. THROWERS OF THE BASH.
WE'RE STOKED TO HAVE YOU HERE.
OOOKAY... BUT WHERE IS HERE?
WELCOME TO THE GREATEST PARTY IN THE UNIVERSE. WELCOME TO PLANET OYAH!
WHOA.

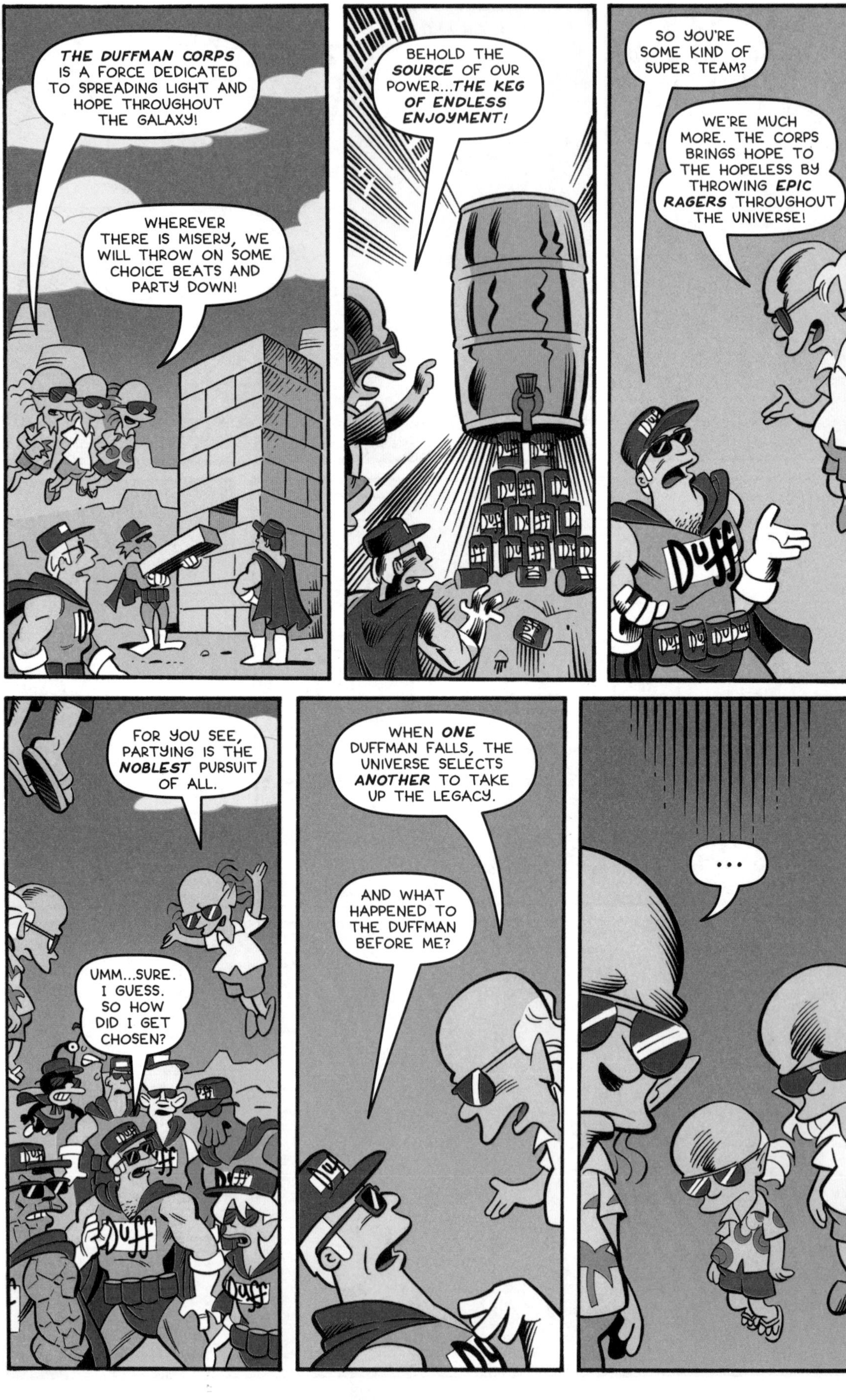
THE DUFFMAN CORPS IS A FORCE DEDICATED TO SPREADING LIGHT AND HOPE THROUGHOUT THE GALAXY!
WHEREVER THERE IS MISERY, WE WILL THROW ON SOME CHOICE BEATS AND PARTY DOWN!
BEHOLD THE SOURCE OF OUR POWER...THE KEG OF ENDLESS ENJOYMENT!
DUFF
SO YOU'RE SOME KIND OF SUPER TEAM?
WE'RE MUCH MORE. THE CORPS BRINGS HOPE TO THE HOPELESS BY THROWING EPIC RAGERS THROUGHOUT THE UNIVERSE!
DUFF
FOR YOU SEE, PARTYING IS THE NOBLEST PURSUIT OF ALL.
UMM...SURE. I GUESS. SO HOW DID I GET CHOSEN?
WHEN ONE DUFFMAN FALLS, THE UNIVERSE SELECTS ANOTHER TO TAKE UP THE LEGACY.
AND WHAT HAPPENED TO THE DUFFMAN BEFORE ME?
...

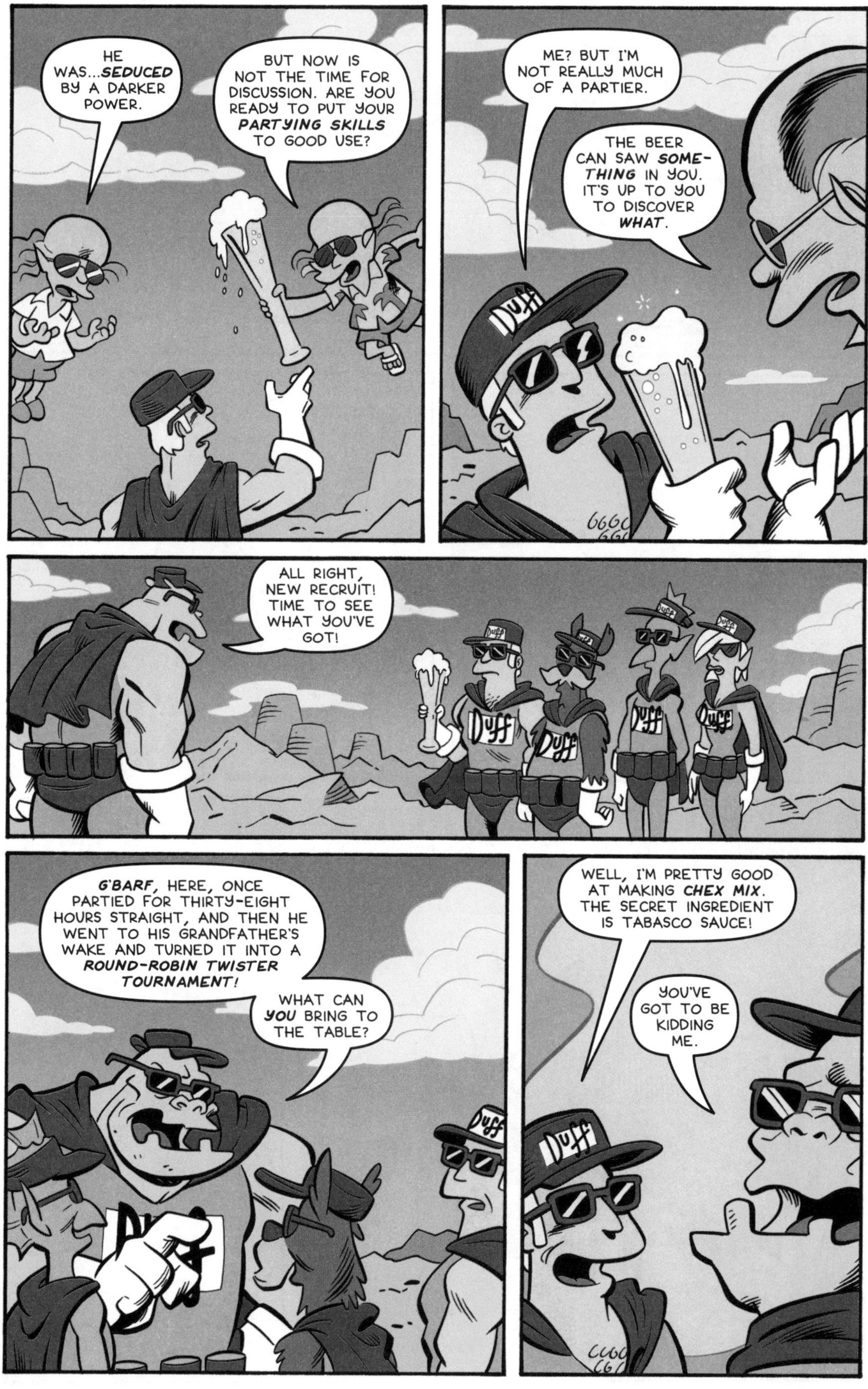
HE WAS...SEDUCED BY A DARKER POWER.
BUT NOW IS NOT THE TIME FOR DISCUSSION. ARE YOU READY TO PUT YOUR PARTYING SKILLS TO GOOD USE?
ME? BUT I'M NOT REALLY MUCH OF A PARTIER.
THE BEER CAN SAW SOME-THING IN YOU. IT'S UP TO YOU TO DISCOVER WHAT.
DUFF
ALL RIGHT, NEW RECRUIT! TIME TO SEE WHAT YOU'VE GOT!
G'BARF, HERE, ONCE PARTIED FOR THIRTY-EIGHT HOURS STRAIGHT, AND THEN HE WENT TO HIS GRANDFATHER'S WAKE AND TURNED IT INTO A ROUND-ROBIN TWISTER TOURNAMENT!
WHAT CAN YOU BRING TO THE TABLE?
WELL, I'M PRETTY GOOD AT MAKING CHEX MIX. THE SECRET INGREDIENT IS TABASCO SAUCE!
YOU'VE GOT TO BE KIDDING ME.

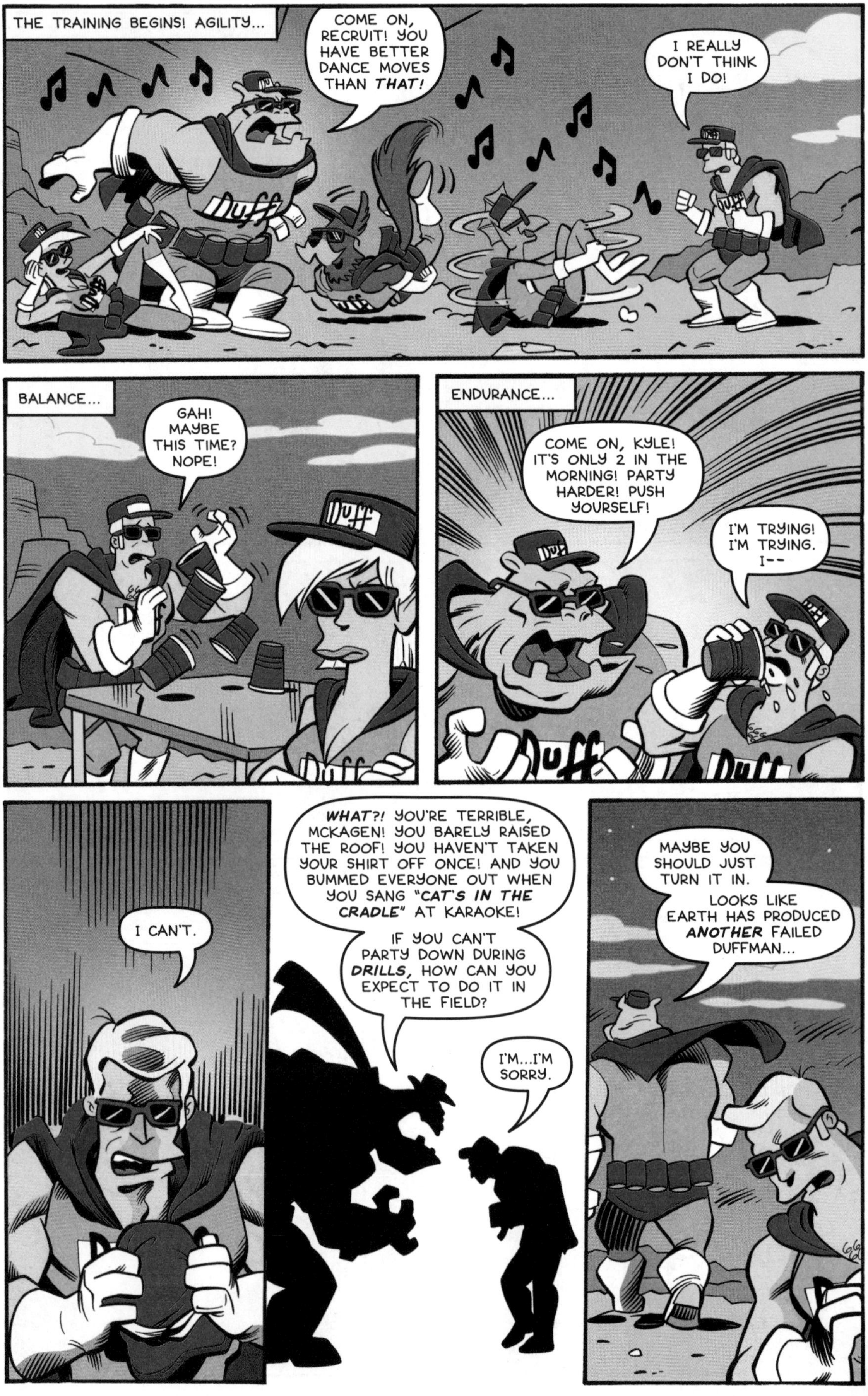
THE TRAINING BEGINS! AGILITY...
COME ON, RECRUIT! YOU HAVE BETTER DANCE MOVES THAN *THAT!*
I REALLY DON'T THINK I DO!
BALANCE...
GAH! MAYBE THIS TIME? NOPE!
ENDURANCE...
COME ON, KYLE! IT'S ONLY 2 IN THE MORNING! PARTY HARDER! PUSH YOURSELF!
I'M TRYING! I'M TRYING. I--
I CAN'T.
WHAT?! YOU'RE TERRIBLE, MCKAGEN! YOU BARELY RAISED THE ROOF! YOU HAVEN'T TAKEN YOUR SHIRT OFF ONCE! AND YOU BUMMED EVERYONE OUT WHEN YOU SANG "*CAT'S IN THE CRADLE*" AT KARAOKE!
IF YOU CAN'T PARTY DOWN DURING *DRILLS,* HOW CAN YOU EXPECT TO DO IT IN THE FIELD?
I'M...I'M SORRY.
MAYBE YOU SHOULD JUST TURN IT IN.
LOOKS LIKE EARTH HAS PRODUCED *ANOTHER* FAILED DUFFMAN...

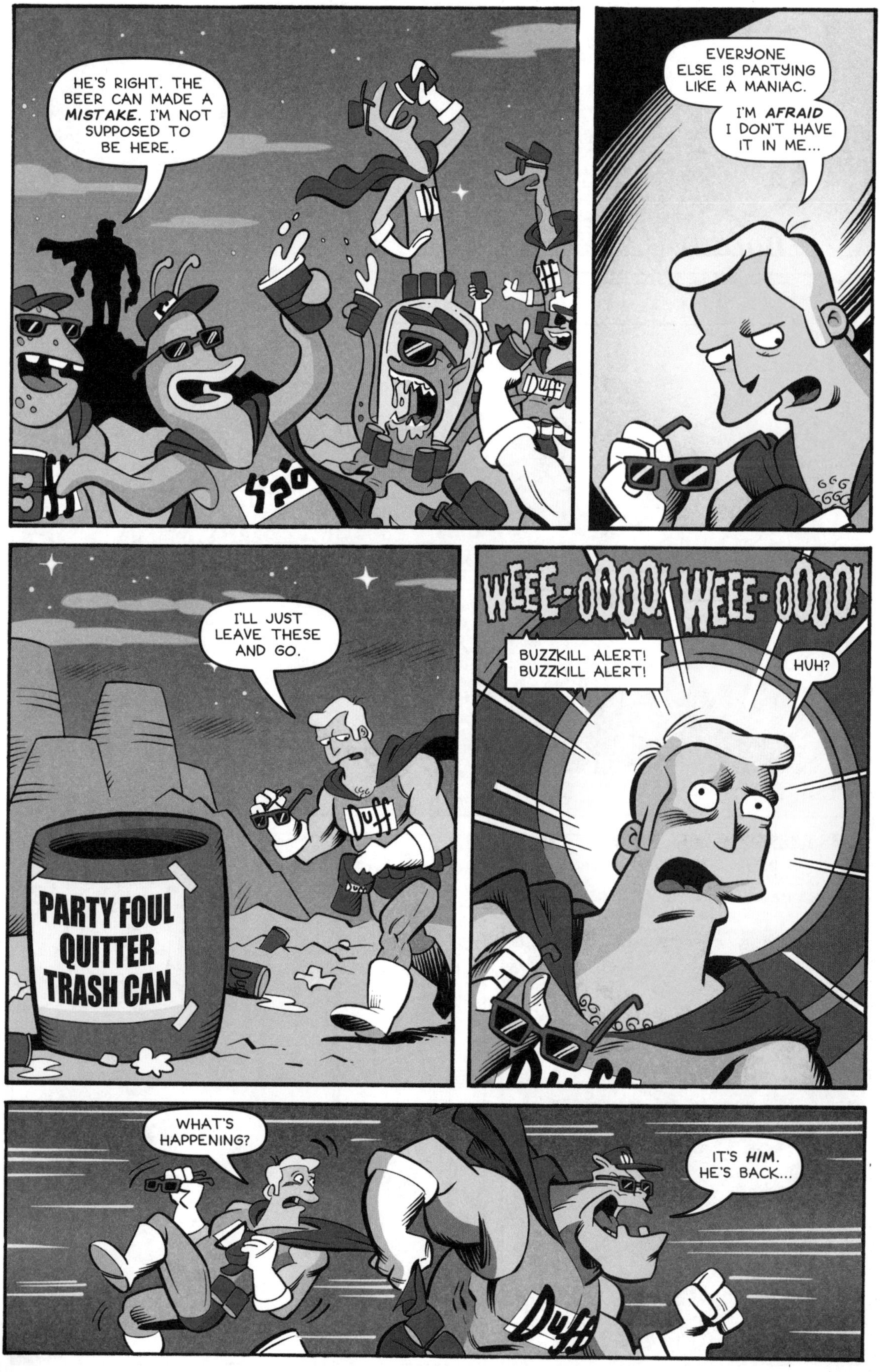
HE'S RIGHT. THE BEER CAN MADE A *MISTAKE*. I'M NOT SUPPOSED TO BE HERE.
EVERYONE ELSE IS PARTYING LIKE A MANIAC.
I'M *AFRAID* I DON'T HAVE IT IN ME...
I'LL JUST LEAVE THESE AND GO.
PARTY FOUL QUITTER TRASH CAN
WEEE-OOOO! WEEE-OOOO!
BUZZKILL ALERT! BUZZKILL ALERT!
HUH?
WHAT'S HAPPENING?
IT'S *HIM*. HE'S BACK...

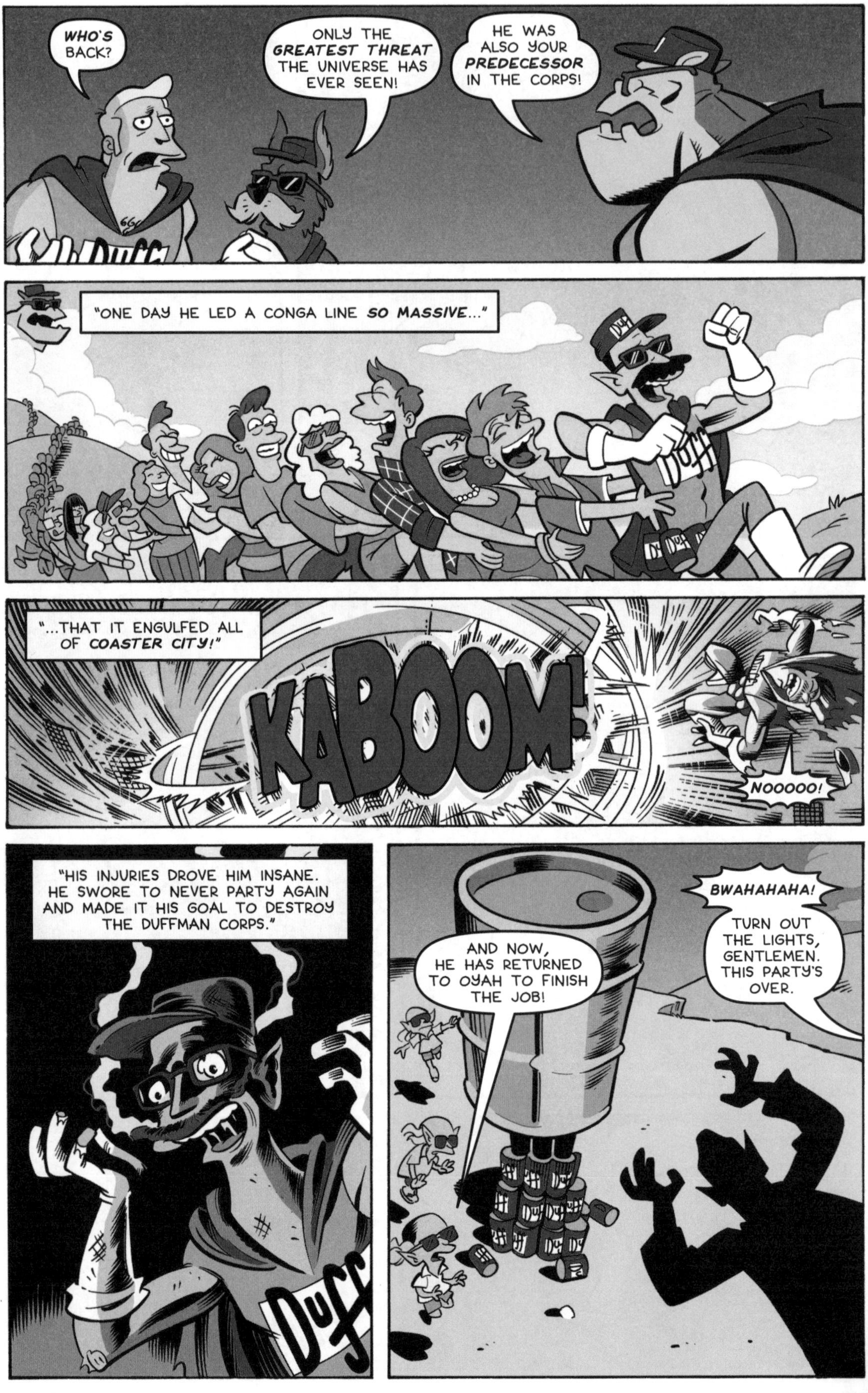
WHO'S BACK?
ONLY THE GREATEST THREAT THE UNIVERSE HAS EVER SEEN!
HE WAS ALSO YOUR PREDECESSOR IN THE CORPS!
"ONE DAY HE LED A CONGA LINE SO MASSIVE..."
"...THAT IT ENGULFED ALL OF COASTER CITY!"
KABOOM!
NOOOOO!
"HIS INJURIES DROVE HIM INSANE. HE SWORE TO NEVER PARTY AGAIN AND MADE IT HIS GOAL TO DESTROY THE DUFFMAN CORPS."
AND NOW, HE HAS RETURNED TO OYAH TO FINISH THE JOB!
BWAHAHAHA!
TURN OUT THE LIGHTS, GENTLEMEN. THIS PARTY'S OVER.

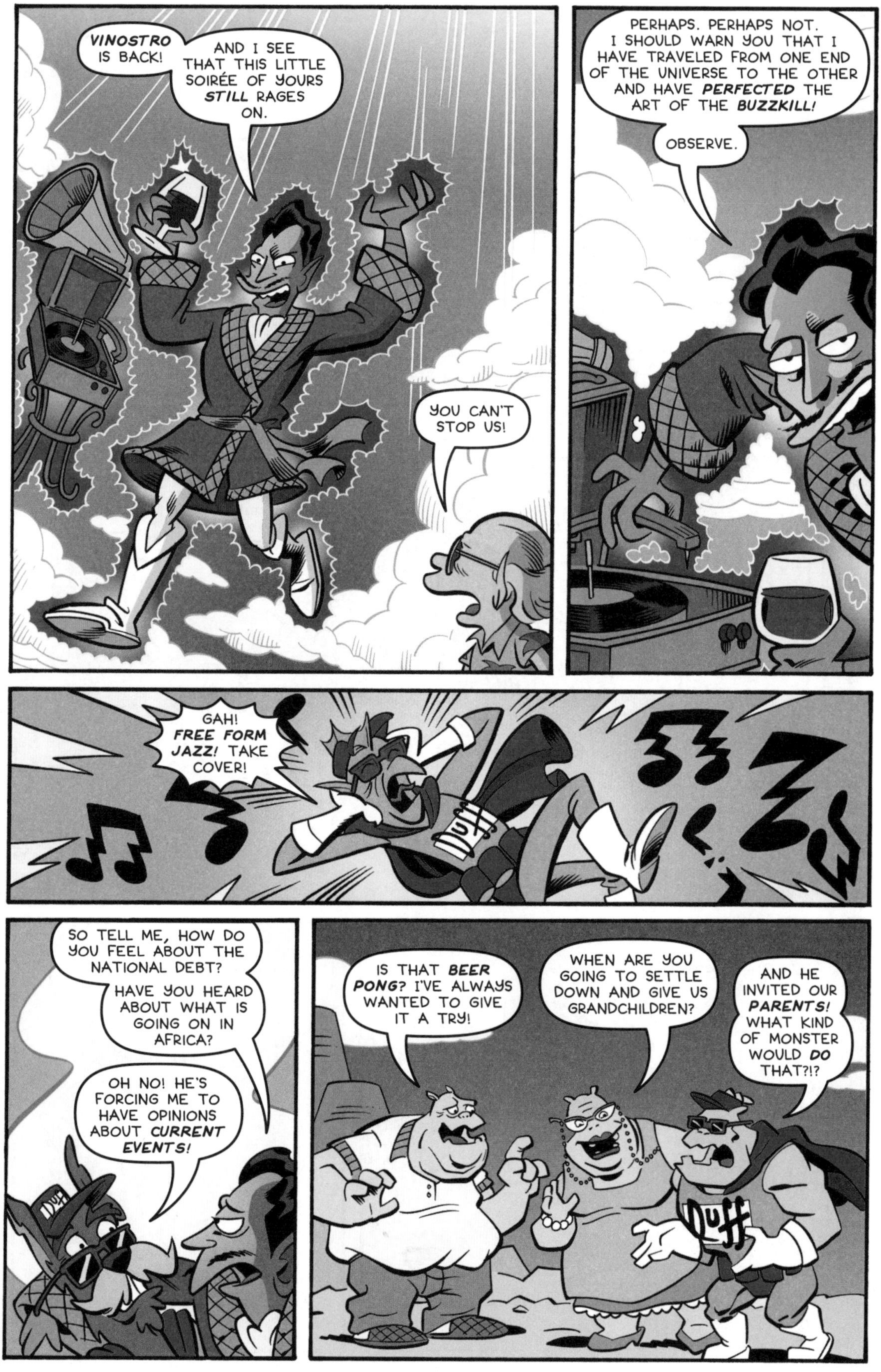
VINOSTRO IS BACK!
AND I SEE THAT THIS LITTLE SOIRÉE OF YOURS STILL RAGES ON.
YOU CAN'T STOP US!
PERHAPS. PERHAPS NOT. I SHOULD WARN YOU THAT I HAVE TRAVELED FROM ONE END OF THE UNIVERSE TO THE OTHER AND HAVE PERFECTED THE ART OF THE BUZZKILL!
OBSERVE.
GAH! FREE FORM JAZZ! TAKE COVER!
SO TELL ME, HOW DO YOU FEEL ABOUT THE NATIONAL DEBT?
HAVE YOU HEARD ABOUT WHAT IS GOING ON IN AFRICA?
OH NO! HE'S FORCING ME TO HAVE OPINIONS ABOUT CURRENT EVENTS!
IS THAT BEER PONG? I'VE ALWAYS WANTED TO GIVE IT A TRY!
WHEN ARE YOU GOING TO SETTLE DOWN AND GIVE US GRANDCHILDREN?
AND HE INVITED OUR PARENTS! WHAT KIND OF MONSTER WOULD DO THAT?!?

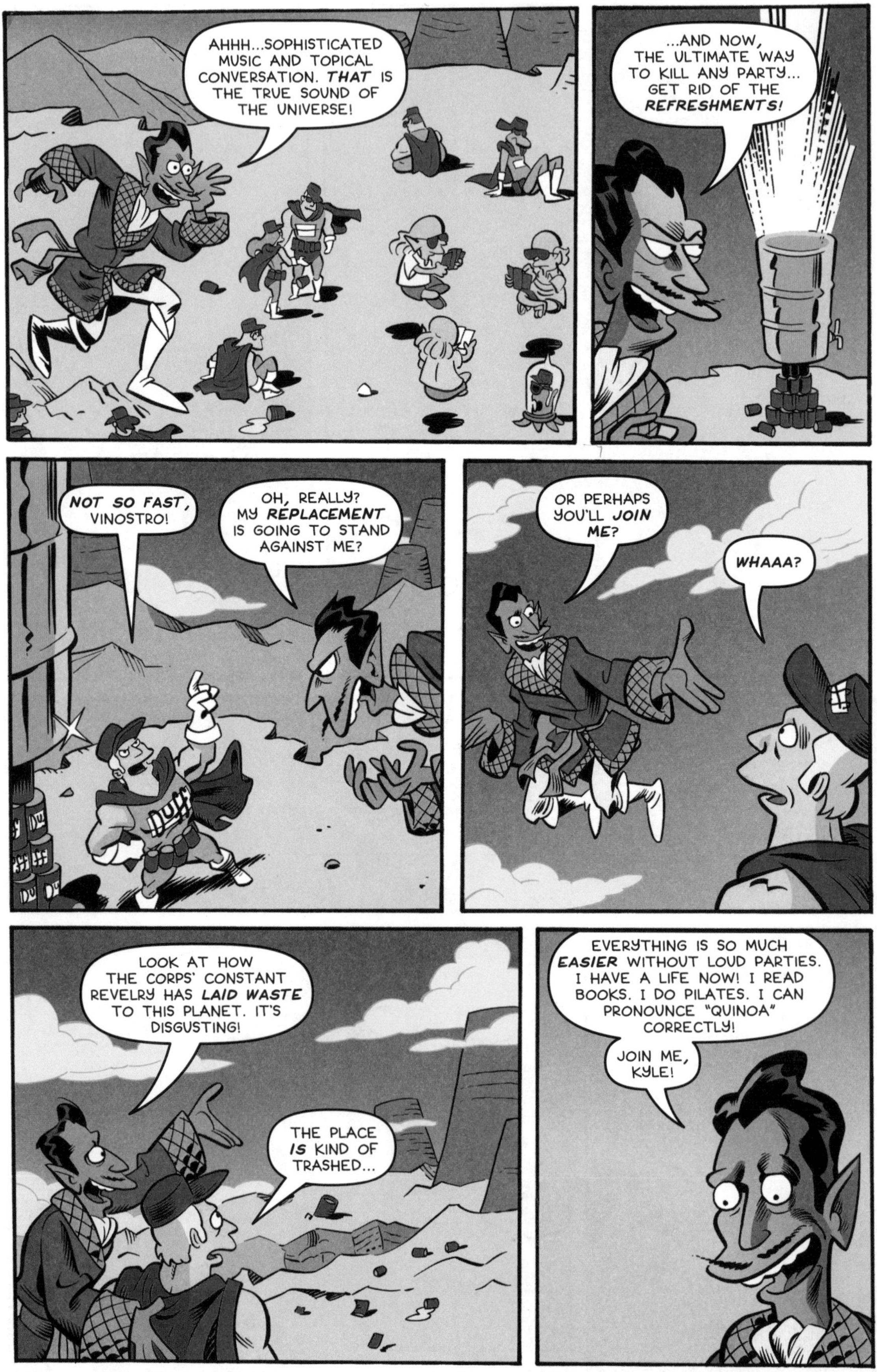
AHHH...SOPHISTICATED MUSIC AND TOPICAL CONVERSATION. *THAT* IS THE TRUE SOUND OF THE UNIVERSE!
...AND NOW, THE ULTIMATE WAY TO KILL ANY PARTY... GET RID OF THE *REFRESHMENTS!*
NOT SO FAST, VINOSTRO!
OH, REALLY? MY *REPLACEMENT* IS GOING TO STAND AGAINST ME?
OR PERHAPS YOU'LL *JOIN ME*?
WHAAA?
LOOK AT HOW THE CORPS' CONSTANT REVELRY HAS *LAID WASTE* TO THIS PLANET. IT'S DISGUSTING!
THE PLACE *IS* KIND OF TRASHED...
EVERYTHING IS SO MUCH *EASIER* WITHOUT LOUD PARTIES. I HAVE A LIFE NOW! I READ BOOKS. I DO PILATES. I CAN PRONOUNCE "QUINOA" CORRECTLY!
JOIN ME, KYLE!

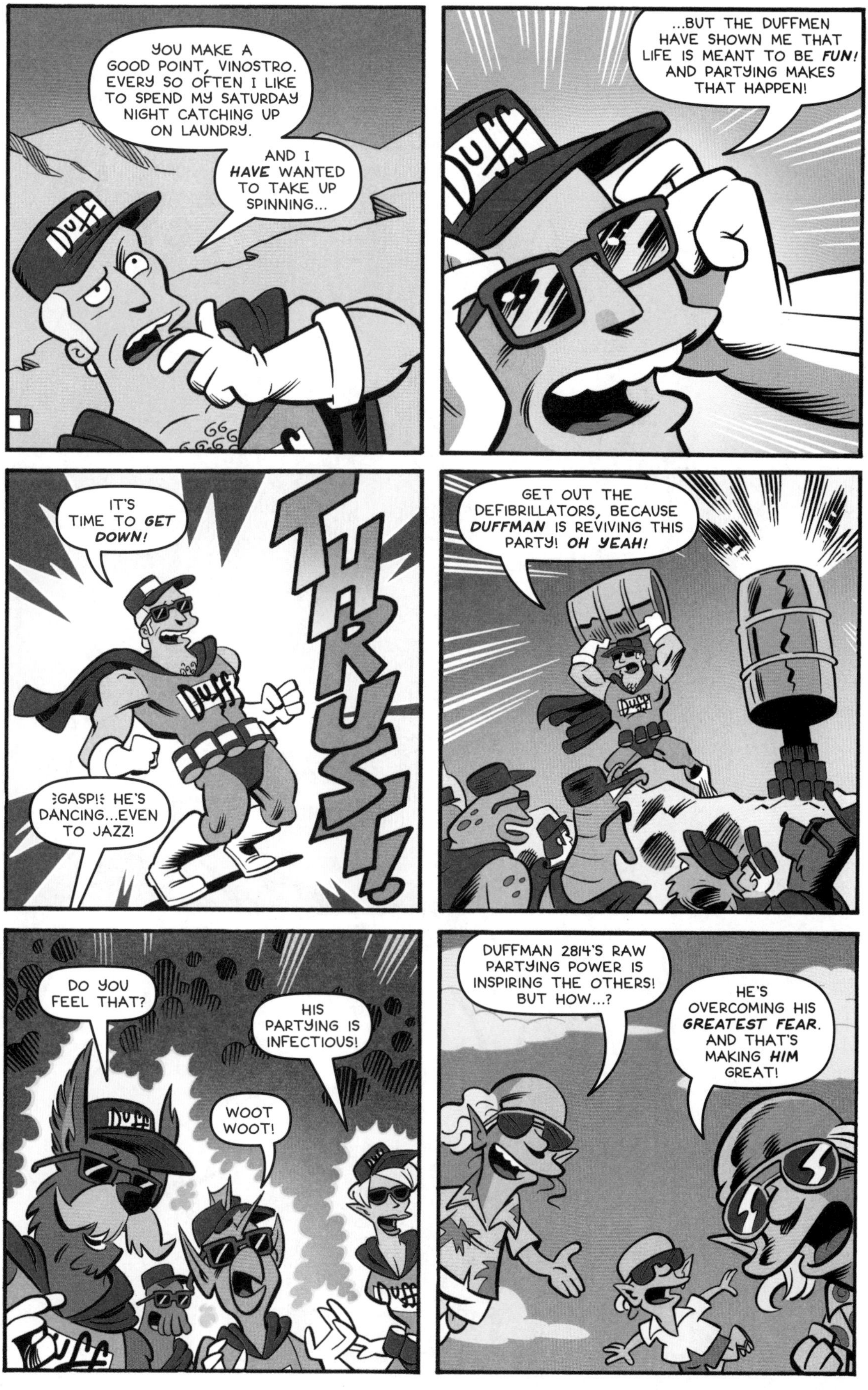

YOU MAKE A GOOD POINT, VINOSTRO. EVERY SO OFTEN I LIKE TO SPEND MY SATURDAY NIGHT CATCHING UP ON LAUNDRY.
AND I HAVE WANTED TO TAKE UP SPINNING...
...BUT THE DUFFMEN HAVE SHOWN ME THAT LIFE IS MEANT TO BE FUN! AND PARTYING MAKES THAT HAPPEN!
IT'S TIME TO GET DOWN!
THRUST!
:GASP!: HE'S DANCING...EVEN TO JAZZ!
GET OUT THE DEFIBRILLATORS, BECAUSE DUFFMAN IS REVIVING THIS PARTY! OH YEAH!
DO YOU FEEL THAT?
HIS PARTYING IS INFECTIOUS!
WOOT WOOT!
DUFFMAN 2814'S RAW PARTYING POWER IS INSPIRING THE OTHERS! BUT HOW...?
HE'S OVERCOMING HIS GREATEST FEAR. AND THAT'S MAKING HIM GREAT!

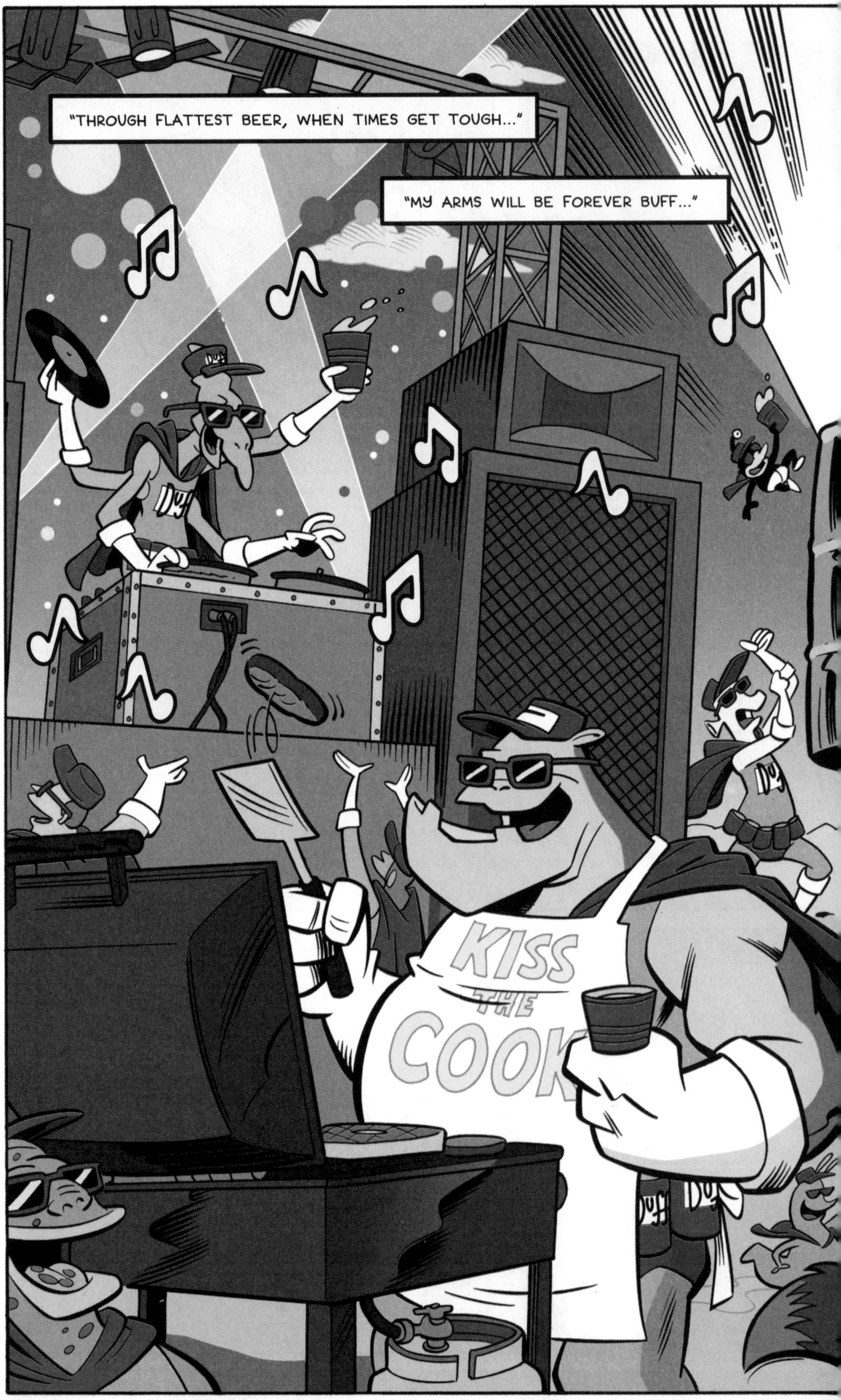
"THROUGH FLATTEST BEER, WHEN TIMES GET TOUGH..."
"MY ARMS WILL BE FOREVER BUFF..."
KISS THE COOK

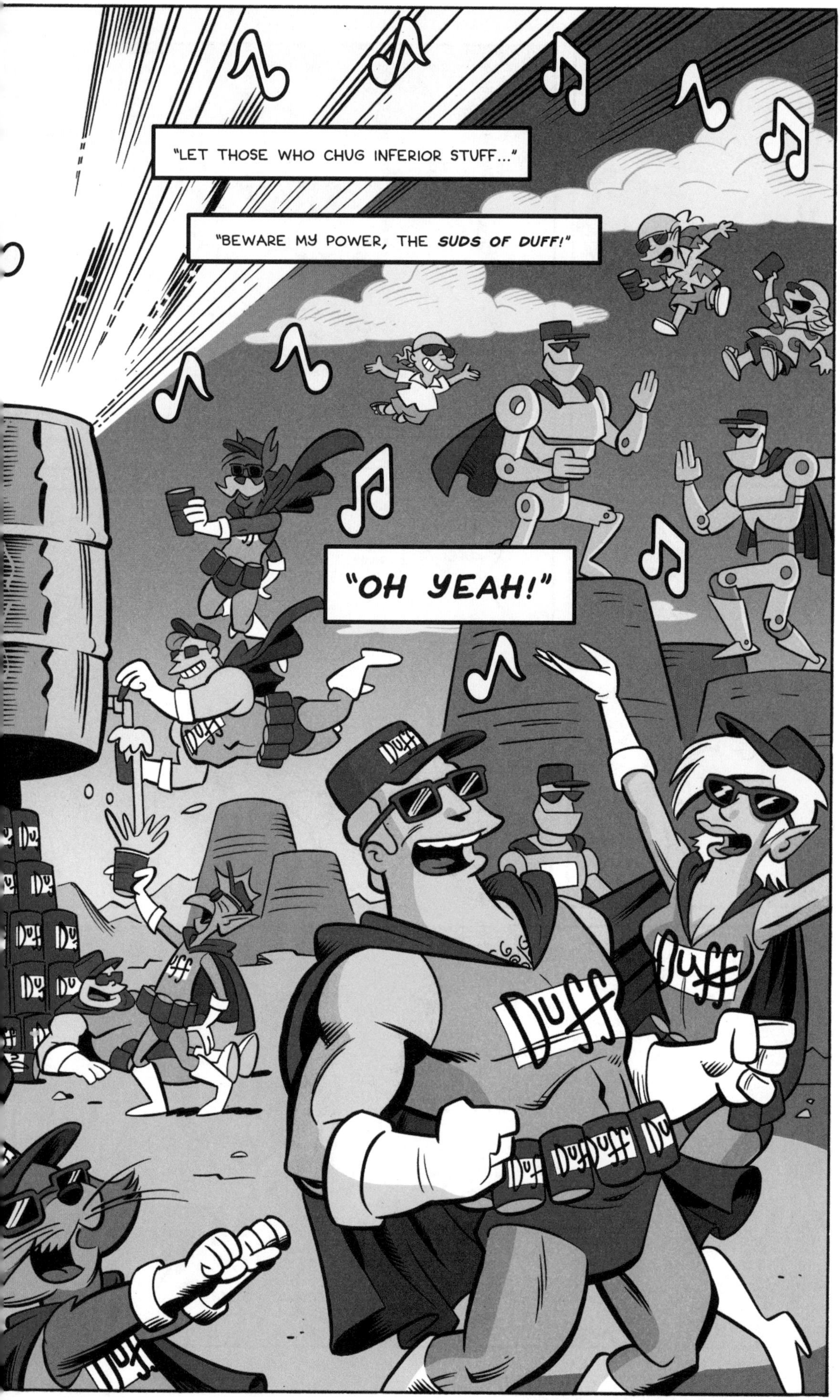
"LET THOSE WHO CHUG INFERIOR STUFF..."
"BEWARE MY POWER, THE SUDS OF DUFF!"
"OH YEAH!"

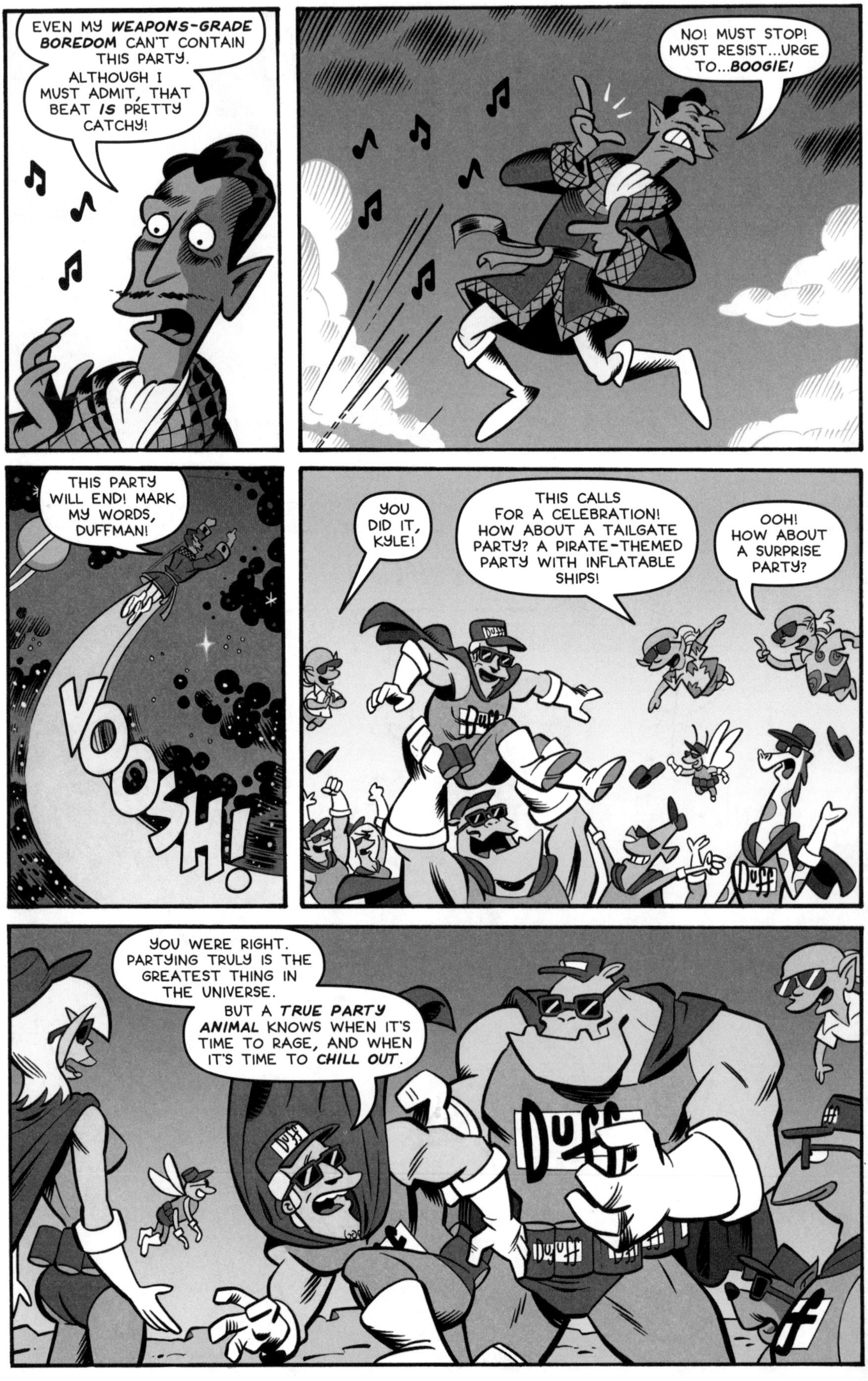
EVEN MY WEAPONS-GRADE BOREDOM CAN'T CONTAIN THIS PARTY.
ALTHOUGH I MUST ADMIT, THAT BEAT IS PRETTY CATCHY!
NO! MUST STOP! MUST RESIST...URGE TO...BOOGIE!
THIS PARTY WILL END! MARK MY WORDS, DUFFMAN!
VOOSH!
YOU DID IT, KYLE!
THIS CALLS FOR A CELEBRATION! HOW ABOUT A TAILGATE PARTY? A PIRATE-THEMED PARTY WITH INFLATABLE SHIPS!
OOH! HOW ABOUT A SURPRISE PARTY?
YOU WERE RIGHT. PARTYING TRULY IS THE GREATEST THING IN THE UNIVERSE.
BUT A TRUE PARTY ANIMAL KNOWS WHEN IT'S TIME TO RAGE, AND WHEN IT'S TIME TO CHILL OUT.

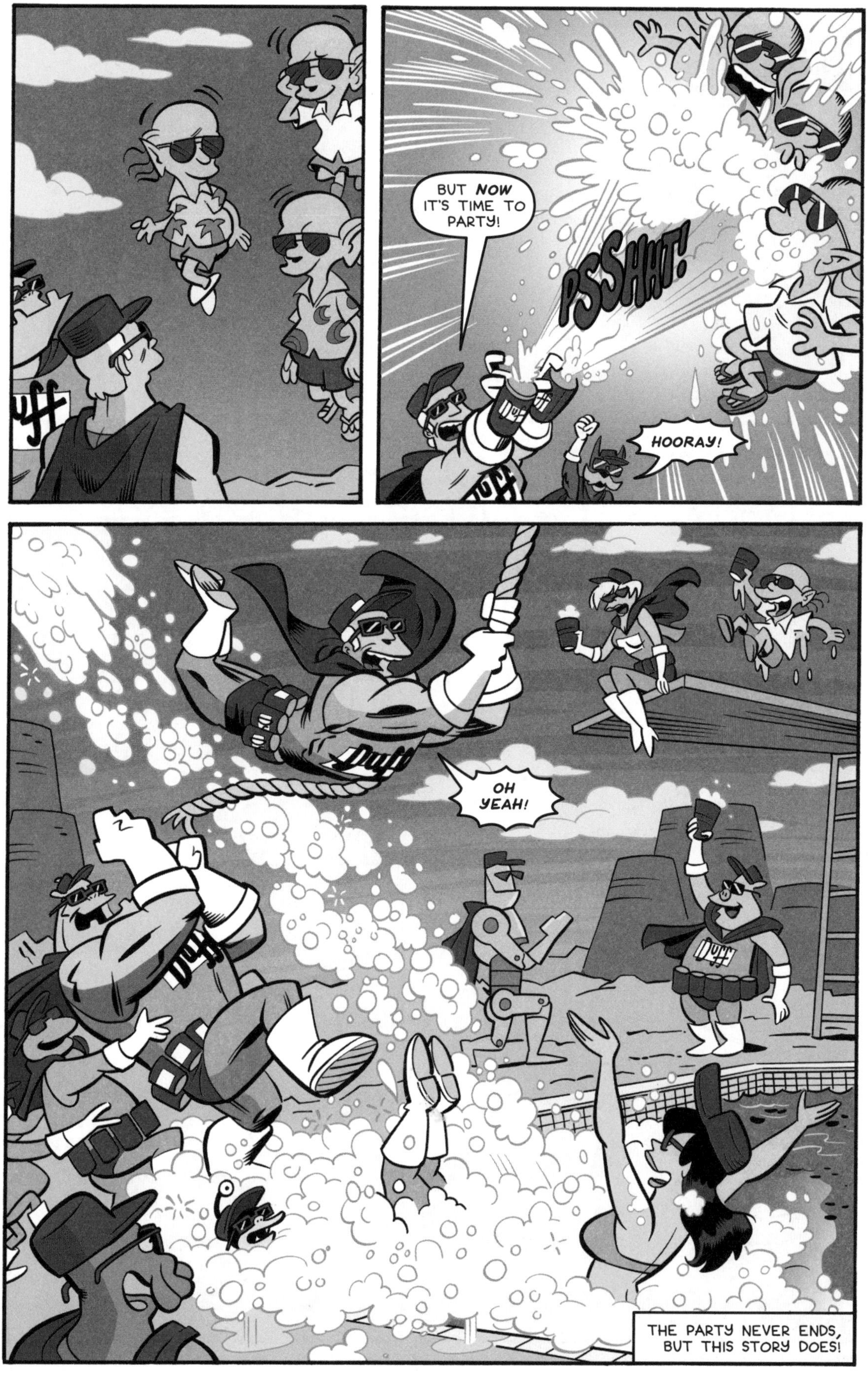
BUT NOW IT'S TIME TO PARTY!
PSSHHT!
HOORAY!
OH YEAH!
THE PARTY NEVER ENDS, BUT THIS STORY DOES!

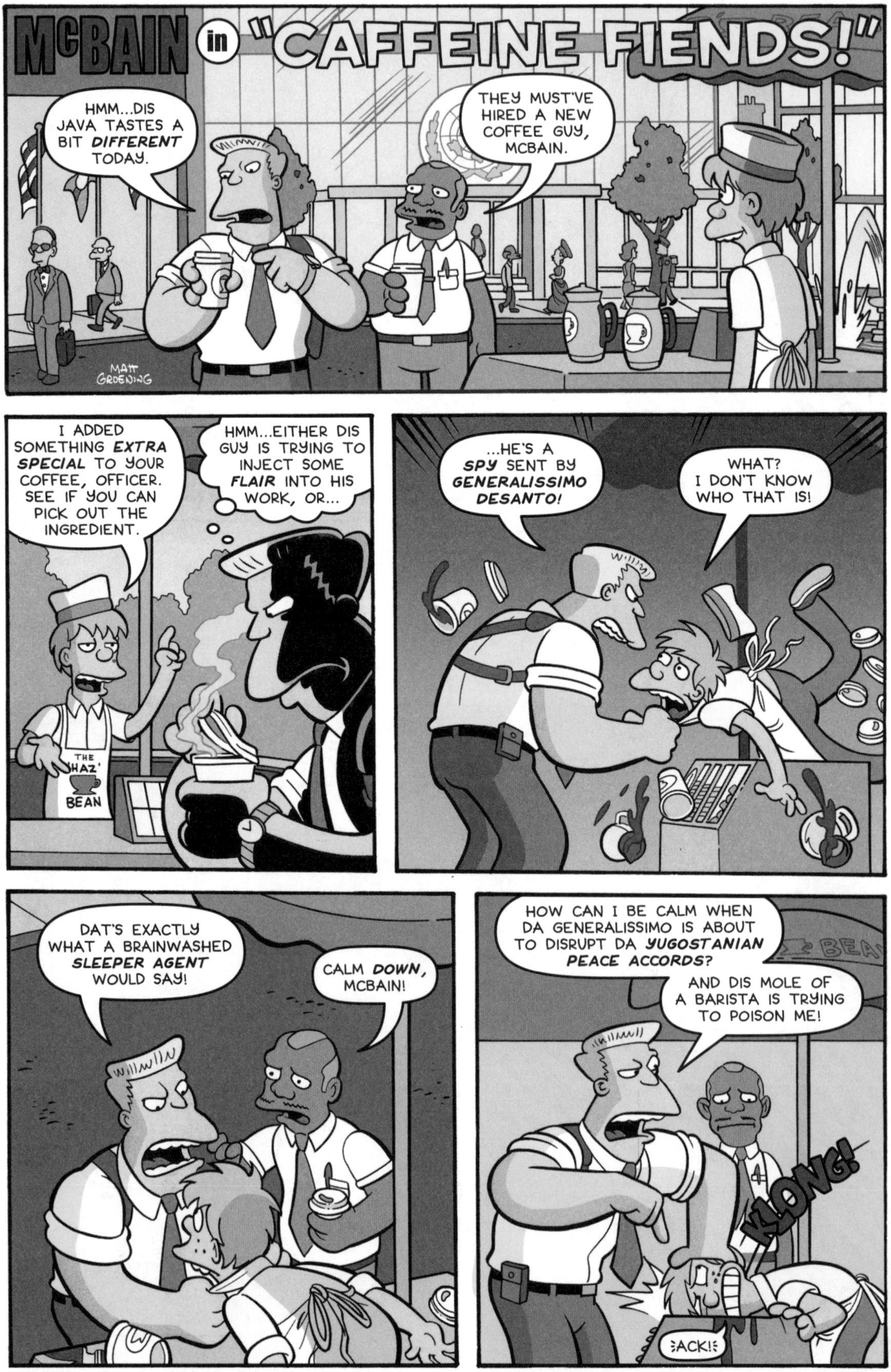
McBAIN in "CAFFEINE FIENDS!"
HMM...DIS JAVA TASTES A BIT DIFFERENT TODAY.
THEY MUST'VE HIRED A NEW COFFEE GUY, MCBAIN.
MATT GROENING
I ADDED SOMETHING EXTRA SPECIAL TO YOUR COFFEE, OFFICER. SEE IF YOU CAN PICK OUT THE INGREDIENT.
HMM...EITHER DIS GUY IS TRYING TO INJECT SOME FLAIR INTO HIS WORK, OR...
THE HAZ' BEAN
...HE'S A SPY SENT BY GENERALISSIMO DESANTO!
WHAT? I DON'T KNOW WHO THAT IS!
DAT'S EXACTLY WHAT A BRAINWASHED SLEEPER AGENT WOULD SAY!
CALM DOWN, MCBAIN!
HOW CAN I BE CALM WHEN DA GENERALISSIMO IS ABOUT TO DISRUPT DA YUGOSTANIAN PEACE ACCORDS?
AND DIS MOLE OF A BARISTA IS TRYING TO POISON ME!
KLONG!
ACK!

MAX DAVISON SCRIPT | ***JAMES LLOYD*** PENCILS | ***ANDREW PEPOY*** INKS | ***NATHAN HAMILL*** COLORS | ***KAREN BATES*** LETTERS | ***NATHAN KANE*** EDITOR

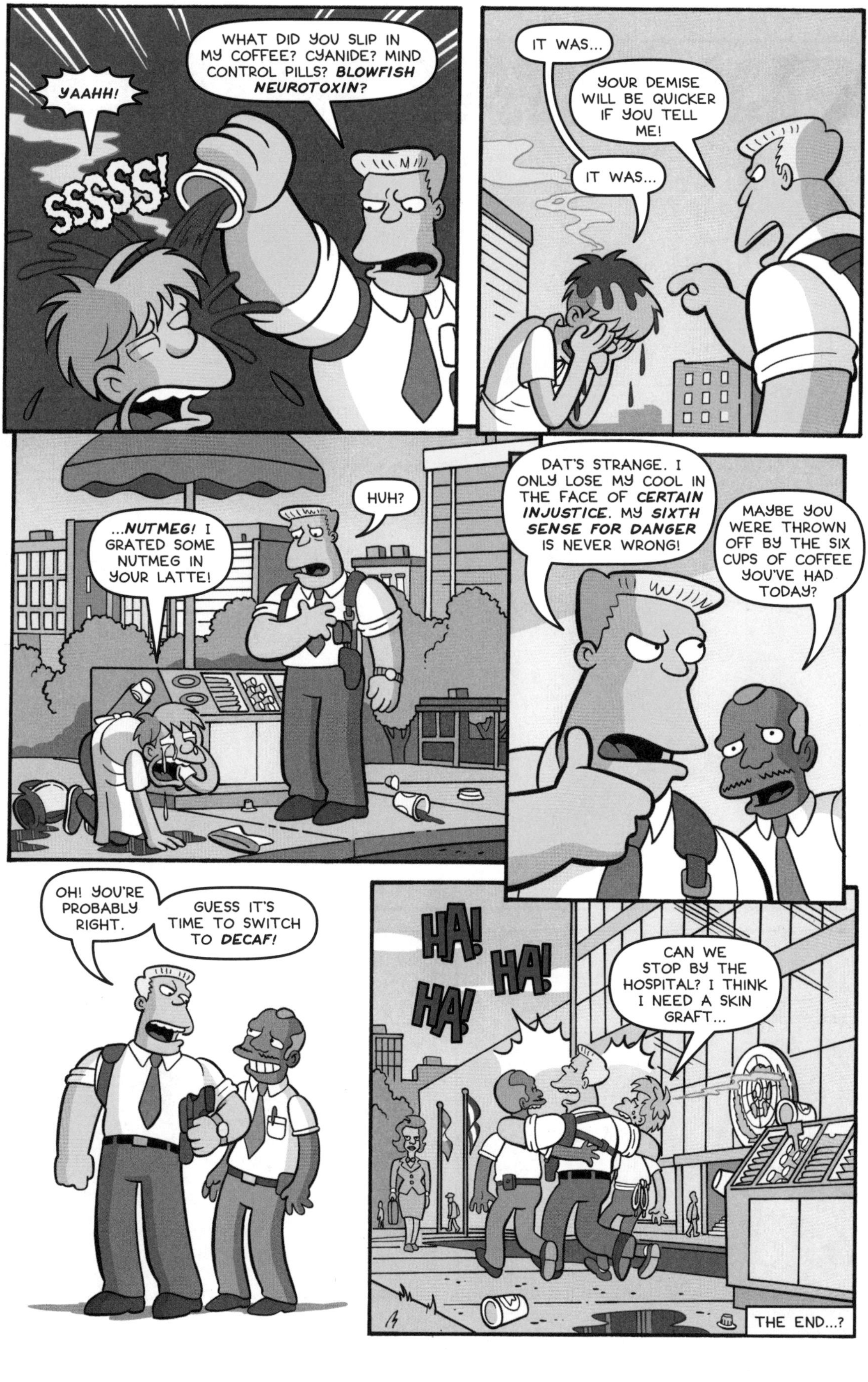
WHAT DID YOU SLIP IN MY COFFEE? CYANIDE? MIND CONTROL PILLS? **BLOWFISH NEUROTOXIN**?
YAAHH!
SSSSS!
IT WAS...
YOUR DEMISE WILL BE QUICKER IF YOU TELL ME!
IT WAS...
...**NUTMEG!** I GRATED SOME NUTMEG IN YOUR LATTE!
HUH?
DAT'S STRANGE. I ONLY LOSE MY COOL IN THE FACE OF **CERTAIN INJUSTICE**. MY **SIXTH SENSE FOR DANGER** IS NEVER WRONG!
MAYBE YOU WERE THROWN OFF BY THE SIX CUPS OF COFFEE YOU'VE HAD TODAY?
OH! YOU'RE PROBABLY RIGHT.
GUESS IT'S TIME TO SWITCH TO **DECAF!**
HA! HA! HA!
CAN WE STOP BY THE HOSPITAL? I THINK I NEED A SKIN GRAFT...
THE END...?

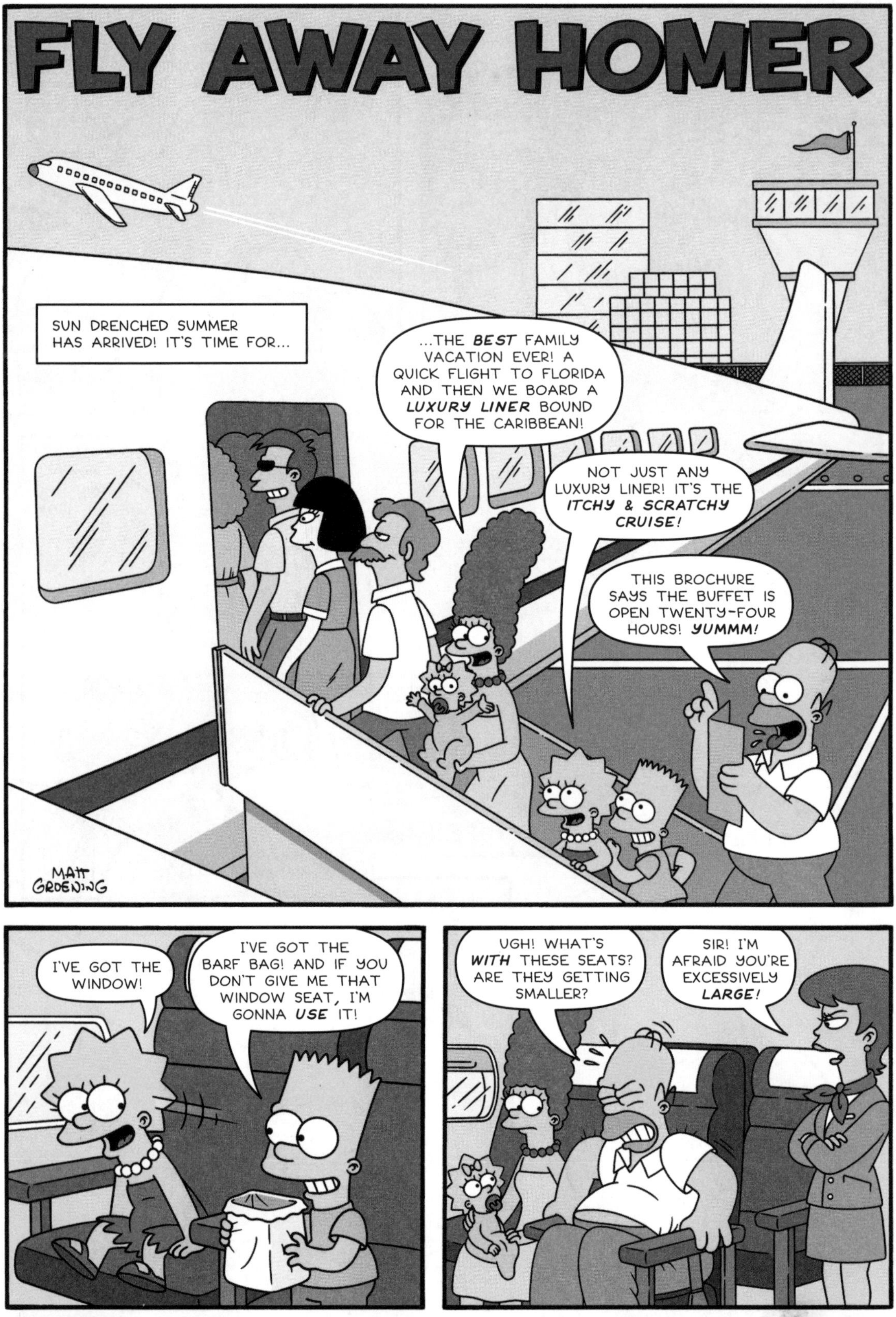
FLY AWAY HOMER
SUN DRENCHED SUMMER HAS ARRIVED! IT'S TIME FOR...
...THE BEST FAMILY VACATION EVER! A QUICK FLIGHT TO FLORIDA AND THEN WE BOARD A LUXURY LINER BOUND FOR THE CARIBBEAN!
NOT JUST ANY LUXURY LINER! IT'S THE ITCHY & SCRATCHY CRUISE!
THIS BROCHURE SAYS THE BUFFET IS OPEN TWENTY-FOUR HOURS! YUMMM!
MATT GROENING
I'VE GOT THE WINDOW!
I'VE GOT THE BARF BAG! AND IF YOU DON'T GIVE ME THAT WINDOW SEAT, I'M GONNA USE IT!
UGH! WHAT'S WITH THESE SEATS? ARE THEY GETTING SMALLER?
SIR! I'M AFRAID YOU'RE EXCESSIVELY LARGE!

PAT MCGREAL SCRIPT · ***PHIL ORTIZ*** PENCILS · ***MIKE ROTE*** INKS · ***NATHAN HAMILL*** COLORS · ***KAREN BATES*** LETTERS · ***BILL MORRISON*** EDITOR

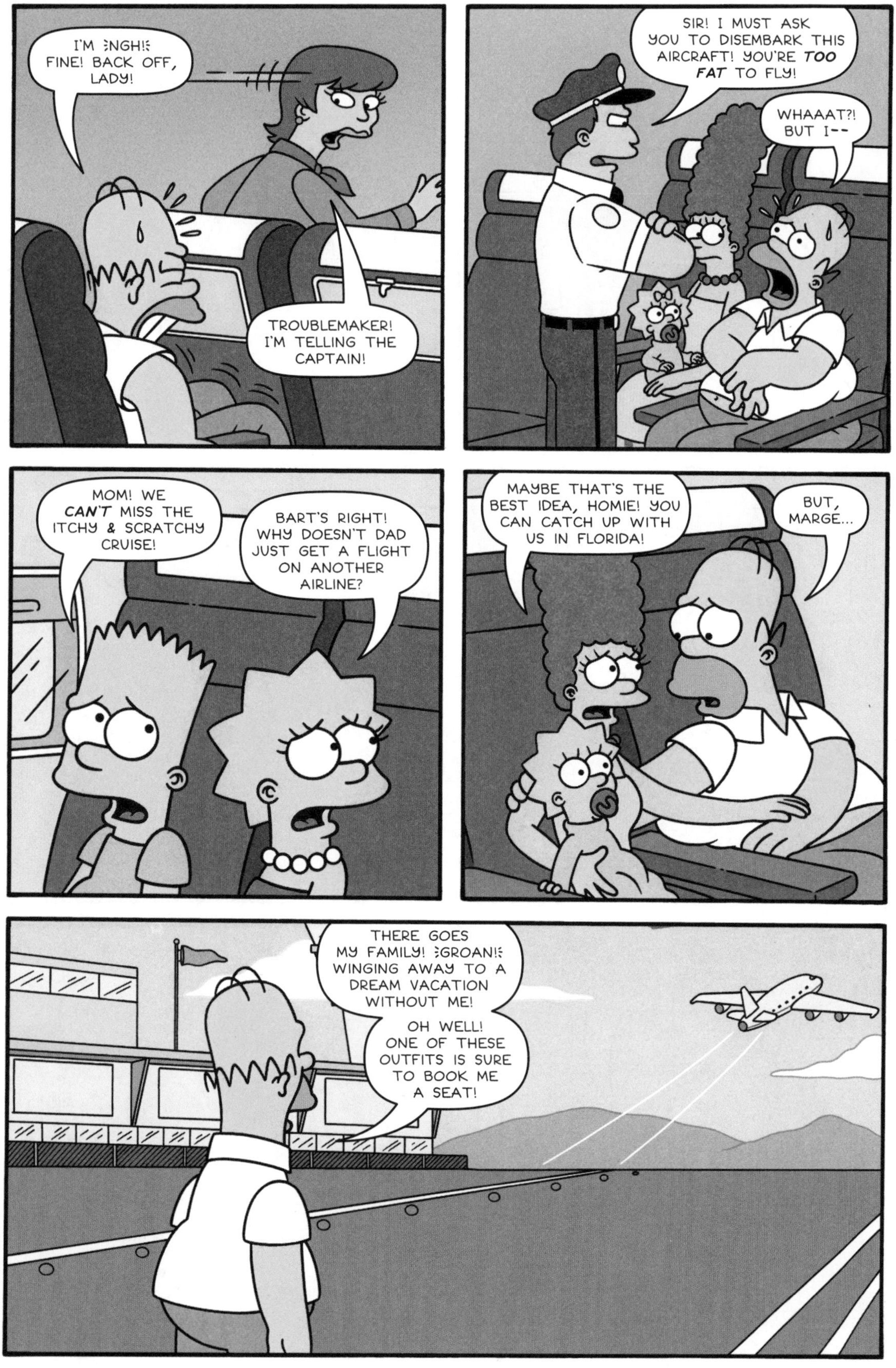
I'M ⁝NGH!⁝ FINE! BACK OFF, LADY!
TROUBLEMAKER! I'M TELLING THE CAPTAIN!
SIR! I MUST ASK YOU TO DISEMBARK THIS AIRCRAFT! YOU'RE *TOO FAT* TO FLY!
WHAAAT?! BUT I--
MOM! WE *CAN'T* MISS THE ITCHY & SCRATCHY CRUISE!
BART'S RIGHT! WHY DOESN'T DAD JUST GET A FLIGHT ON ANOTHER AIRLINE?
MAYBE THAT'S THE BEST IDEA, HOMIE! YOU CAN CATCH UP WITH US IN FLORIDA!
BUT, MARGE...
THERE GOES MY FAMILY! ⁝GROAN!⁝ WINGING AWAY TO A DREAM VACATION WITHOUT ME!
OH WELL! ONE OF THESE OUTFITS IS SURE TO BOOK ME A SEAT!

SORRY, SIR! YOUR GIRTH IS TOO...GIRTHY!

D'OH!

Sky Blah

A LUMP OF LARD LIKE YOU?! FORGET IT!

NO FAIR!

IN FLORIDA...

MOM! THE BOAT IS LEAVING! *MOM! THE BOAT IS LEAVING! MOM! THE BOAT IS LEAVING*

OH DEAR! STILL NO SIGN OF YOUR FATHER! WE *CAN'T* GO WITHOUT HIM!

FINAL BOARDING CALL!

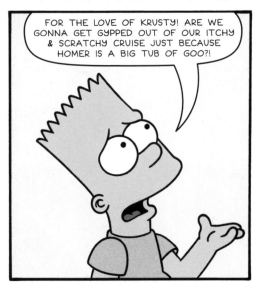

FOR THE LOVE OF KRUSTY! ARE WE GONNA GET GYPPED OUT OF OUR ITCHY & SCRATCHY CRUISE JUST BECAUSE HOMER IS A BIG TUB OF GOO?!

ALL RIGHT, KIDS! COME ON! MAYBE HE WILL STILL SHOW UP! MAYBE A MIRACLE WILL HAPPEN!

RIGHT! AND MAYBE PIGS WILL DROP OUT OF THE SKY!

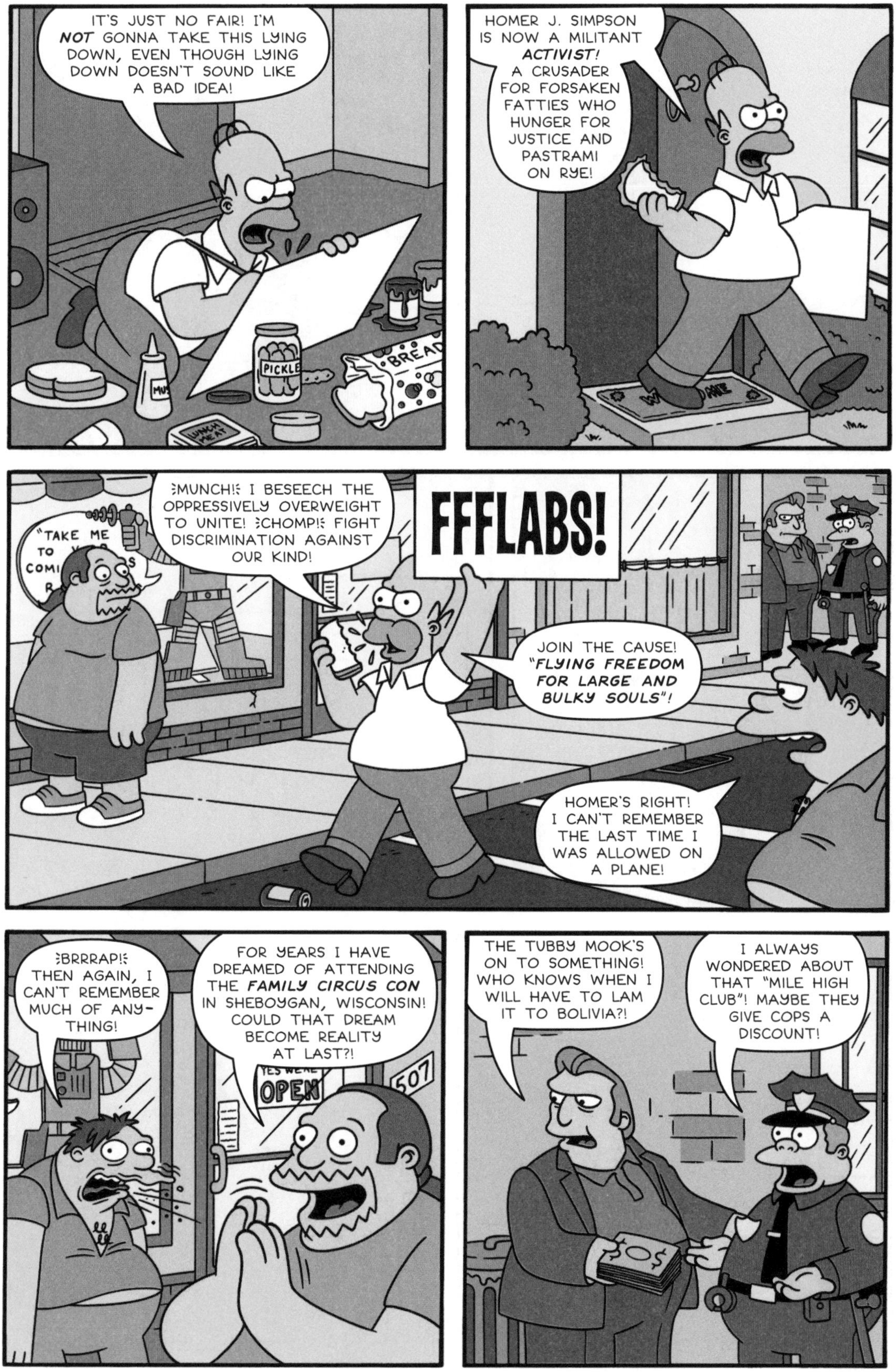

IT'S JUST NO FAIR! I'M **NOT** GONNA TAKE THIS LYING DOWN, EVEN THOUGH LYING DOWN DOESN'T SOUND LIKE A BAD IDEA!
PICKLE
BREAD
LUNCH MEAT
HOMER J. SIMPSON IS NOW A MILITANT ***ACTIVIST!*** A CRUSADER FOR FORSAKEN FATTIES WHO HUNGER FOR JUSTICE AND PASTRAMI ON RYE!
MUNCH! I BESEECH THE OPPRESSIVELY OVERWEIGHT TO UNITE! CHOMP! FIGHT DISCRIMINATION AGAINST OUR KIND!
FFFLABS!
JOIN THE CAUSE! "***FLYING FREEDOM FOR LARGE AND BULKY SOULS***"!
HOMER'S RIGHT! I CAN'T REMEMBER THE LAST TIME I WAS ALLOWED ON A PLANE!
BRRRAP! THEN AGAIN, I CAN'T REMEMBER MUCH OF ANY-THING!
FOR YEARS I HAVE DREAMED OF ATTENDING THE ***FAMILY CIRCUS CON*** IN SHEBOYGAN, WISCONSIN! COULD THAT DREAM BECOME REALITY AT LAST?!
OPEN
507
THE TUBBY MOOK'S ON TO SOMETHING! WHO KNOWS WHEN I WILL HAVE TO LAM IT TO BOLIVIA?!
I ALWAYS WONDERED ABOUT THAT "MILE HIGH CLUB"! MAYBE THEY GIVE COPS A DISCOUNT!

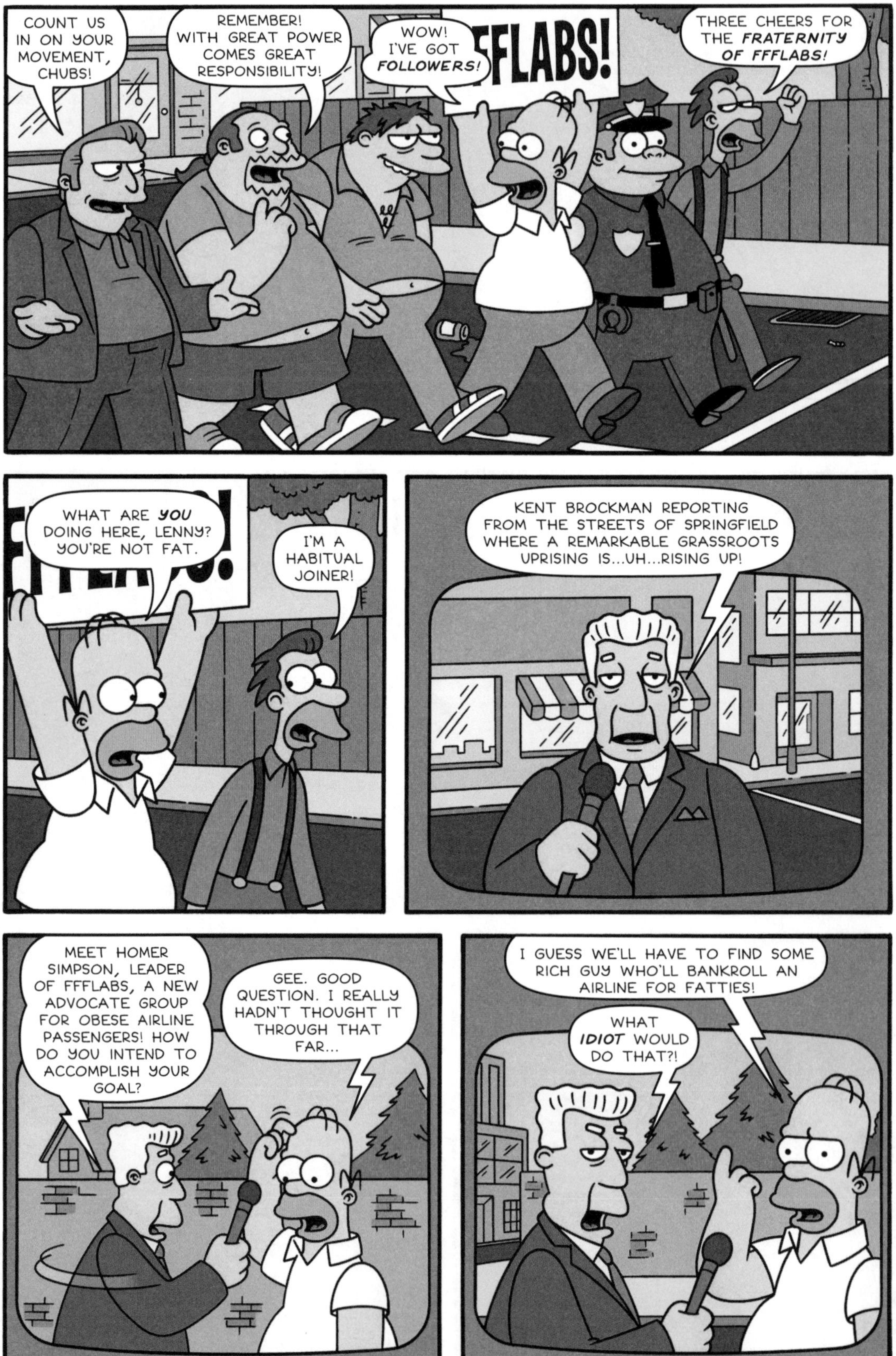

COUNT US IN ON YOUR MOVEMENT, CHUBS!
REMEMBER! WITH GREAT POWER COMES GREAT RESPONSIBILITY!
WOW! I'VE GOT *FOLLOWERS!*
FFLABS!
THREE CHEERS FOR THE *FRATERNITY OF FFFLABS!*
WHAT ARE *YOU* DOING HERE, LENNY? YOU'RE NOT FAT.
I'M A HABITUAL JOINER!
KENT BROCKMAN REPORTING FROM THE STREETS OF SPRINGFIELD WHERE A REMARKABLE GRASSROOTS UPRISING IS...UH...RISING UP!
MEET HOMER SIMPSON, LEADER OF FFFLABS, A NEW ADVOCATE GROUP FOR OBESE AIRLINE PASSENGERS! HOW DO YOU INTEND TO ACCOMPLISH YOUR GOAL?
GEE. GOOD QUESTION. I REALLY HADN'T THOUGHT IT THROUGH THAT FAR...
I GUESS WE'LL HAVE TO FIND SOME RICH GUY WHO'LL BANKROLL AN AIRLINE FOR FATTIES!
WHAT *IDIOT* WOULD DO THAT?!

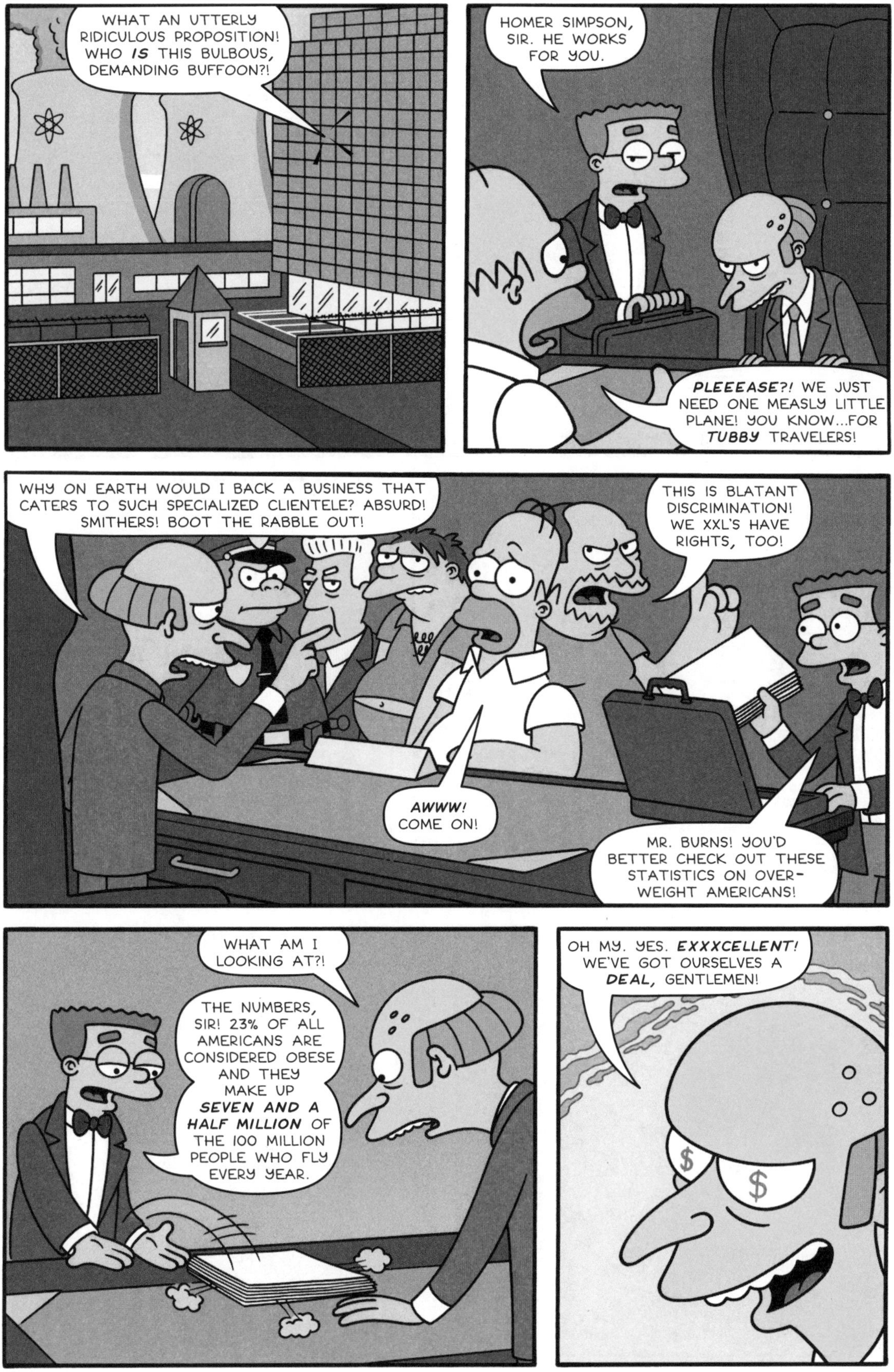
WHAT AN UTTERLY RIDICULOUS PROPOSITION! WHO *IS* THIS BULBOUS, DEMANDING BUFFOON?!
HOMER SIMPSON, SIR. HE WORKS FOR YOU.
PLEEEASE?! WE JUST NEED ONE MEASLY LITTLE PLANE! YOU KNOW...FOR *TUBBY* TRAVELERS!
WHY ON EARTH WOULD I BACK A BUSINESS THAT CATERS TO SUCH SPECIALIZED CLIENTELE? ABSURD! SMITHERS! BOOT THE RABBLE OUT!
THIS IS BLATANT DISCRIMINATION! WE XXL'S HAVE RIGHTS, TOO!
AWWW! COME ON!
MR. BURNS! YOU'D BETTER CHECK OUT THESE STATISTICS ON OVER-WEIGHT AMERICANS!
WHAT AM I LOOKING AT?!
THE NUMBERS, SIR! 23% OF ALL AMERICANS ARE CONSIDERED OBESE AND THEY MAKE UP *SEVEN AND A HALF MILLION* OF THE 100 MILLION PEOPLE WHO FLY EVERY YEAR.
OH MY. YES. *EXXXCELLENT!* WE'VE GOT OURSELVES A *DEAL,* GENTLEMEN!

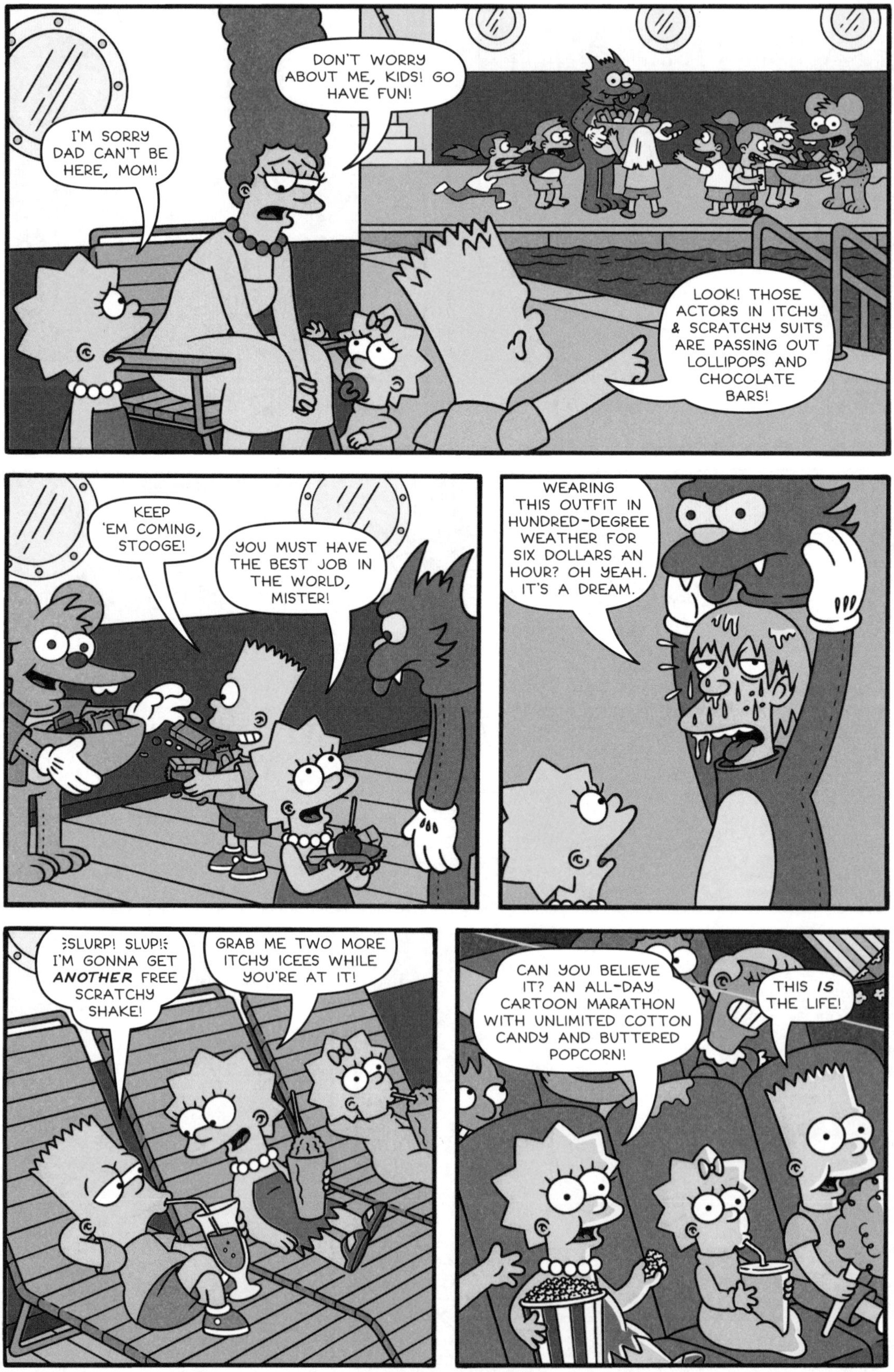
I'M SORRY DAD CAN'T BE HERE, MOM!
DON'T WORRY ABOUT ME, KIDS! GO HAVE FUN!
LOOK! THOSE ACTORS IN ITCHY & SCRATCHY SUITS ARE PASSING OUT LOLLIPOPS AND CHOCOLATE BARS!
KEEP 'EM COMING, STOOGE!
YOU MUST HAVE THE BEST JOB IN THE WORLD, MISTER!
WEARING THIS OUTFIT IN HUNDRED-DEGREE WEATHER FOR SIX DOLLARS AN HOUR? OH YEAH. IT'S A DREAM.
SLURP! SLUP! I'M GONNA GET **ANOTHER** FREE SCRATCHY SHAKE!
GRAB ME TWO MORE ITCHY ICEES WHILE YOU'RE AT IT!
CAN YOU BELIEVE IT? AN ALL-DAY CARTOON MARATHON WITH UNLIMITED COTTON CANDY AND BUTTERED POPCORN!
THIS *IS* THE LIFE!

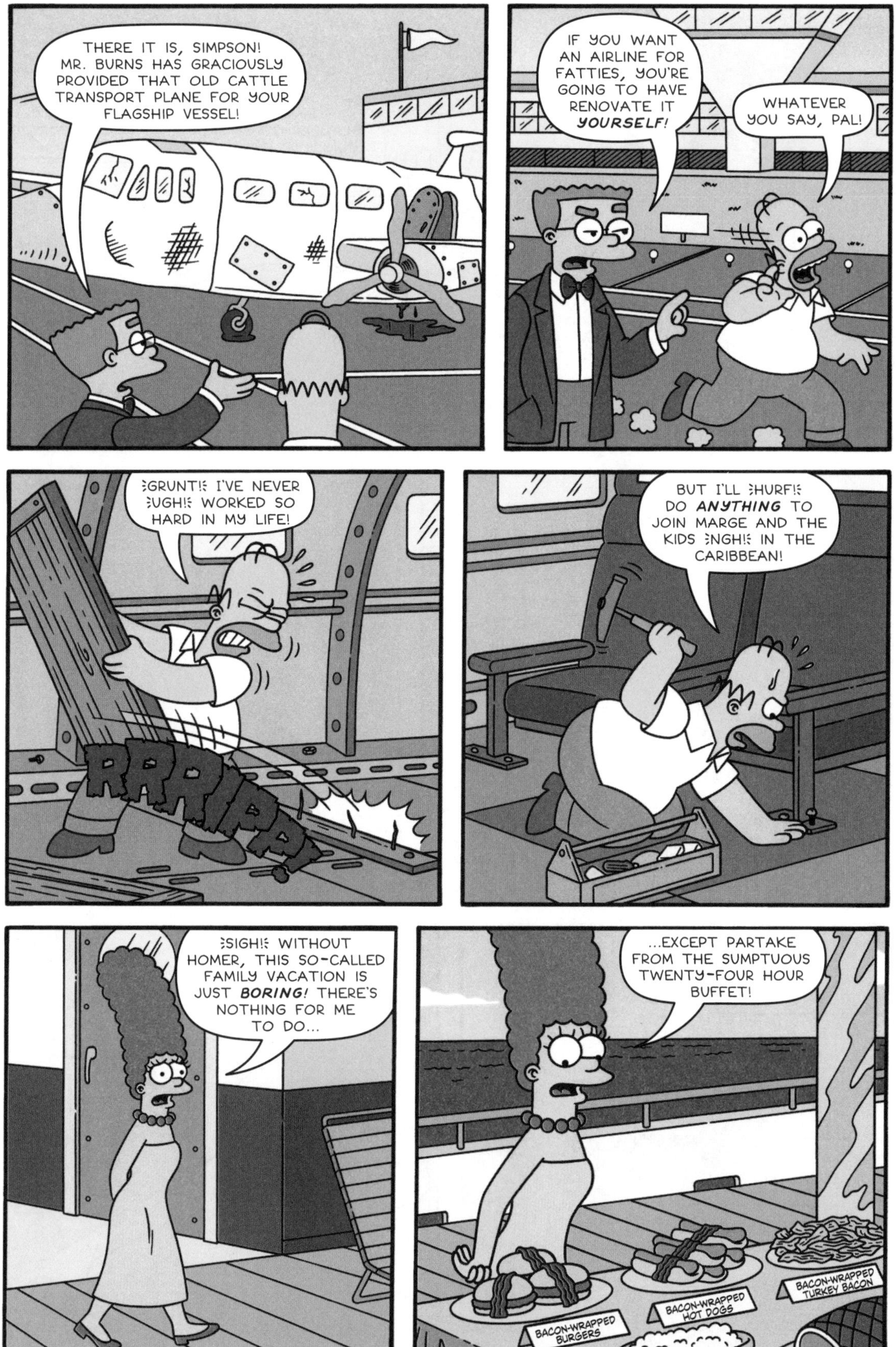
THERE IT IS, SIMPSON! MR. BURNS HAS GRACIOUSLY PROVIDED THAT OLD CATTLE TRANSPORT PLANE FOR YOUR FLAGSHIP VESSEL!
IF YOU WANT AN AIRLINE FOR FATTIES, YOU'RE GOING TO HAVE RENOVATE IT *YOURSELF!*
WHATEVER YOU SAY, PAL!
⁝GRUNT!⁝ I'VE NEVER ⁝UGH!⁝ WORKED SO HARD IN MY LIFE!
RRRIPP!
BUT I'LL ⁝HURF!⁝ DO *ANYTHING* TO JOIN MARGE AND THE KIDS ⁝NGH!⁝ IN THE CARIBBEAN!
⁝SIGH!⁝ WITHOUT HOMER, THIS SO-CALLED FAMILY VACATION IS JUST *BORING!* THERE'S NOTHING FOR ME TO DO...
...EXCEPT PARTAKE FROM THE SUMPTUOUS TWENTY-FOUR HOUR BUFFET!
BACON-WRAPPED BURGERS
BACON-WRAPPED HOT DOGS
BACON-WRAPPED TURKEY BACON

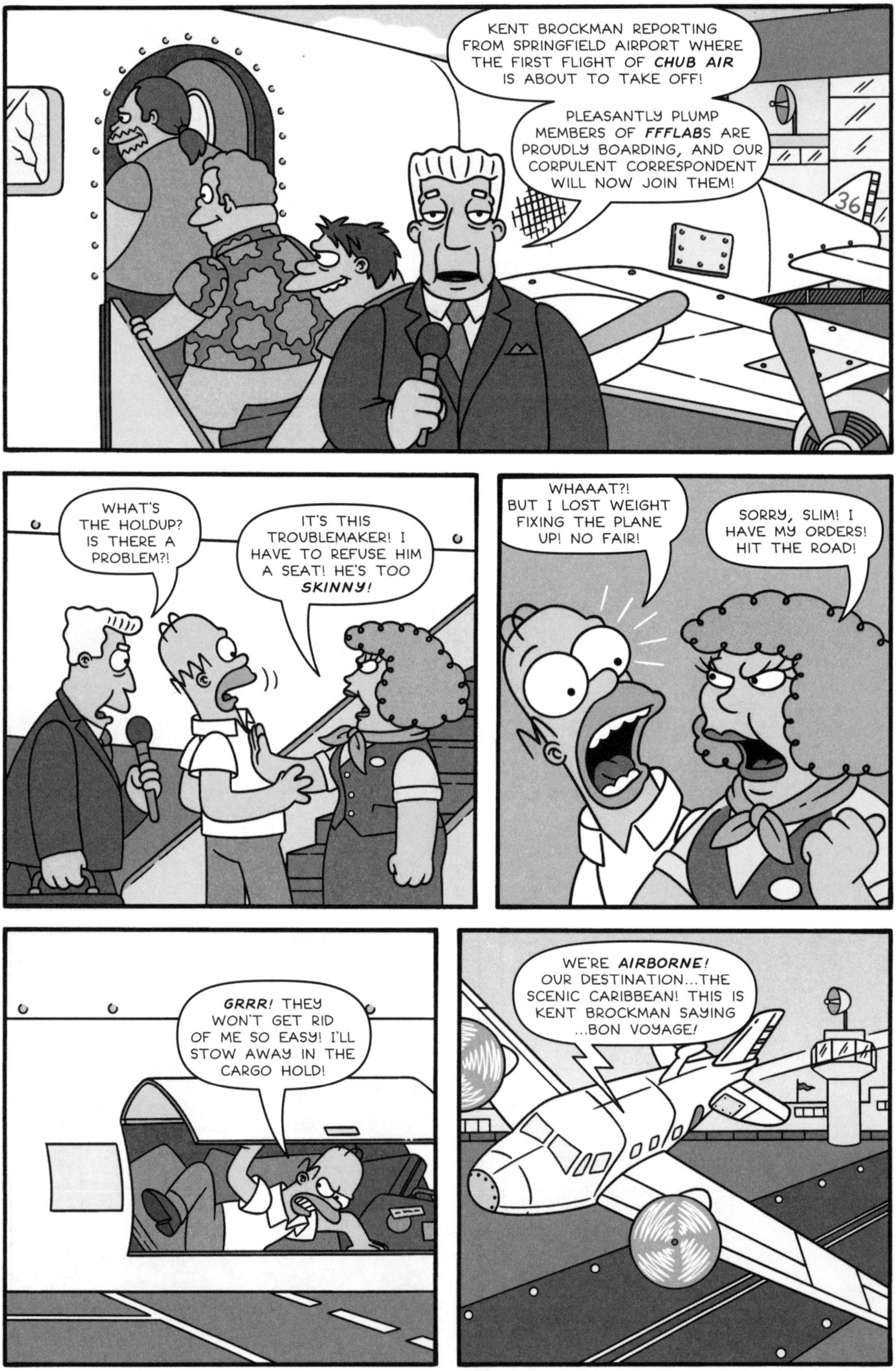
KENT BROCKMAN REPORTING FROM SPRINGFIELD AIRPORT WHERE THE FIRST FLIGHT OF **CHUB AIR** IS ABOUT TO TAKE OFF!
PLEASANTLY PLUMP MEMBERS OF **FFFLAB**S ARE PROUDLY BOARDING, AND OUR CORPULENT CORRESPONDENT WILL NOW JOIN THEM!
36
WHAT'S THE HOLDUP? IS THERE A PROBLEM?!
IT'S THIS TROUBLEMAKER! I HAVE TO REFUSE HIM A SEAT! HE'S TOO ***SKINNY!***
WHAAAT?! BUT I LOST WEIGHT FIXING THE PLANE UP! NO FAIR!
SORRY, SLIM! I HAVE MY ORDERS! HIT THE ROAD!
GRRR! THEY WON'T GET RID OF ME SO EASY! I'LL STOW AWAY IN THE CARGO HOLD!
WE'RE ***AIRBORNE!*** OUR DESTINATION...THE SCENIC CARIBBEAN! THIS IS KENT BROCKMAN SAYING ...BON VOYAGE!

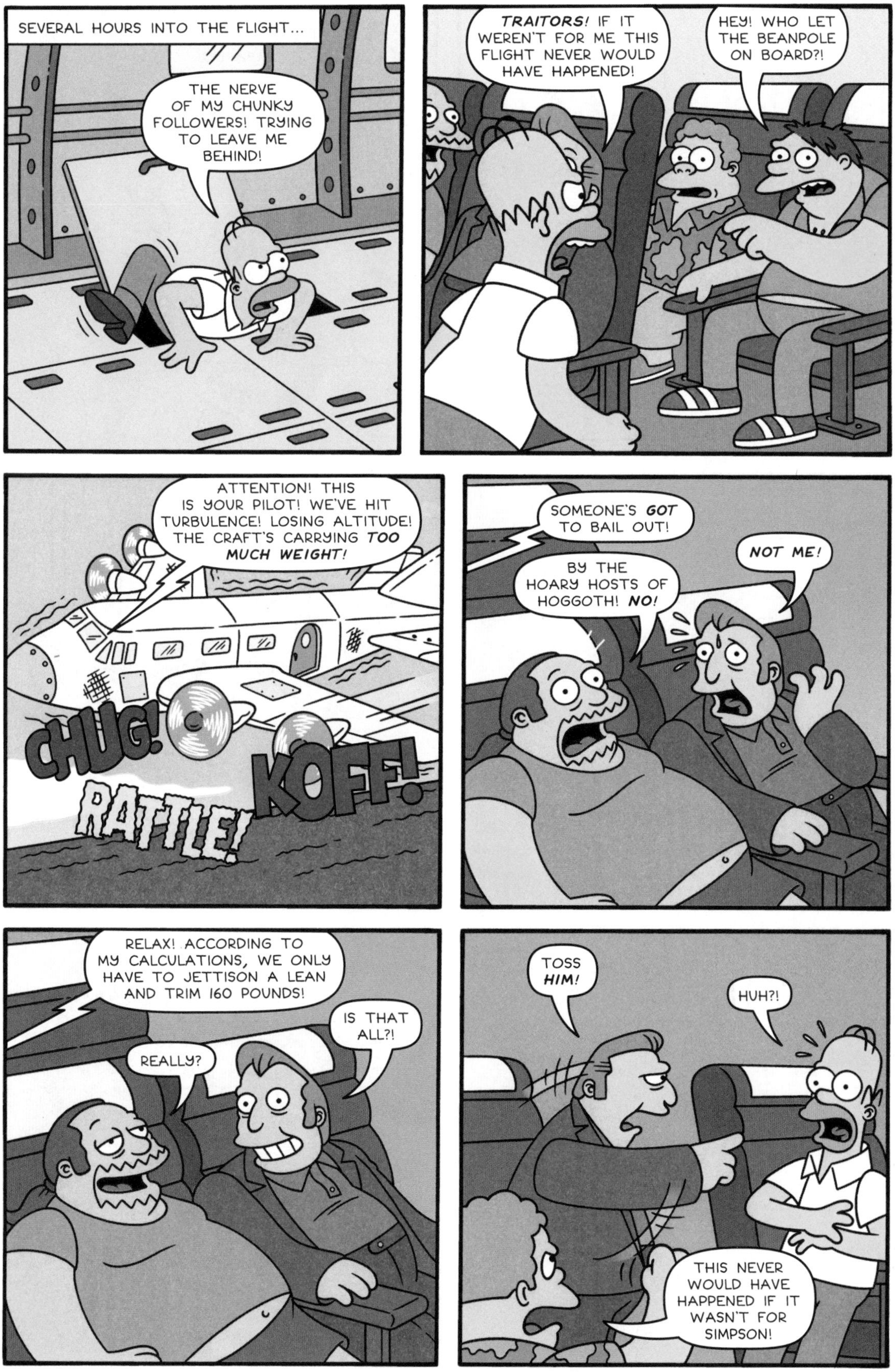
SEVERAL HOURS INTO THE FLIGHT...
THE NERVE OF MY CHUNKY FOLLOWERS! TRYING TO LEAVE ME BEHIND!
TRAITORS! IF IT WEREN'T FOR ME THIS FLIGHT NEVER WOULD HAVE HAPPENED!
HEY! WHO LET THE BEANPOLE ON BOARD?!
ATTENTION! THIS IS YOUR PILOT! WE'VE HIT TURBULENCE! LOSING ALTITUDE! THE CRAFT'S CARRYING *TOO MUCH WEIGHT!*
CHUG!
RATTLE!
KOFF!
SOMEONE'S *GOT* TO BAIL OUT!
BY THE HOARY HOSTS OF HOGGOTH! *NO!*
NOT ME!
RELAX! ACCORDING TO MY CALCULATIONS, WE ONLY HAVE TO JETTISON A LEAN AND TRIM 160 POUNDS!
REALLY?
IS THAT ALL?!
TOSS *HIM!*
HUH?!
THIS NEVER WOULD HAVE HAPPENED IF IT WASN'T FOR SIMPSON!

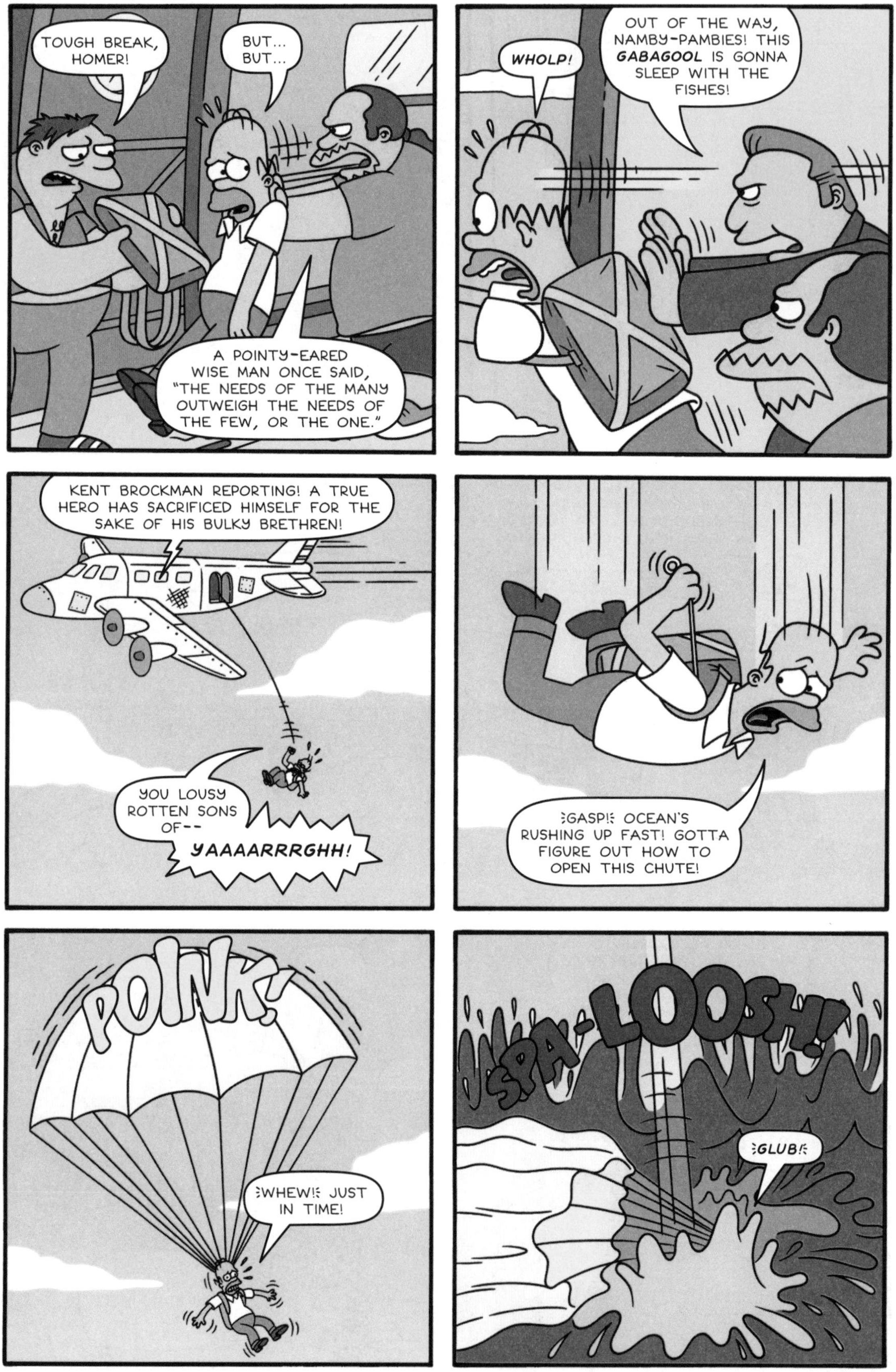
TOUGH BREAK, HOMER!
BUT... BUT...
A POINTY-EARED WISE MAN ONCE SAID, "THE NEEDS OF THE MANY OUTWEIGH THE NEEDS OF THE FEW, OR THE ONE."
WHOLP!
OUT OF THE WAY, NAMBY-PAMBIES! THIS GABAGOOL IS GONNA SLEEP WITH THE FISHES!
KENT BROCKMAN REPORTING! A TRUE HERO HAS SACRIFICED HIMSELF FOR THE SAKE OF HIS BULKY BRETHREN!
YOU LOUSY ROTTEN SONS OF--
YAAAARRRGHH!
GASP! OCEAN'S RUSHING UP FAST! GOTTA FIGURE OUT HOW TO OPEN THIS CHUTE!
POINK!
WHEW! JUST IN TIME!
SPA-LOOSH!
GLUB!

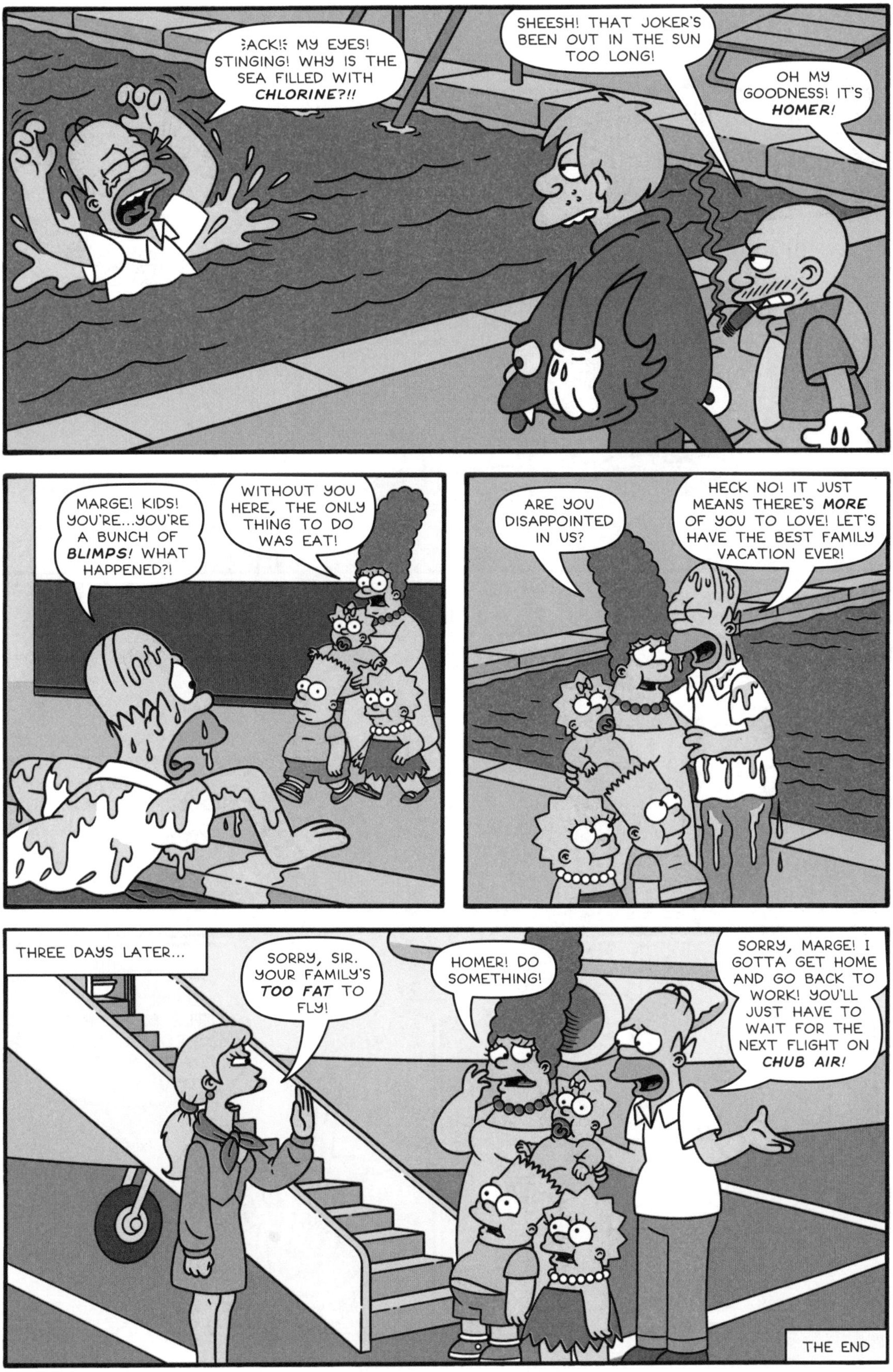
ACK!! MY EYES! STINGING! WHY IS THE SEA FILLED WITH CHLORINE?!!
SHEESH! THAT JOKER'S BEEN OUT IN THE SUN TOO LONG!
OH MY GOODNESS! IT'S HOMER!
MARGE! KIDS! YOU'RE...YOU'RE A BUNCH OF BLIMPS! WHAT HAPPENED?!
WITHOUT YOU HERE, THE ONLY THING TO DO WAS EAT!
ARE YOU DISAPPOINTED IN US?
HECK NO! IT JUST MEANS THERE'S MORE OF YOU TO LOVE! LET'S HAVE THE BEST FAMILY VACATION EVER!
THREE DAYS LATER...
SORRY, SIR. YOUR FAMILY'S TOO FAT TO FLY!
HOMER! DO SOMETHING!
SORRY, MARGE! I GOTTA GET HOME AND GO BACK TO WORK! YOU'LL JUST HAVE TO WAIT FOR THE NEXT FLIGHT ON CHUB AIR!
THE END

MR. BURNS BEARS IT ALL

DEAN RANKINE STORY & ART
KAREN BATES LETTERS
NATHAN KANE EDITOR

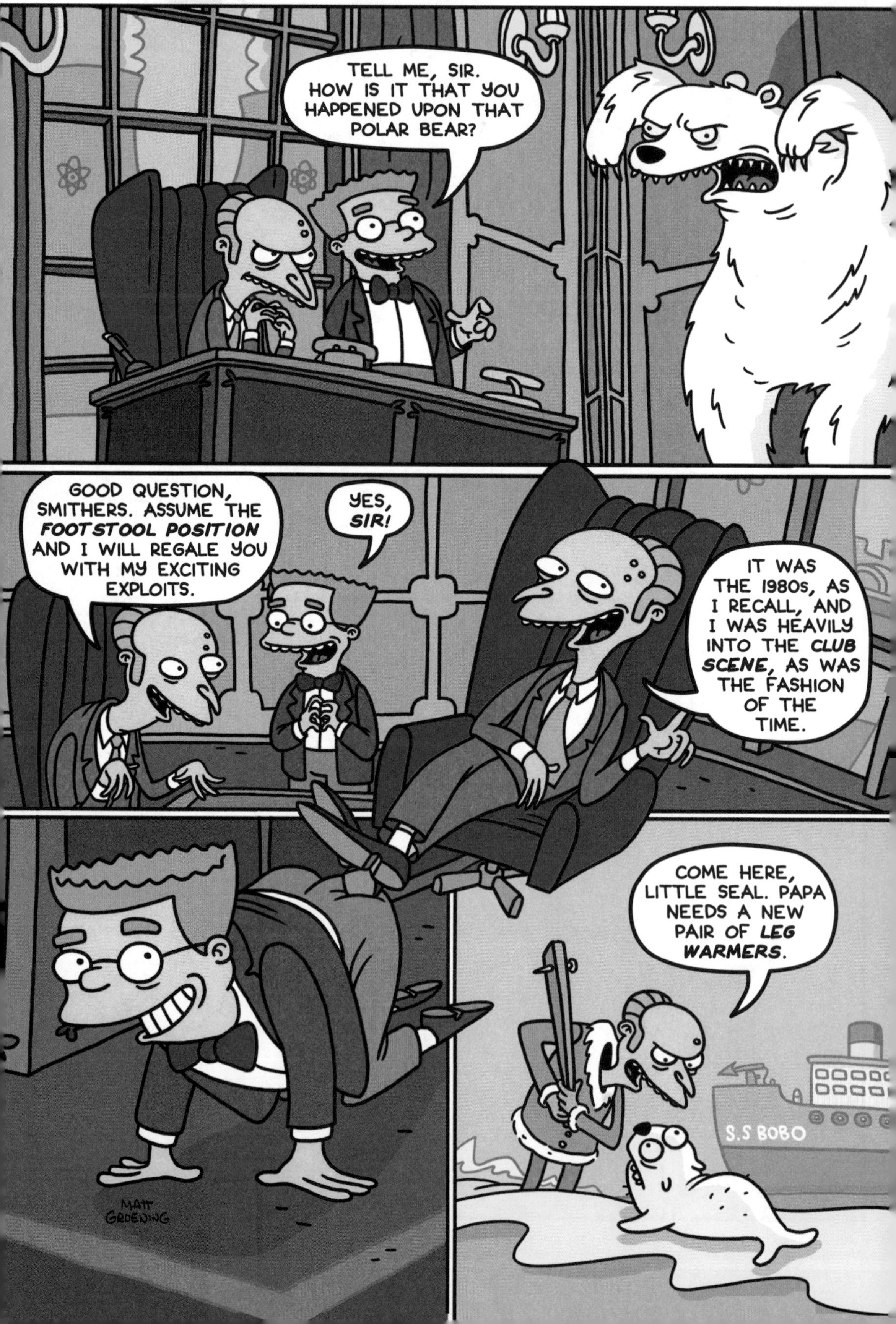
TELL ME, SIR. HOW IS IT THAT YOU HAPPENED UPON THAT POLAR BEAR?
GOOD QUESTION, SMITHERS. ASSUME THE FOOTSTOOL POSITION AND I WILL REGALE YOU WITH MY EXCITING EXPLOITS.
YES, SIR!
IT WAS THE 1980s, AS I RECALL, AND I WAS HEAVILY INTO THE CLUB SCENE, AS WAS THE FASHION OF THE TIME.
COME HERE, LITTLE SEAL. PAPA NEEDS A NEW PAIR OF LEG WARMERS.
S.S BOBO
MATT GROENING

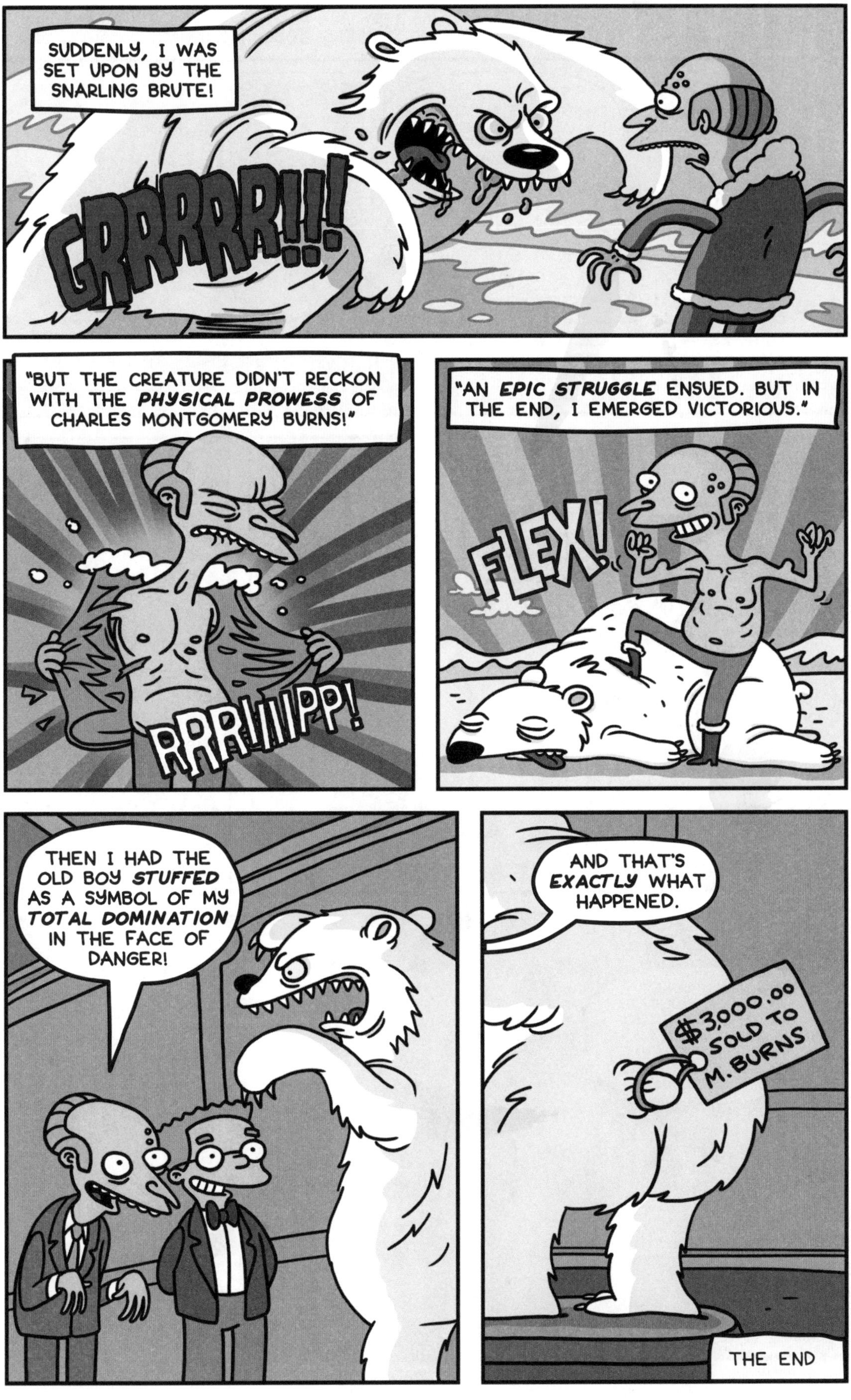
SUDDENLY, I WAS SET UPON BY THE SNARLING BRUTE!
GRRRRRR!!!
"BUT THE CREATURE DIDN'T RECKON WITH THE PHYSICAL PROWESS OF CHARLES MONTGOMERY BURNS!"
RRRIIIIPP!
"AN EPIC STRUGGLE ENSUED. BUT IN THE END, I EMERGED VICTORIOUS."
FLEX!
THEN I HAD THE OLD BOY STUFFED AS A SYMBOL OF MY TOTAL DOMINATION IN THE FACE OF DANGER!
AND THAT'S EXACTLY WHAT HAPPENED.
$3,000.00 SOLD TO M. BURNS
THE END

McBAIN in "REDUCE, REUSE, RE-VENGEANCE!"

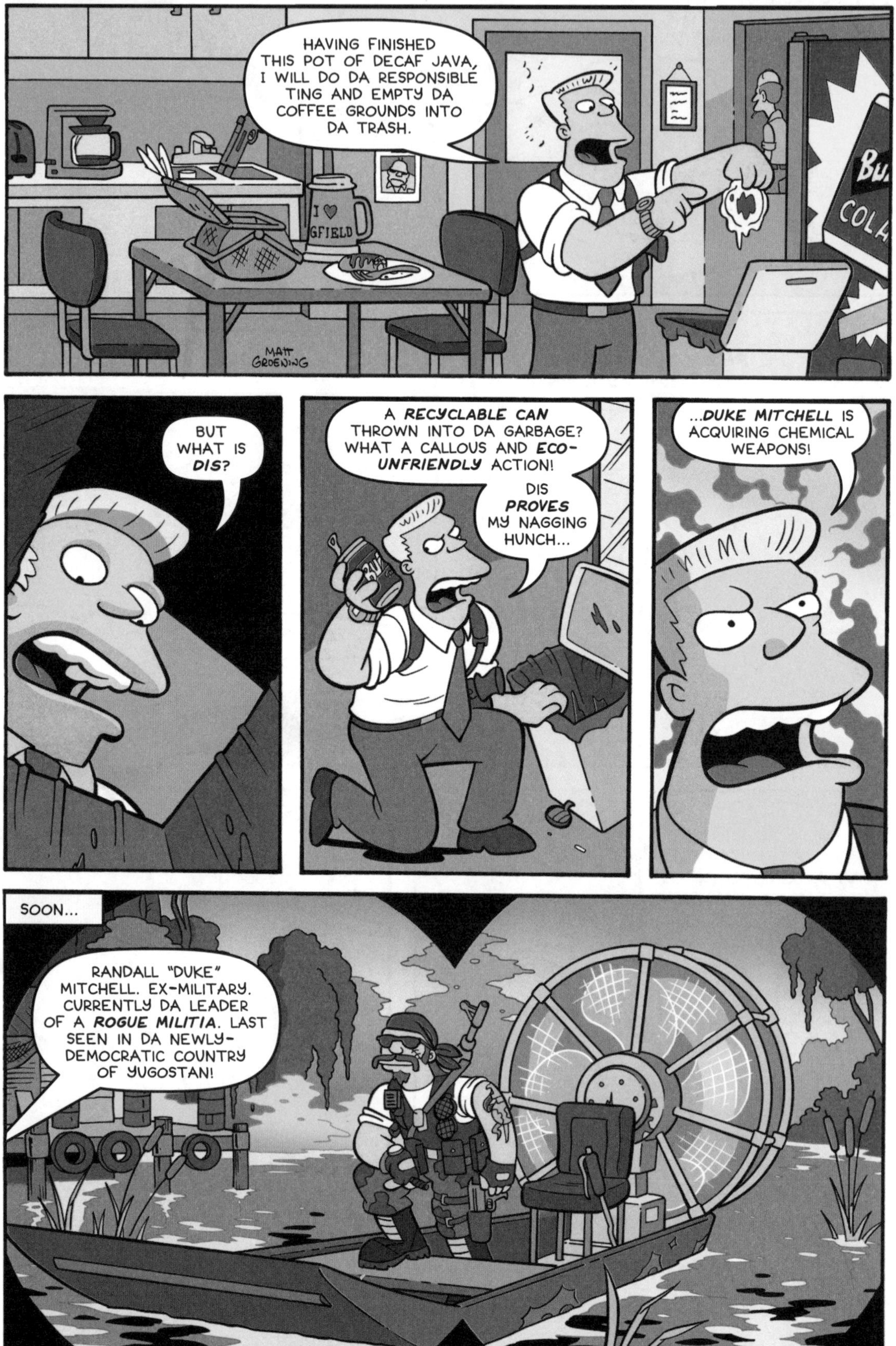
HAVING FINISHED THIS POT OF DECAF JAVA, I WILL DO DA RESPONSIBLE TING AND EMPTY DA COFFEE GROUNDS INTO DA TRASH.
MATT GROENING
BUT WHAT IS *DIS*?
A ***RECYCLABLE CAN*** THROWN INTO DA GARBAGE? WHAT A CALLOUS AND ***ECO-UNFRIENDLY*** ACTION!
DIS ***PROVES*** MY NAGGING HUNCH...
...***DUKE MITCHELL*** IS ACQUIRING CHEMICAL WEAPONS!
SOON...
RANDALL "DUKE" MITCHELL. EX-MILITARY. CURRENTLY DA LEADER OF A ***ROGUE MILITIA***. LAST SEEN IN DA NEWLY-DEMOCRATIC COUNTRY OF YUGOSTAN!

MAX DAVISON SCRIPT | ***JAMES LLOYD*** PENCILS | ***ANDREW PEPOY*** INKS | ***NATHAN HAMILL*** COLORS | ***KAREN BATES*** LETTERS | ***NATHAN KANE*** EDITOR

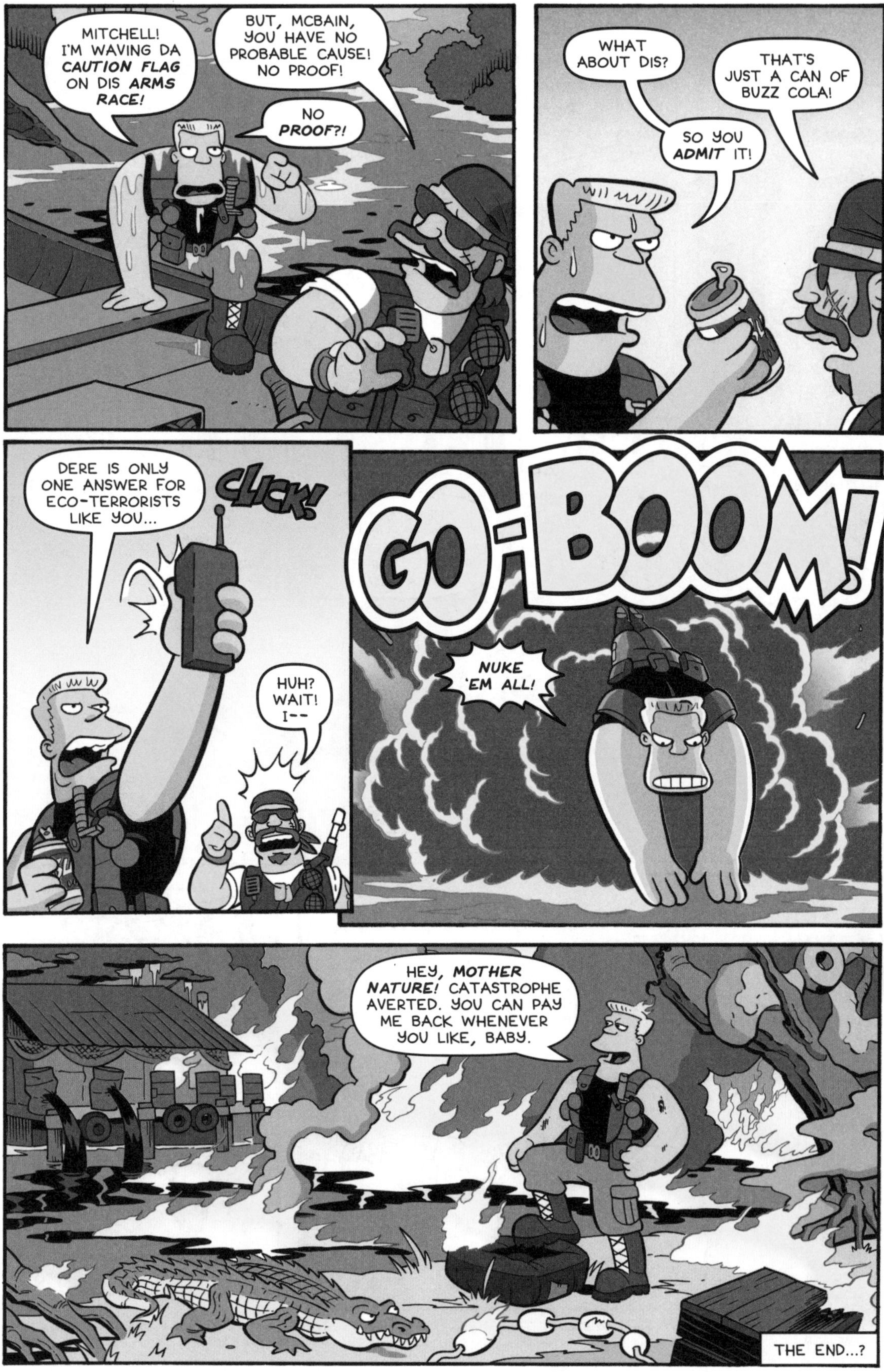

MITCHELL! I'M WAVING DA **CAUTION FLAG** ON DIS **ARMS RACE!**
BUT, MCBAIN, YOU HAVE NO PROBABLE CAUSE! NO PROOF!
NO ***PROOF?!***
WHAT ABOUT DIS?
THAT'S JUST A CAN OF BUZZ COLA!
SO YOU **ADMIT** IT!
DERE IS ONLY ONE ANSWER FOR ECO-TERRORISTS LIKE YOU...
CLICK!
HUH? WAIT! I--
GO-BOOM!
NUKE 'EM ALL!
HEY, **MOTHER NATURE!** CATASTROPHE AVERTED. YOU CAN PAY ME BACK WHENEVER YOU LIKE, BABY.
THE END...?

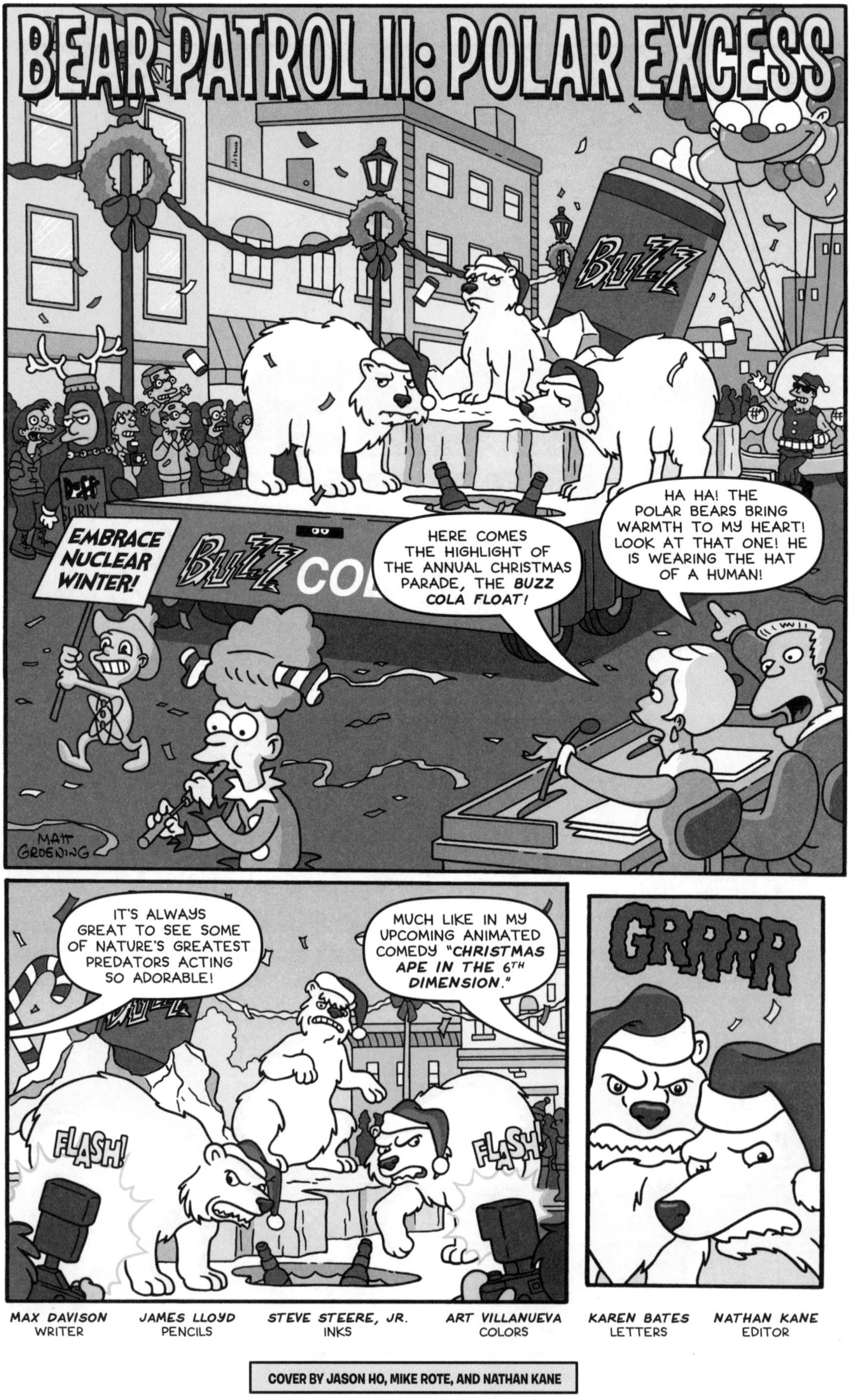
BEAR PATROL II: POLAR EXCESS
EMBRACE NUCLEAR WINTER!
HERE COMES THE HIGHLIGHT OF THE ANNUAL CHRISTMAS PARADE, THE *BUZZ COLA FLOAT!*
HA HA! THE POLAR BEARS BRING WARMTH TO MY HEART! LOOK AT THAT ONE! HE IS WEARING THE HAT OF A HUMAN!
MATT GROENING
IT'S ALWAYS GREAT TO SEE SOME OF NATURE'S GREATEST PREDATORS ACTING SO ADORABLE!
MUCH LIKE IN MY UPCOMING ANIMATED COMEDY "*CHRISTMAS APE IN THE 6TH DIMENSION*."
FLASH!
FLASH!
GRRRR

MAX DAVISON WRITER · *JAMES LLOYD* PENCILS · *STEVE STEERE, JR.* INKS · *ART VILLANUEVA* COLORS · *KAREN BATES* LETTERS · *NATHAN KANE* EDITOR

COVER BY JASON HO, MIKE ROTE, AND NATHAN KANE

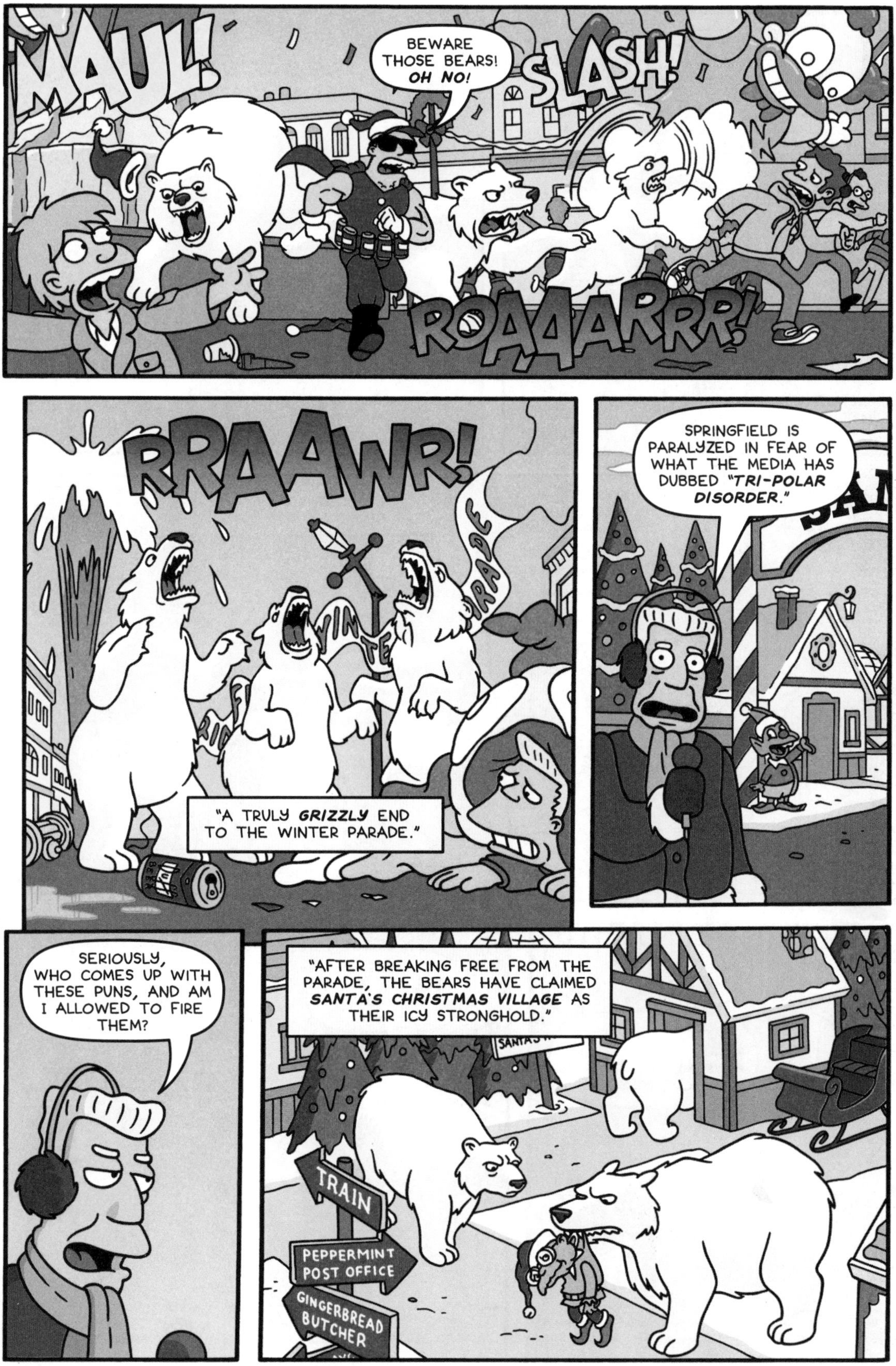
MAUL!
BEWARE THOSE BEARS! OH NO!
SLASH!
ROAAARRR!
RRAAWR!
"A TRULY GRIZZLY END TO THE WINTER PARADE."
SPRINGFIELD IS PARALYZED IN FEAR OF WHAT THE MEDIA HAS DUBBED "TRI-POLAR DISORDER."
SERIOUSLY, WHO COMES UP WITH THESE PUNS, AND AM I ALLOWED TO FIRE THEM?
"AFTER BREAKING FREE FROM THE PARADE, THE BEARS HAVE CLAIMED SANTA'S CHRISTMAS VILLAGE AS THEIR ICY STRONGHOLD."
TRAIN
PEPPERMINT POST OFFICE
GINGERBREAD BUTCHER

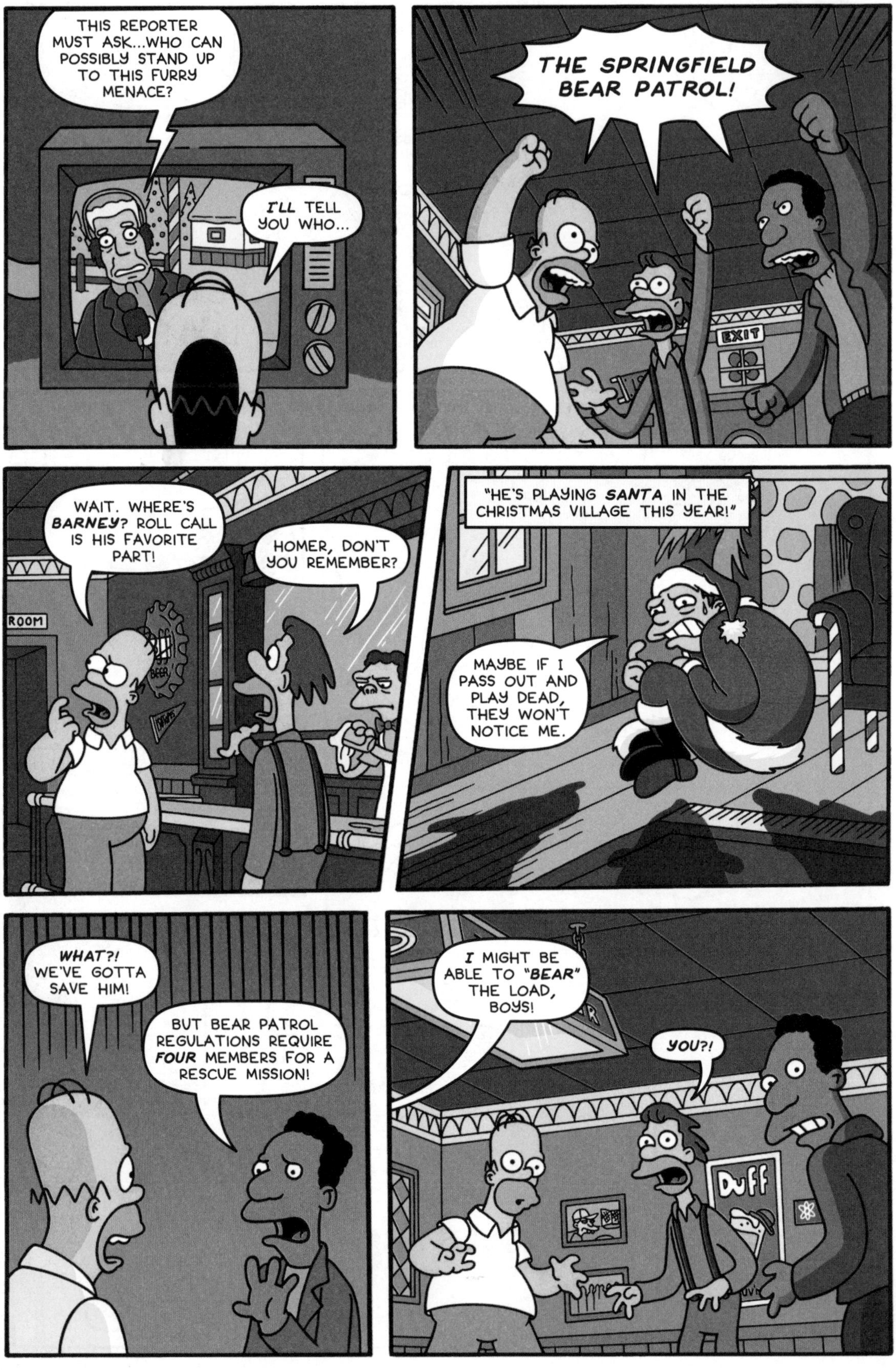
THIS REPORTER MUST ASK...WHO CAN POSSIBLY STAND UP TO THIS FURRY MENACE?
I'LL TELL YOU WHO...
THE SPRINGFIELD BEAR PATROL!
EXIT
WAIT. WHERE'S BARNEY? ROLL CALL IS HIS FAVORITE PART!
HOMER, DON'T YOU REMEMBER?
ROOM
"HE'S PLAYING SANTA IN THE CHRISTMAS VILLAGE THIS YEAR!"
MAYBE IF I PASS OUT AND PLAY DEAD, THEY WON'T NOTICE ME.
WHAT?! WE'VE GOTTA SAVE HIM!
BUT BEAR PATROL REGULATIONS REQUIRE FOUR MEMBERS FOR A RESCUE MISSION!
I MIGHT BE ABLE TO "BEAR" THE LOAD, BOYS!
YOU?!
DUFF

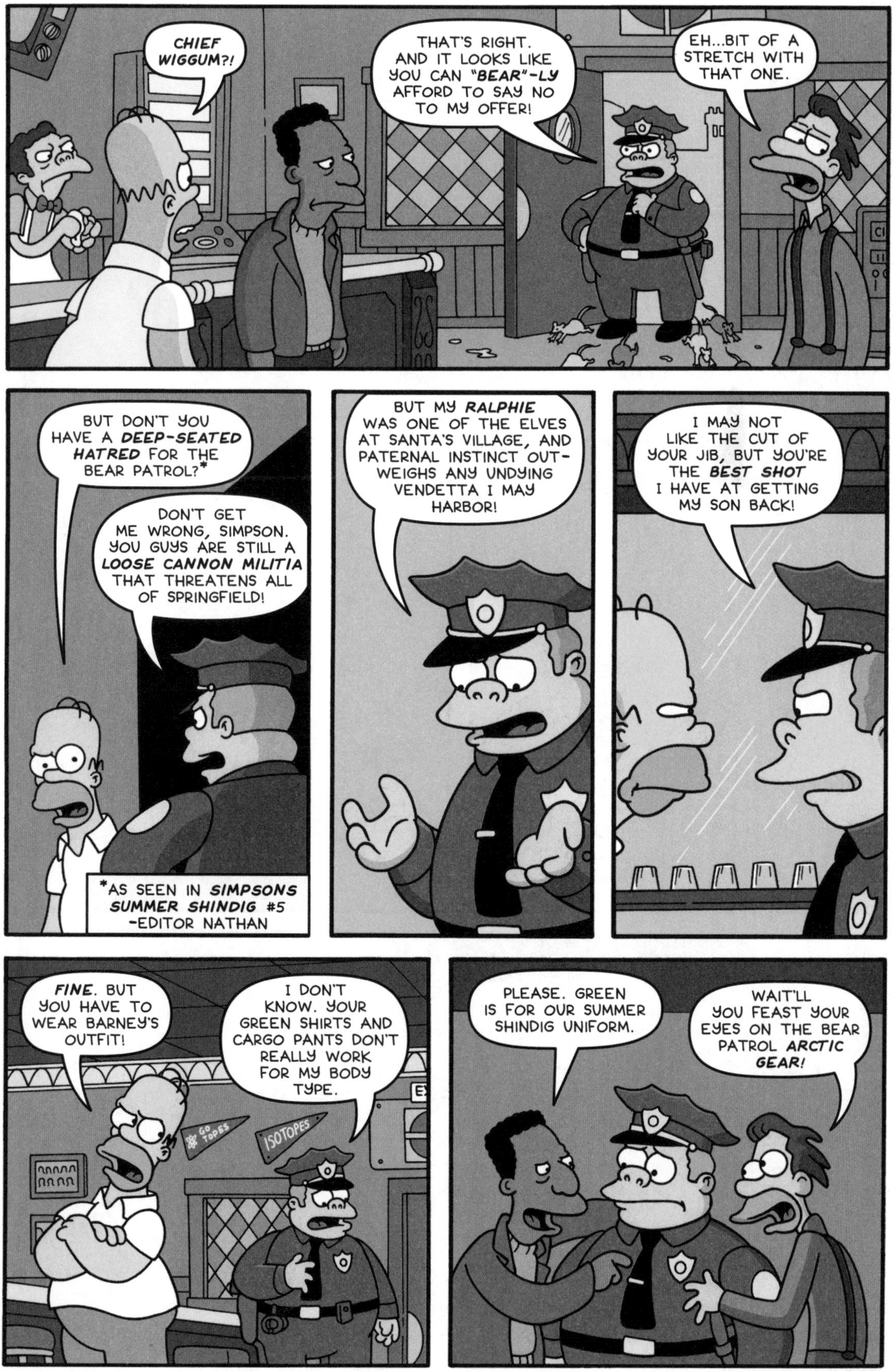
CHIEF WIGGUM?!
THAT'S RIGHT. AND IT LOOKS LIKE YOU CAN "BEAR"-LY AFFORD TO SAY NO TO MY OFFER!
EH...BIT OF A STRETCH WITH THAT ONE.
BUT DON'T YOU HAVE A DEEP-SEATED HATRED FOR THE BEAR PATROL?*
DON'T GET ME WRONG, SIMPSON. YOU GUYS ARE STILL A LOOSE CANNON MILITIA THAT THREATENS ALL OF SPRINGFIELD!
*AS SEEN IN SIMPSONS SUMMER SHINDIG #5 -EDITOR NATHAN
BUT MY RALPHIE WAS ONE OF THE ELVES AT SANTA'S VILLAGE, AND PATERNAL INSTINCT OUTWEIGHS ANY UNDYING VENDETTA I MAY HARBOR!
I MAY NOT LIKE THE CUT OF YOUR JIB, BUT YOU'RE THE BEST SHOT I HAVE AT GETTING MY SON BACK!
FINE. BUT YOU HAVE TO WEAR BARNEY'S OUTFIT!
I DON'T KNOW. YOUR GREEN SHIRTS AND CARGO PANTS DON'T REALLY WORK FOR MY BODY TYPE.
GO TOPES
ISOTOPES
PLEASE. GREEN IS FOR OUR SUMMER SHINDIG UNIFORM.
WAIT'LL YOU FEAST YOUR EYES ON THE BEAR PATROL ARCTIC GEAR!

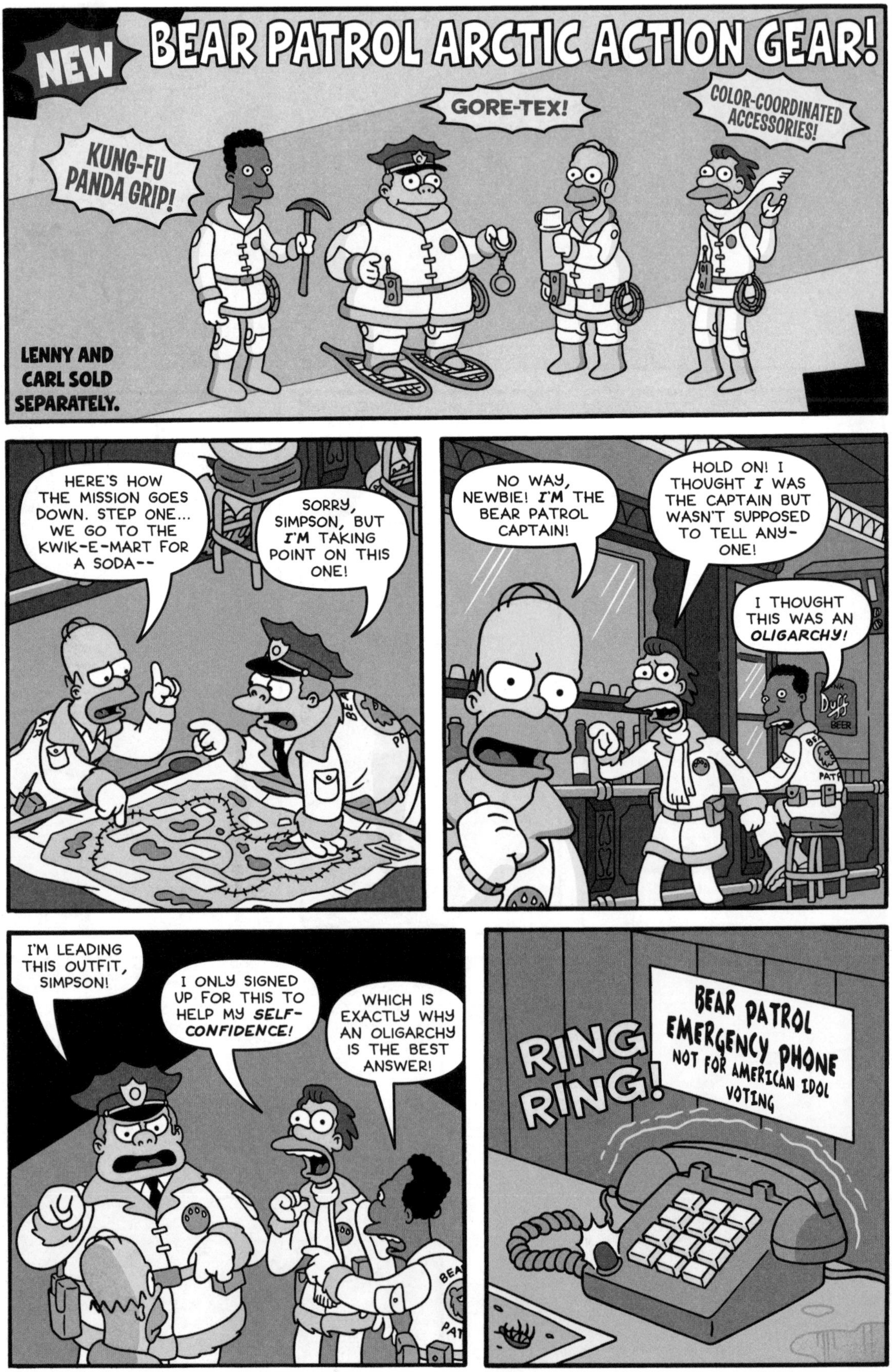

NEW
BEAR PATROL ARCTIC ACTION GEAR!
KUNG-FU PANDA GRIP!
GORE-TEX!
COLOR-COORDINATED ACCESSORIES!
LENNY AND CARL SOLD SEPARATELY.
HERE'S HOW THE MISSION GOES DOWN. STEP ONE... WE GO TO THE KWIK-E-MART FOR A SODA--
SORRY, SIMPSON, BUT I'M TAKING POINT ON THIS ONE!
NO WAY, NEWBIE! I'M THE BEAR PATROL CAPTAIN!
HOLD ON! I THOUGHT I WAS THE CAPTAIN BUT WASN'T SUPPOSED TO TELL ANY-ONE!
I THOUGHT THIS WAS AN OLIGARCHY!
I'M LEADING THIS OUTFIT, SIMPSON!
I ONLY SIGNED UP FOR THIS TO HELP MY SELF-CONFIDENCE!
WHICH IS EXACTLY WHY AN OLIGARCHY IS THE BEST ANSWER!
RING RING!
BEAR PATROL EMERGENCY PHONE
NOT FOR AMERICAN IDOL VOTING

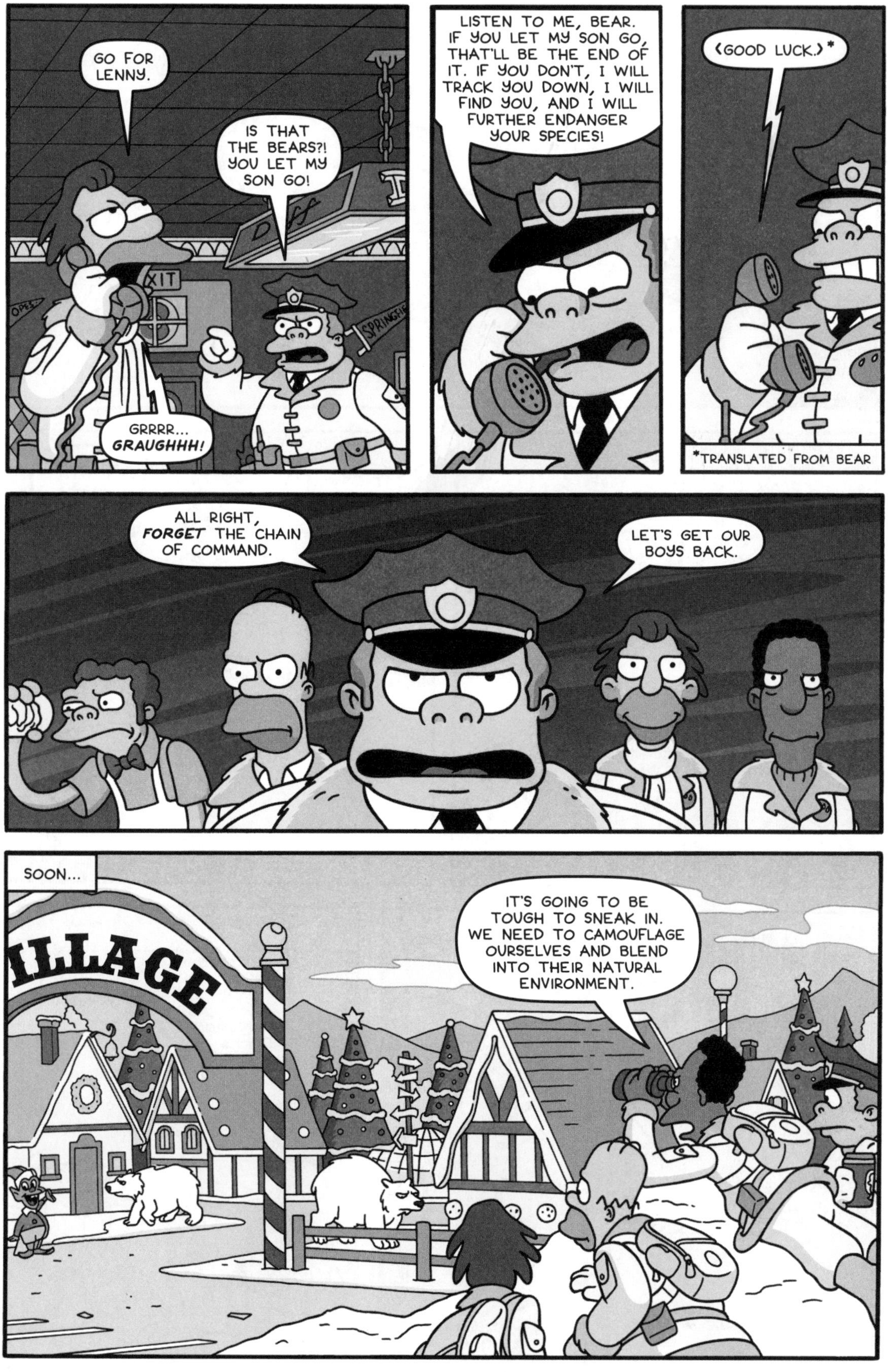

GO FOR LENNY.
IS THAT THE BEARS?! YOU LET MY SON GO!
GRRRR... GRAUGHHH!
LISTEN TO ME, BEAR. IF YOU LET MY SON GO, THAT'LL BE THE END OF IT. IF YOU DON'T, I WILL TRACK YOU DOWN, I WILL FIND YOU, AND I WILL FURTHER ENDANGER YOUR SPECIES!
‹GOOD LUCK.›*
*TRANSLATED FROM BEAR
ALL RIGHT, FORGET THE CHAIN OF COMMAND.
LET'S GET OUR BOYS BACK.
SOON...
ILLAGE
IT'S GOING TO BE TOUGH TO SNEAK IN. WE NEED TO CAMOUFLAGE OURSELVES AND BLEND INTO THEIR NATURAL ENVIRONMENT.

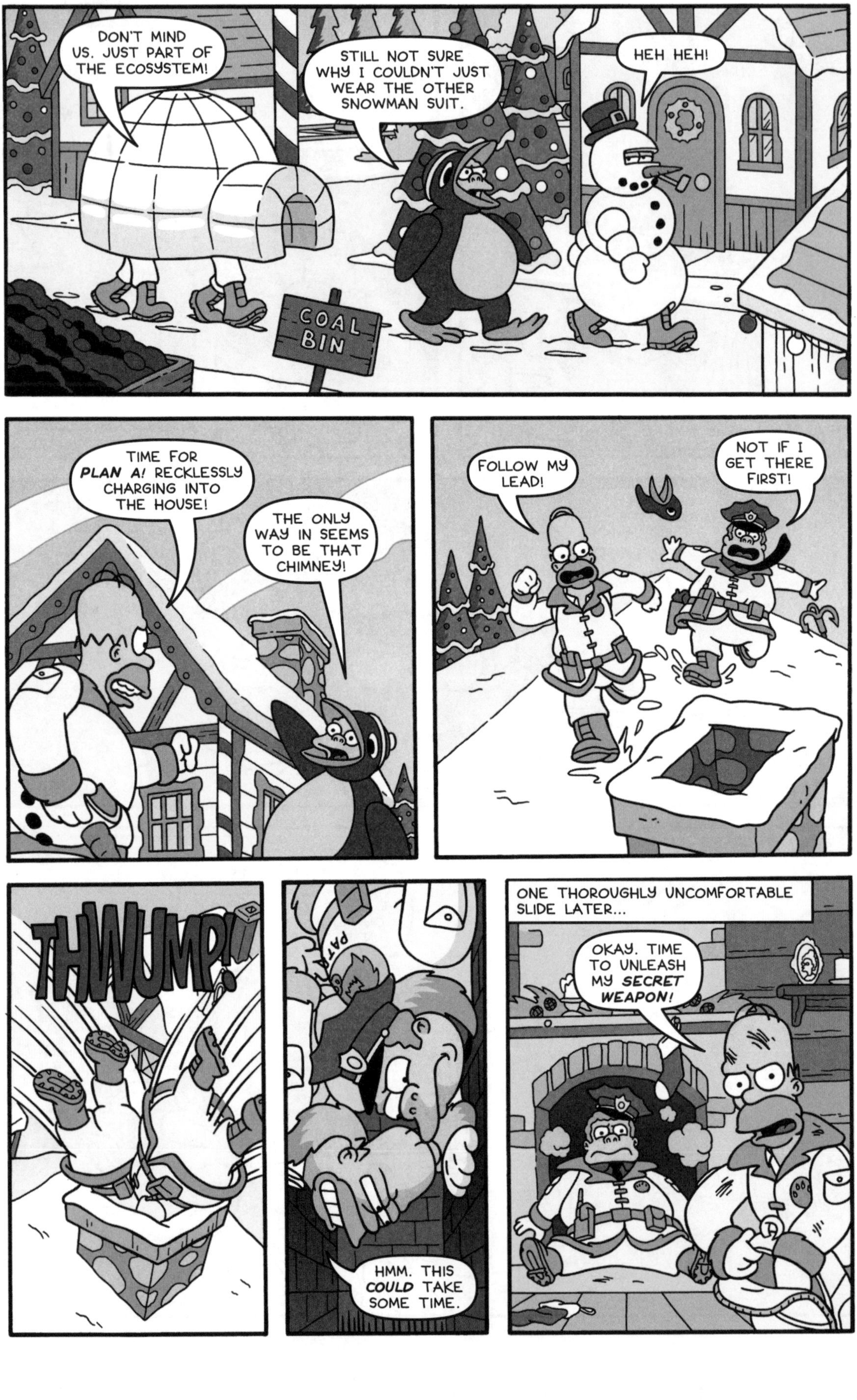
DON'T MIND US. JUST PART OF THE ECOSYSTEM!
STILL NOT SURE WHY I COULDN'T JUST WEAR THE OTHER SNOWMAN SUIT.
HEH HEH!
COAL BIN
TIME FOR PLAN A! RECKLESSLY CHARGING INTO THE HOUSE!
THE ONLY WAY IN SEEMS TO BE THAT CHIMNEY!
FOLLOW MY LEAD!
NOT IF I GET THERE FIRST!
THWUMP!
HMM. THIS COULD TAKE SOME TIME.
ONE THOROUGHLY UNCOMFORTABLE SLIDE LATER...
OKAY. TIME TO UNLEASH MY SECRET WEAPON!

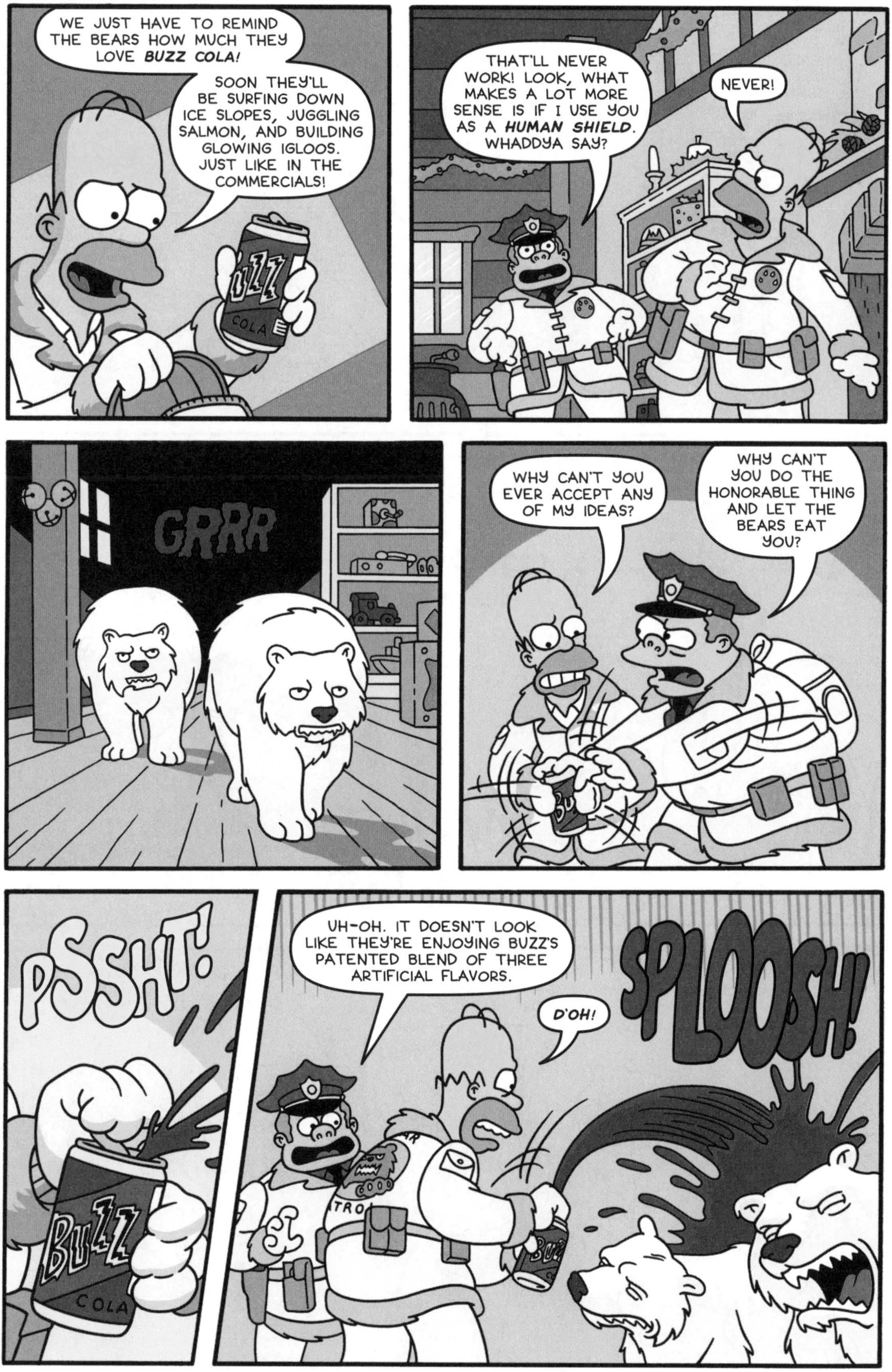
WE JUST HAVE TO REMIND THE BEARS HOW MUCH THEY LOVE *BUZZ COLA!*
SOON THEY'LL BE SURFING DOWN ICE SLOPES, JUGGLING SALMON, AND BUILDING GLOWING IGLOOS. JUST LIKE IN THE COMMERCIALS!
BUZZ
COLA
THAT'LL NEVER WORK! LOOK, WHAT MAKES A LOT MORE SENSE IS IF I USE YOU AS A ***HUMAN SHIELD***. WHADDYA SAY?
NEVER!
GRRR
WHY CAN'T YOU EVER ACCEPT ANY OF MY IDEAS?
WHY CAN'T YOU DO THE HONORABLE THING AND LET THE BEARS EAT YOU?
PSSHT!
BUZZ
COLA
UH-OH. IT DOESN'T LOOK LIKE THEY'RE ENJOYING BUZZ'S PATENTED BLEND OF THREE ARTIFICIAL FLAVORS.
D'OH!
SPLOOSH!

LENNY, PLEASE TELL ME YOUR MISSION IS GOING WELL!

NO LUCK, HOMER!

DESTROYING THEIR HABITAT WITH *GLOBAL WARMING* IS TAKING WAY TOO LONG!

HOW DOES *AL GORE* MAKE THIS SEEM SO EASY?

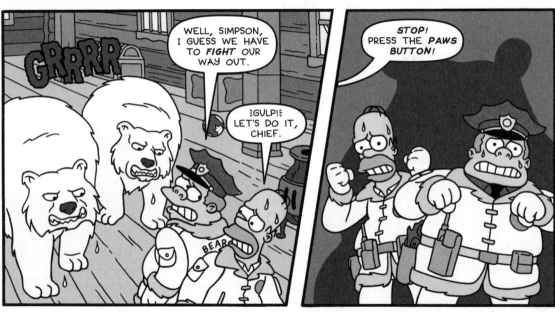

GRRRR

WELL, SIMPSON, I GUESS WE HAVE TO *FIGHT* OUR WAY OUT.

⁅GULP!⁆ LET'S DO IT, CHIEF.

BEAR

STOP! PRESS THE *PAWS* BUTTON!

WATCH OUT, RALPHIE! YOU DON'T KNOW WHAT THESE BEARS MIGHT DO!

OF COURSE I KNOW THEM! THEY'RE MY FAVORITES!

FROM THE COMMERCIALS?

BEAR

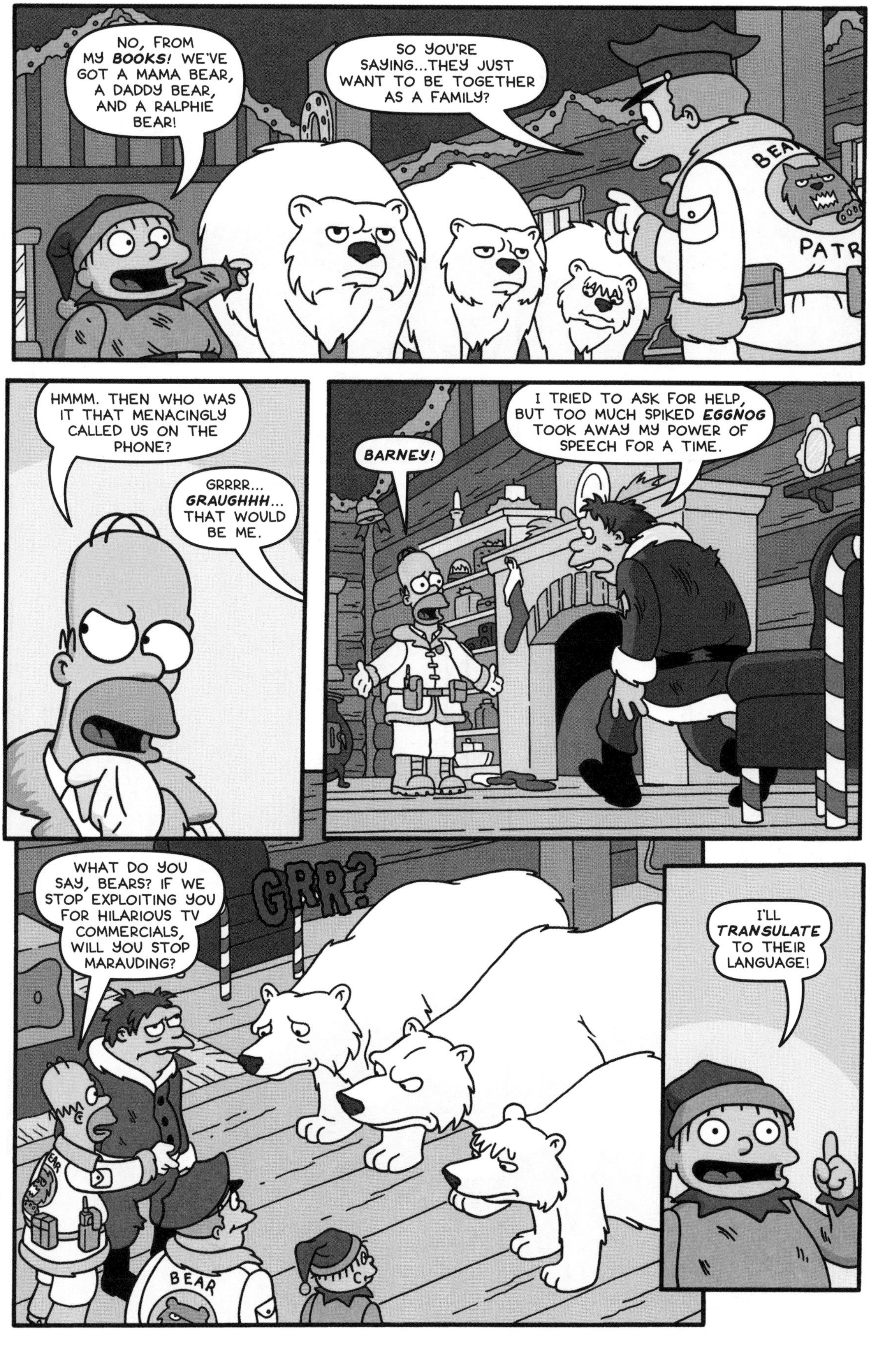

NO, FROM MY **BOOKS!** WE'VE GOT A MAMA BEAR, A DADDY BEAR, AND A RALPHIE BEAR!
SO YOU'RE SAYING...THEY JUST WANT TO BE TOGETHER AS A FAMILY?
BEAR PATR
HMMM. THEN WHO WAS IT THAT MENACINGLY CALLED US ON THE PHONE?
GRRRR... **GRAUGHHH**... THAT WOULD BE ME.
BARNEY!
I TRIED TO ASK FOR HELP, BUT TOO MUCH SPIKED **EGGNOG** TOOK AWAY MY POWER OF SPEECH FOR A TIME.
WHAT DO YOU SAY, BEARS? IF WE STOP EXPLOITING YOU FOR HILARIOUS TV COMMERCIALS, WILL YOU STOP MARAUDING?
GRR?
BEAR
I'LL ***TRANSULATE*** TO THEIR LANGUAGE!

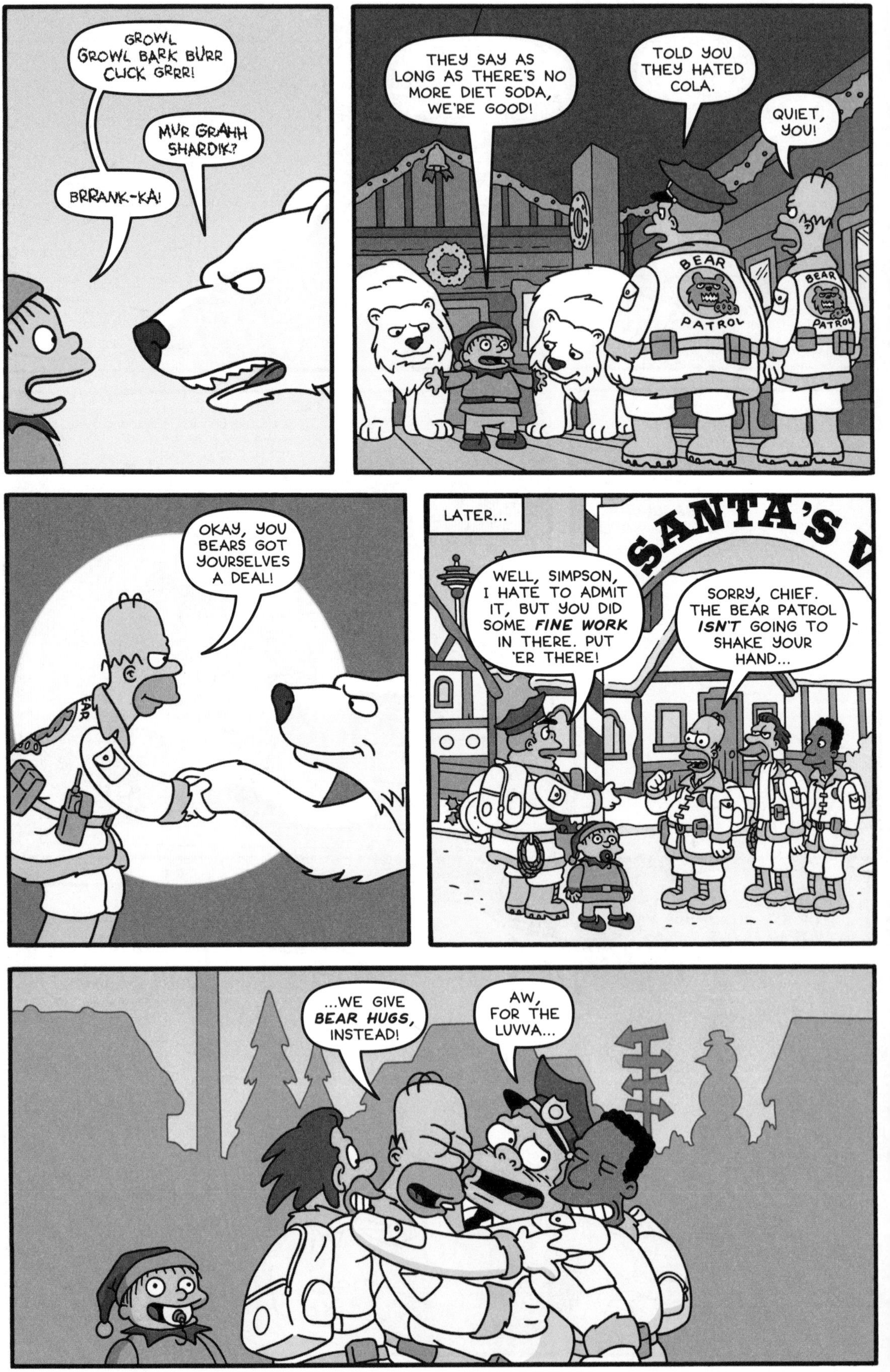
GROWL GROWL BARK BURR CLICK GRRR!
MUR GRAHH SHARDIK?
BRRANK-KA!
THEY SAY AS LONG AS THERE'S NO MORE DIET SODA, WE'RE GOOD!
TOLD YOU THEY HATED COLA.
QUIET, YOU!
BEAR PATROL
OKAY, YOU BEARS GOT YOURSELVES A DEAL!
LATER...
SANTA'S V
WELL, SIMPSON, I HATE TO ADMIT IT, BUT YOU DID SOME FINE WORK IN THERE. PUT 'ER THERE!
SORRY, CHIEF. THE BEAR PATROL ISN'T GOING TO SHAKE YOUR HAND...
...WE GIVE BEAR HUGS, INSTEAD!
AW, FOR THE LUVVA...

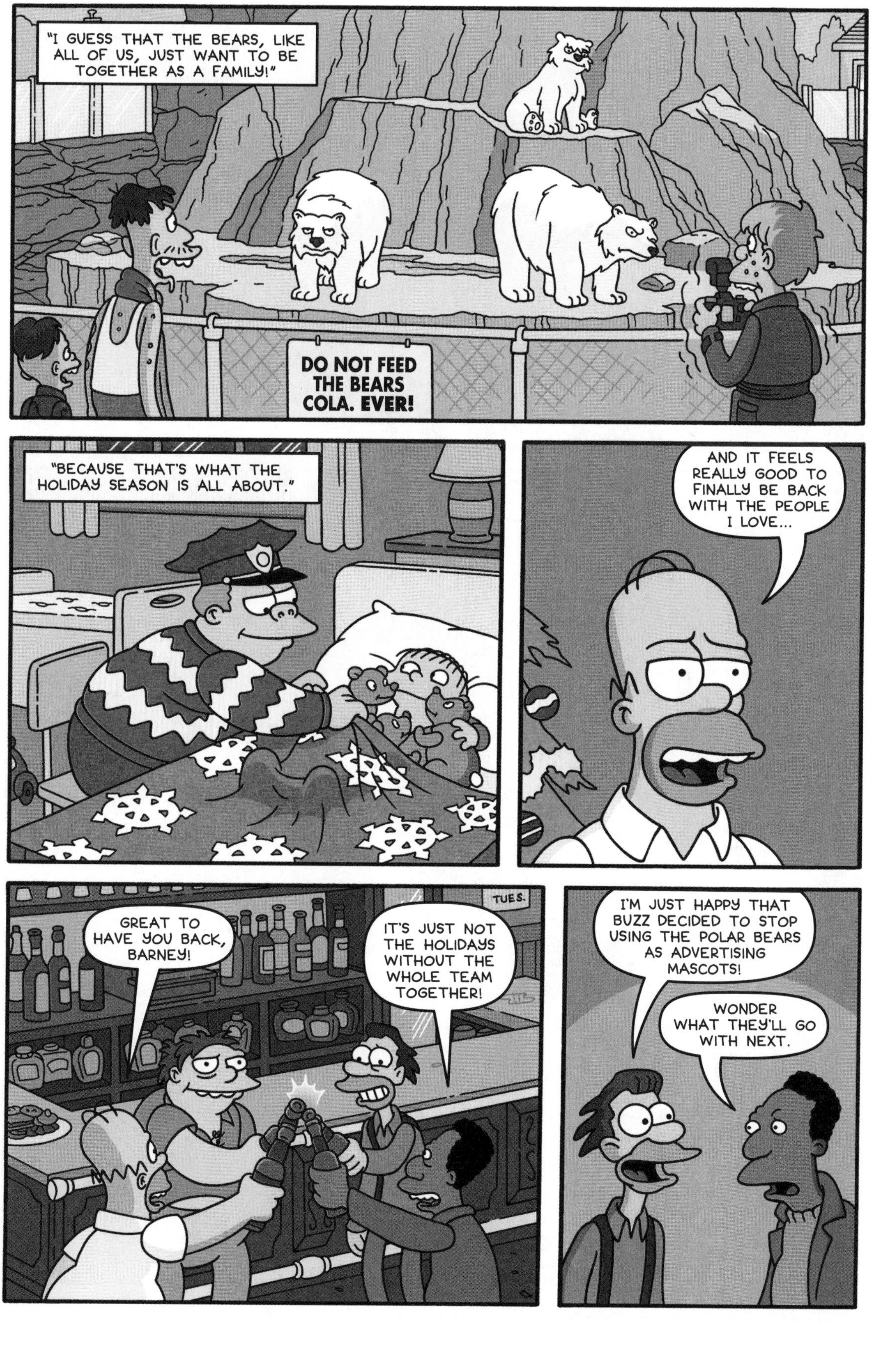
"I GUESS THAT THE BEARS, LIKE ALL OF US, JUST WANT TO BE TOGETHER AS A FAMILY!"
DO NOT FEED THE BEARS COLA. EVER!
"BECAUSE THAT'S WHAT THE HOLIDAY SEASON IS ALL ABOUT."
AND IT FEELS REALLY GOOD TO FINALLY BE BACK WITH THE PEOPLE I LOVE...
TUES.
GREAT TO HAVE YOU BACK, BARNEY!
IT'S JUST NOT THE HOLIDAYS WITHOUT THE WHOLE TEAM TOGETHER!
I'M JUST HAPPY THAT BUZZ DECIDED TO STOP USING THE POLAR BEARS AS ADVERTISING MASCOTS!
WONDER WHAT THEY'LL GO WITH NEXT.

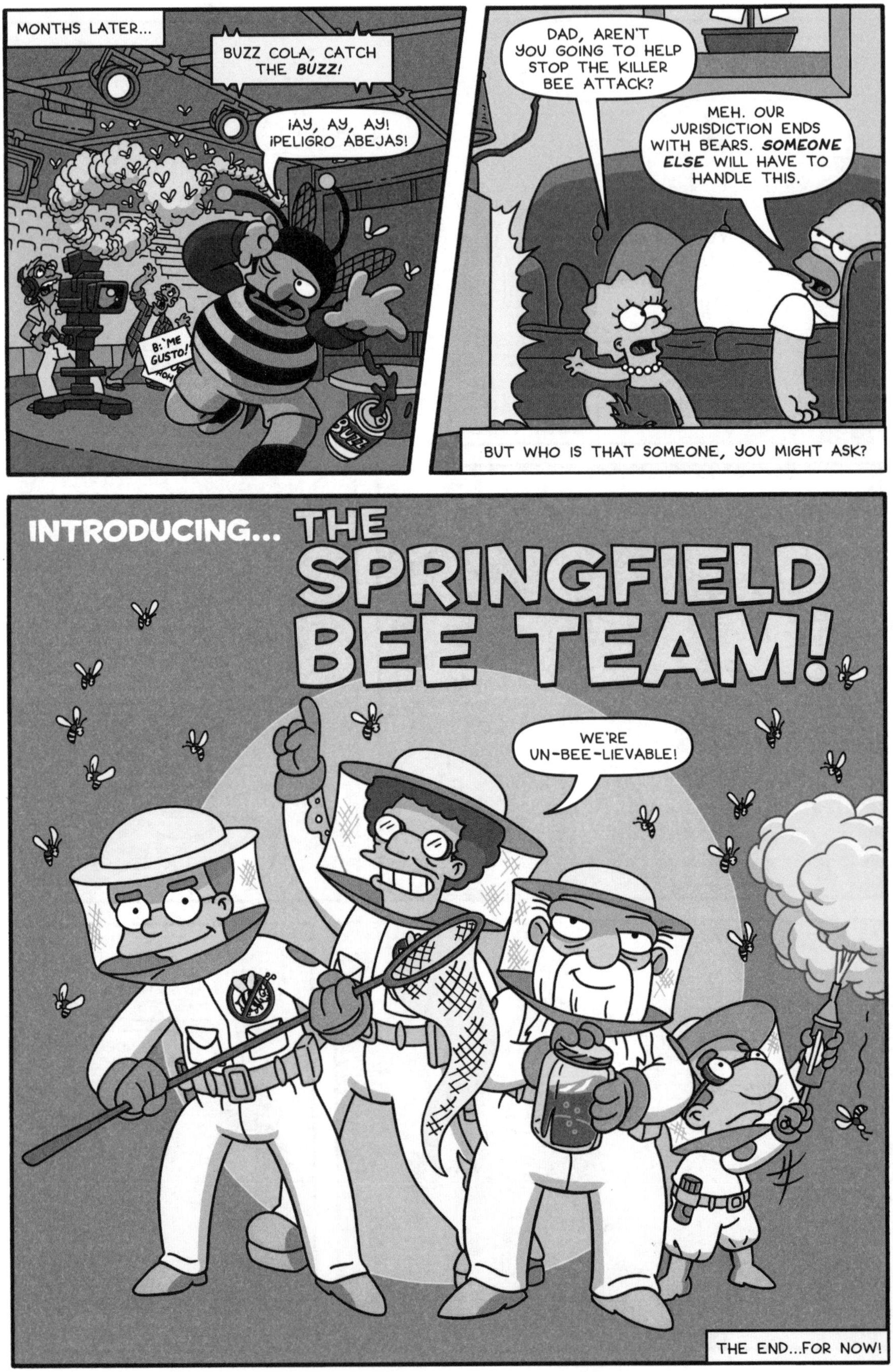

MONTHS LATER...
BUZZ COLA, CATCH THE *BUZZ!*
¡AY, AY, AY! ¡PELIGRO ABEJAS!
DAD, AREN'T YOU GOING TO HELP STOP THE KILLER BEE ATTACK?
MEH. OUR JURISDICTION ENDS WITH BEARS. ***SOMEONE ELSE*** WILL HAVE TO HANDLE THIS.
BUT WHO IS THAT SOMEONE, YOU MIGHT ASK?
INTRODUCING... THE SPRINGFIELD BEE TEAM!
WE'RE UN-BEE-LIEVABLE!
THE END...FOR NOW!

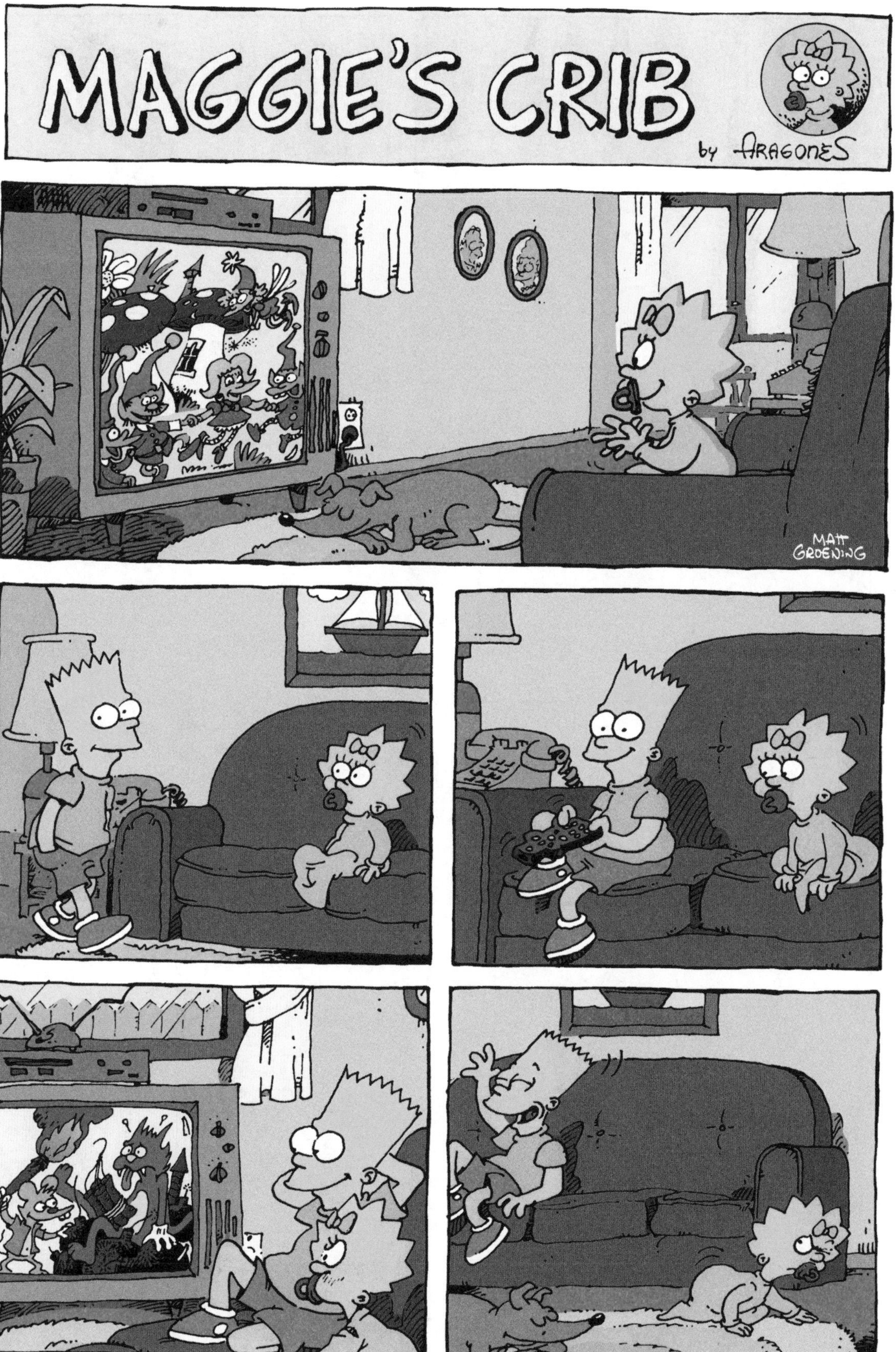
MAGGIE'S CRIB
by ARAGONES
MATT GROENING

SERGIO ARAGONÉS
STORY & ART

NATHAN HAMILL
COLORS

NATHAN KANE
EDITOR

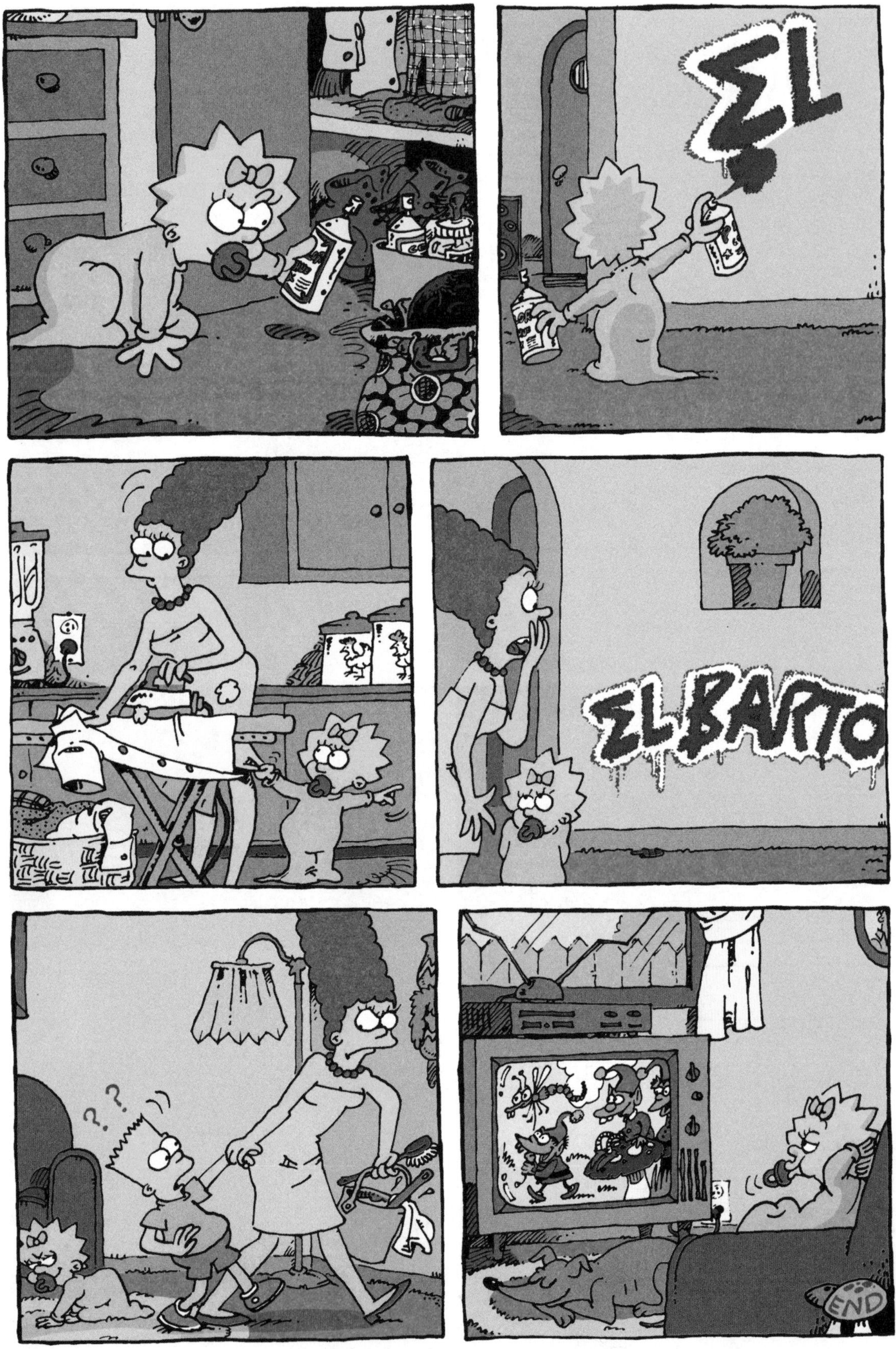
EL
EL BARTO
??
END

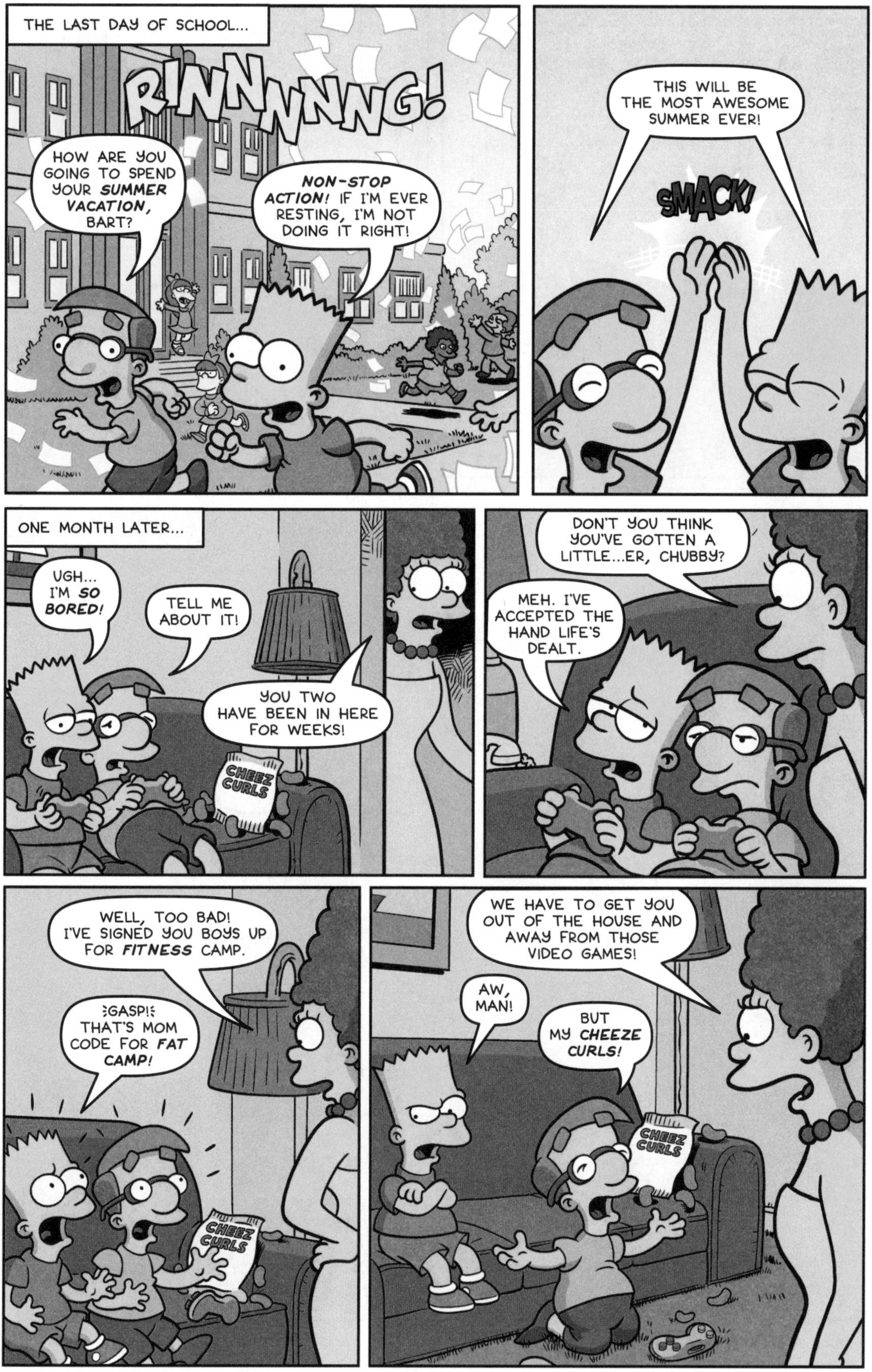
THE LAST DAY OF SCHOOL...
RINNNNNG!
HOW ARE YOU GOING TO SPEND YOUR SUMMER VACATION, BART?
NON-STOP ACTION! IF I'M EVER RESTING, I'M NOT DOING IT RIGHT!
THIS WILL BE THE MOST AWESOME SUMMER EVER!
SMACK!
ONE MONTH LATER...
UGH... I'M SO BORED!
TELL ME ABOUT IT!
YOU TWO HAVE BEEN IN HERE FOR WEEKS!
CHEEZ CURLS
DON'T YOU THINK YOU'VE GOTTEN A LITTLE...ER, CHUBBY?
MEH. I'VE ACCEPTED THE HAND LIFE'S DEALT.
WELL, TOO BAD! I'VE SIGNED YOU BOYS UP FOR FITNESS CAMP.
GASP! THAT'S MOM CODE FOR FAT CAMP!
CHEEZ CURLS
WE HAVE TO GET YOU OUT OF THE HOUSE AND AWAY FROM THOSE VIDEO GAMES!
AW, MAN!
BUT MY CHEEZE CURLS!
CHEEZ CURLS

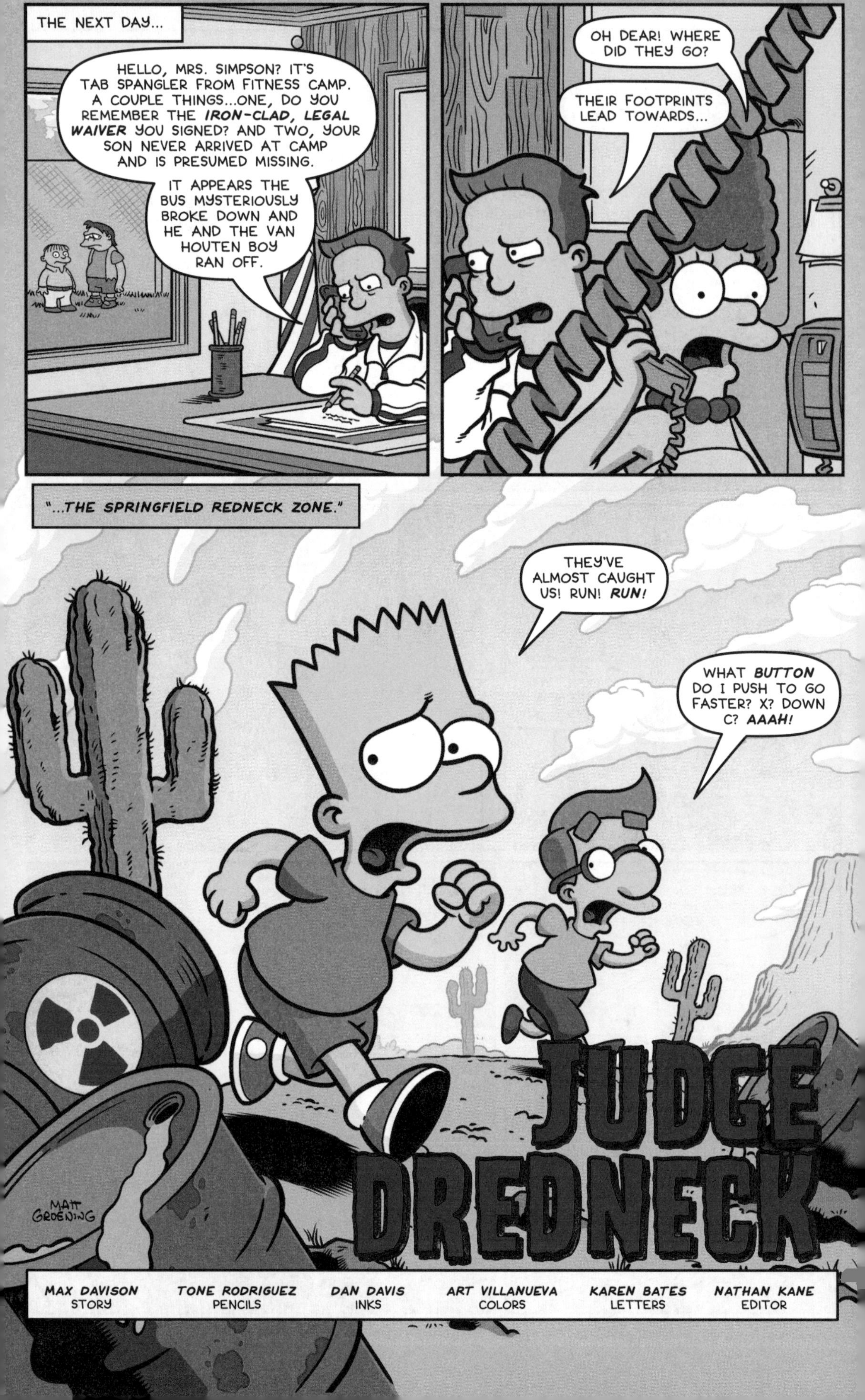
THE NEXT DAY...
HELLO, MRS. SIMPSON? IT'S TAB SPANGLER FROM FITNESS CAMP. A COUPLE THINGS...ONE, DO YOU REMEMBER THE IRON-CLAD, LEGAL WAIVER YOU SIGNED? AND TWO, YOUR SON NEVER ARRIVED AT CAMP AND IS PRESUMED MISSING.
IT APPEARS THE BUS MYSTERIOUSLY BROKE DOWN AND HE AND THE VAN HOUTEN BOY RAN OFF.
OH DEAR! WHERE DID THEY GO?
THEIR FOOTPRINTS LEAD TOWARDS...
"...THE SPRINGFIELD REDNECK ZONE."
THEY'VE ALMOST CAUGHT US! RUN! RUN!
WHAT BUTTON DO I PUSH TO GO FASTER? X? DOWN C? AAAH!
MATT GROENING
JUDGE DREDNECK
MAX DAVISON STORY
TONE RODRIGUEZ PENCILS
DAN DAVIS INKS
ART VILLANUEVA COLORS
KAREN BATES LETTERS
NATHAN KANE EDITOR

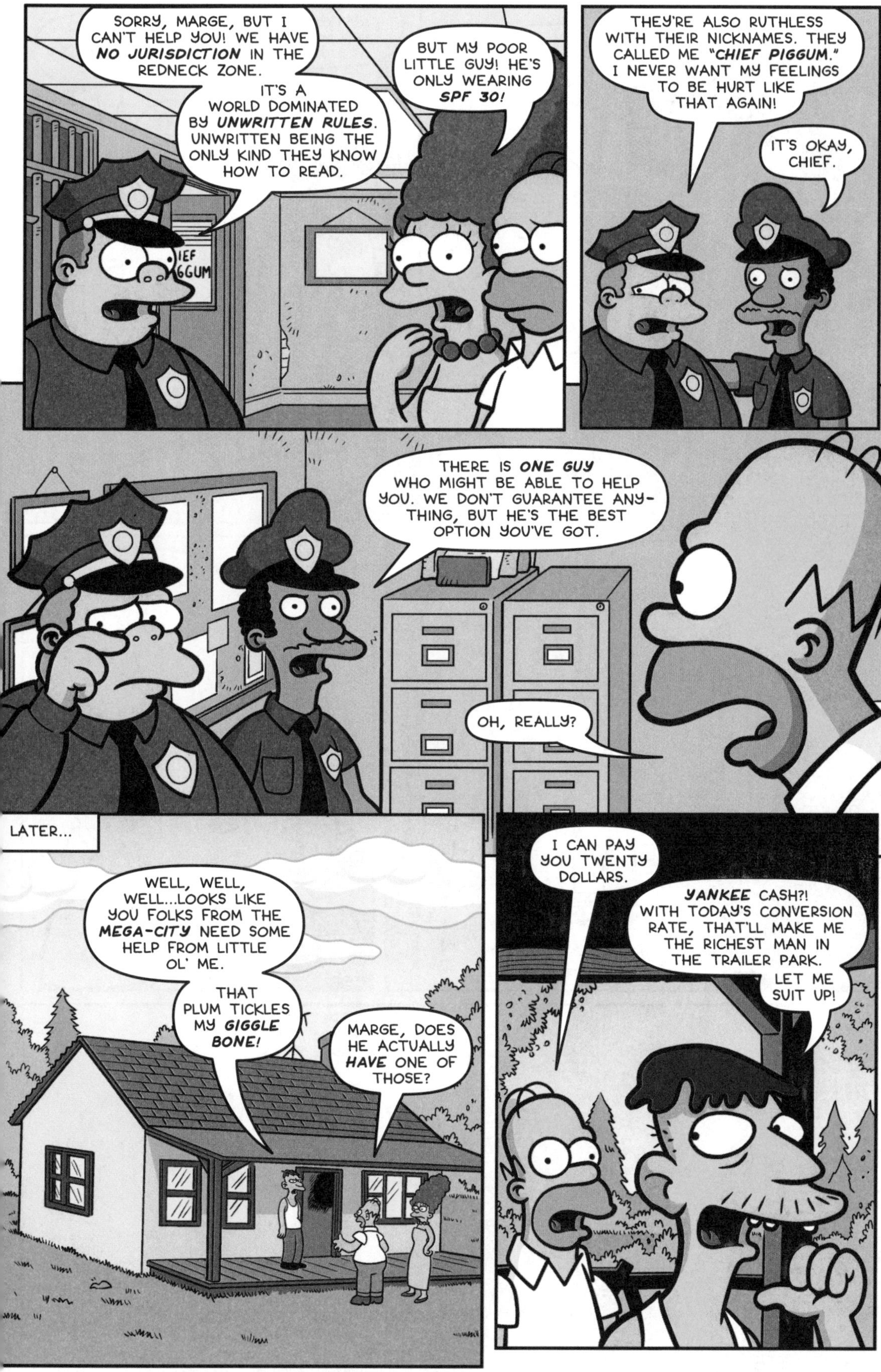
SORRY, MARGE, BUT I CAN'T HELP YOU! WE HAVE **NO JURISDICTION** IN THE REDNECK ZONE.
IT'S A WORLD DOMINATED BY **UNWRITTEN RULES**. UNWRITTEN BEING THE ONLY KIND THEY KNOW HOW TO READ.
IEF GGUM
BUT MY POOR LITTLE GUY! HE'S ONLY WEARING **SPF 30!**
THEY'RE ALSO RUTHLESS WITH THEIR NICKNAMES. THEY CALLED ME **"CHIEF PIGGUM."** I NEVER WANT MY FEELINGS TO BE HURT LIKE THAT AGAIN!
IT'S OKAY, CHIEF.
THERE IS **ONE GUY** WHO MIGHT BE ABLE TO HELP YOU. WE DON'T GUARANTEE ANYTHING, BUT HE'S THE BEST OPTION YOU'VE GOT.
OH, REALLY?
LATER...
WELL, WELL, WELL...LOOKS LIKE YOU FOLKS FROM THE **MEGA-CITY** NEED SOME HELP FROM LITTLE OL' ME.
THAT PLUM TICKLES MY **GIGGLE BONE!**
MARGE, DOES HE ACTUALLY **HAVE** ONE OF THOSE?
I CAN PAY YOU TWENTY DOLLARS.
YANKEE CASH?! WITH TODAY'S CONVERSION RATE, THAT'LL MAKE ME THE RICHEST MAN IN THE TRAILER PARK.
LET ME SUIT UP!

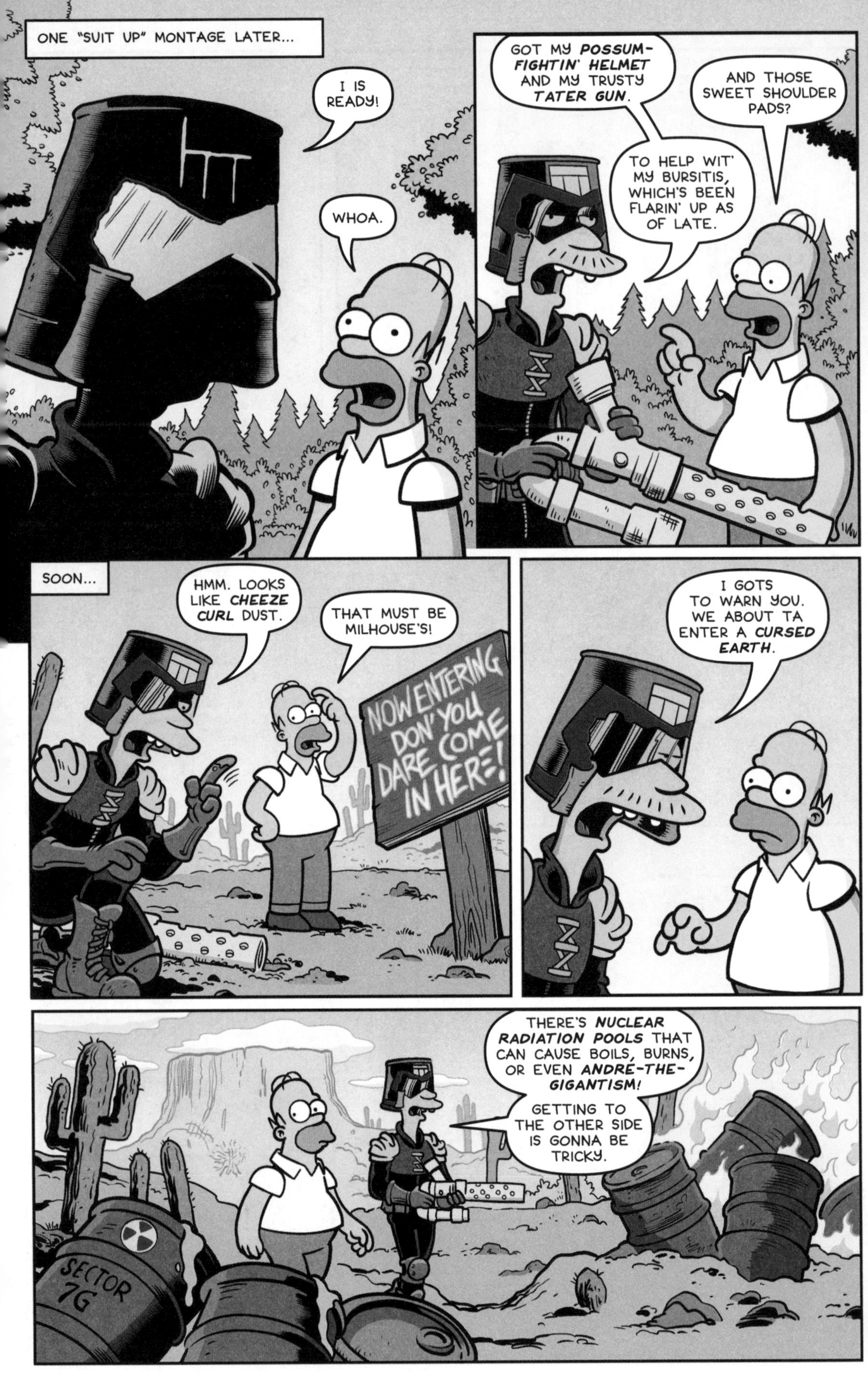
ONE "SUIT UP" MONTAGE LATER...
I IS READY!
WHOA.
GOT MY **POSSUM-FIGHTIN' HELMET** AND MY TRUSTY **TATER GUN**.
AND THOSE SWEET SHOULDER PADS?
TO HELP WIT' MY BURSITIS, WHICH'S BEEN FLARIN' UP AS OF LATE.
SOON...
HMM. LOOKS LIKE **CHEEZE CURL** DUST.
THAT MUST BE MILHOUSE'S!
NOW ENTERING DON' YOU DARE COME IN HERE!
I GOTS TO WARN YOU. WE ABOUT TA ENTER A **CURSED EARTH**.
THERE'S **NUCLEAR RADIATION POOLS** THAT CAN CAUSE BOILS, BURNS, OR EVEN **ANDRE-THE-GIGANTISM**!
GETTING TO THE OTHER SIDE IS GONNA BE TRICKY.
SECTOR 7G

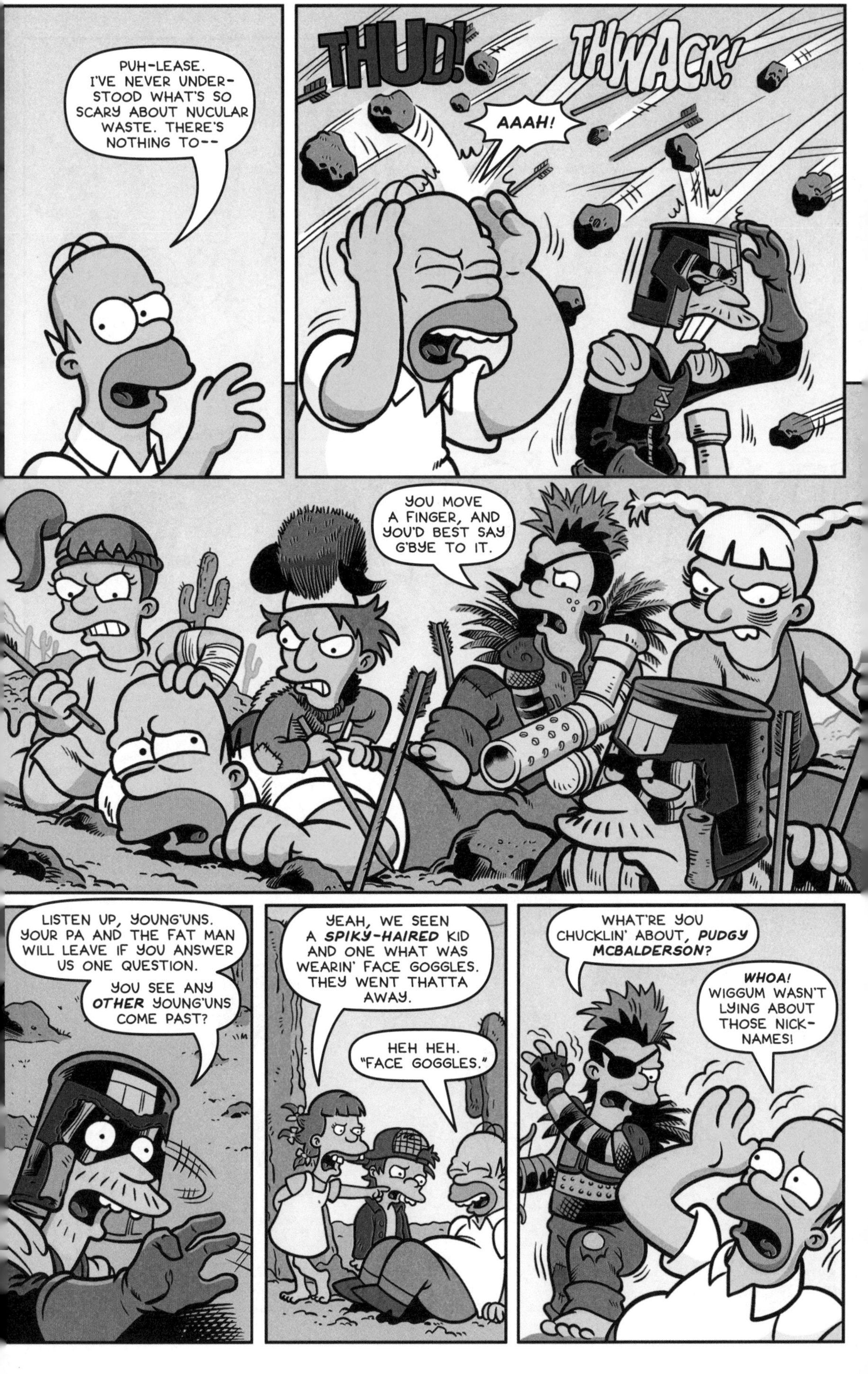
PUH-LEASE. I'VE NEVER UNDER-STOOD WHAT'S SO SCARY ABOUT NUCULAR WASTE. THERE'S NOTHING TO--
THUD!
THWACK!
AAAH!
YOU MOVE A FINGER, AND YOU'D BEST SAY G'BYE TO IT.
LISTEN UP, YOUNG'UNS. YOUR PA AND THE FAT MAN WILL LEAVE IF YOU ANSWER US ONE QUESTION.
YOU SEE ANY OTHER YOUNG'UNS COME PAST?
YEAH, WE SEEN A SPIKY-HAIRED KID AND ONE WHAT WAS WEARIN' FACE GOGGLES. THEY WENT THATTA AWAY.
HEH HEH. "FACE GOGGLES."
WHAT'RE YOU CHUCKLIN' ABOUT, PUDGY MCBALDERSON?
WHOA! WIGGUM WASN'T LYING ABOUT THOSE NICK-NAMES!

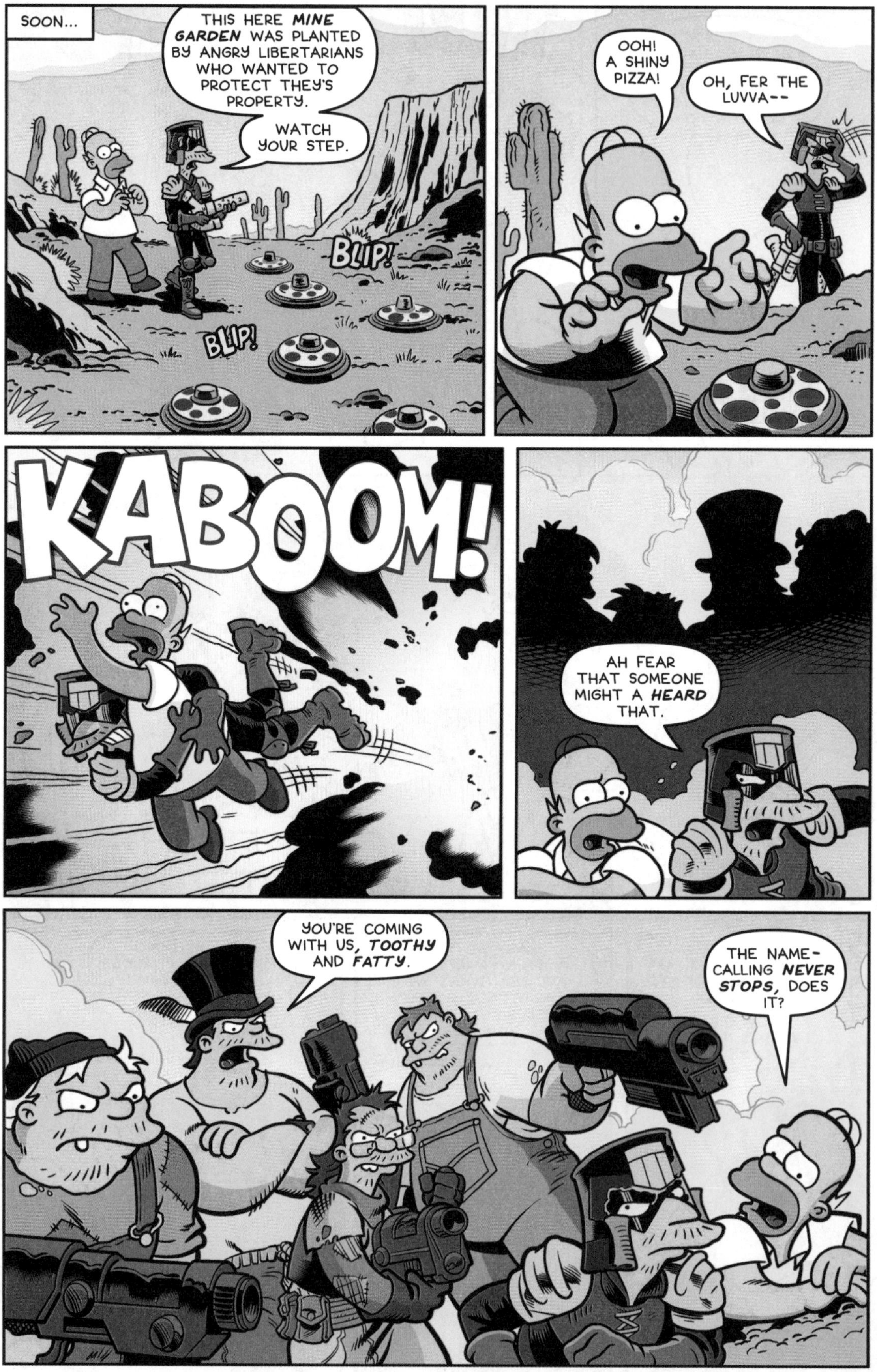
SOON...
THIS HERE *MINE GARDEN* WAS PLANTED BY ANGRY LIBERTARIANS WHO WANTED TO PROTECT THEY'S PROPERTY.
WATCH YOUR STEP.
BLIP!
BLIP!
OOH! A SHINY PIZZA!
OH, FER THE LUVVA--
KABOOM!
AH FEAR THAT SOMEONE MIGHT A *HEARD* THAT.
YOU'RE COMING WITH US, *TOOTHY* AND *FATTY*.
THE NAME-CALLING *NEVER STOPS*, DOES IT?

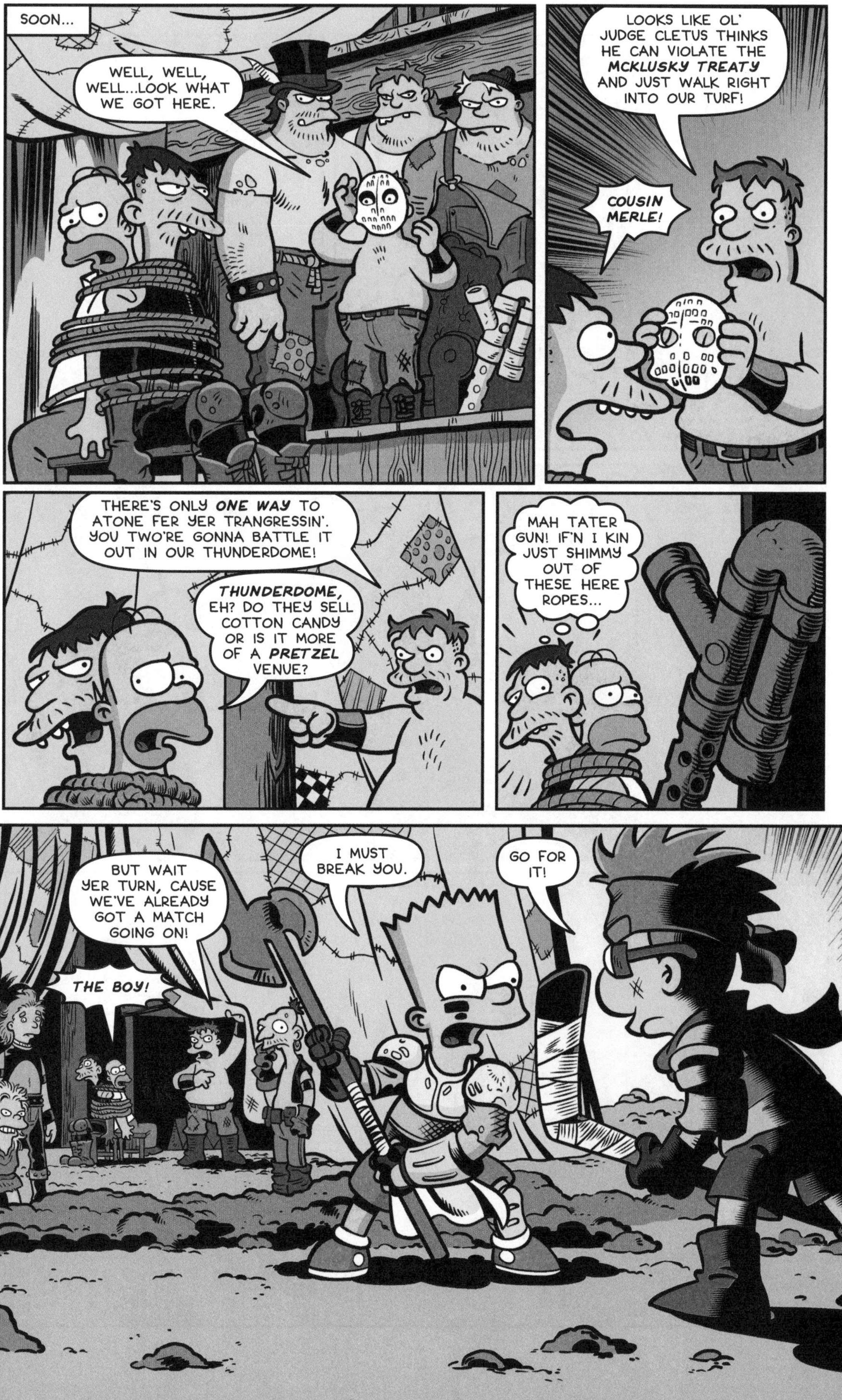
SOON...
WELL, WELL, WELL...LOOK WHAT WE GOT HERE.
LOOKS LIKE OL' JUDGE CLETUS THINKS HE CAN VIOLATE THE MCKLUSKY TREATY AND JUST WALK RIGHT INTO OUR TURF!
COUSIN MERLE!
THERE'S ONLY ONE WAY TO ATONE FER YER TRANGRESSIN'. YOU TWO'RE GONNA BATTLE IT OUT IN OUR THUNDERDOME!
THUNDERDOME, EH? DO THEY SELL COTTON CANDY OR IS IT MORE OF A PRETZEL VENUE?
MAH TATER GUN! IF'N I KIN JUST SHIMMY OUT OF THESE HERE ROPES...
BUT WAIT YER TURN, CAUSE WE'VE ALREADY GOT A MATCH GOING ON!
THE BOY!
I MUST BREAK YOU.
GO FOR IT!

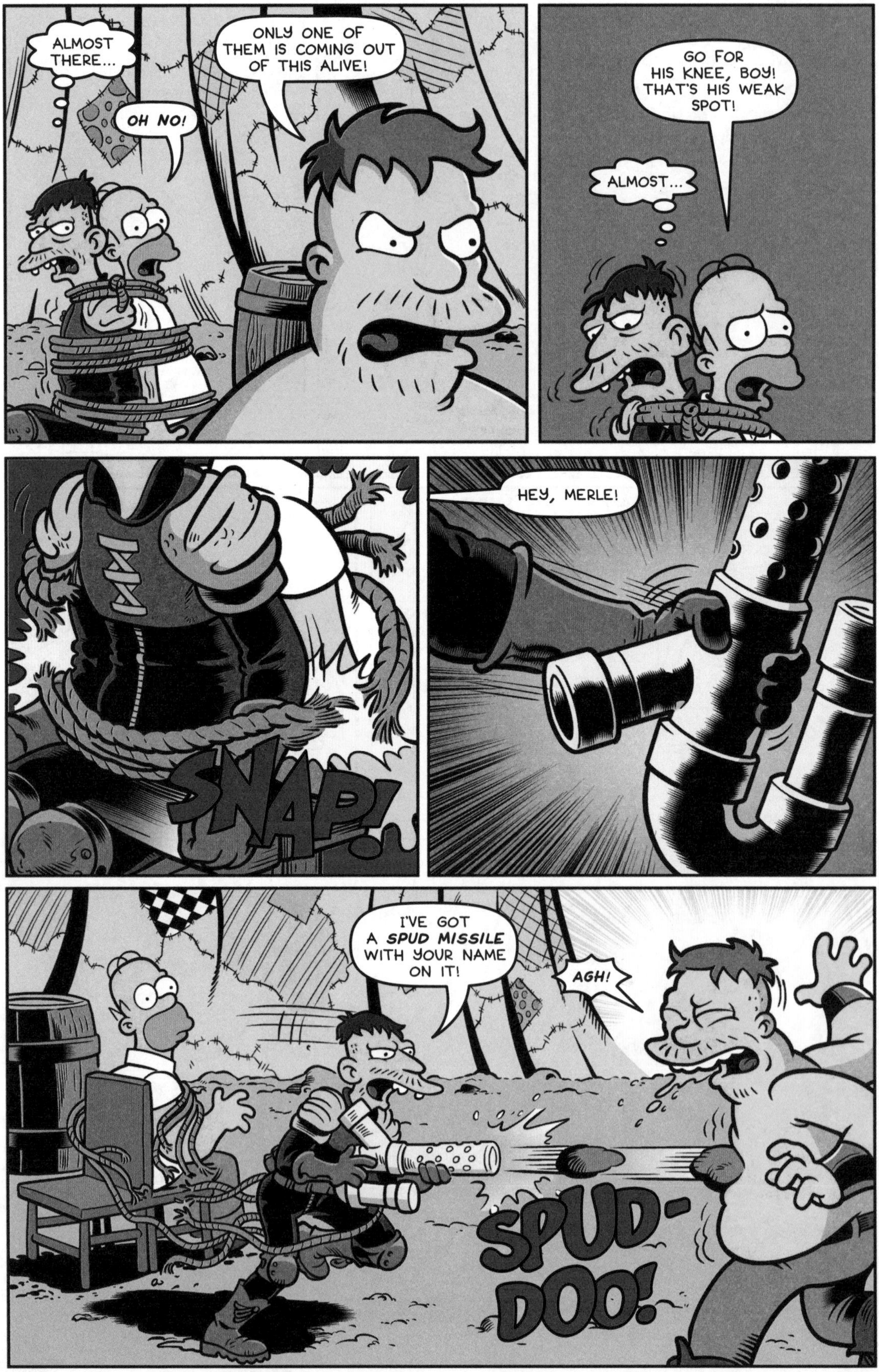
ALMOST THERE...
OH NO!
ONLY ONE OF THEM IS COMING OUT OF THIS ALIVE!
GO FOR HIS KNEE, BOY! THAT'S HIS WEAK SPOT!
ALMOST...
SNAP!
HEY, MERLE!
I'VE GOT A SPUD MISSILE WITH YOUR NAME ON IT!
AGH!
SPUD-DOO!

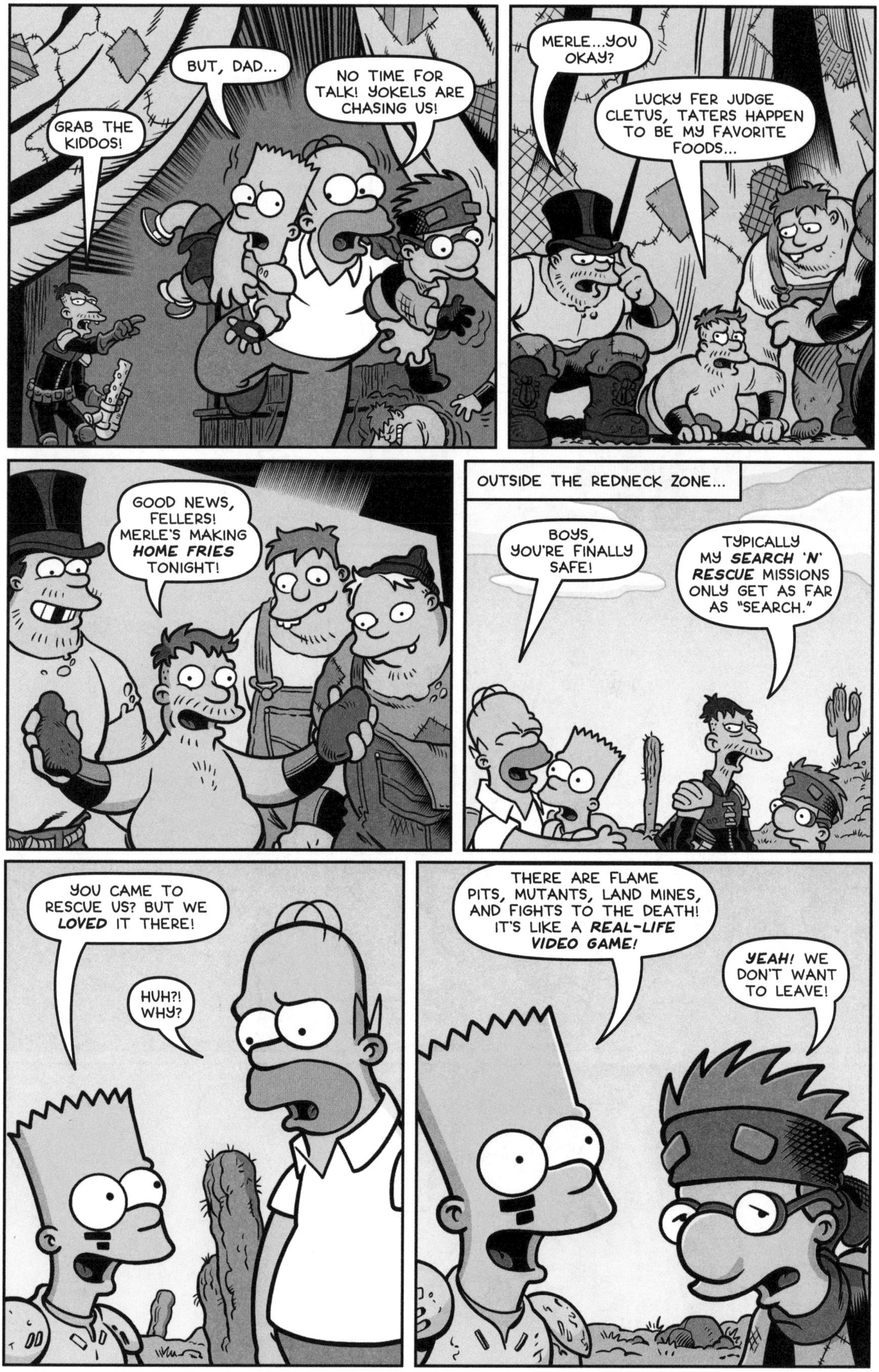

GRAB THE KIDDOS!
BUT, DAD...
NO TIME FOR TALK! YOKELS ARE CHASING US!
MERLE...YOU OKAY?
LUCKY FER JUDGE CLETUS, TATERS HAPPEN TO BE MY FAVORITE FOODS...
GOOD NEWS, FELLERS! MERLE'S MAKING **HOME FRIES** TONIGHT!
OUTSIDE THE REDNECK ZONE...
BOYS, YOU'RE FINALLY SAFE!
TYPICALLY MY **SEARCH 'N' RESCUE** MISSIONS ONLY GET AS FAR AS "SEARCH."
YOU CAME TO RESCUE US? BUT WE **LOVED** IT THERE!
HUH?! WHY?
THERE ARE FLAME PITS, MUTANTS, LAND MINES, AND FIGHTS TO THE DEATH! IT'S LIKE A **REAL-LIFE VIDEO GAME!**
YEAH! WE DON'T WANT TO LEAVE!

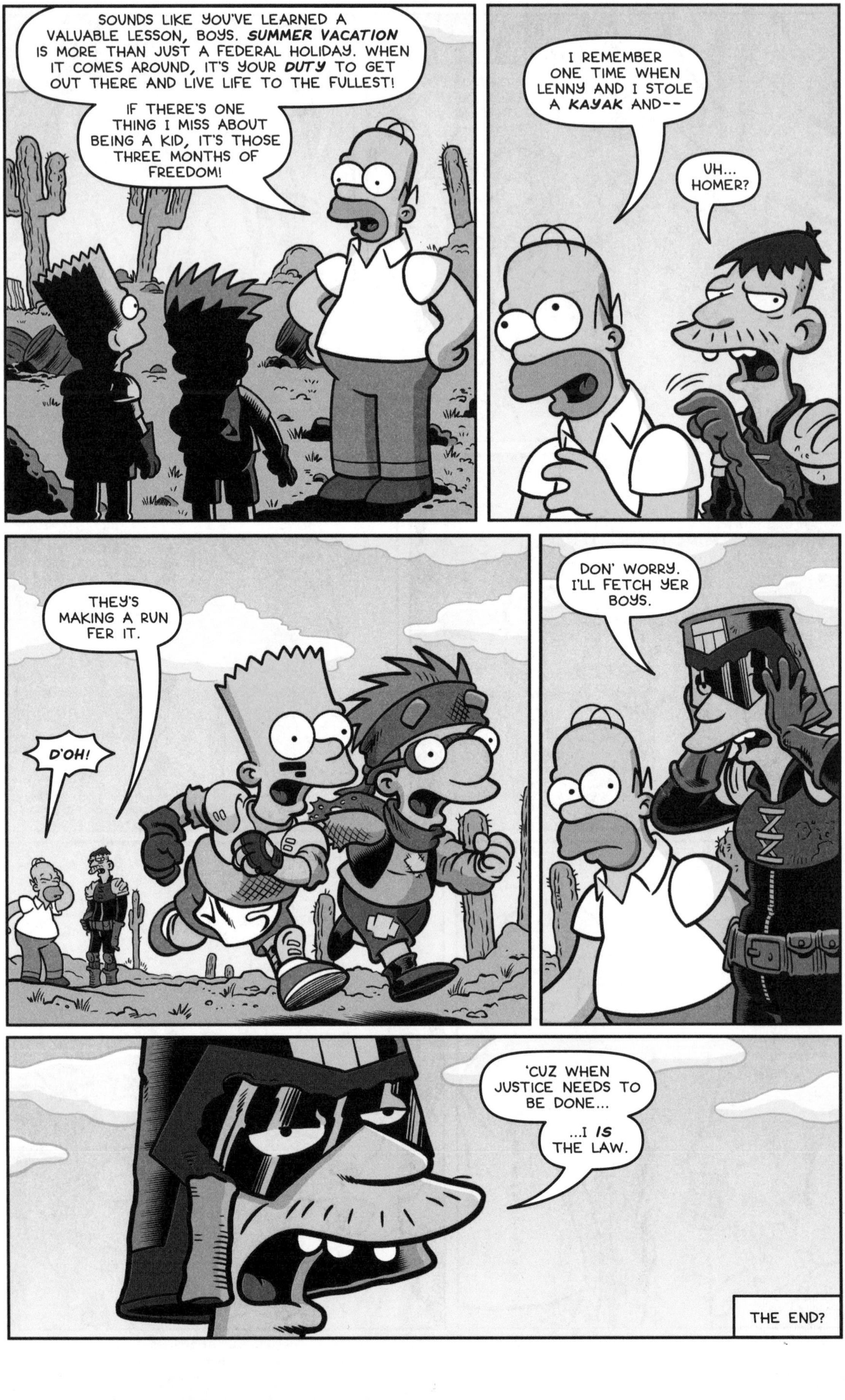

SOUNDS LIKE YOU'VE LEARNED A VALUABLE LESSON, BOYS. **SUMMER VACATION** IS MORE THAN JUST A FEDERAL HOLIDAY. WHEN IT COMES AROUND, IT'S YOUR **DUTY** TO GET OUT THERE AND LIVE LIFE TO THE FULLEST!
IF THERE'S ONE THING I MISS ABOUT BEING A KID, IT'S THOSE THREE MONTHS OF FREEDOM!
I REMEMBER ONE TIME WHEN LENNY AND I STOLE A **KAYAK** AND--
UH... HOMER?
THEY'S MAKING A RUN FER IT.
D'OH!
DON' WORRY. I'LL FETCH YER BOYS.
'CUZ WHEN JUSTICE NEEDS TO BE DONE...
...I ***IS*** THE LAW.
THE END?

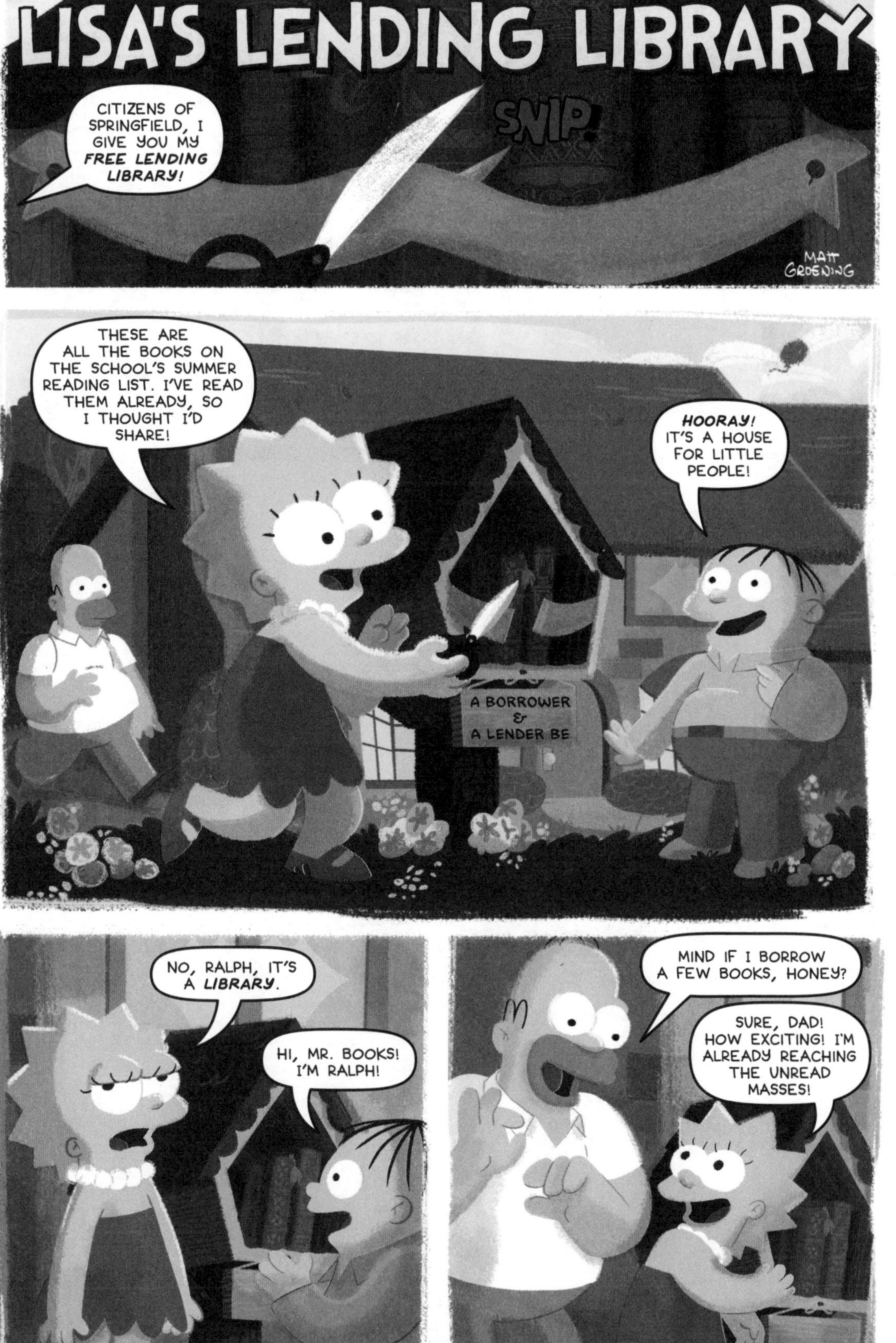
LISA'S LENDING LIBRARY
CITIZENS OF SPRINGFIELD, I GIVE YOU MY FREE LENDING LIBRARY!
SNIP!
MATT GROENING
THESE ARE ALL THE BOOKS ON THE SCHOOL'S SUMMER READING LIST. I'VE READ THEM ALREADY, SO I THOUGHT I'D SHARE!
HOORAY! IT'S A HOUSE FOR LITTLE PEOPLE!
A BORROWER & A LENDER BE
NO, RALPH, IT'S A LIBRARY.
HI, MR. BOOKS! I'M RALPH!
MIND IF I BORROW A FEW BOOKS, HONEY?
SURE, DAD! HOW EXCITING! I'M ALREADY REACHING THE UNREAD MASSES!

SHERRI L. SMITH WRITER | **KASSANDRA HELLER** ART | **KAREN BATES** LETTERS | **NATHAN KANE** EDITOR

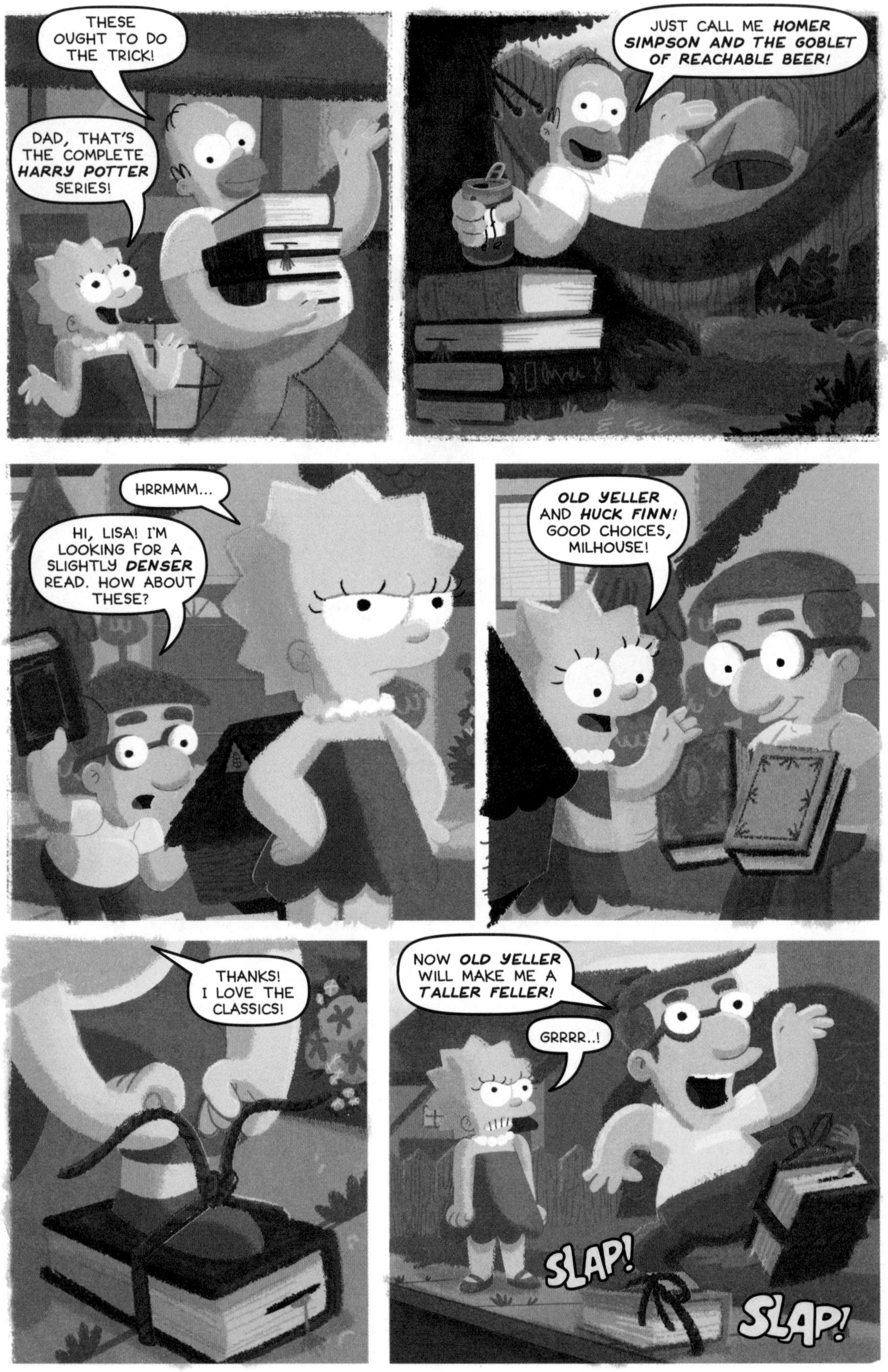
THESE OUGHT TO DO THE TRICK!
DAD, THAT'S THE COMPLETE ***HARRY POTTER*** SERIES!
JUST CALL ME ***HOMER SIMPSON AND THE GOBLET OF REACHABLE BEER!***
HRRMMM...
HI, LISA! I'M LOOKING FOR A SLIGHTLY ***DENSER*** READ. HOW ABOUT THESE?
OLD YELLER AND ***HUCK FINN!*** GOOD CHOICES, MILHOUSE!
THANKS! I LOVE THE CLASSICS!
NOW ***OLD YELLER*** WILL MAKE ME A ***TALLER FELLER!***
GRRRR..!
SLAP!
SLAP!

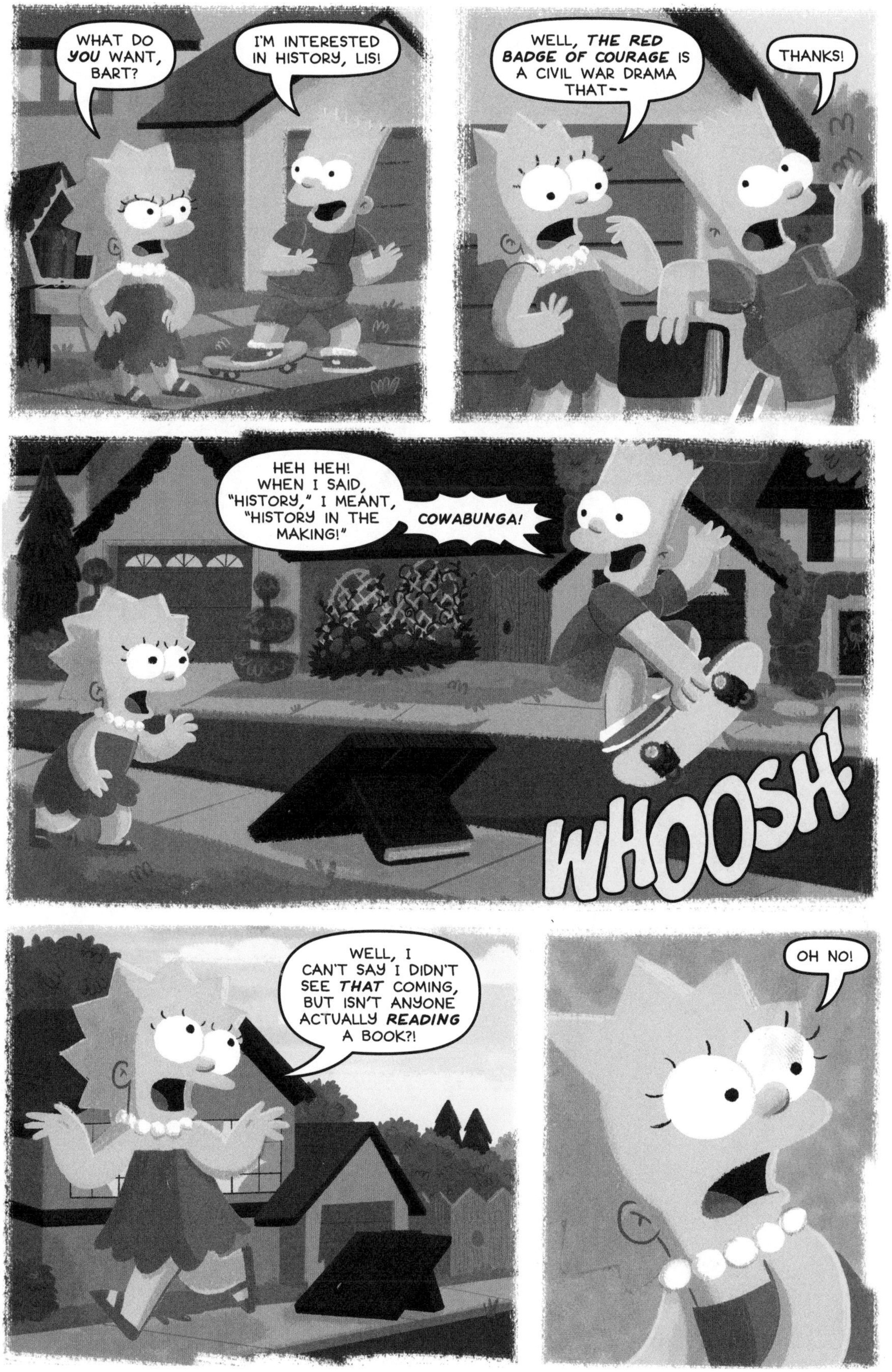
WHAT DO *YOU* WANT, BART?
I'M INTERESTED IN HISTORY, LIS!
WELL, ***THE RED BADGE OF COURAGE*** IS A CIVIL WAR DRAMA THAT--
THANKS!
HEH HEH! WHEN I SAID, "HISTORY," I MEANT, "HISTORY IN THE MAKING!"
COWABUNGA!
WHOOSH!
WELL, I CAN'T SAY I DIDN'T SEE *THAT* COMING, BUT ISN'T ANYONE ACTUALLY ***READING*** A BOOK?!
OH NO!

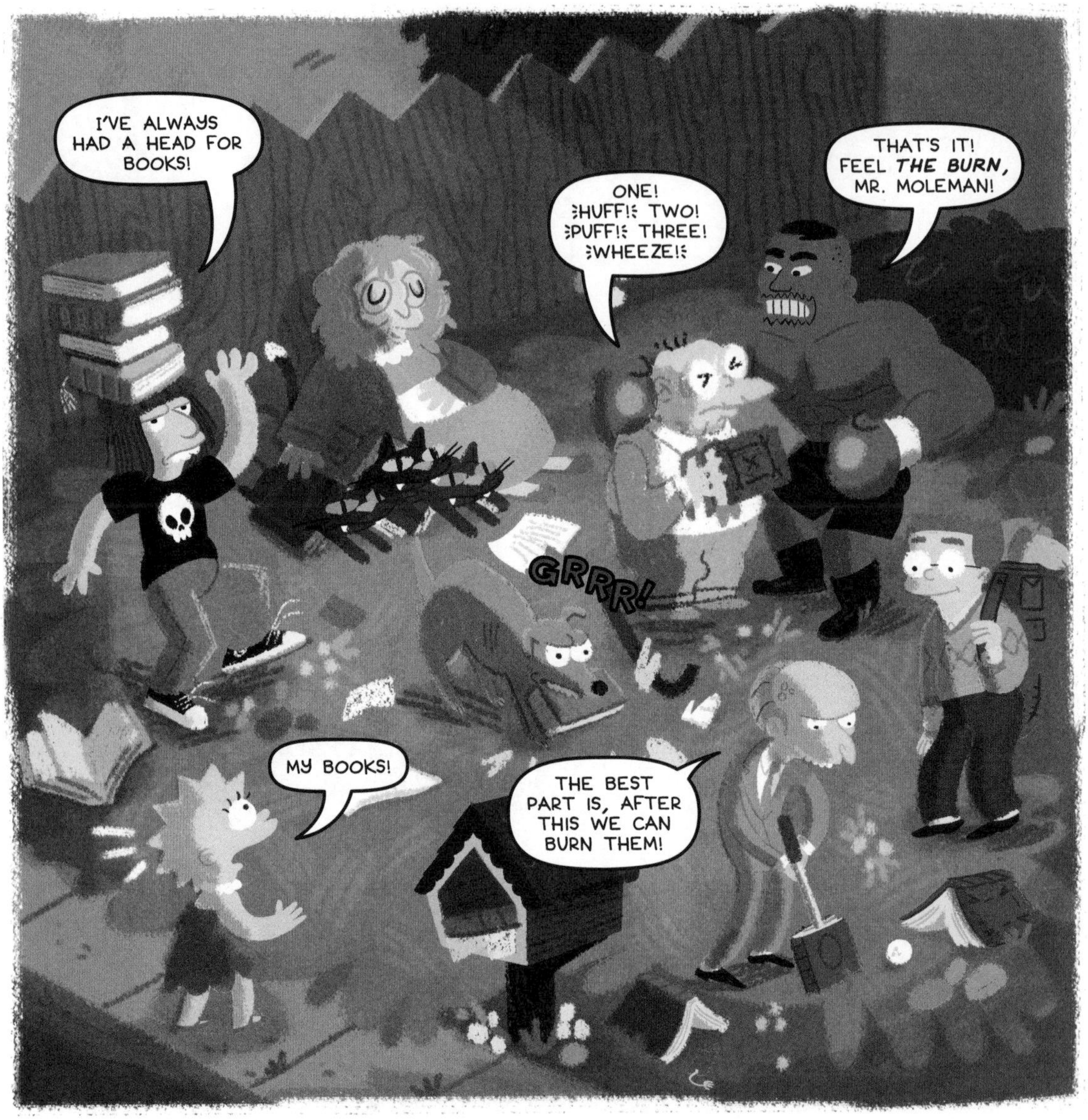
I'VE ALWAYS HAD A HEAD FOR BOOKS!
ONE! HUFF! TWO! PUFF! THREE! WHEEZE!
THAT'S IT! FEEL **THE BURN,** MR. MOLEMAN!
GRRRR!
MY BOOKS!
THE BEST PART IS, AFTER THIS WE CAN BURN THEM!

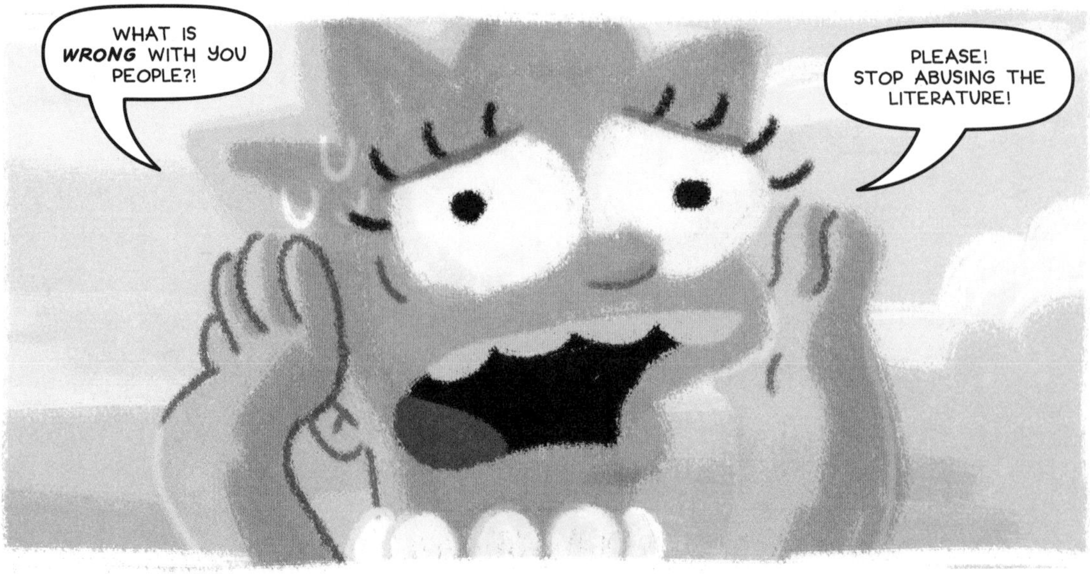
WHAT IS **WRONG** WITH YOU PEOPLE?!
PLEASE! STOP ABUSING THE LITERATURE!

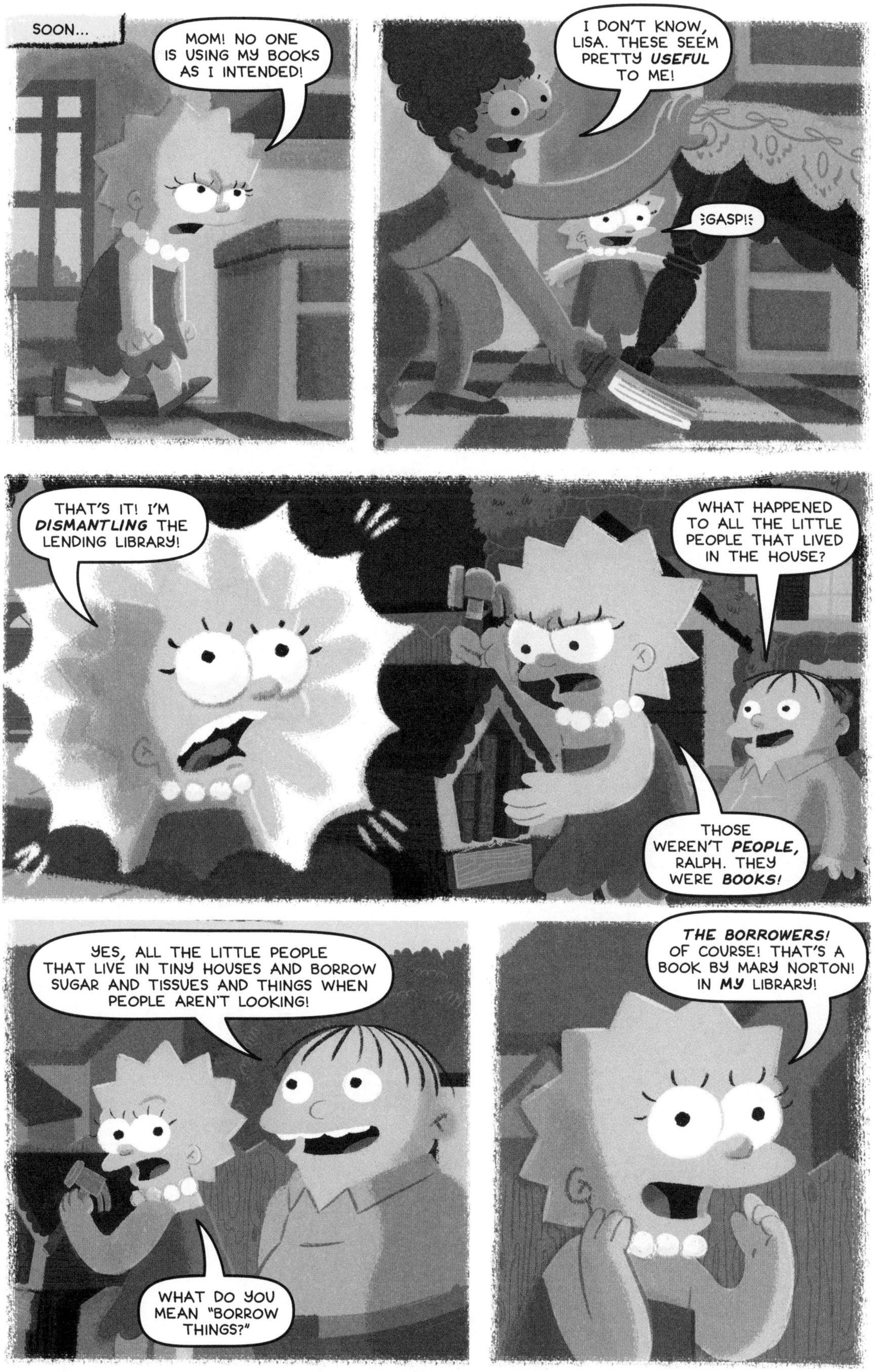
SOON...
MOM! NO ONE IS USING MY BOOKS AS I INTENDED!
I DON'T KNOW, LISA. THESE SEEM PRETTY *USEFUL* TO ME!
GASP!
THAT'S IT! I'M *DISMANTLING* THE LENDING LIBRARY!
WHAT HAPPENED TO ALL THE LITTLE PEOPLE THAT LIVED IN THE HOUSE?
THOSE WEREN'T *PEOPLE,* RALPH. THEY WERE *BOOKS!*
YES, ALL THE LITTLE PEOPLE THAT LIVE IN TINY HOUSES AND BORROW SUGAR AND TISSUES AND THINGS WHEN PEOPLE AREN'T LOOKING!
WHAT DO YOU MEAN "BORROW THINGS?"
THE BORROWERS! OF COURSE! THAT'S A BOOK BY MARY NORTON! IN *MY* LIBRARY!

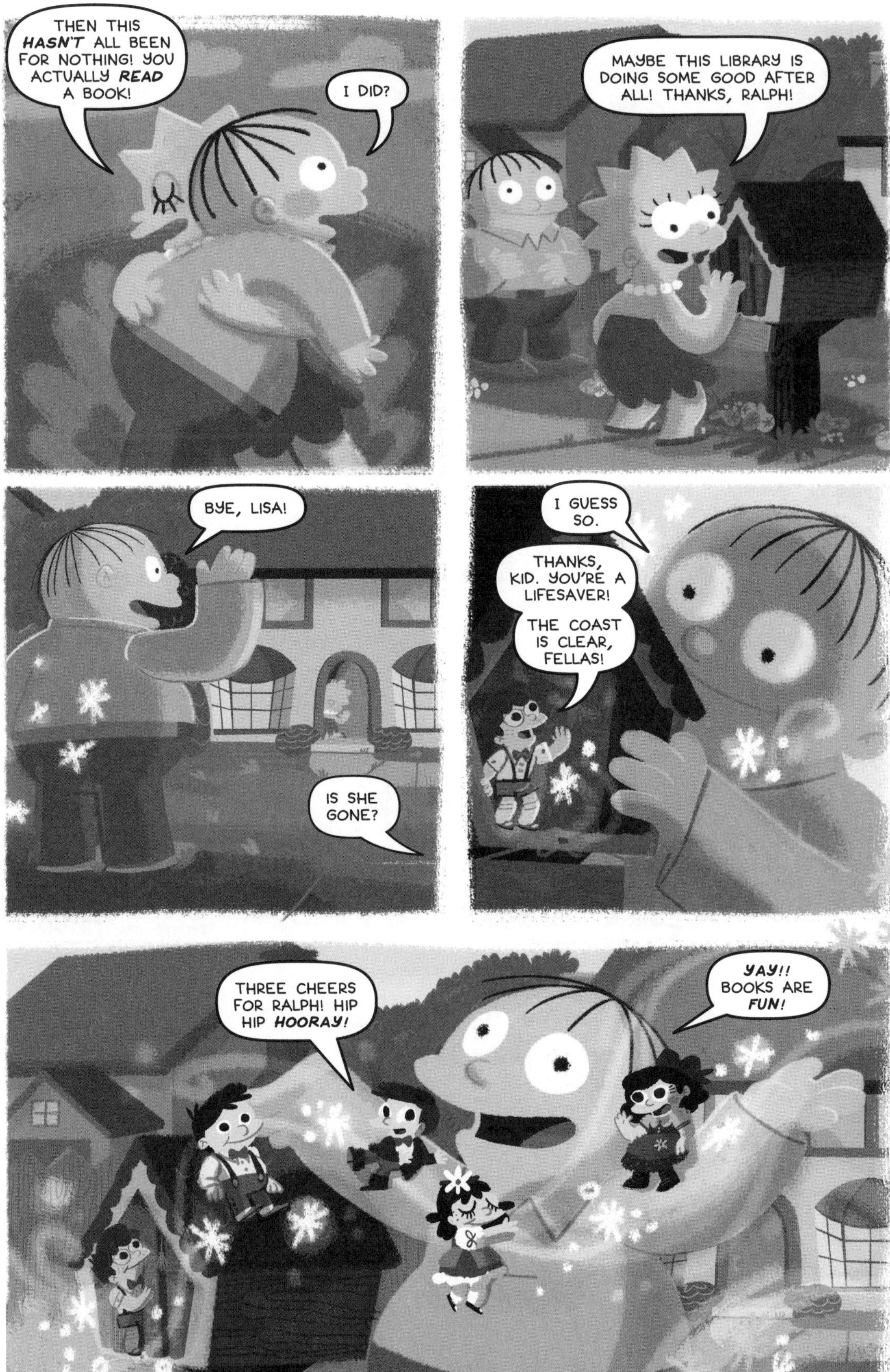
THEN THIS **HASN'T** ALL BEEN FOR NOTHING! YOU ACTUALLY **READ** A BOOK!
I DID?
MAYBE THIS LIBRARY IS DOING SOME GOOD AFTER ALL! THANKS, RALPH!
BYE, LISA!
IS SHE GONE?
I GUESS SO.
THANKS, KID. YOU'RE A LIFESAVER!
THE COAST IS CLEAR, FELLAS!
THREE CHEERS FOR RALPH! HIP HIP **HOORAY**!
YAY!! BOOKS ARE **FUN**!
THE END

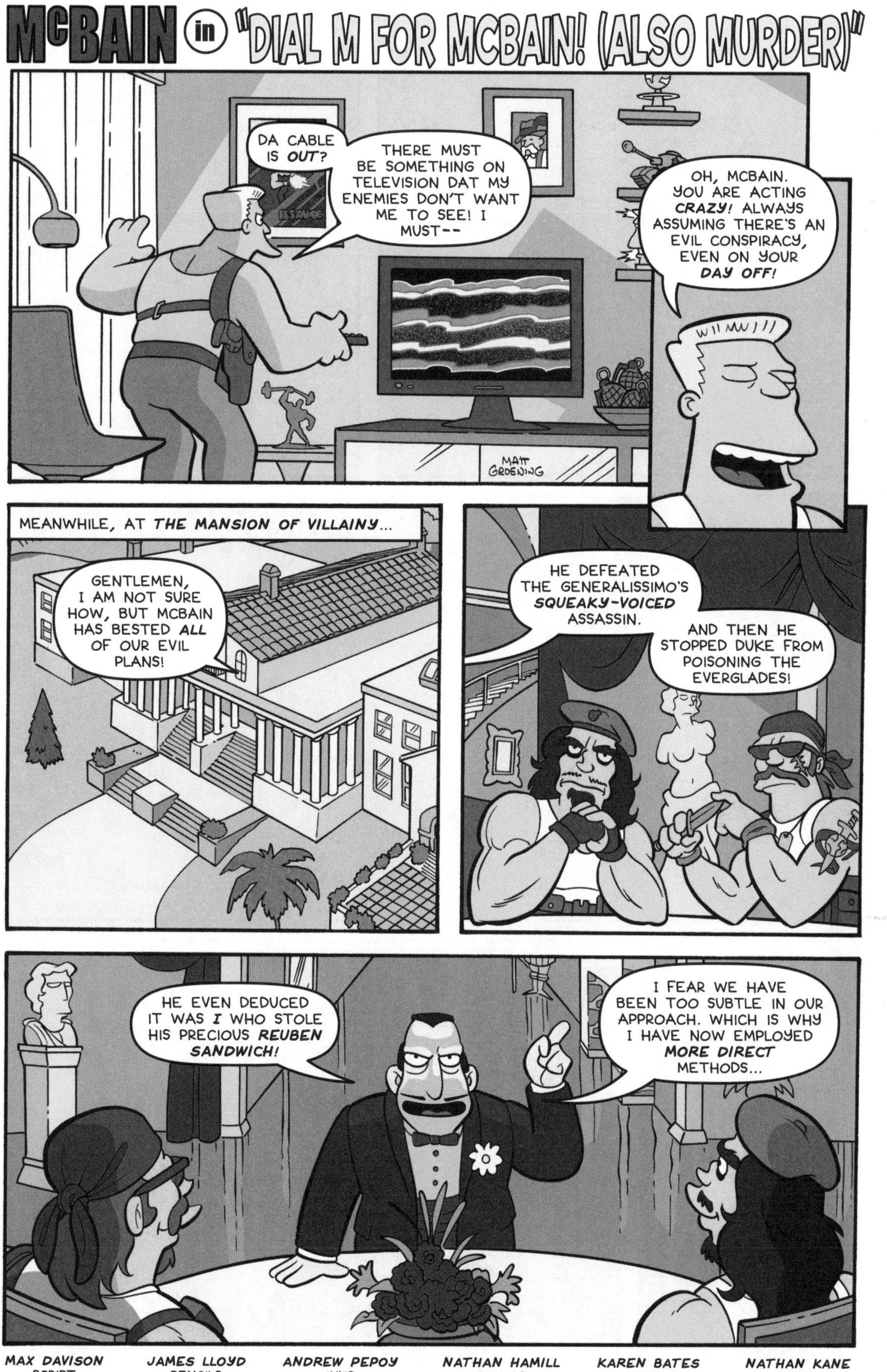
McBAIN in "DIAL M FOR MCBAIN! (ALSO MURDER)"
DA CABLE IS OUT?
THERE MUST BE SOMETHING ON TELEVISION DAT MY ENEMIES DON'T WANT ME TO SEE! I MUST--
OH, MCBAIN. YOU ARE ACTING CRAZY! ALWAYS ASSUMING THERE'S AN EVIL CONSPIRACY, EVEN ON YOUR DAY OFF!
MATT GROENING
MEANWHILE, AT THE MANSION OF VILLAINY...
GENTLEMEN, I AM NOT SURE HOW, BUT MCBAIN HAS BESTED ALL OF OUR EVIL PLANS!
HE DEFEATED THE GENERALISSIMO'S SQUEAKY-VOICED ASSASSIN.
AND THEN HE STOPPED DUKE FROM POISONING THE EVERGLADES!
HE EVEN DEDUCED IT WAS I WHO STOLE HIS PRECIOUS REUBEN SANDWICH!
I FEAR WE HAVE BEEN TOO SUBTLE IN OUR APPROACH. WHICH IS WHY I HAVE NOW EMPLOYED MORE DIRECT METHODS...

MAX DAVISON SCRIPT · **JAMES LLOYD** PENCILS · **ANDREW PEPOY** INKS · **NATHAN HAMILL** COLORS · **KAREN BATES** LETTERS · **NATHAN KANE** EDITOR

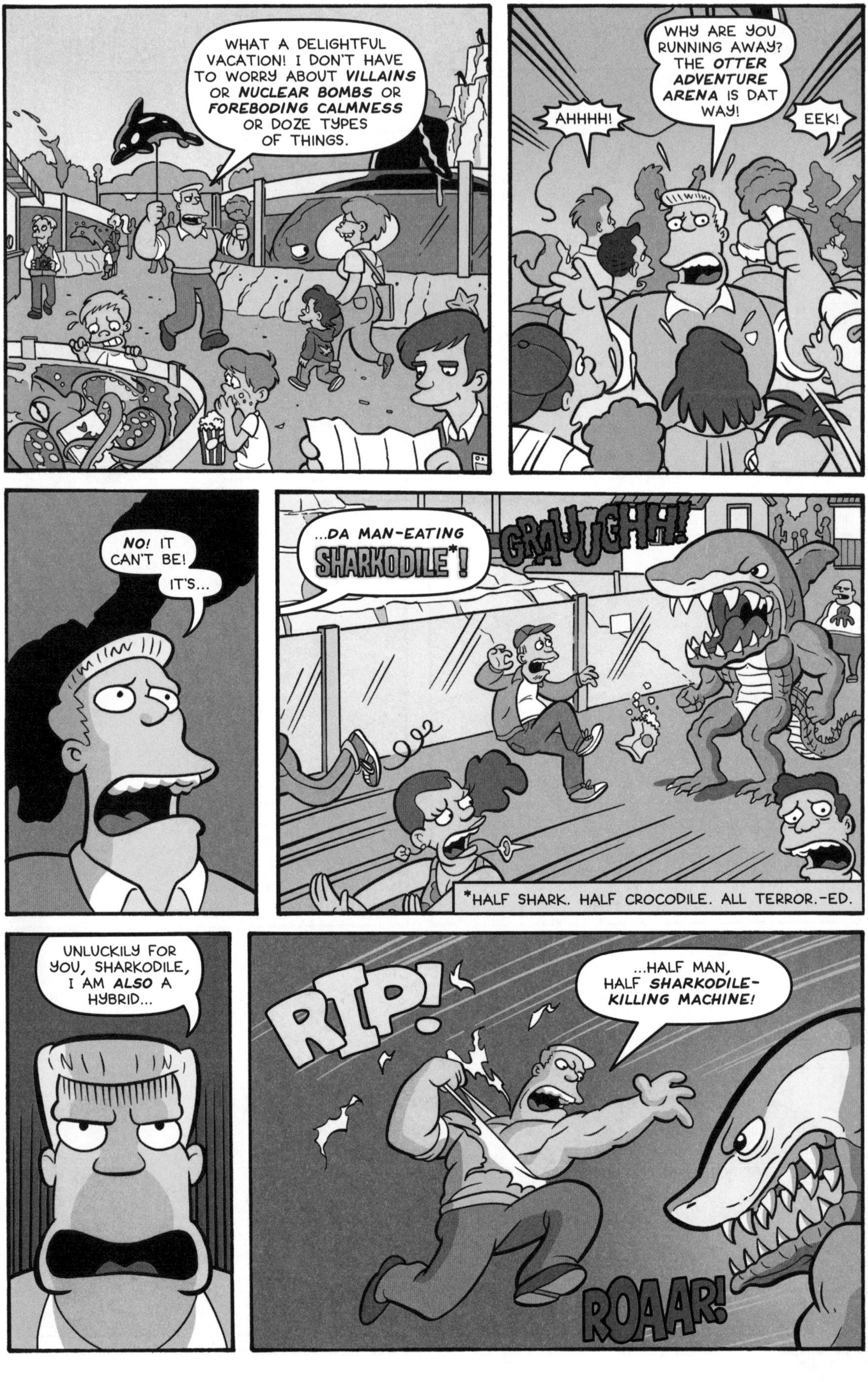
WHAT A DELIGHTFUL VACATION! I DON'T HAVE TO WORRY ABOUT VILLAINS OR NUCLEAR BOMBS OR FOREBODING CALMNESS OR DOZE TYPES OF THINGS.
AHHHH!
WHY ARE YOU RUNNING AWAY? THE OTTER ADVENTURE ARENA IS DAT WAY!
EEK!
NO! IT CAN'T BE!
IT'S...
...DA MAN-EATING SHARKODILE*!
GRAUUGHH!
*HALF SHARK. HALF CROCODILE. ALL TERROR.-ED.
UNLUCKILY FOR YOU, SHARKODILE, I AM ALSO A HYBRID...
RIP!
...HALF MAN, HALF SHARKODILE-KILLING MACHINE!
ROAAR!

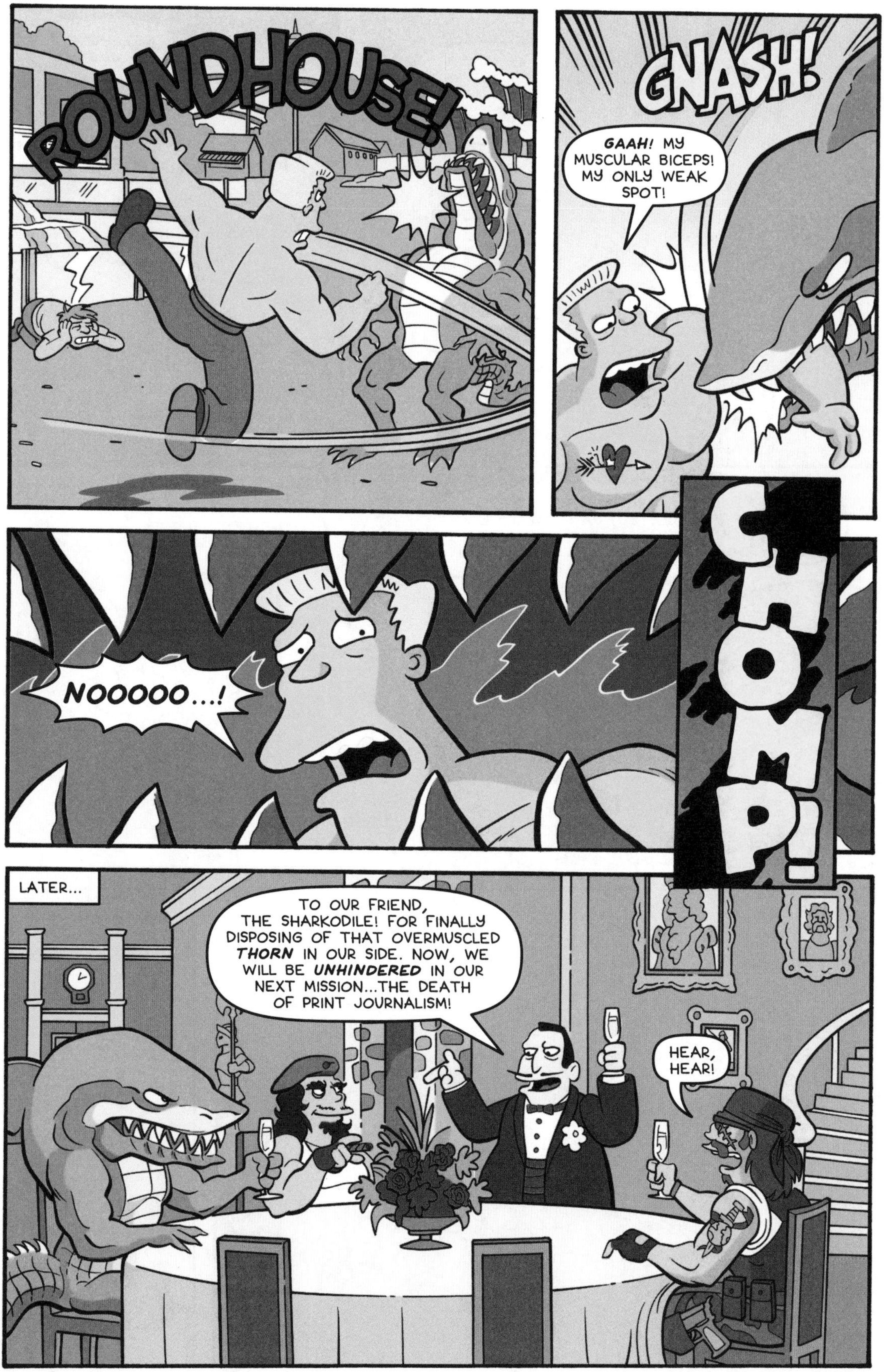
ROUNDHOUSE!
GNASH!
GAAH! MY MUSCULAR BICEPS! MY ONLY WEAK SPOT!
NOOOOO...!
CHOMP!
LATER...
TO OUR FRIEND, THE SHARKODILE! FOR FINALLY DISPOSING OF THAT OVERMUSCLED THORN IN OUR SIDE. NOW, WE WILL BE UNHINDERED IN OUR NEXT MISSION...THE DEATH OF PRINT JOURNALISM!
HEAR, HEAR!

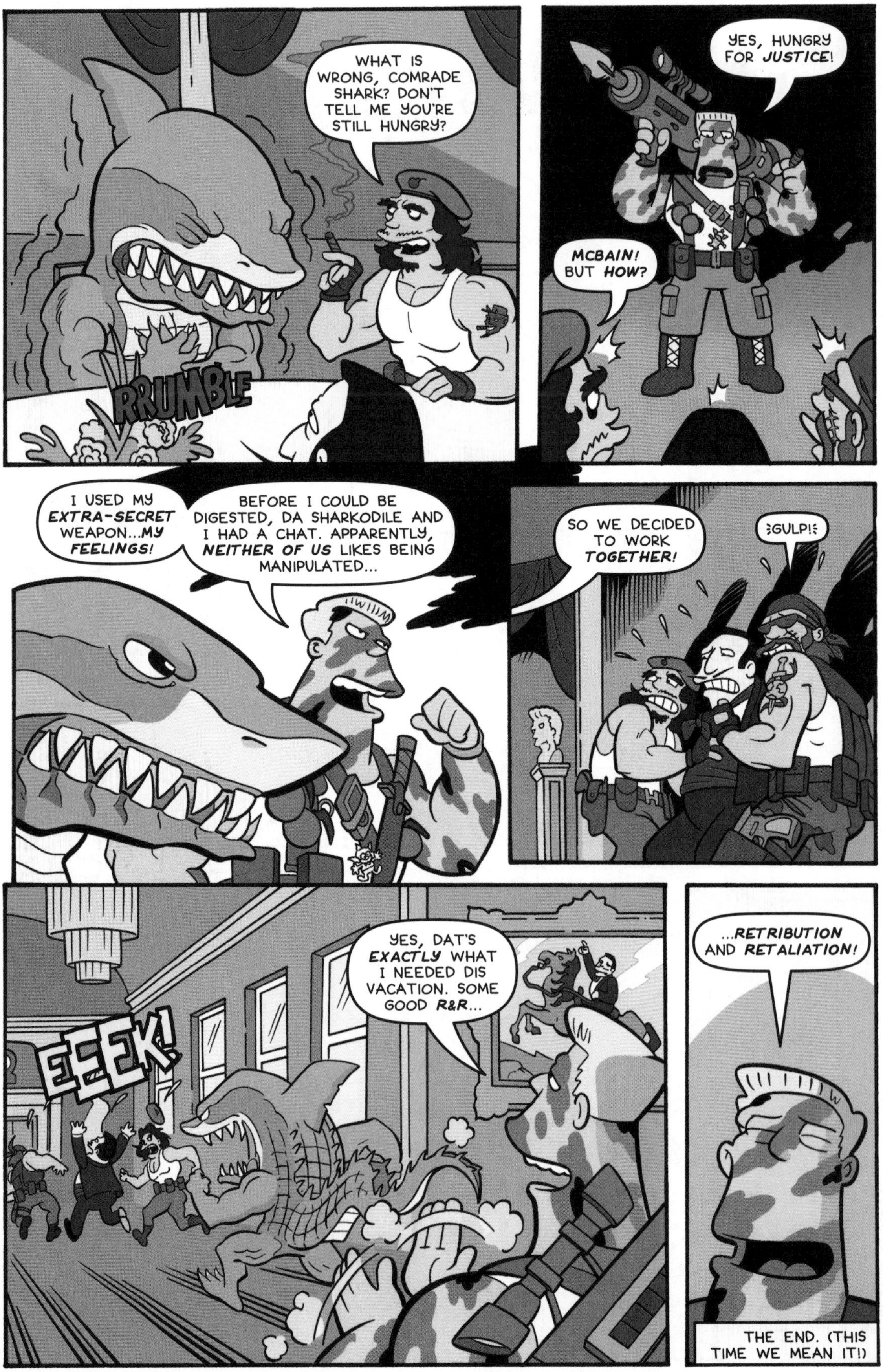
WHAT IS WRONG, COMRADE SHARK? DON'T TELL ME YOU'RE STILL HUNGRY?
RRUMBLE
YES, HUNGRY FOR JUSTICE!
MCBAIN! BUT HOW?
I USED MY EXTRA-SECRET WEAPON...MY FEELINGS!
BEFORE I COULD BE DIGESTED, DA SHARKODILE AND I HAD A CHAT. APPARENTLY, NEITHER OF US LIKES BEING MANIPULATED...
SO WE DECIDED TO WORK TOGETHER!
GULP!
YES, DAT'S EXACTLY WHAT I NEEDED DIS VACATION. SOME GOOD R&R...
EEEK!
...RETRIBUTION AND RETALIATION!
THE END. (THIS TIME WE MEAN IT!)

HOMER SIMPSON: CANINE DECODER

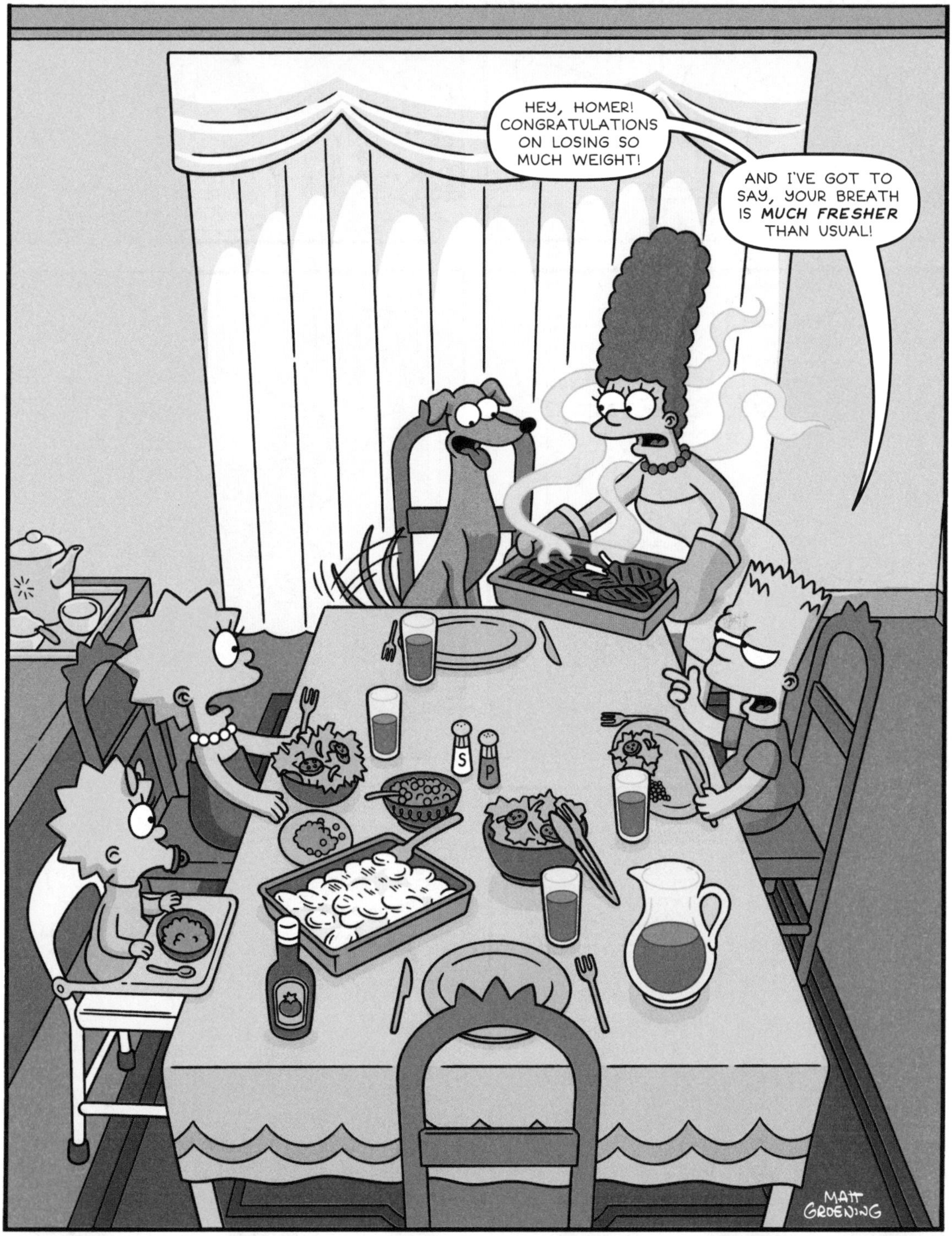
HEY, HOMER! CONGRATULATIONS ON LOSING SO MUCH WEIGHT!
AND I'VE GOT TO SAY, YOUR BREATH IS ***MUCH FRESHER*** THAN USUAL!
S
P
MATT GROENING

IAN **BOOTHBY** SCRIPT
NINA **MATSUMOTO** PENCILS
MIKE **ROTE** INKS
ART **VILLANUEVA** COLORS
KAREN **BATES** LETTERS
NATHAN **KANE** EDITOR

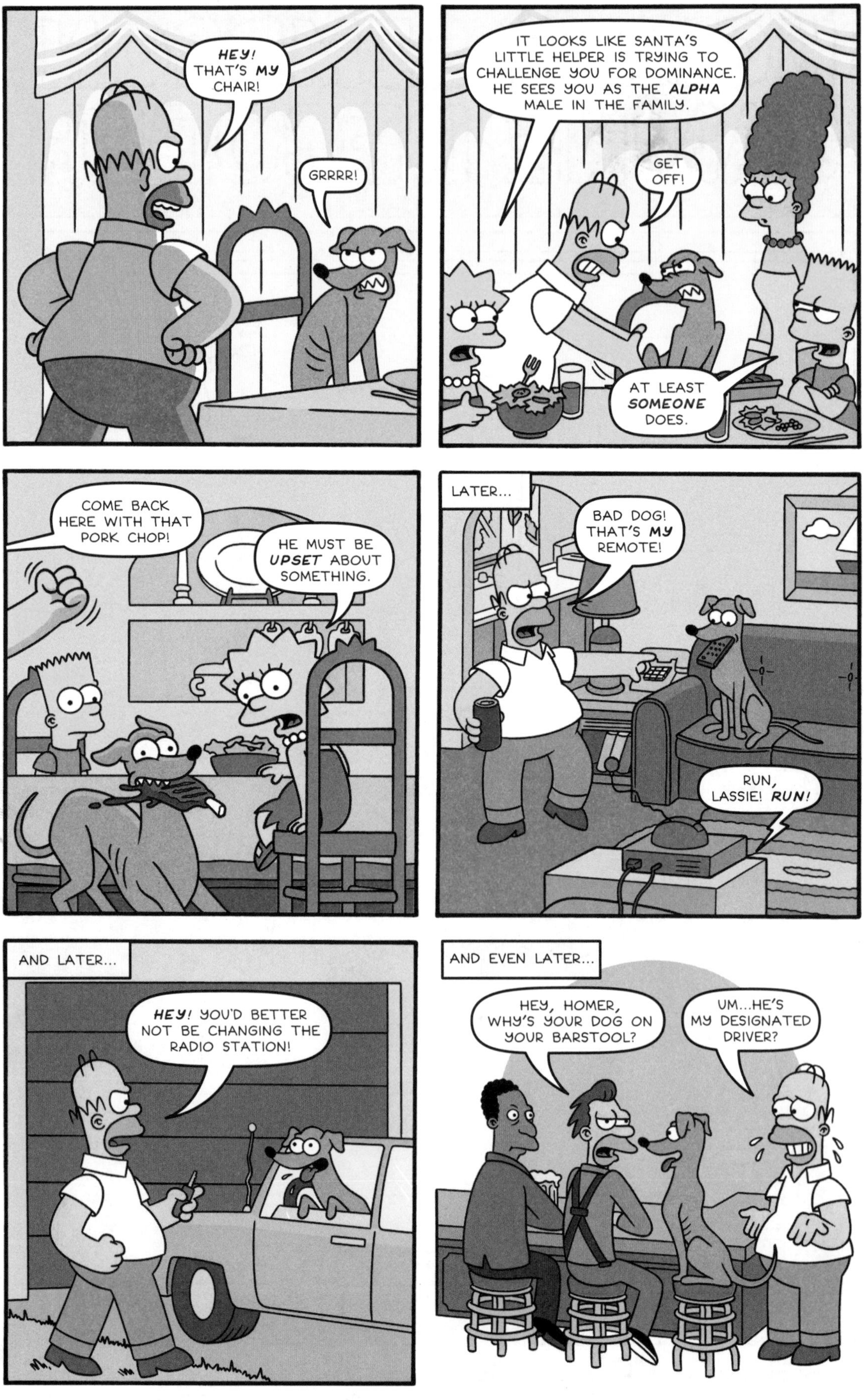
HEY! THAT'S MY CHAIR!
GRRRR!
IT LOOKS LIKE SANTA'S LITTLE HELPER IS TRYING TO CHALLENGE YOU FOR DOMINANCE. HE SEES YOU AS THE ALPHA MALE IN THE FAMILY.
GET OFF!
AT LEAST SOMEONE DOES.
COME BACK HERE WITH THAT PORK CHOP!
HE MUST BE UPSET ABOUT SOMETHING.
LATER...
BAD DOG! THAT'S MY REMOTE!
RUN, LASSIE! RUN!
AND LATER...
HEY! YOU'D BETTER NOT BE CHANGING THE RADIO STATION!
AND EVEN LATER...
HEY, HOMER, WHY'S YOUR DOG ON YOUR BARSTOOL?
UM...HE'S MY DESIGNATED DRIVER?

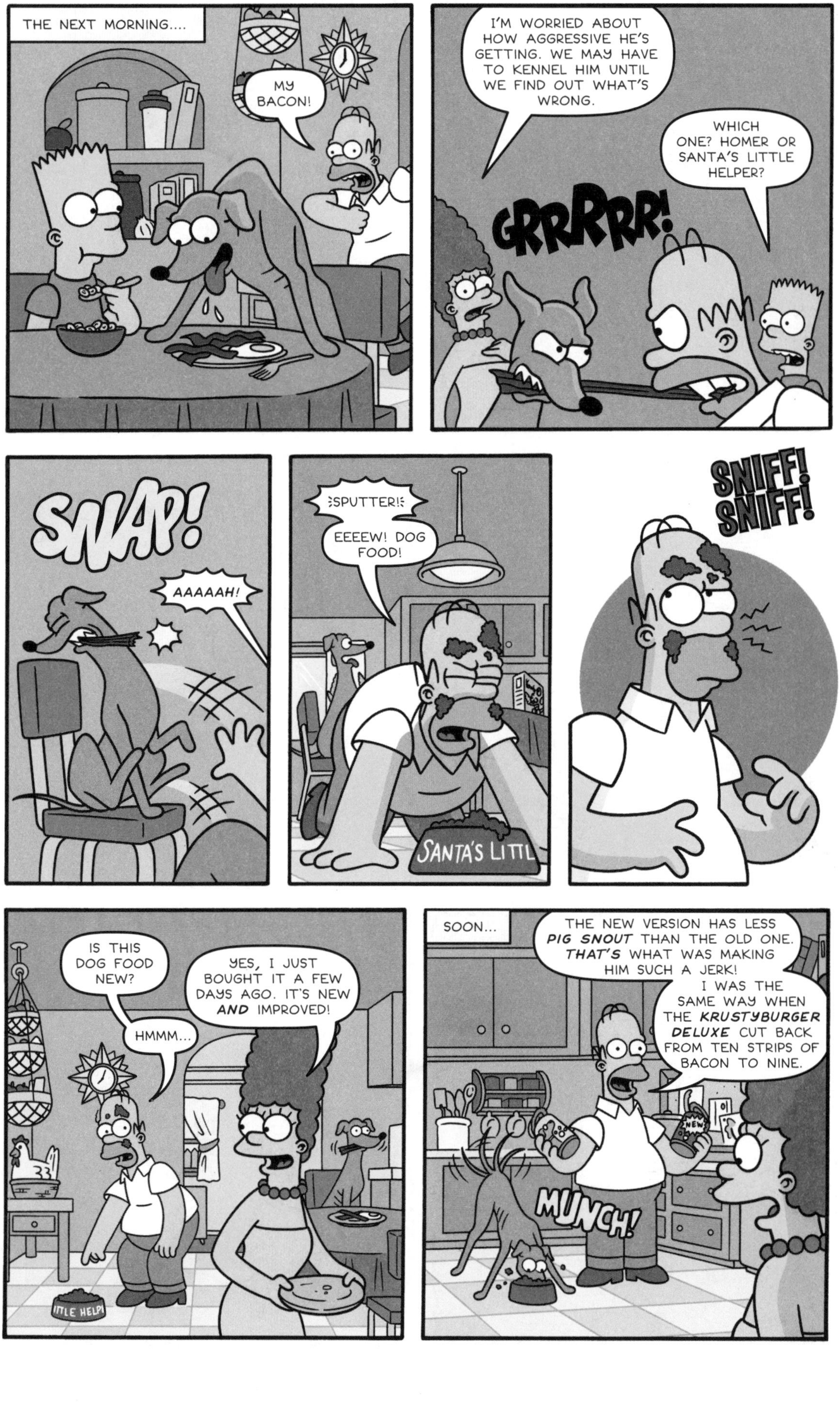
THE NEXT MORNING....
MY BACON!
I'M WORRIED ABOUT HOW AGGRESSIVE HE'S GETTING. WE MAY HAVE TO KENNEL HIM UNTIL WE FIND OUT WHAT'S WRONG.
WHICH ONE? HOMER OR SANTA'S LITTLE HELPER?
GRRRRR!
SNAP!
AAAAAH!
SPUTTER!
EEEEW! DOG FOOD!
SANTA'S LITTL
SNIFF! SNIFF!
IS THIS DOG FOOD NEW?
HMMM...
YES, I JUST BOUGHT IT A FEW DAYS AGO. IT'S NEW ***AND*** IMPROVED!
ITLE HELP
SOON...
THE NEW VERSION HAS LESS ***PIG SNOUT*** THAN THE OLD ONE. ***THAT'S*** WHAT WAS MAKING HIM SUCH A JERK!
I WAS THE SAME WAY WHEN THE ***KRUSTYBURGER DELUXE*** CUT BACK FROM TEN STRIPS OF BACON TO NINE.
NEW
MUNCH!

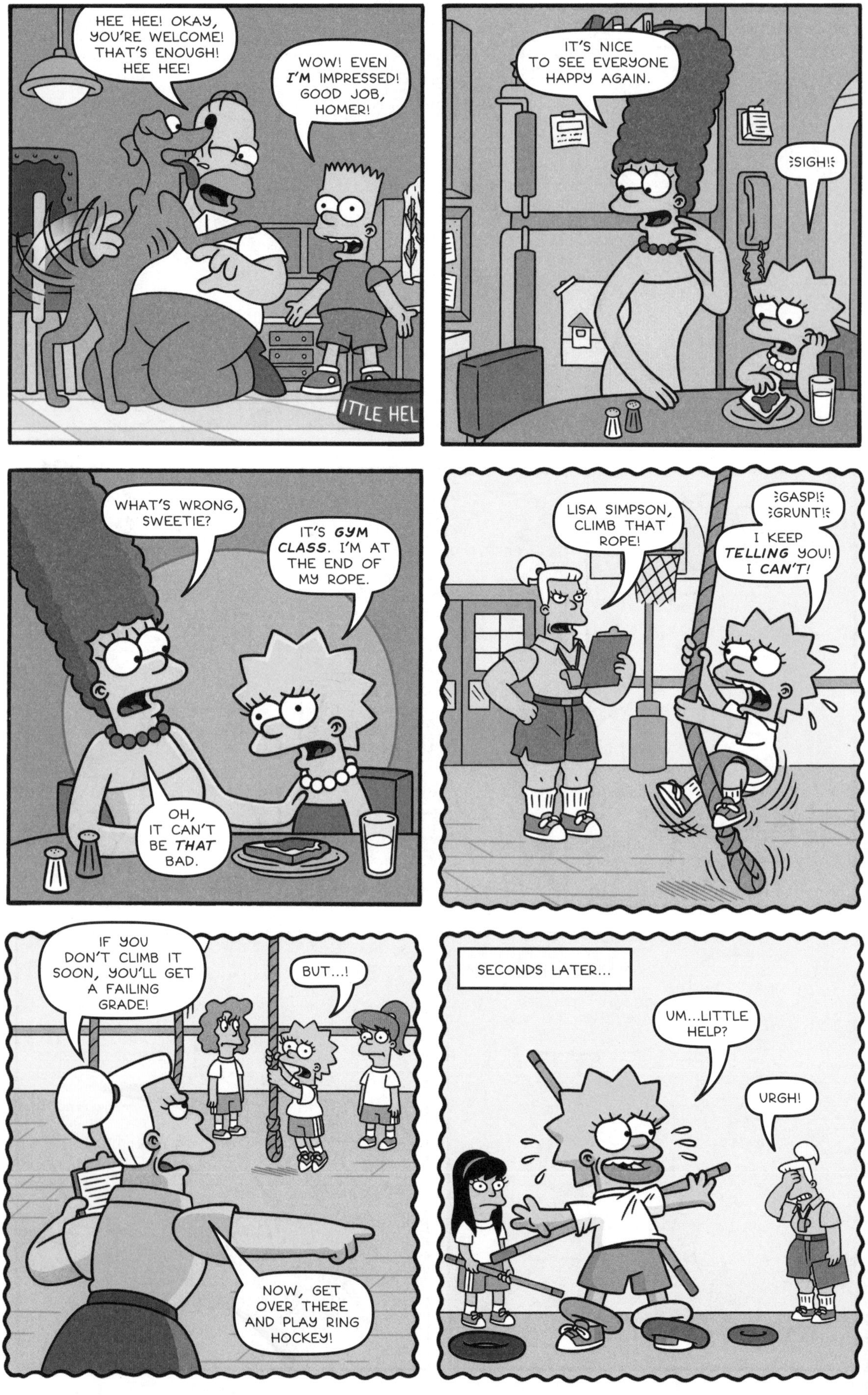
HEE HEE! OKAY, YOU'RE WELCOME! THAT'S ENOUGH! HEE HEE!
WOW! EVEN *I'M* IMPRESSED! GOOD JOB, HOMER!
ITTLE HEL
IT'S NICE TO SEE EVERYONE HAPPY AGAIN.
SIGH!
WHAT'S WRONG, SWEETIE?
IT'S *GYM CLASS*. I'M AT THE END OF MY ROPE.
OH, IT CAN'T BE *THAT* BAD.
LISA SIMPSON, CLIMB THAT ROPE!
GASP! GRUNT! I KEEP *TELLING* YOU! I *CAN'T*!
IF YOU DON'T CLIMB IT SOON, YOU'LL GET A FAILING GRADE!
BUT...!
NOW, GET OVER THERE AND PLAY RING HOCKEY!
SECONDS LATER...
UM...LITTLE HELP?
URGH!

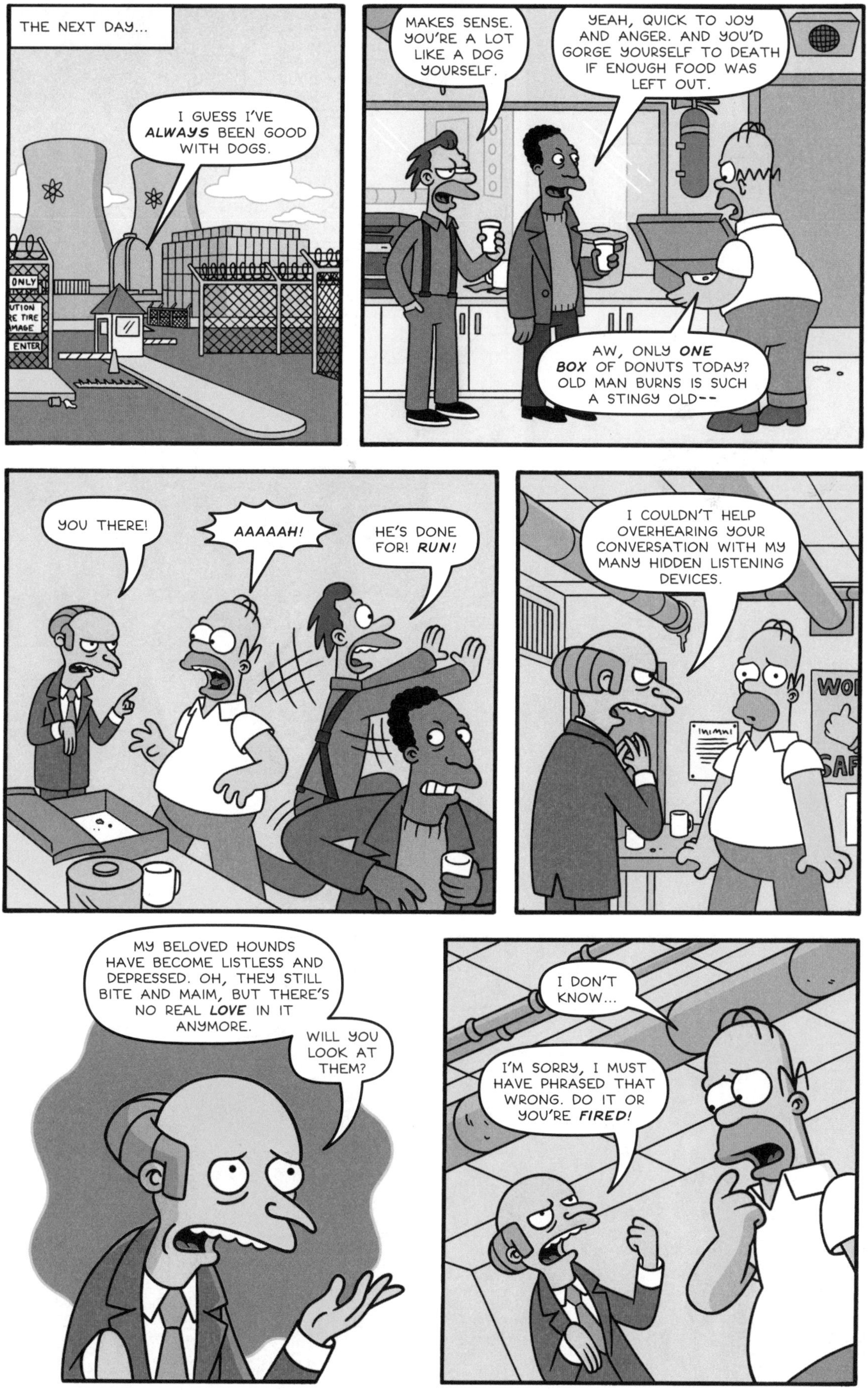

THE NEXT DAY...
I GUESS I'VE ALWAYS BEEN GOOD WITH DOGS.
ONLY
ENTER
MAKES SENSE. YOU'RE A LOT LIKE A DOG YOURSELF.
YEAH, QUICK TO JOY AND ANGER. AND YOU'D GORGE YOURSELF TO DEATH IF ENOUGH FOOD WAS LEFT OUT.
AW, ONLY ONE BOX OF DONUTS TODAY? OLD MAN BURNS IS SUCH A STINGY OLD--
YOU THERE!
AAAAAH!
HE'S DONE FOR! RUN!
I COULDN'T HELP OVERHEARING YOUR CONVERSATION WITH MY MANY HIDDEN LISTENING DEVICES.
MY BELOVED HOUNDS HAVE BECOME LISTLESS AND DEPRESSED. OH, THEY STILL BITE AND MAIM, BUT THERE'S NO REAL LOVE IN IT ANYMORE.
WILL YOU LOOK AT THEM?
I DON'T KNOW...
I'M SORRY, I MUST HAVE PHRASED THAT WRONG. DO IT OR YOU'RE FIRED!

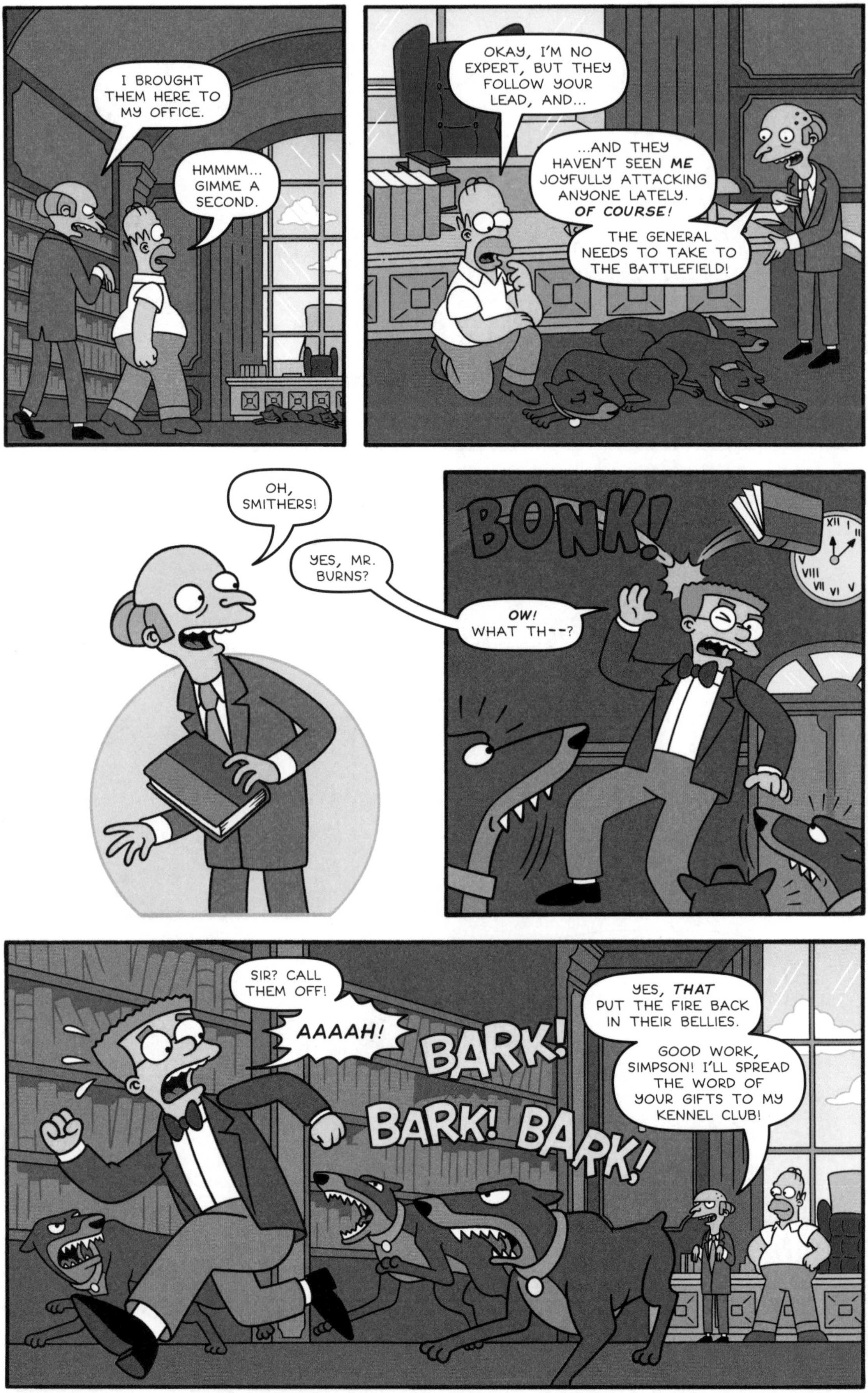

I BROUGHT THEM HERE TO MY OFFICE.
HMMMM... GIMME A SECOND.
OKAY, I'M NO EXPERT, BUT THEY FOLLOW YOUR LEAD, AND...
...AND THEY HAVEN'T SEEN **ME** JOYFULLY ATTACKING ANYONE LATELY. ***OF COURSE!***
THE GENERAL NEEDS TO TAKE TO THE BATTLEFIELD!
OH, SMITHERS!
YES, MR. BURNS?
BONK!
OW! WHAT TH--?
SIR? CALL THEM OFF!
AAAAH!
BARK!
BARK! BARK!
YES, ***THAT*** PUT THE FIRE BACK IN THEIR BELLIES.
GOOD WORK, SIMPSON! I'LL SPREAD THE WORD OF YOUR GIFTS TO MY KENNEL CLUB!

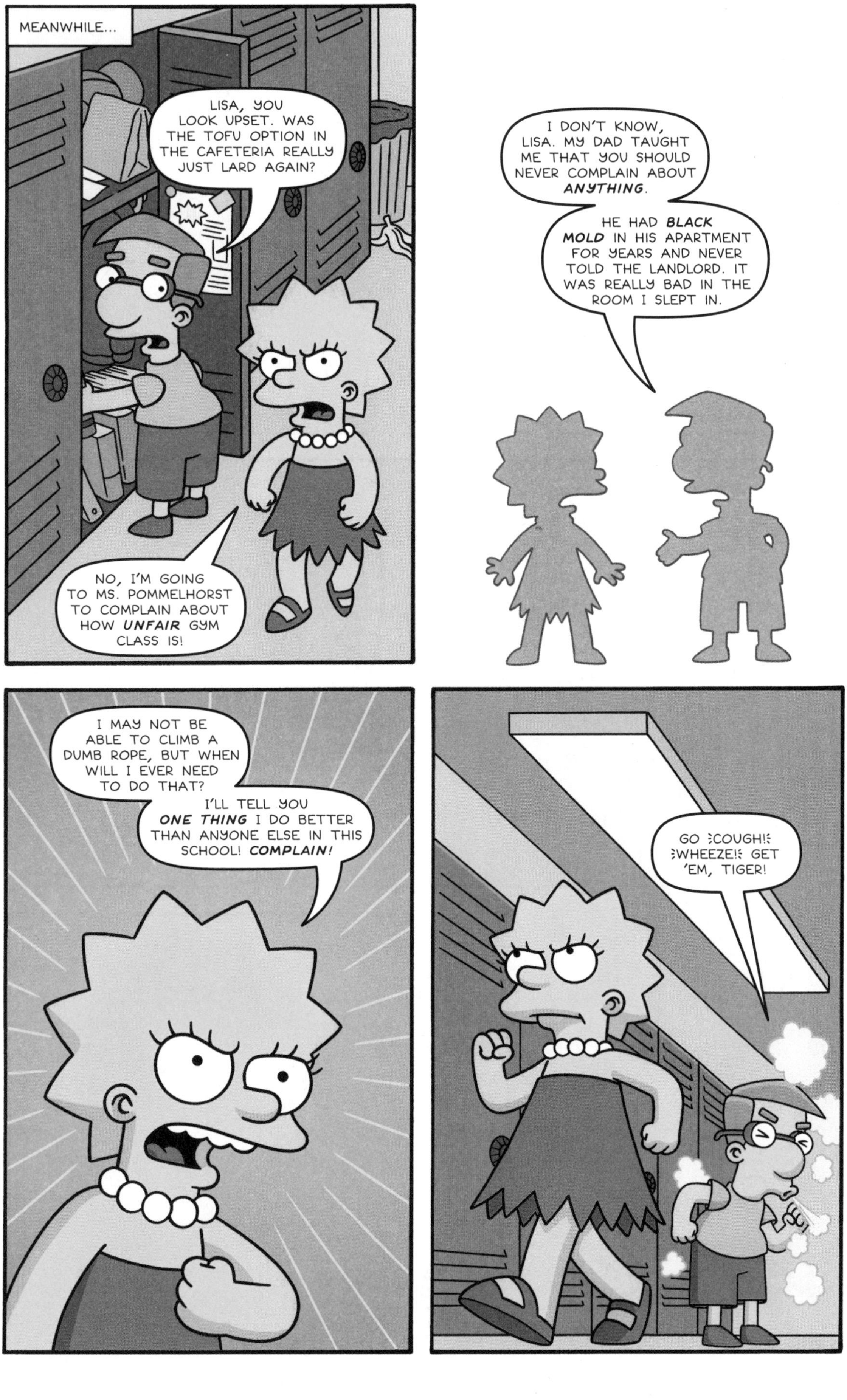

MEANWHILE...
LISA, YOU LOOK UPSET. WAS THE TOFU OPTION IN THE CAFETERIA REALLY JUST LARD AGAIN?
NO, I'M GOING TO MS. POMMELHORST TO COMPLAIN ABOUT HOW *UNFAIR* GYM CLASS IS!
I DON'T KNOW, LISA. MY DAD TAUGHT ME THAT YOU SHOULD NEVER COMPLAIN ABOUT *ANYTHING*.
HE HAD *BLACK MOLD* IN HIS APARTMENT FOR YEARS AND NEVER TOLD THE LANDLORD. IT WAS REALLY BAD IN THE ROOM I SLEPT IN.
I MAY NOT BE ABLE TO CLIMB A DUMB ROPE, BUT WHEN WILL I EVER NEED TO DO THAT?
I'LL TELL YOU *ONE THING* I DO BETTER THAN ANYONE ELSE IN THIS SCHOOL! *COMPLAIN*!
GO COUGH! WHEEZE! GET 'EM, TIGER!

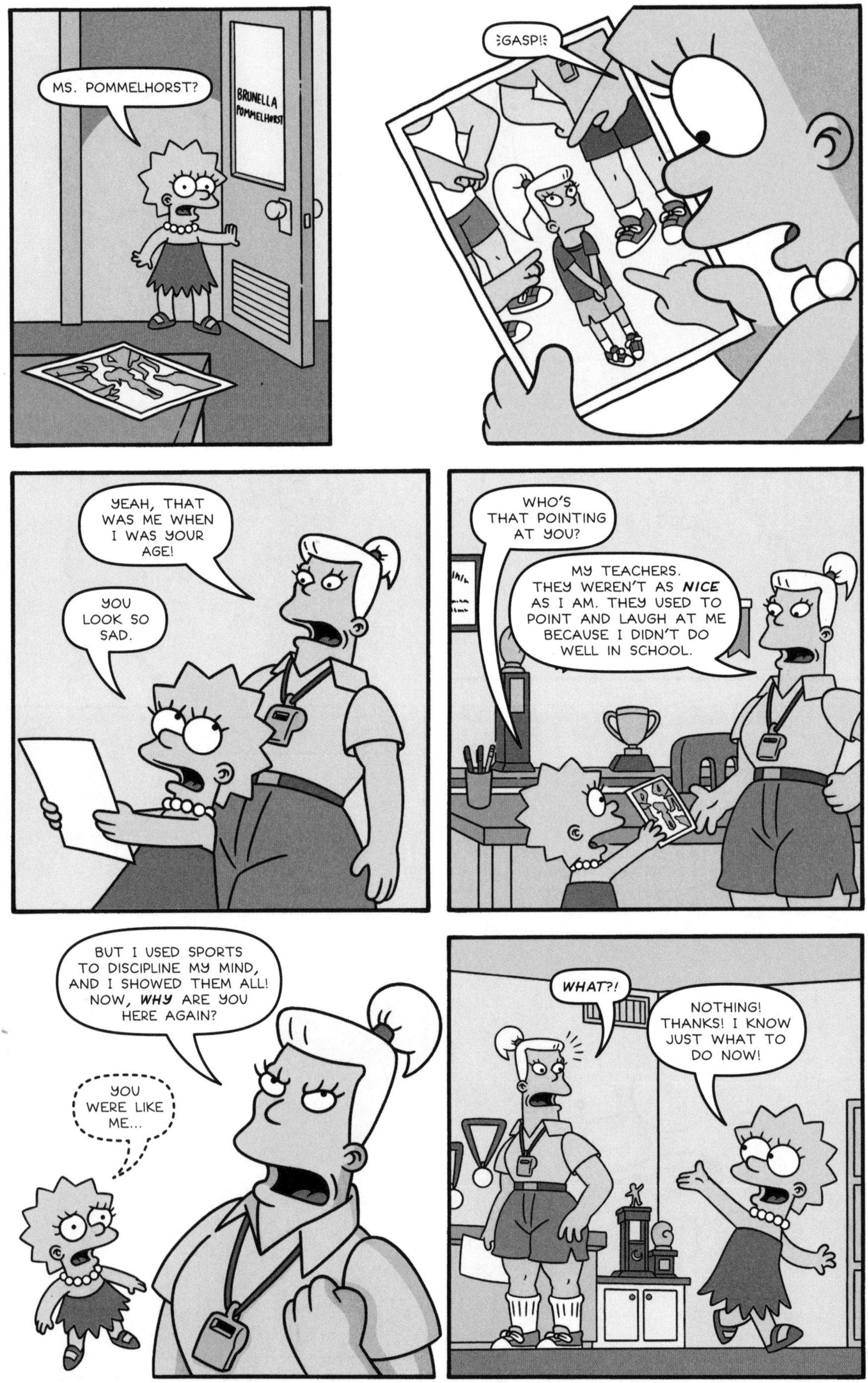
MS. POMMELHORST?
BRUNELLA POMMELHORST
GASP!
YEAH, THAT WAS ME WHEN I WAS YOUR AGE!
YOU LOOK SO SAD.
WHO'S THAT POINTING AT YOU?
MY TEACHERS. THEY WEREN'T AS NICE AS I AM. THEY USED TO POINT AND LAUGH AT ME BECAUSE I DIDN'T DO WELL IN SCHOOL.
BUT I USED SPORTS TO DISCIPLINE MY MIND, AND I SHOWED THEM ALL! NOW, WHY ARE YOU HERE AGAIN?
YOU WERE LIKE ME...
WHAT?!
NOTHING! THANKS! I KNOW JUST WHAT TO DO NOW!

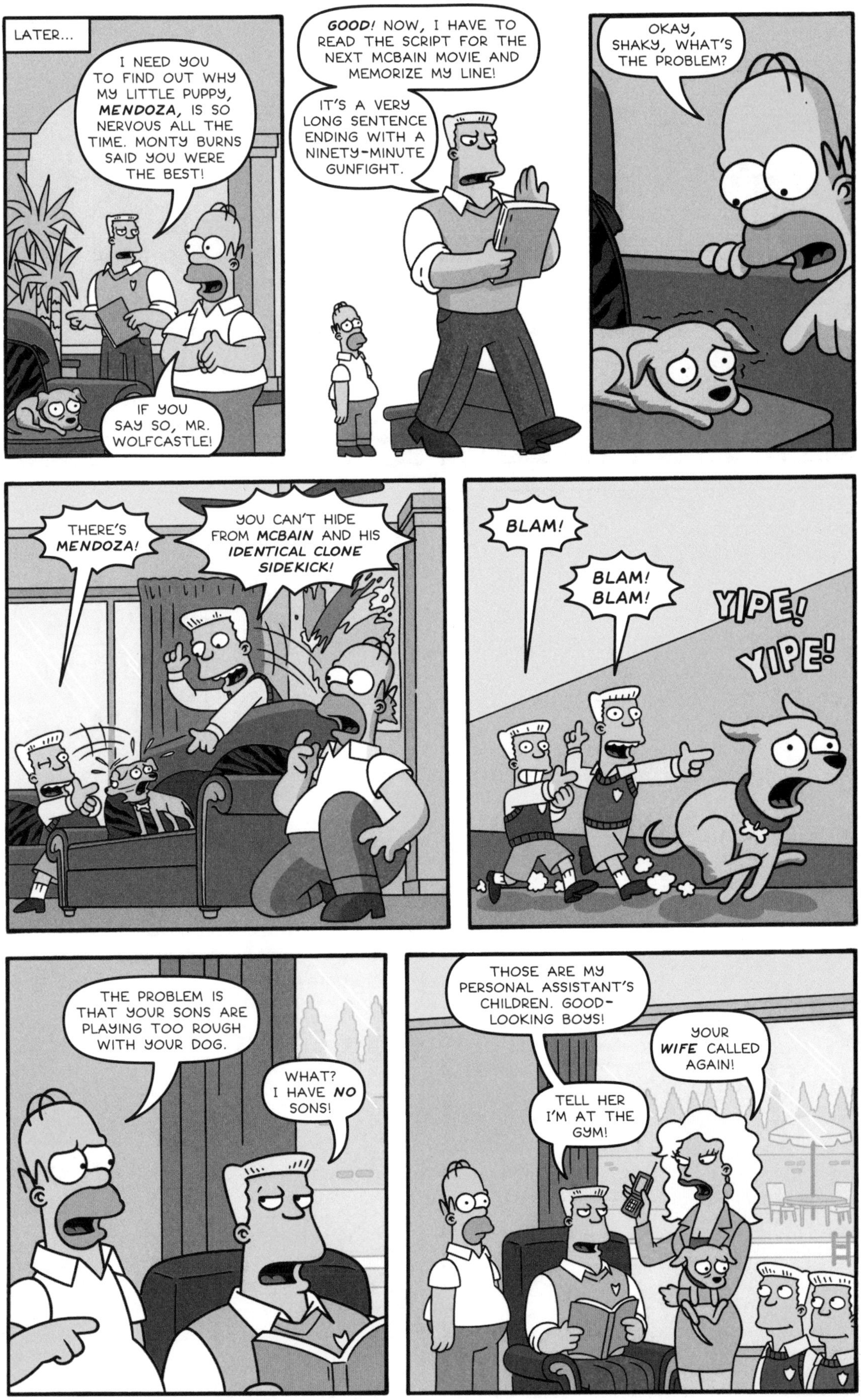
LATER...
I NEED YOU TO FIND OUT WHY MY LITTLE PUPPY, MENDOZA, IS SO NERVOUS ALL THE TIME. MONTY BURNS SAID YOU WERE THE BEST!
IF YOU SAY SO, MR. WOLFCASTLE!
GOOD! NOW, I HAVE TO READ THE SCRIPT FOR THE NEXT MCBAIN MOVIE AND MEMORIZE MY LINE!
IT'S A VERY LONG SENTENCE ENDING WITH A NINETY-MINUTE GUNFIGHT.
OKAY, SHAKY, WHAT'S THE PROBLEM?
THERE'S MENDOZA!
YOU CAN'T HIDE FROM MCBAIN AND HIS IDENTICAL CLONE SIDEKICK!
BLAM!
BLAM! BLAM!
YIPE!
YIPE!
THE PROBLEM IS THAT YOUR SONS ARE PLAYING TOO ROUGH WITH YOUR DOG.
WHAT? I HAVE NO SONS!
THOSE ARE MY PERSONAL ASSISTANT'S CHILDREN. GOOD-LOOKING BOYS!
YOUR WIFE CALLED AGAIN!
TELL HER I'M AT THE GYM!

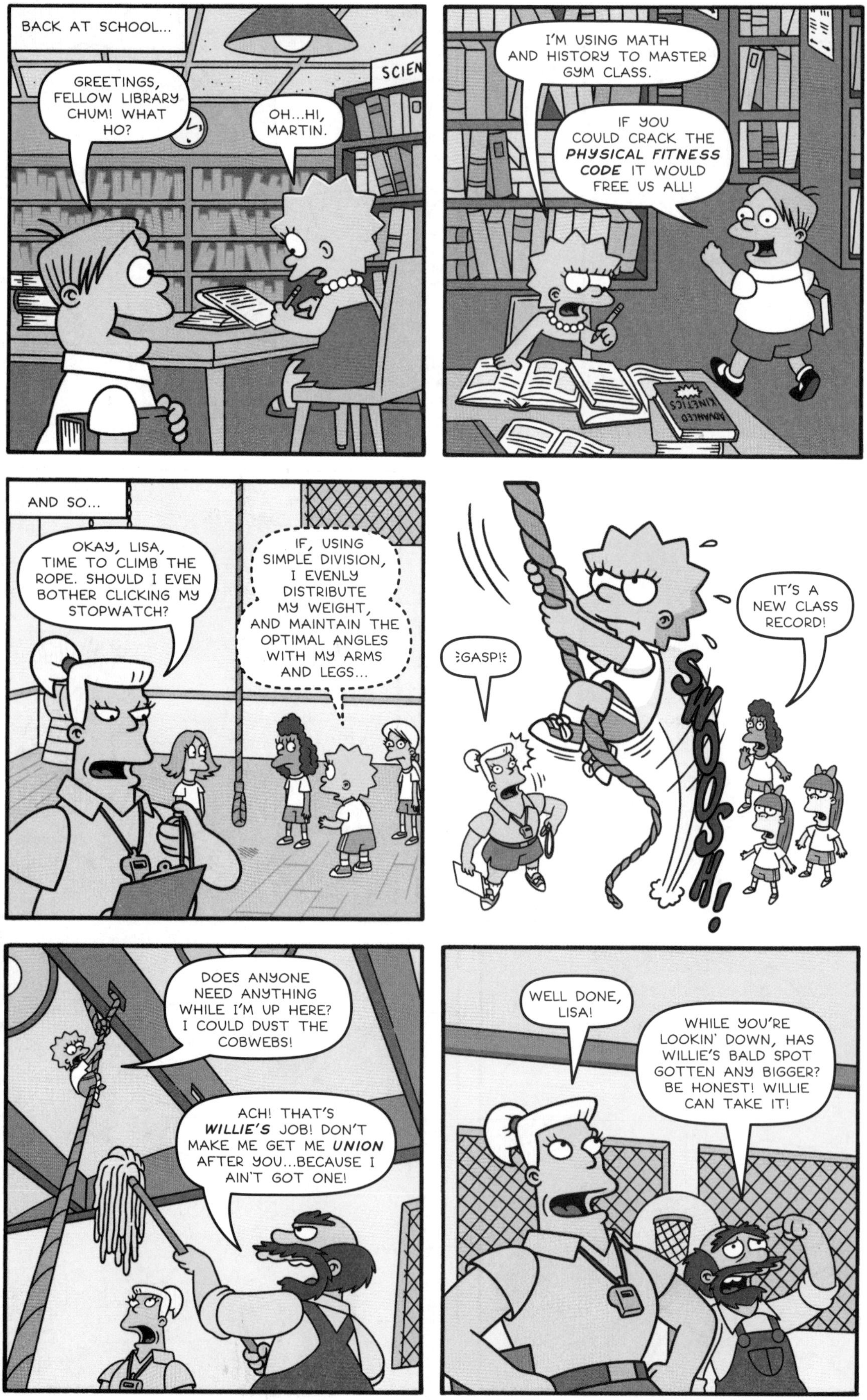
BACK AT SCHOOL...
GREETINGS, FELLOW LIBRARY CHUM! WHAT HO?
OH...HI, MARTIN.
SCIEN
I'M USING MATH AND HISTORY TO MASTER GYM CLASS.
IF YOU COULD CRACK THE PHYSICAL FITNESS CODE IT WOULD FREE US ALL!
ADVANCED KINETICS
AND SO...
OKAY, LISA, TIME TO CLIMB THE ROPE. SHOULD I EVEN BOTHER CLICKING MY STOPWATCH?
IF, USING SIMPLE DIVISION, I EVENLY DISTRIBUTE MY WEIGHT, AND MAINTAIN THE OPTIMAL ANGLES WITH MY ARMS AND LEGS...
GASP!
IT'S A NEW CLASS RECORD!
SWOOSH!
DOES ANYONE NEED ANYTHING WHILE I'M UP HERE? I COULD DUST THE COBWEBS!
ACH! THAT'S WILLIE'S JOB! DON'T MAKE ME GET ME UNION AFTER YOU...BECAUSE I AIN'T GOT ONE!
WELL DONE, LISA!
WHILE YOU'RE LOOKIN' DOWN, HAS WILLIE'S BALD SPOT GOTTEN ANY BIGGER? BE HONEST! WILLIE CAN TAKE IT!

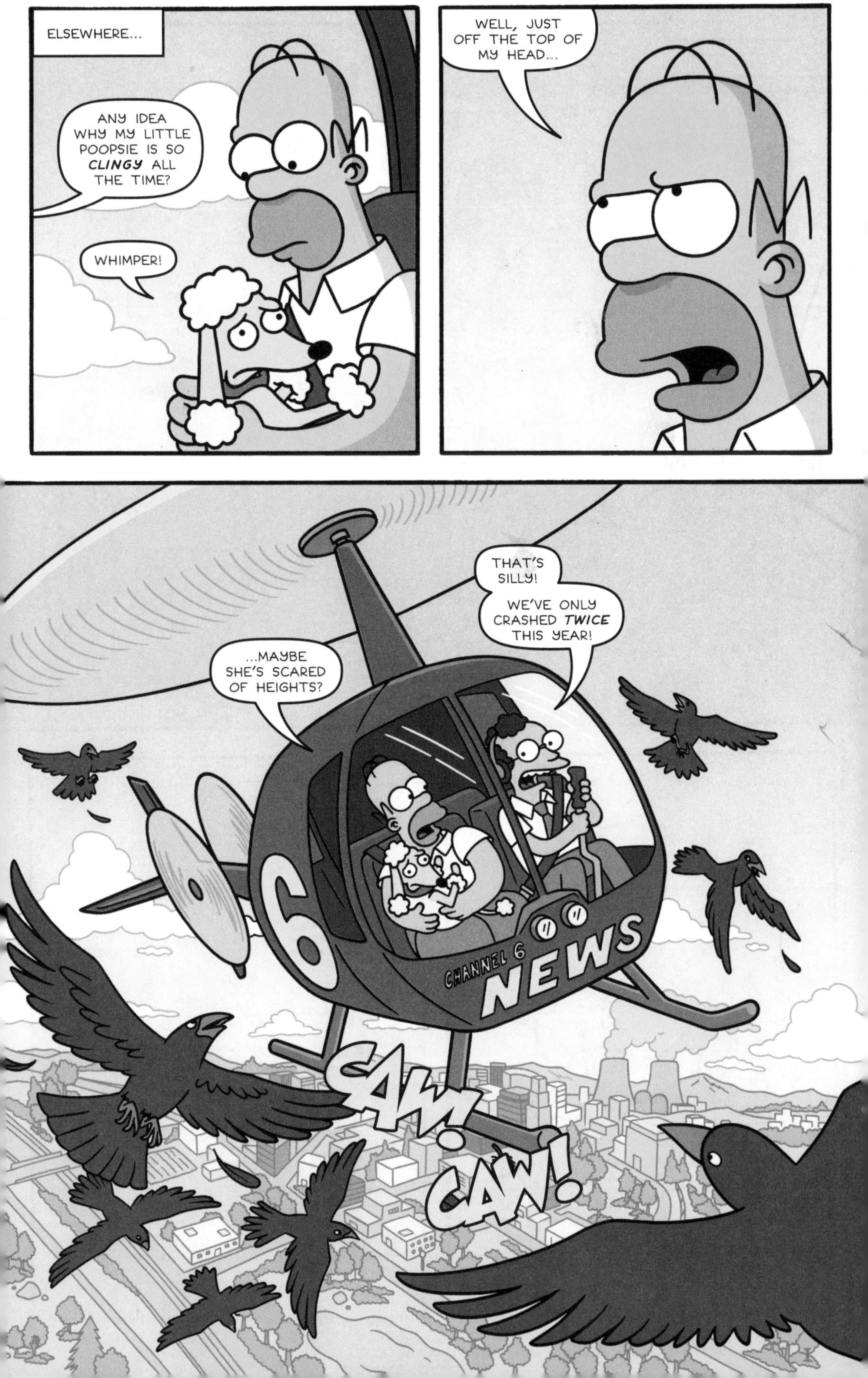
ELSEWHERE...
ANY IDEA WHY MY LITTLE POOPSIE IS SO *CLINGY* ALL THE TIME?
WHIMPER!
WELL, JUST OFF THE TOP OF MY HEAD...
...MAYBE SHE'S SCARED OF HEIGHTS?
THAT'S SILLY!
WE'VE ONLY CRASHED *TWICE* THIS YEAR!
CHANNEL 6
NEWS
6
CAW!
CAW!

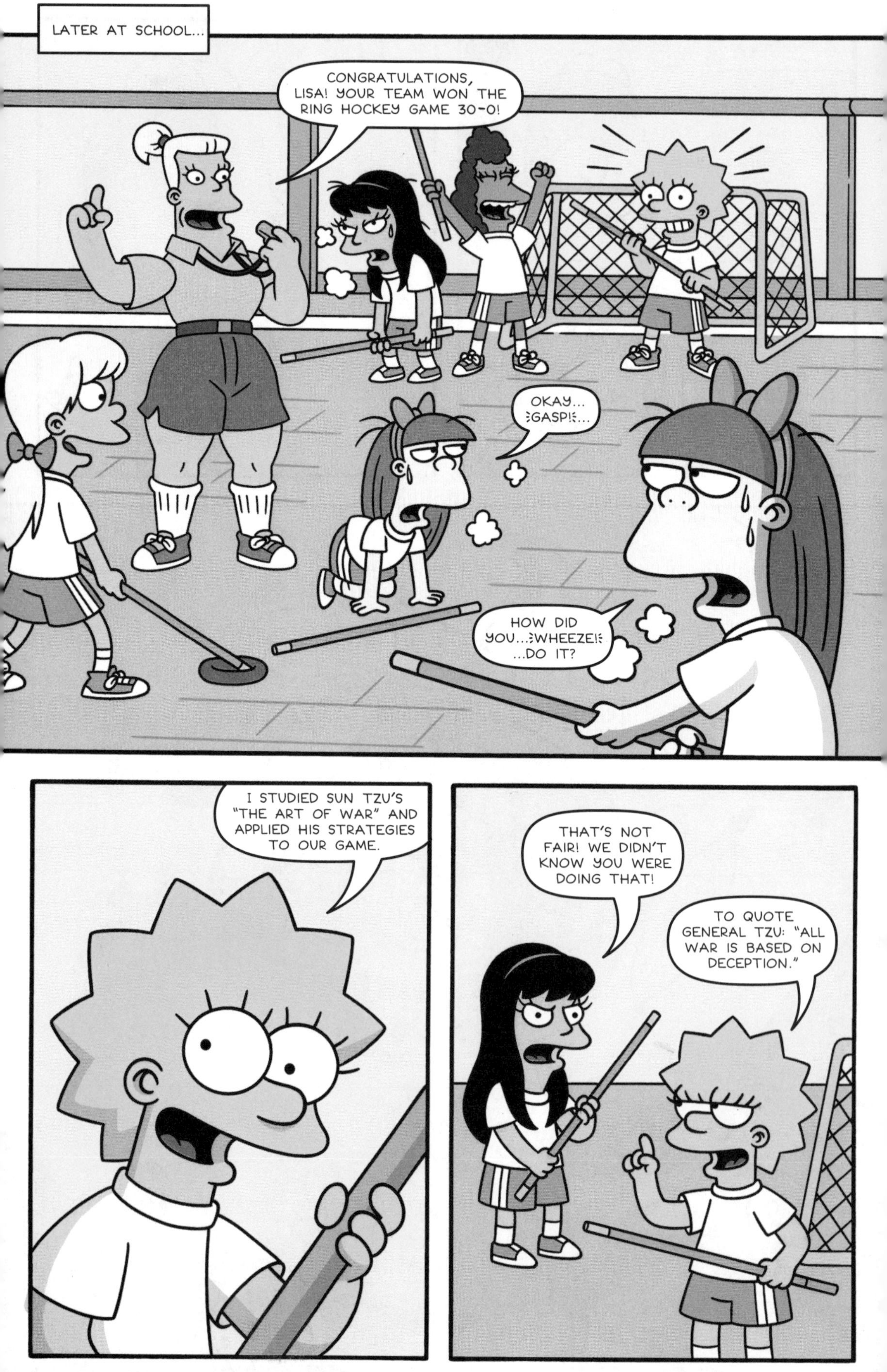
LATER AT SCHOOL...
CONGRATULATIONS, LISA! YOUR TEAM WON THE RING HOCKEY GAME 30-0!
OKAY... GASP!...
HOW DID YOU... WHEEZE! ...DO IT?
I STUDIED SUN TZU'S "THE ART OF WAR" AND APPLIED HIS STRATEGIES TO OUR GAME.
THAT'S NOT FAIR! WE DIDN'T KNOW YOU WERE DOING THAT!
TO QUOTE GENERAL TZU: "ALL WAR IS BASED ON DECEPTION."

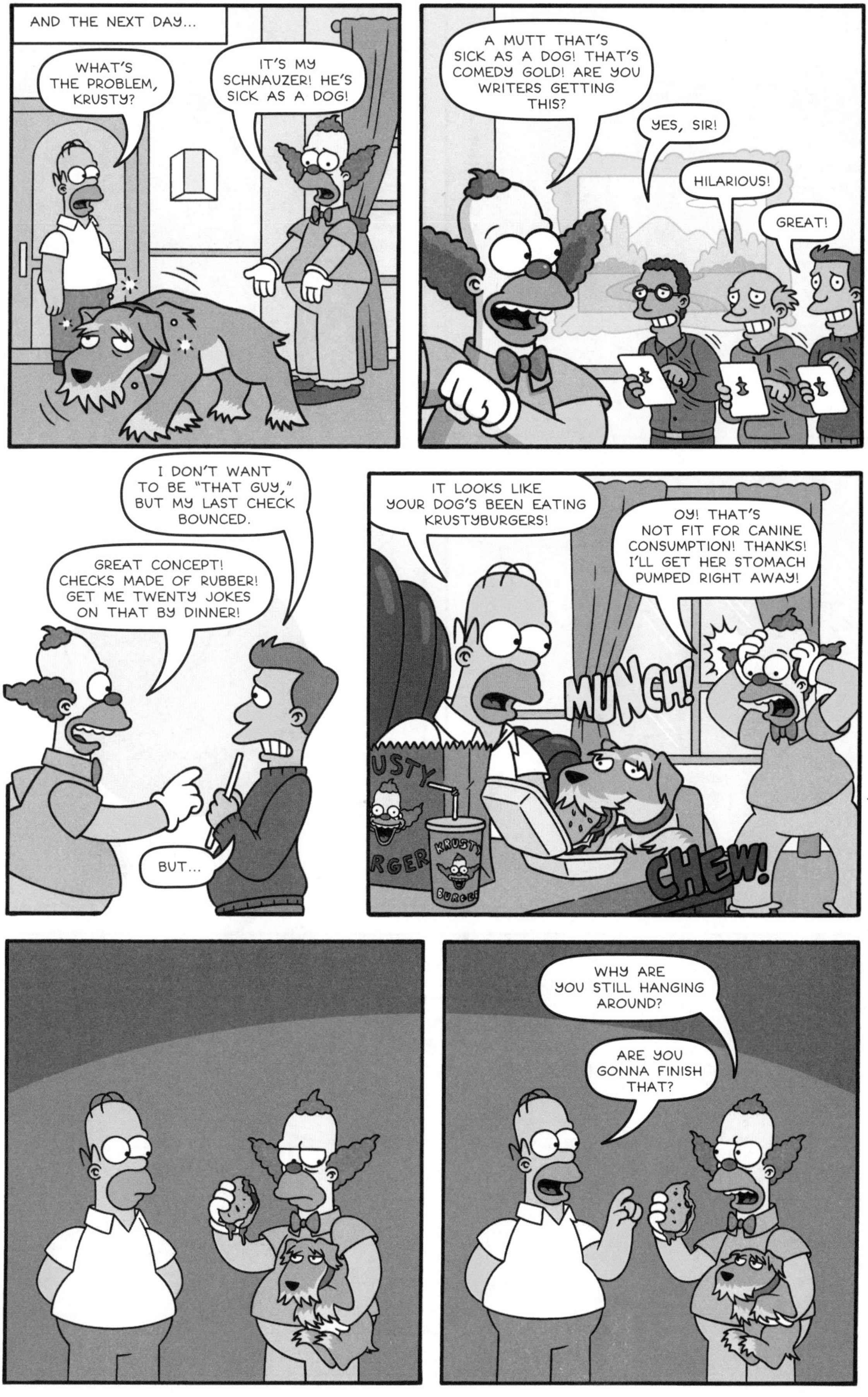
AND THE NEXT DAY...
WHAT'S THE PROBLEM, KRUSTY?
IT'S MY SCHNAUZER! HE'S SICK AS A DOG!
A MUTT THAT'S SICK AS A DOG! THAT'S COMEDY GOLD! ARE YOU WRITERS GETTING THIS?
YES, SIR!
HILARIOUS!
GREAT!
I DON'T WANT TO BE "THAT GUY," BUT MY LAST CHECK BOUNCED.
GREAT CONCEPT! CHECKS MADE OF RUBBER! GET ME TWENTY JOKES ON THAT BY DINNER!
BUT...
IT LOOKS LIKE YOUR DOG'S BEEN EATING KRUSTYBURGERS!
OY! THAT'S NOT FIT FOR CANINE CONSUMPTION! THANKS! I'LL GET HER STOMACH PUMPED RIGHT AWAY!
MUNCH!
CHEW!
WHY ARE YOU STILL HANGING AROUND?
ARE YOU GONNA FINISH THAT?

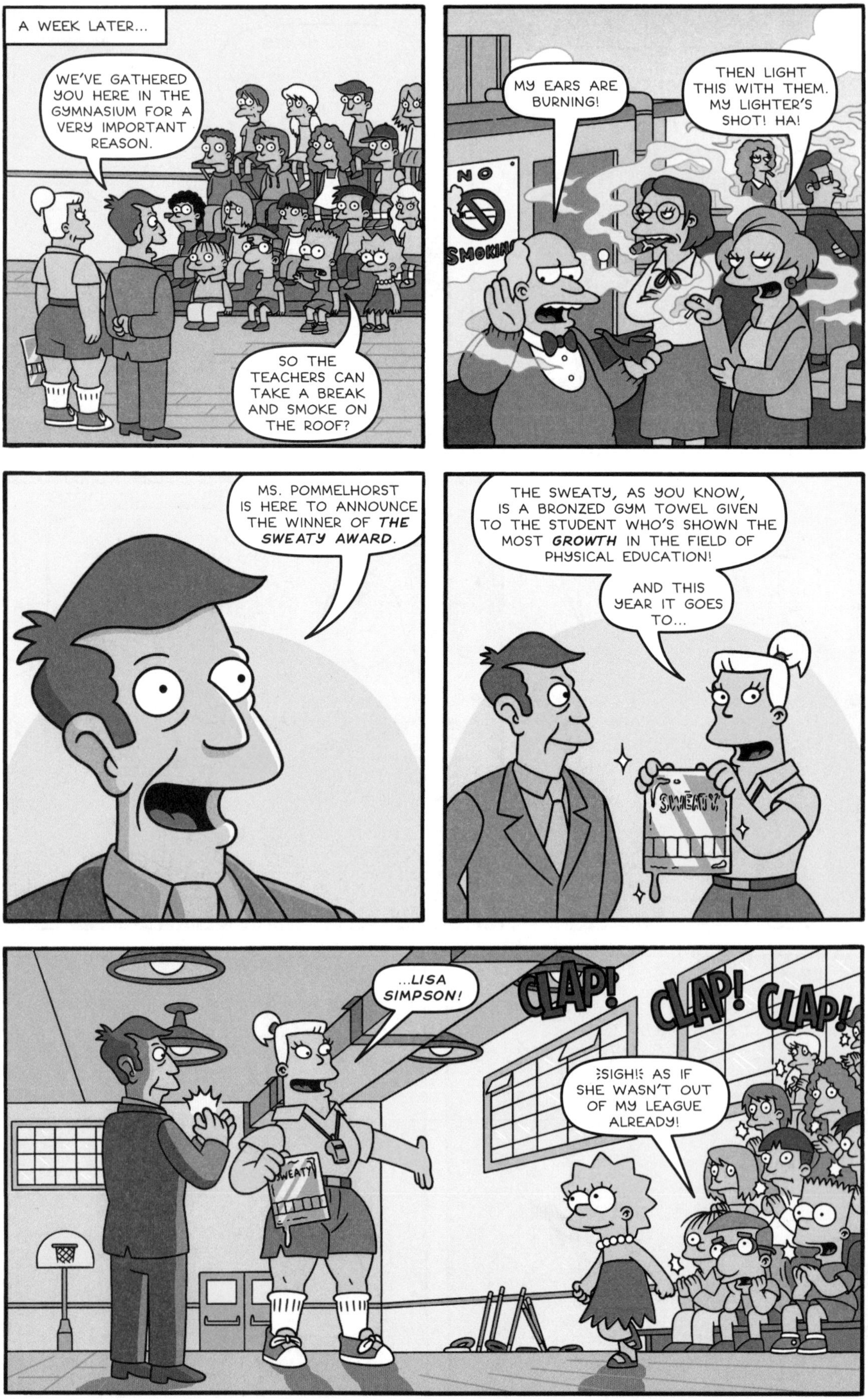
A WEEK LATER...
WE'VE GATHERED YOU HERE IN THE GYMNASIUM FOR A VERY IMPORTANT REASON.
SO THE TEACHERS CAN TAKE A BREAK AND SMOKE ON THE ROOF?
NO SMOKING
MY EARS ARE BURNING!
THEN LIGHT THIS WITH THEM. MY LIGHTER'S SHOT! HA!
MS. POMMELHORST IS HERE TO ANNOUNCE THE WINNER OF THE SWEATY AWARD.
THE SWEATY, AS YOU KNOW, IS A BRONZED GYM TOWEL GIVEN TO THE STUDENT WHO'S SHOWN THE MOST GROWTH IN THE FIELD OF PHYSICAL EDUCATION!
AND THIS YEAR IT GOES TO...
SWEATY
...LISA SIMPSON!
CLAP! CLAP! CLAP!
SWEATY
SIGH! AS IF SHE WASN'T OUT OF MY LEAGUE ALREADY!

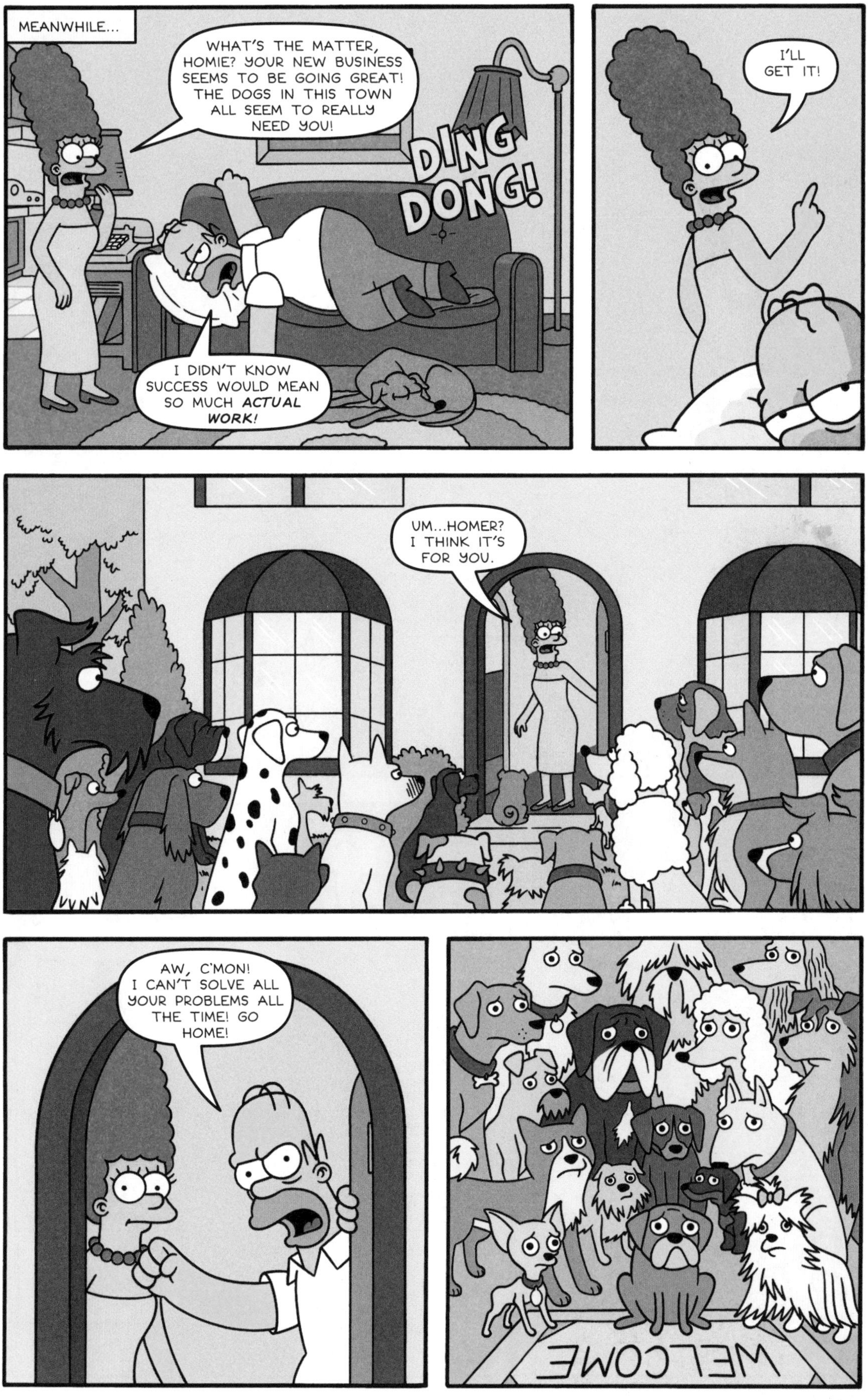
MEANWHILE...
WHAT'S THE MATTER, HOMIE? YOUR NEW BUSINESS SEEMS TO BE GOING GREAT! THE DOGS IN THIS TOWN ALL SEEM TO REALLY NEED YOU!
I DIDN'T KNOW SUCCESS WOULD MEAN SO MUCH *ACTUAL WORK!*
DING DONG!
I'LL GET IT!
UM...HOMER? I THINK IT'S FOR YOU.
AW, C'MON! I CAN'T SOLVE ALL YOUR PROBLEMS ALL THE TIME! GO HOME!
WELCOME

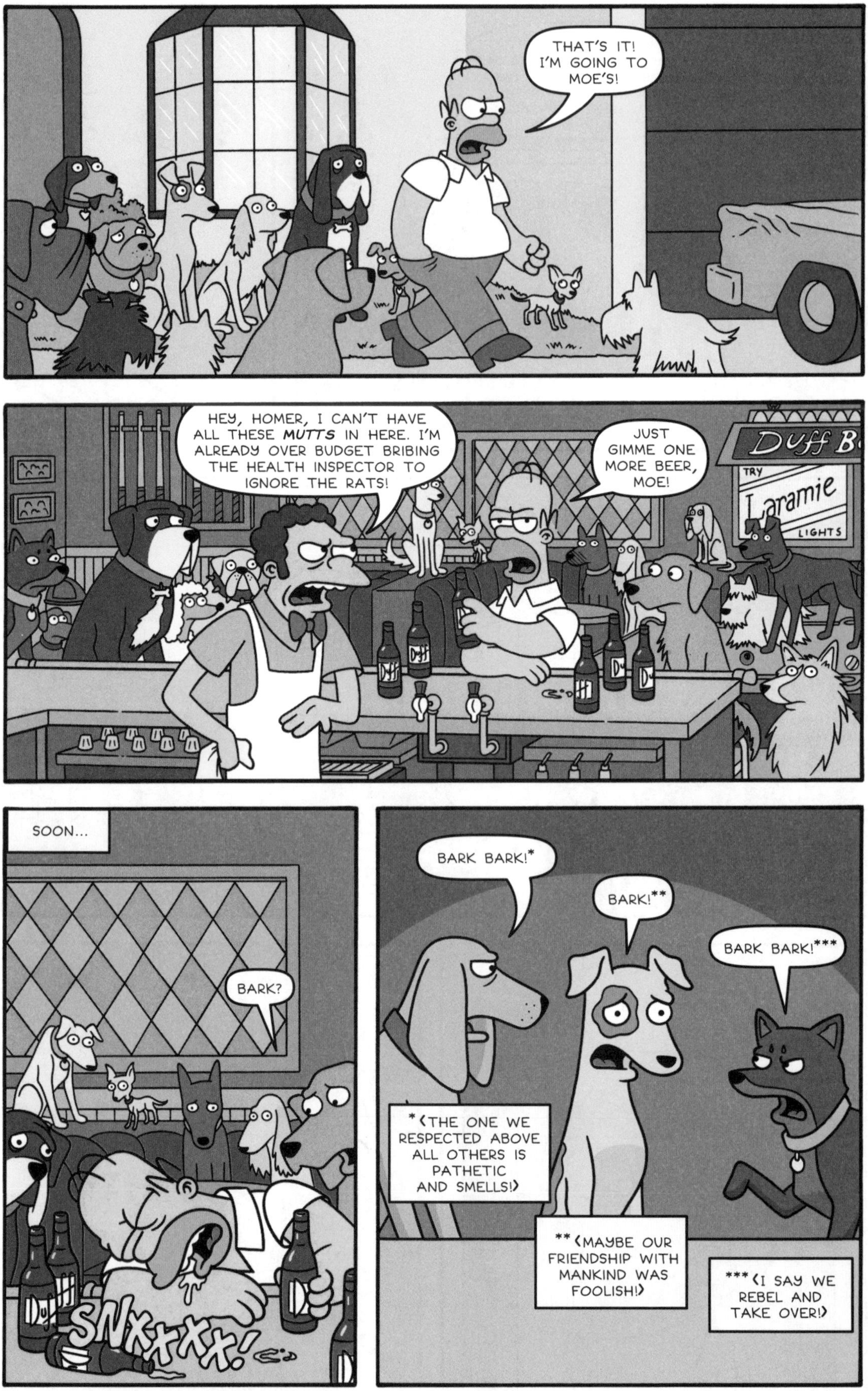
THAT'S IT! I'M GOING TO MOE'S!
HEY, HOMER, I CAN'T HAVE ALL THESE *MUTTS* IN HERE. I'M ALREADY OVER BUDGET BRIBING THE HEALTH INSPECTOR TO IGNORE THE RATS!
JUST GIMME ONE MORE BEER, MOE!
Duff B
TRY Laramie LIGHTS
SOON...
BARK?
SNXXXXX!
BARK BARK!*
BARK!**
BARK BARK!***
*(THE ONE WE RESPECTED ABOVE ALL OTHERS IS PATHETIC AND SMELLS!)
**(MAYBE OUR FRIENDSHIP WITH MANKIND WAS FOOLISH!)
***(I SAY WE REBEL AND TAKE OVER!)

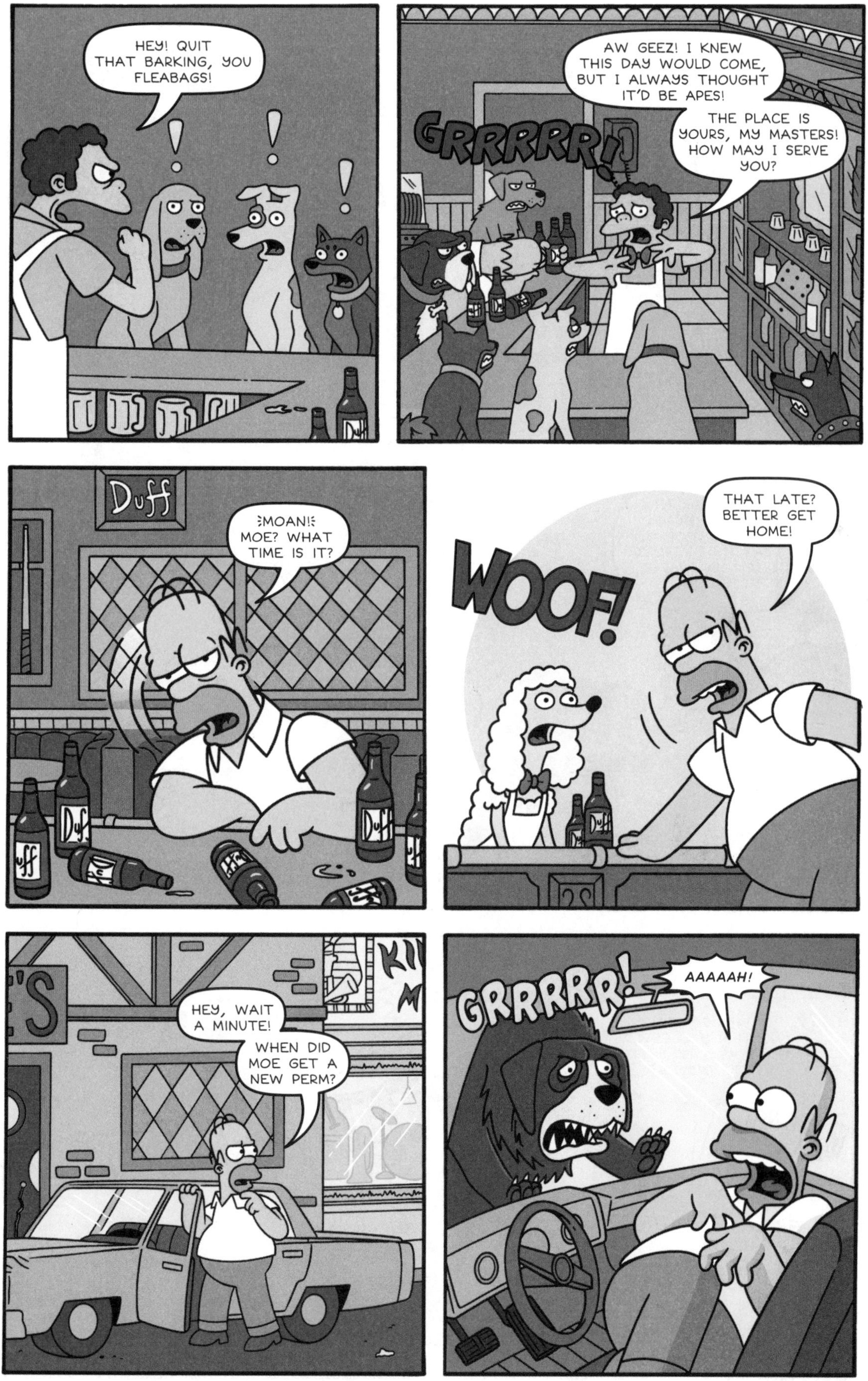
HEY! QUIT THAT BARKING, YOU FLEABAGS!
GRRRRR!
AW GEEZ! I KNEW THIS DAY WOULD COME, BUT I ALWAYS THOUGHT IT'D BE APES!
THE PLACE IS YOURS, MY MASTERS! HOW MAY I SERVE YOU?
Duff
MOAN! MOE? WHAT TIME IS IT?
WOOF!
THAT LATE? BETTER GET HOME!
HEY, WAIT A MINUTE!
WHEN DID MOE GET A NEW PERM?
GRRRRR!
AAAAAH!

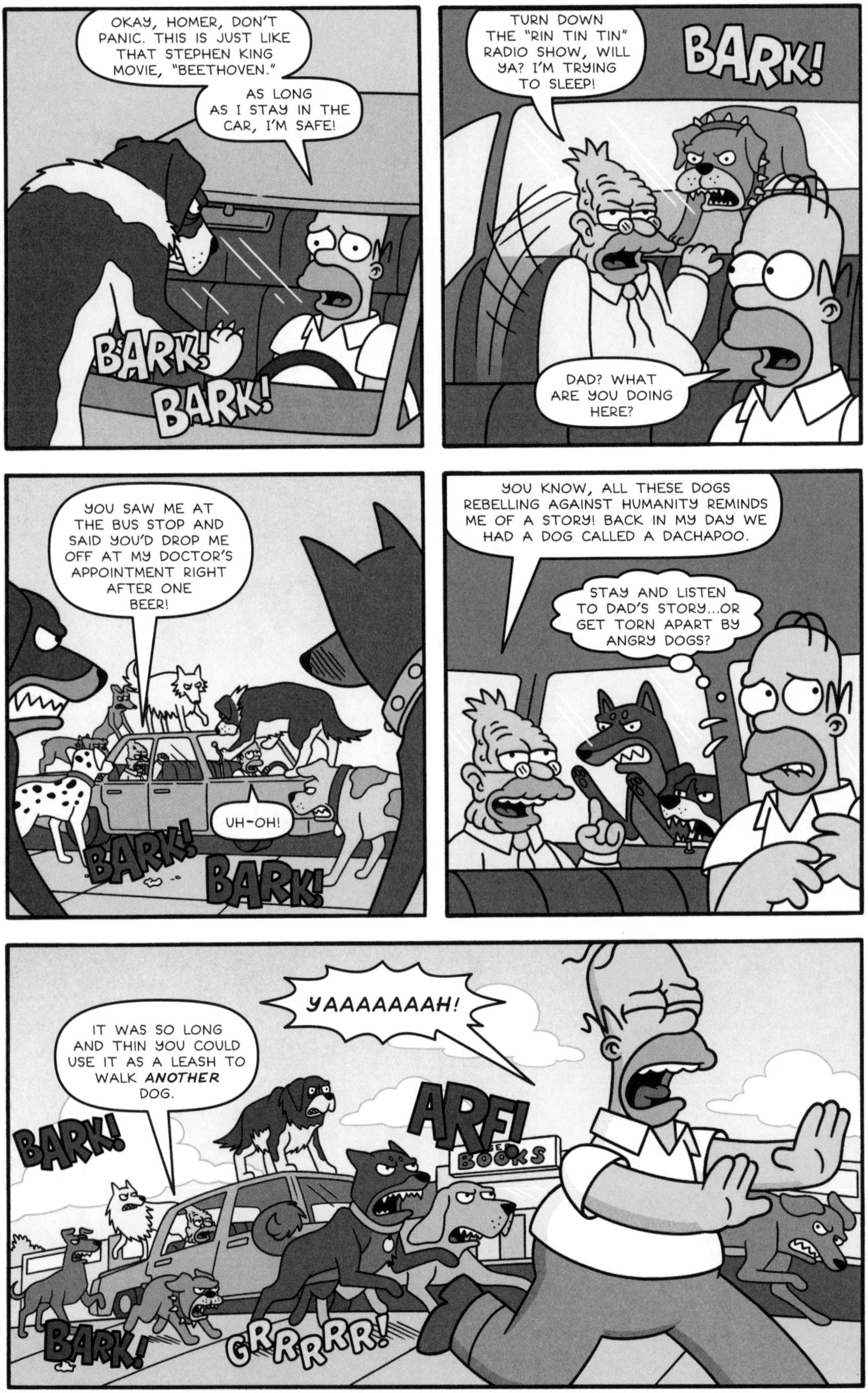
OKAY, HOMER, DON'T PANIC. THIS IS JUST LIKE THAT STEPHEN KING MOVIE, "BEETHOVEN."
AS LONG AS I STAY IN THE CAR, I'M SAFE!
BARK!
BARK!
TURN DOWN THE "RIN TIN TIN" RADIO SHOW, WILL YA? I'M TRYING TO SLEEP!
BARK!
DAD? WHAT ARE YOU DOING HERE?
YOU SAW ME AT THE BUS STOP AND SAID YOU'D DROP ME OFF AT MY DOCTOR'S APPOINTMENT RIGHT AFTER ONE BEER!
UH-OH!
BARK!
BARK!
YOU KNOW, ALL THESE DOGS REBELLING AGAINST HUMANITY REMINDS ME OF A STORY! BACK IN MY DAY WE HAD A DOG CALLED A DACHAPOO.
STAY AND LISTEN TO DAD'S STORY...OR GET TORN APART BY ANGRY DOGS?
IT WAS SO LONG AND THIN YOU COULD USE IT AS A LEASH TO WALK *ANOTHER* DOG.
YAAAAAAAH!
BARK!
ARF!
BOOKS
BARK!
GRRRRRR!

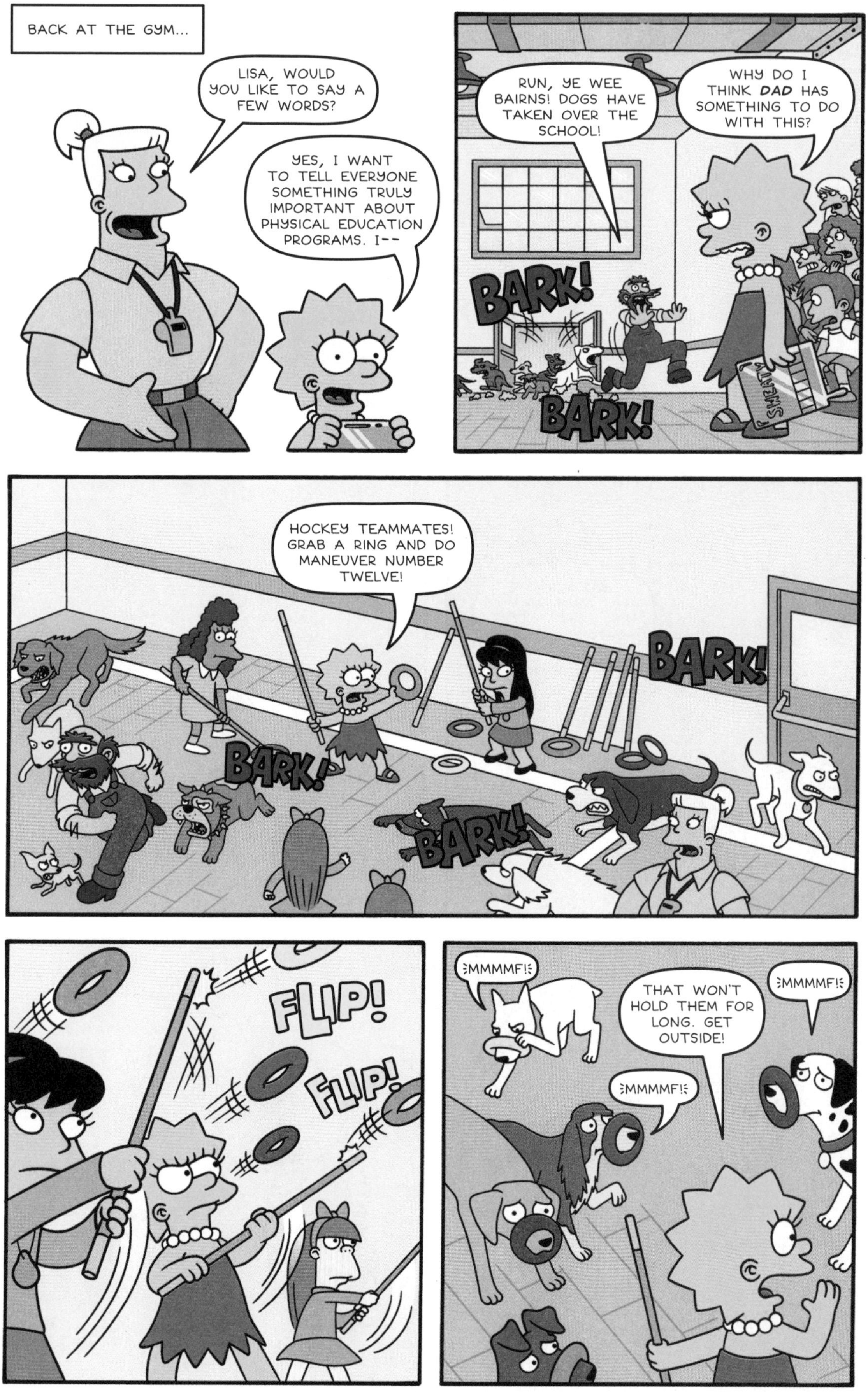
BACK AT THE GYM...
LISA, WOULD YOU LIKE TO SAY A FEW WORDS?
YES, I WANT TO TELL EVERYONE SOMETHING TRULY IMPORTANT ABOUT PHYSICAL EDUCATION PROGRAMS. I--
RUN, YE WEE BAIRNS! DOGS HAVE TAKEN OVER THE SCHOOL!
WHY DO I THINK DAD HAS SOMETHING TO DO WITH THIS?
BARK!
BARK!
SWEATY
HOCKEY TEAMMATES! GRAB A RING AND DO MANEUVER NUMBER TWELVE!
BARK!
BARK!
BARK!
FLIP!
FLIP!
MMMMF!
THAT WON'T HOLD THEM FOR LONG. GET OUTSIDE!
MMMMF!
MMMMF!

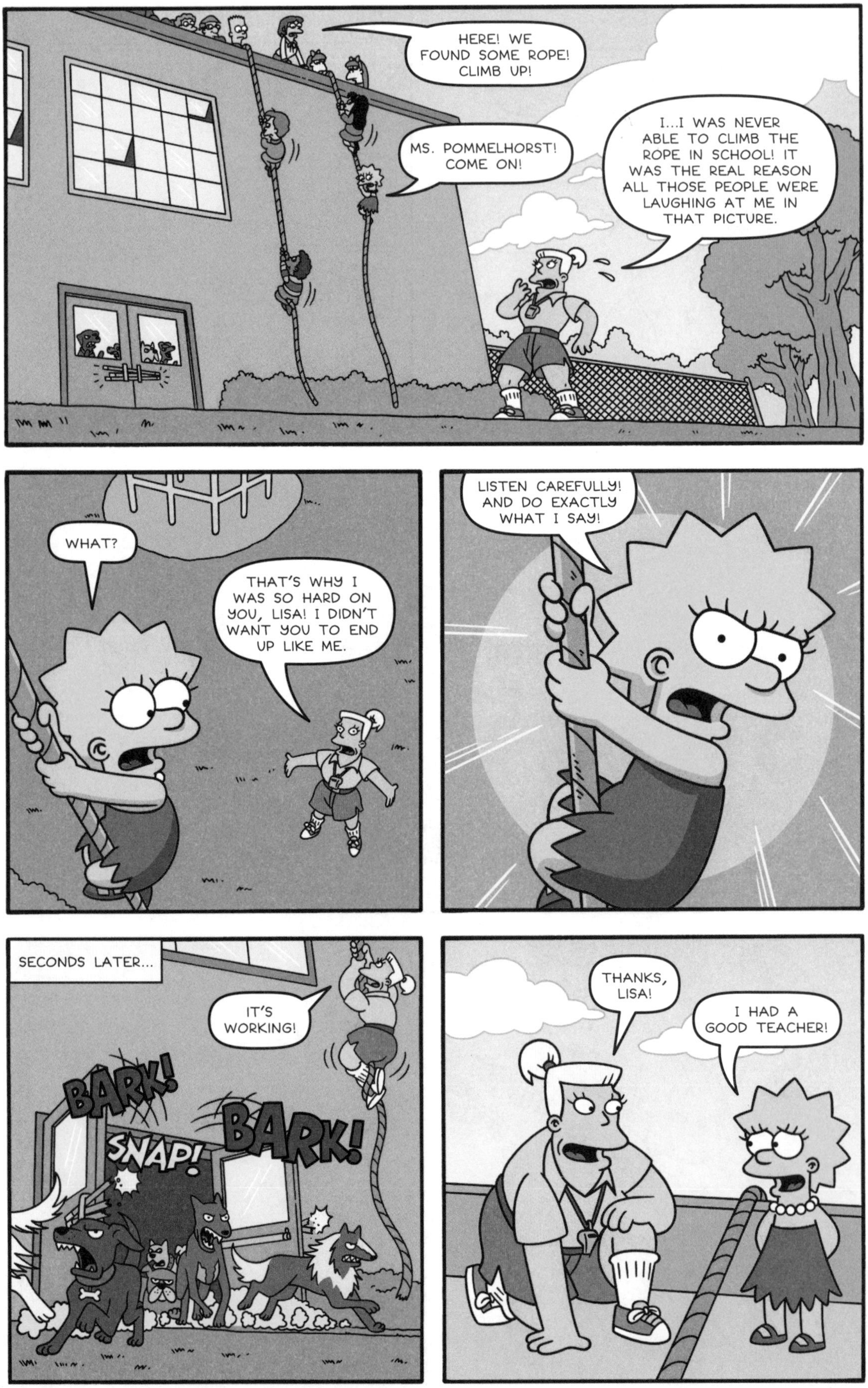
HERE! WE FOUND SOME ROPE! CLIMB UP!
MS. POMMELHORST! COME ON!
I...I WAS NEVER ABLE TO CLIMB THE ROPE IN SCHOOL! IT WAS THE REAL REASON ALL THOSE PEOPLE WERE LAUGHING AT ME IN THAT PICTURE.
WHAT?
THAT'S WHY I WAS SO HARD ON YOU, LISA! I DIDN'T WANT YOU TO END UP LIKE ME.
LISTEN CAREFULLY! AND DO EXACTLY WHAT I SAY!
SECONDS LATER...
IT'S WORKING!
BARK!
SNAP!
BARK!
THANKS, LISA!
I HAD A GOOD TEACHER!

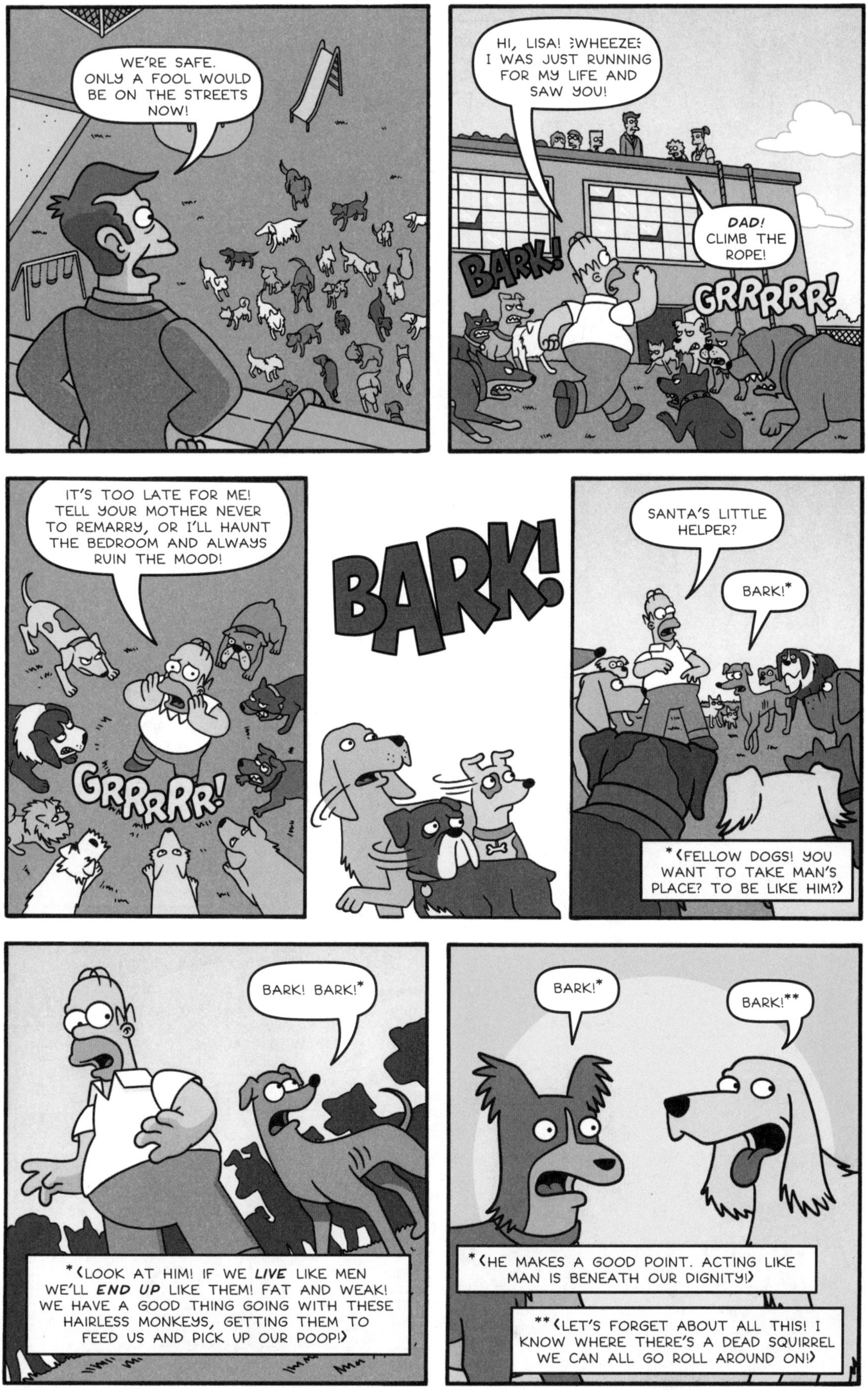

WE'RE SAFE. ONLY A FOOL WOULD BE ON THE STREETS NOW!
HI, LISA! ⁝WHEEZE⁝ I WAS JUST RUNNING FOR MY LIFE AND SAW YOU!
BARK!
DAD! CLIMB THE ROPE!
GRRRRRR!
IT'S TOO LATE FOR ME! TELL YOUR MOTHER NEVER TO REMARRY, OR I'LL HAUNT THE BEDROOM AND ALWAYS RUIN THE MOOD!
GRRRRRR!
BARK!
SANTA'S LITTLE HELPER?
BARK!*
*(FELLOW DOGS! YOU WANT TO TAKE MAN'S PLACE? TO BE LIKE HIM?)
BARK! BARK!*
*(LOOK AT HIM! IF WE LIVE LIKE MEN WE'LL END UP LIKE THEM! FAT AND WEAK! WE HAVE A GOOD THING GOING WITH THESE HAIRLESS MONKEYS, GETTING THEM TO FEED US AND PICK UP OUR POOP!)
BARK!*
BARK!**
*(HE MAKES A GOOD POINT. ACTING LIKE MAN IS BENEATH OUR DIGNITY!)
**(LET'S FORGET ABOUT ALL THIS! I KNOW WHERE THERE'S A DEAD SQUIRREL WE CAN ALL GO ROLL AROUND ON!)

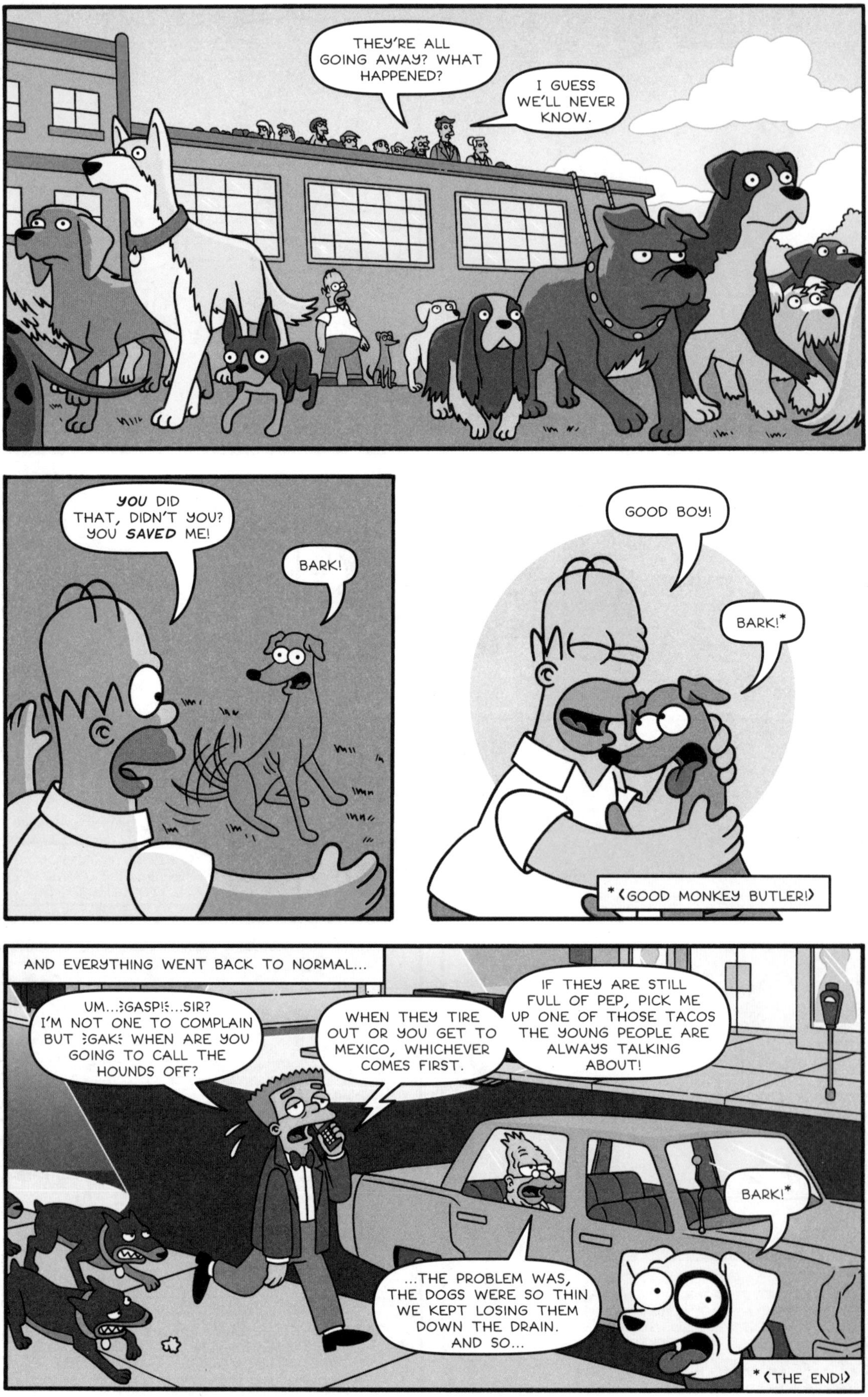
THEY'RE ALL GOING AWAY? WHAT HAPPENED?
I GUESS WE'LL NEVER KNOW.
YOU DID THAT, DIDN'T YOU? YOU SAVED ME!
BARK!
GOOD BOY!
BARK!*
*(GOOD MONKEY BUTLER!)
AND EVERYTHING WENT BACK TO NORMAL...
UM...{GASP!}...SIR? I'M NOT ONE TO COMPLAIN BUT {GAK} WHEN ARE YOU GOING TO CALL THE HOUNDS OFF?
WHEN THEY TIRE OUT OR YOU GET TO MEXICO, WHICHEVER COMES FIRST.
IF THEY ARE STILL FULL OF PEP, PICK ME UP ONE OF THOSE TACOS THE YOUNG PEOPLE ARE ALWAYS TALKING ABOUT!
BARK!*
...THE PROBLEM WAS, THE DOGS WERE SO THIN WE KEPT LOSING THEM DOWN THE DRAIN. AND SO...
*(THE END!)

WHERE'S RALPH?

RALPH'S HIDING SOMEWHERE IN THIS PICTURE. CAN YOU FIND HIM?

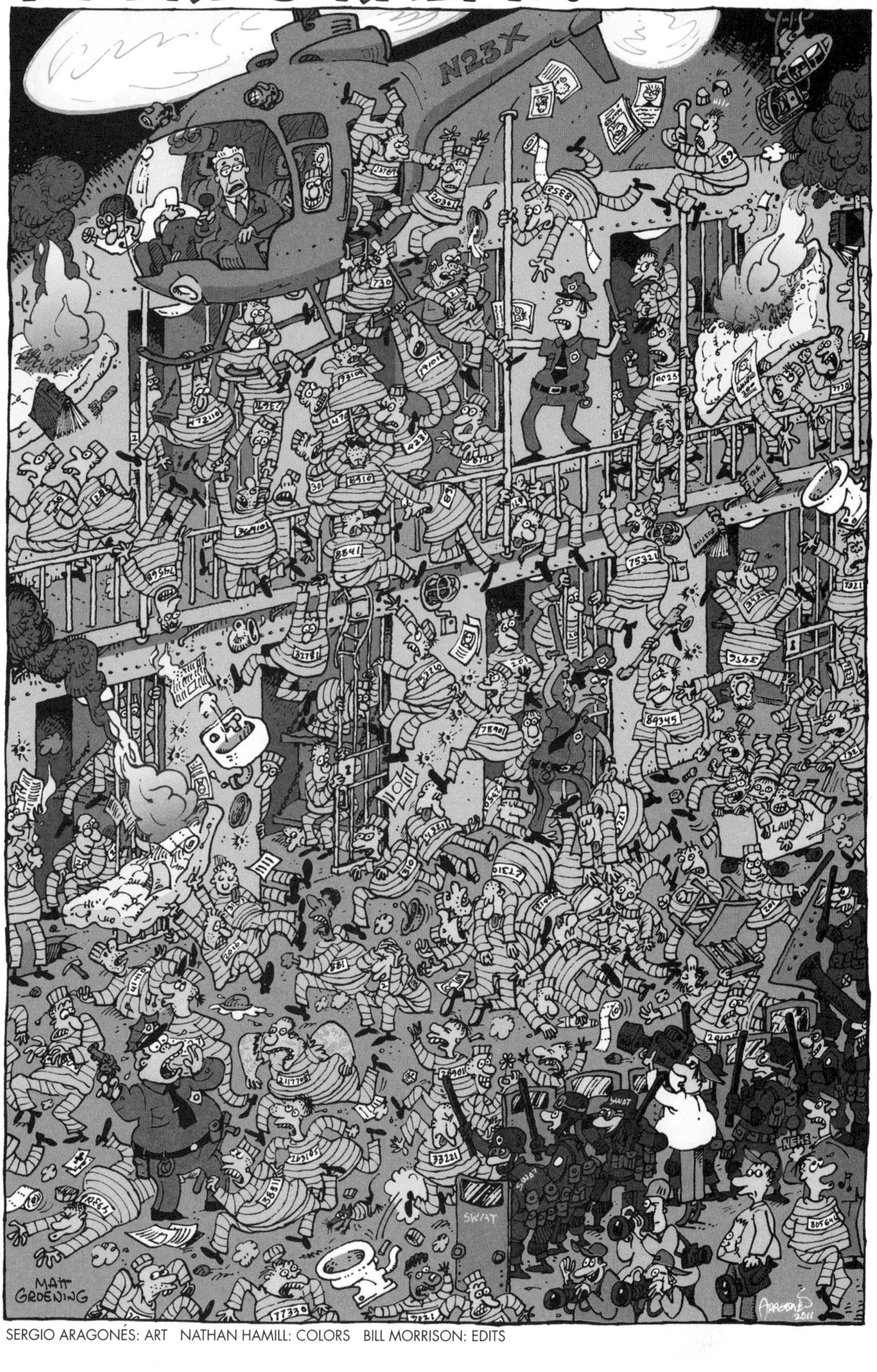
N23X
LAUNDRY
SWAT
SWAT
MATT GROENING
ARAGONÉS 2011

SERGIO ARAGONÉS: ART NATHAN HAMILL: COLORS BILL MORRISON: EDITS

HEY, HEY, NEW MEMBER OF TEAM KRUSTY*!
NOW YOU CAN GET MOVING IN THE FAST LANE TO SUCCESS**
WITH YOUR VERY OWN POP-UP† KRUSTYBURGER
FAST FOOD FRANCHISE, COURTESY OF THE

BUSY HANDS¥ PAPERCRAFT PROJECT!

*The term "Team Krusty" and any other term related to or suggestive of the KrustyCo Brand® heretofore and herewith does not expressly denote or acknowledge any personal affiliation and/or legal representation or liability for the aforementioned "member"! • ** Franchise success, not assured and/or guaranteed! • † This is not a fully functional restaurant, but a mere paper miniature representation of said franchise, which can be assembled with adhesive tape and scissors. Be warned: Sharp instruments should only be used under the supervision of a responsible adult! • ¥ You cut yourself, didn't you? Did your mother leave you home alone with that "no-good" uncle of yours again? I knew it! Oy! My lawyers are going to have a field day with this. Do you know how much they charge an hour? Do you...?

WHAT YOU WILL NEED:
- Scissors, adhesive tape, and a straight edge (such as a ruler).
- An ability to fold along straight lines.
- An additional "mint condition" copy of this book secured elsewhere!

1. Cut out figures and bases.
2. Cut along the dotted line at the base of each figure and also the center of each curved base. (Be careful not to cut too far!)
3. Connect base to figure as shown (Fig. 1).
4. Before cutting out the shapes, use a ruler and a slightly rounded metal tool (like the edge of a key) to first score, and then fold lightly along all the interior lines (this will make final folds much easier).
5. Cut along the exterior shape. Make sure to cut all the way to where the walls, the roof, and the flap lines meet (Fig. 2).

Fig. 1

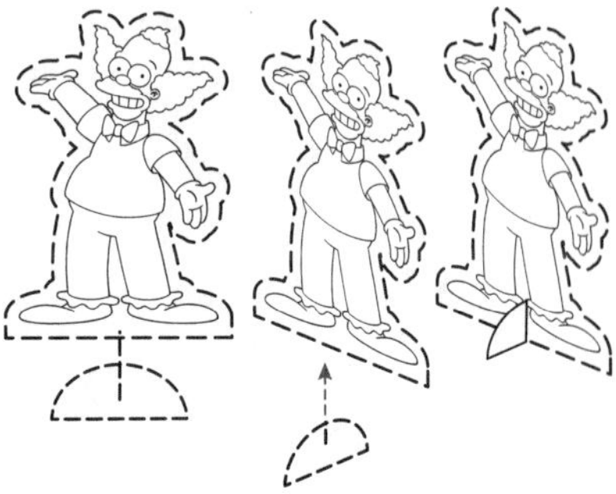

6. Form building by folding walls into place (Fig. 3) and secure all tabs to the interior of the building with tape (Fig. 4).

7. Cut and fold awning shape as shown (Fig. 5), and secure with tape. Then, place on top of building and secure with looped tape between the roof and awning (Fig. 6). For added strength, you can run a small piece of tape along the back edge of the awning shape and the back wall of the building (Fig. 7).

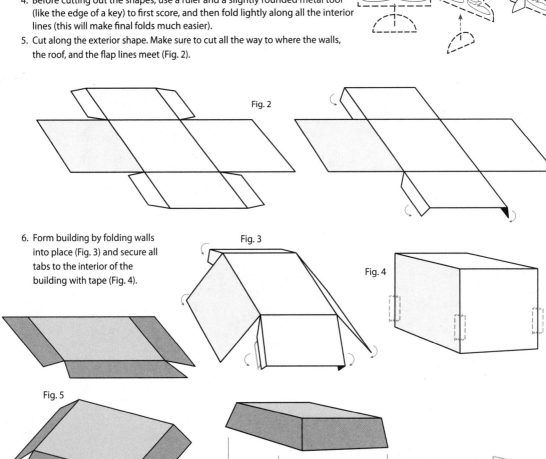

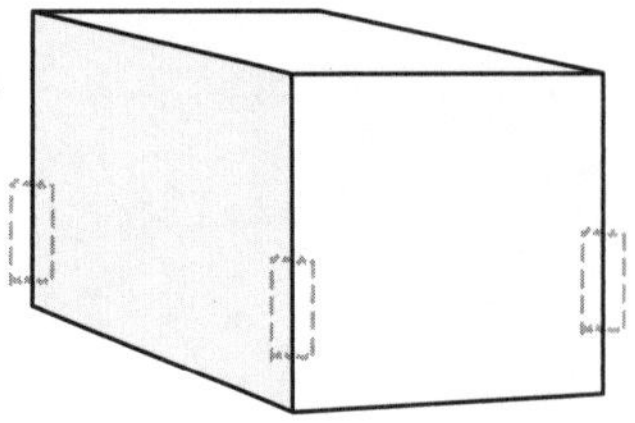

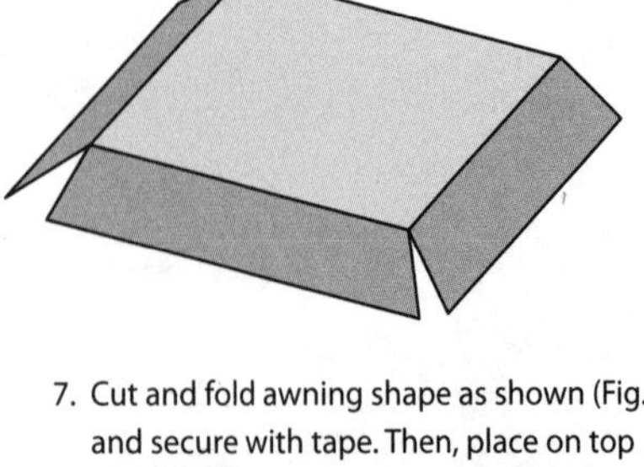

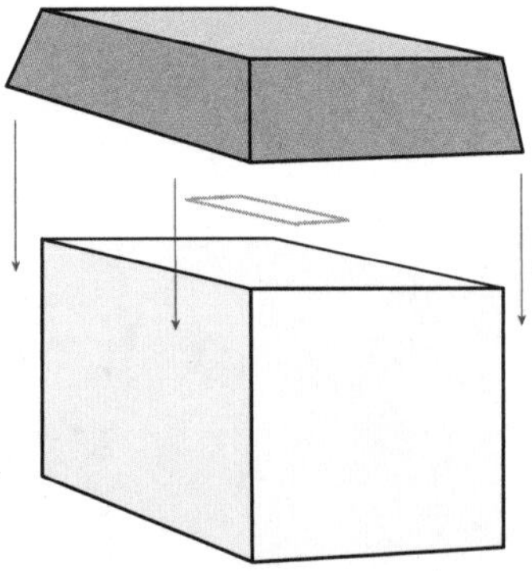

Fig. 2

Fig. 3

Fig. 4

Fig. 5

Fig. 6

Fig. 7

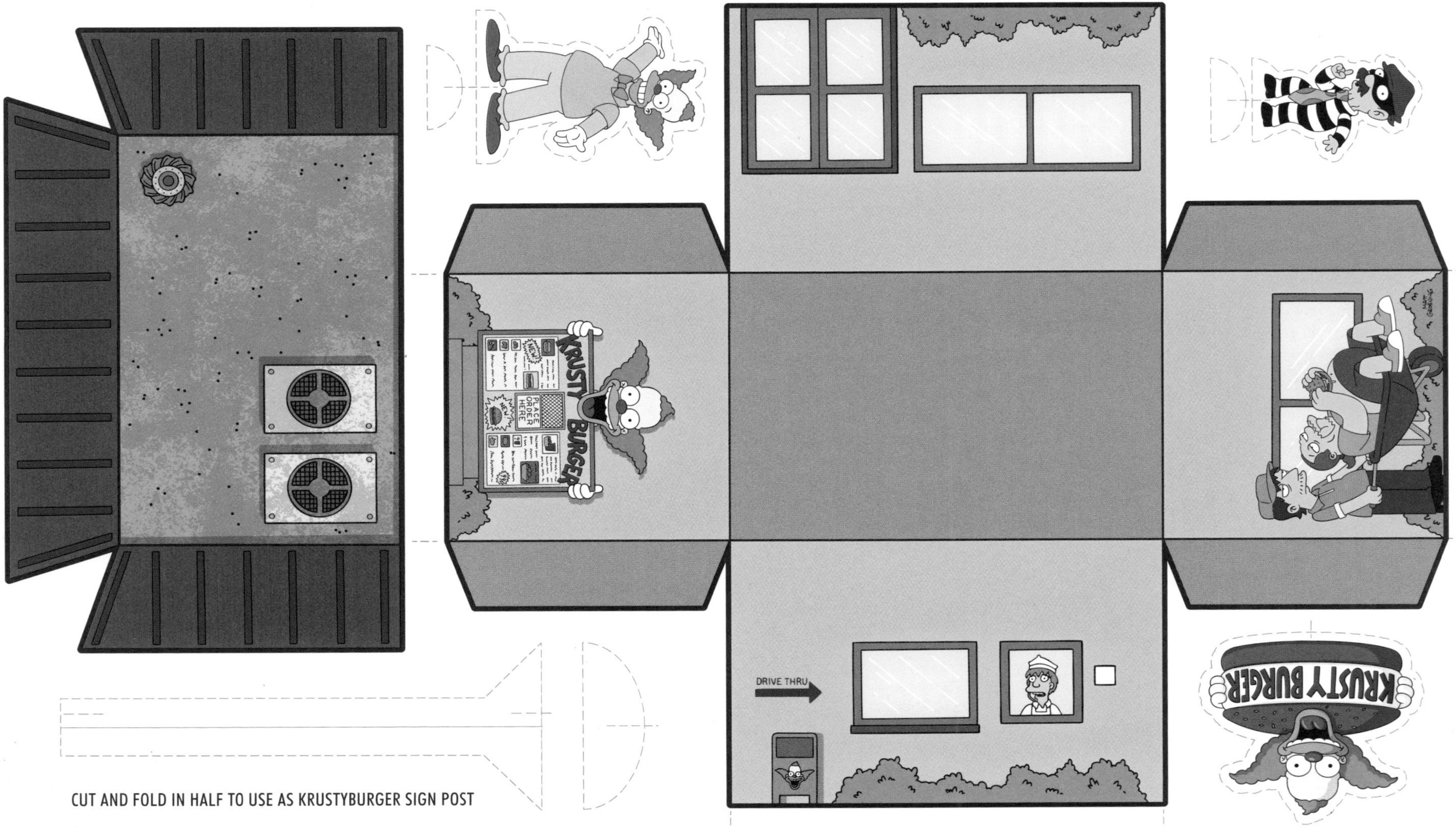
KRUSTY BURGER
PLACE ORDER HERE
NEW!
NEW!
DRIVE THRU
KRUSTY BURGER

CUT AND FOLD IN HALF TO USE AS KRUSTYBURGER SIGN POST